Public Human Resource Management

Public Human Resource Management

Strategies and Practices in the 21st Century

R. Paul Battaglio, Jr.
University of Texas–Dallas

Los Angeles | London | New Delhi
Singapore | Washington DC

Los Angeles | London | New Delhi
Singapore | Washington DC

FOR INFORMATION:

CQ Press
2455 Teller Road
Thousand Oaks, California 91320
E-mail: order@sagepub.com

SAGE Publications Ltd.
1 Oliver's Yard
55 City Road
London EC1Y 1SP
United Kingdom

SAGE Publications India Pvt. Ltd.
B 1/I 1 Mohan Cooperative Industrial Area
Mathura Road, New Delhi 110 044
India

SAGE Publications Asia-Pacific Pte. Ltd.
3 Church Street
#10-04 Samsung Hub
Singapore 049483

Printed in the United States of America

Library of Congress Cataloging-in-Publication Data

Battaglio, R. Paul Jr.
Public human resource management : strategies and practices in the 21st century / R. Paul Battaglio Jr., University of Texas, Dallas.

pages cm

ISBN 978-1-4522-1823-6 (hardcover)

1. Civil service—Personnel management. I. Title.

JF1601.B38 2015
352.6—dc23   2014019197

This book is printed on acid-free paper.

Acquisitions Editor: Suzanne Flinchbaugh
Editorial Assistant: Davia Grant
Production Editor: Kelly DeRosa
Copy Editor: Paula L. Fleming
Typesetter: C&M Digitals (P) Ltd.
Proofreader: Ellen Brink
Indexer: Rick Hurd
Cover Designer: Janet Kiesel
Marketing Manager: Amy Whitaker

14 15 16 17 18 10 9 8 7 6 5 4 3 2 1

Detailed Contents

List of Tables, Figures, and Boxes

Tables

Figures

Boxes

The desire to write *Public Human Resource Management: Strategies and Practices in the 21st Century* was a result of continued requests from students to review material that was relevant to the personnel challenges they were experiencing in their day-to-day work activities. The students frequently questioned why textbooks rarely addressed the practical impact of personnel reforms on practices such as recruitment, pay, and performance appraisal. Students were also eager to learn more about emerging issues such as nonprofit human resources, motivation, privatization, and human resource information systems. When I asked colleagues if they knew of any texts that addressed contemporary public sector personnel issues, they invariably replied no. Tired of having to incorporate a potpourri of material into the classroom to address student concerns for practical guidance, I decided to take on the endeavor of writing a text that brought attention to the changing landscape of public human resource management. My goal was simple: to put together a text that covered the traditional personnel material; include subjects that were rarely or never addressed in public personnel; and most importantly, apply a personnel reform framework for examining each chapter.

The reform framework for the book—decentralization, performance-based pay, declassification, deregulation, and privatization—is meant to prepare the next generation of human resource managers for careers in the public and nonprofit sectors. The framework addresses one of the most important issues raised by students and managers over the last few decades—how do we operate in an environment that is increasingly hostile to traditional personnel practices? As is often the case in MPA programs, my students came to class from their day jobs in government and nonprofit organizations. Keen to put in place best practices, my students want more from the traditional texts in personnel administration. They wanted material that addressed implementing contemporary reform practices such as performance-based pay, employment at-will, diversity plans, motivational tools, contracting out, human resource information systems, and strategic plans. Moreover, many of my students were increasingly exploring employment options in the nonprofit sector. Students who secured employment in nonprofit organizations quickly realized the difference in personnel practices in their sector in contrast to the public and private sector. The text also explores these differences in each chapter, taking up trending issues in nonprofit human resource management. The result is a labor of love that I believe finally takes up the current challenges public and nonprofit managers are increasingly facing in their everyday work environments.

Organization of the Book

I have organized the book into three sections: *Foundations*, *Functions*, and *The Future*. The *Foundations* chapters bring the reader through the history of public human resource management in the United States. Most importantly, Chapter 1 establishes the reform framework that will be used throughout the text: decentralization, performance-based pay, declassification, deregulation, and privatization. While civil service systems have afforded employees job protections, merit-based employment, political neutrality, open and competitive examination processes, and equal pay, these ideals have rapidly changed (and in some cases radically so) over the turn of the last century as a result of public human resource management reforms. The reform framework provides an updated assessment of what reforms mean for successfully operating in the contemporary workplace. With the promise of efficiency, personnel reforms also bring about the potential for significant costs in terms of legal and fiscal uncertainties. Providing practical human resource solutions for coping with an increasingly complex environment is a key aim of the text.

The second section—*Functions*—puts the framework to work in earnest, taking up the impact reforms have had on routine human resource activities. These chapters highlight the difficulties of *recruiting and maintaining* qualified personnel in an increasingly reform-oriented environment; adequately *compensating* employees based on their organizational performance; employing appropriate *performance appraisals*; tapping the potential of public service *motivation*; and understanding the challenges contemporary reforms pose for *labor management relations* in the public sector.

Finally, I focus on *The Future* of public human resource management by reviewing topics that are trending and seldom covered in traditional textbooks. Among these trends is the increased reliance in the public sector on both private and nonprofit firms to provide HR functions in a bid for greater efficiency. Regardless of the merits of *privatization,* the public sector has embraced it as a viable alternative necessitating greater awareness among HR managers as the best way to manage the process. *Technology* has also tasked HR managers with a greater appreciation for HRIS software that can be applied to both routine and complex tasks in a bid to become more strategic in managing the future workforce. Accordingly, *strategic human resource management* (SHRM) considers the merits of strategic planning, improving internal processes and employee capacity, workforce planning, and accountability—features now considered essential to the future of PHRM. Given the changes taking place, scholars and instructors need to take stock of traditional subject areas and competencies and refocus our attention on topics such as data analysis, managerial economics, labor market analysis, communication, and international public human resource management. I conclude the text with an assessment of the potential challenges and opportunities public HR managers will face in the 21st century, tying together the analysis of PHRM reforms in each chapter into an overall analysis.

One final note about the organization of the text. In response to my students' many in-class questions, I incorporate nonprofit human resource management issues into the text. You will notice that each chapter offers a "Nonprofits in Focus" box. The recurring boxes provide insight into how the issues raised in each chapter affect nonprofits. While nonprofits are frequently included in the public affairs curriculum, they are also governed by a distinct set of legal guidelines. This is indeed the case for human resources in the nonprofit sector, where personnel rules and guidelines do not always mirror those of federal, state, and local PHRM.

Acknowledgments

I'm thankful for the support of colleagues and friends in the academy. If not for their encouragement *Public Human Resource Management: Strategies and Practices in the 21st Century* would have simply been an idea. Their insight and feedback proved instrumental in the delivery of the final product.

Thanks also go to my students in several semesters of PA 6345 Human Resource Management over the course of writing my text. They often served as a sounding board for many of my ideas for case studies and exercises. Ultimately, the text is meant to serve their needs as future stewards in the public and nonprofit sectors.

Working with the editorial team at CQ Press is without a doubt a professional highlight of my career. Publisher Charisse Kiino and development editor Nancy Loh were instrumental in supporting my contribution to academic literature and offered invaluable suggestions. The final version of the text also benefited from the exemplary copy editing expertise of Paula Fleming.

Finally, I am eternally grateful to my family for their patience and support over the duration of this project. Thanks to my wife Leah for her advice and editing suggestions. Thanks go to my son Luca for his patience while Daddy worked on his book instead of having playtime. My daughter Lola was born during the writing process, so once again I am thankful to my wife for answering late-night wake-up calls when Daddy needed to get up early to work on his book.

PART I

Foundations

1

Introduction

Public Human Resource Management in the 21st Century

Human resource management is an essential part of any organization, encompassing a wide range of activities and functions, including staffing and recruiting, administration of benefits and payroll, workforce planning, training and development, performance appraisal, discipline, labor-management relations, and overall employee well-being. In fact, most employer-employee relations in any organization involve some aspect of human resources. This is true regardless of whether the organization is in the public sector (government), the private sector (for-profit companies), or the nonprofit sector. However, **public human resource management (PHRM)**—human resource activities at the federal, state, and local levels of government—can be particularly challenging, as it often entails complex legal guidelines that apply exclusively to public sector employees and public organizations; guidelines that human resource managers must understand, abide by, and enforce. It is the policies, regulations, and practices of PHRM that are the focus of this book.

Furthermore, this text takes a contemporary approach in its coverage of PHRM, recognizing that over the last few decades, traditional PHRM has given way to quite a different landscape, one that looks increasingly like the private sector. Beginning in the late 1970s, a series of reforms has aimed at improving the efficiency of public services. The impetus for these reforms has been a critical view of traditional public management practices, especially of human resource practices. These have often been depicted as archaic and rule bound and as epitomizing the convoluted practices typical of bureaucracy. Traditional PHRM espoused democratic ideals and values, emphasized fair and equitable treatment of all public employees, and protected public employees' rights. However, traditional PHRM also conformed rigidly to rules and regulations and was based on a hierarchical structure, wherein a central personnel office set policy and made decisions that then filtered down to divisions or subordinate offices. Thus, making hiring and termination decisions in the public sector was widely viewed as unnecessarily time-consuming. A classic example of the byzantine human resource process was the rules and procedures governing federal government hiring outlined in the ten-thousand-plus page *Federal Personnel Manual* (Mesch, Perry, and Wise 1995).

The reforms that have been implemented over the last few decades have been referred to as "managerialist" in their focus or as "new public management." The influence of private sector practices aimed at improving productivity is a persistent theme throughout these public sector reform efforts. These reforms were meant to increase efficiency and productivity, and—in contrast to to traditional PHRM, which was more concerned with rules and proper bureaucratic process—they were results driven. Reformers advocated adopting greater flexibility in approaching tasks so as to be more efficient, using more managerial discretion, and embracing a "whatever gets the job done" philosophy. Such reformers have become increasingly commonplace in the public sector.

Given the extent of reform efforts over the last few decades, managing human resources in the public sector has become increasingly difficult to navigate. Changes to civil service laws at the local, state, and federal levels of government have also created confusion among those trying to implement human resource changes in their jurisdictions. Practitioners and scholars are in need of some clarification regarding the current state of PHRM to identify just what are best practices in public human resource management today.

The aim of this text is to provide readers with a foundational knowledge of how PHRM operates and functions, while also highlighting the changes that have been proposed and implemented in PHRM, the scholarly debate surrounding those changes, and the impact they've had on practice. The hope is that by considering the difficulties of navigating the new landscape of PHRM at federal, state, and local levels, scholars and practitioners will have a better road map to guide their work and a toolkit for implementing it.

The chapters that follow will develop a concise analysis of the impact reforms have had on routine practices, addressing changes to pay, benefits, employee rights and labor relations, diversity planning and affirmative action, and performance appraisal. To achieve this goal, the text has distilled these changes down to five specific types of reform that have been implemented in some form or another throughout the public sector: (1) decentralization, (2) deregulation, (3) performance-based pay, (4) declassification, and (5) privatization. We will use these five common reform types, which will each be explained and discussed in turn in the following section of this chapter, as a framework for appreciating the day-to-day impact these changes have had on PHRM operations. Each following chapter will then utilize the framework in light of the topic being reviewed; the final section of each chapter will offer insight into how these reforms have modified practices in the specific human resource area under discussion.

Each chapter will also provide information applicable to nonprofit human resource practices through a "Nonprofits in Focus" box. While not a specific focus of the text, nonprofit organizations are often considered in the broader PHRM discussion, and many readers will appreciate the challenges that managers in these organizations face—challenges that have intensified since the economic collapse of 2008. Finally, the book will address the future of PHRM education in graduate and undergraduate programs in light of recent reforms. Llorens and Battaglio's (2010) assessment of PHRM education in master's of public affairs/administration programs highlighted the shortcomings of graduate programs, which do not always teach the skills necessary to manage in a reform environment. A continued focus on more traditional human resource practices portends a future workforce ill-equipped for taking on future public service challenges. This text takes on these challenges head on.

Public HRM Reform: An Overview

The **civil service system**—the regulations, processes, and institutions that govern public employment—is the foundation of public service. Chapter 2 provides a more detailed account of the evolution of the American civil service system, but here we briefly discuss two landmark pieces of legislation that have been fundamental in shaping our civil service system—the Pendleton Act of 1883 and the Civil Service Reform Act of 1978. Both of the acts marked key points in history when civil service was redefined.

Historically, civil service systems based on professional merit were considered an essential element for government performance (Kellough and Nigro 2006b; Selden 2006). This practice was formally put into law with the Pendleton Act of 1883, which established a civil service system that separated routine work from policy and administrative process and that was based on merit, with open recruitment and competitive examinations (as opposed to the patronage and nepotism that was pervasive at the time) and political neutrality. These principles, which emulated the British tradition that had emerged in the mid-19th century, were deemed essential for effective governance.

These principles held for roughly the next century. In recent decades, however, the traditional association of civil service systems with effective governance has been challenged as being too focused on rules and not focused enough on finding the right person for the job. The Civil Service Reform Act of 1978 marked the beginning of the current reform era of PHRM, effecting a reorganization of the civil service system and increased managerial flexibility. Civil service reformers insist that reforming PHRM is crucial for enhancing government efficiency (Elling and Thompson

2007; Kettl et al. 1996). Functions such as planning, hiring, development, and discipline—typically centralized processes common to most levels of government— have been challenged by the current wave of reforms; they are now seen as civil service practices emblematic of bureaucratic inflexibility, inefficiency, and ineffectiveness. Greater managerial latitude has been afforded politicians and managers alike over personnel decisions and functions. As mentioned above, five distinct reform themes have emerged over the last three decades: decentralization, performance-based pay, declassification, deregulation, and privatization, and all have all challenged the traditional core of PHRM. Table 1.1 provides a summary of the five reform themes. In the

Table 1.1	**Public Human Resource Management Reform Types**
Decentralization	Staffing and compensation decisions are increasingly being made by agency and division level managers.
	Termination, transfer, and demotion decisions have also devolved to lower levels.
	Employment-at-will environments are removing hierarchy-based rules and regulations for staffing and compensation decisions.
Performance-Based Pay	Compensation is increasingly tied to performance.
	There is greater appreciation for effective performance appraisal and job analysis.
	Pay based on annual merit increases is being used as a recruitment, retention, and motivational tool.
Declassification	Salary and benefits are increasingly offered in nontraditional manners, such as broadbanding or paybanding.
	Classic step-in-grade classification and compensation is eschewed in favor of less finite job descriptions and pay.
	Greater skill is required to negotiate employment packages.
Deregulation	The expectation of continued employment is increasingly eroded or eliminated.
	A greater knowledge of the legal environment of PHRM is needed.
	PHRM systems may exhibit a mixture of step-in-grade classified and unclassified personnel, or even an employment-at-will environment.
Privatization	Many HR-related functions are being outsourced to private and nonprofit organizations.
	Negotiation and cost-benefit analysis skills are essential for awarding of contracts.
	HR personnel are often tasked with managing and monitoring contracts and contract employees.
	HR personnel increasingly need knowledge of contract law.

following sections, we review the contemporary reform environment and its potential impact on the traditional core functions of PHRM.

Decentralization

Traditionally, all staffing decisions for a jurisdiction were typically made by a central personnel office. This process could be time-consuming, as all decisions needed to be sent up and down the organizational hierarchy for approval. **Decentralization** entails HR functions being demoted to the lower agency (i.e., division or department). Turning over personnel decisions to agency-level HR directors and political appointees is seen as making government more responsive and effective. Decentralization strategies provide managers at the agency level greater latitude over management issues; they can make decisions more quickly and independently and do not need to wait for approval. This downward transfer of responsibility increases managerial flexibility where it is needed most—at the front line. Decentralization strategies, with their focus on improving innovation and accountability for personnel decisions at lower agency levels, have been a hallmark of public management reform in recent decades (Brudney, Hebert, and Wright 1999; Coggburn 2001; Kettl 2000; Thompson 2001).

At the federal level, decentralization has involved the transition of many programs to lower levels of government, replacing centralized, rule-bound systems with more agency-specific, manager-centered systems. Decentralization of PHRM functions has been advocated by reform proponents since the Civil Service Reform Act of 1978. This act abolished the Central Personnel Office, which had previously overseen the civil service, in favor of a streamlined, management-centered agency—the Office of Personnel Management (OPM)—under the president's purview. Since the creation of OPM, the federal decentralization trend has continued, with greater authority over staffing decisions moving to individual federal agencies while broader, higher-level planning issues remain with OPM.

In the 1990s, reform was spearheaded by the Clinton administration's efforts under the National Performance Review (NPR). Spearheaded by then vice president Al Gore, the NPR was a task force of intellectuals and practitioners of public management whose purpose was to offer recommendations for improving government performance. Initially, the agenda was ambitious, recommending the delegation of recruitment, examinations, position classification, salary adjustments, performance management, due process procedure modifications, and changes to the dismissal process to federal agencies (Gore 1993; Thompson 2001). However, political opposition—led by members of Congress sympathetic to civil service and labor—prevented any widespread change and resulted in more modest changes, coming primarily from reductions in the OPM and the elimination of the *Federal Personnel Manual* (Naff and Newman 2004).

During the George W. Bush presidency, initiatives at the federal level continued the push for decentralization. Legislative exemption from Title V of the US Code—the federal legislation governing civil service protections for federal employees—provided many agencies with the ability to develop more flexible systems, which in some instances resemble private sector practices (Woodard 2005, 113). For instance, the Homeland Security Act of 2002 significantly increased personnel flexibility within the Departments of Homeland Security (DHS) and Defense (DOD), giving the secretaries of both agencies greater latitude in managing labor relations and staffing (Brook and King 2008).

A number of state governments have also decentralized HRM decision making, with variations in which functions (e.g., classification, recruitment, selection, training, labor-management relations) have been targeted and to what extent (Selden, Ingraham, and Jacobson 2001). Voter sentiment for improved accountability in government has been a key component in the demand for greater decentralization, although this force has been tempered by the political environment and the degree of unionization in the respective states (Hou et al. 2000).

Decentralization is not without its drawbacks. Hou et al. (2000) asserted that decentralization at the state level has increased the support, planning, and supervision responsibilities of state personnel offices, overburdening them. Recently, Hays and Sowa (2006) surveyed all fifty states to determine to what extent the HR function was decentralizing. The authors found that a majority of states reported some degree of decentralization, often coupled with additional reform efforts. Given the extent of decentralization reform, it seems prudent to take stock of its ramifications for practice. Each chapter of this book will review the merits of decentralization in light of the topic under discussion.

Performance-Based Pay

Traditionally, PHRM pay structures were based on longevity or time-in-service, focusing on career management and advancement instead of employee performance. High-performing civil servants were not rewarded, and underperforming employees were not given incentives to improve. Since the 1980s, the push for greater accountability has resulted in a greater focus on performance management by rewarding superior performers with pay increases. **Performance-based pay structures** have proven to be an attractive alternative to traditional PHRM practices. Appealing to the logic of market-like mechanisms, proponents of compensation reform suggest that performance-based pay systems have the potential to increase employee performance and therefore organizational productivity. A number of performance-based pay schemes have been implemented by linking individual, team, and/or organizational performance measurement to financial incentives. Financial incentives can be distributed as increases to base pay (i.e., merit pay), one-time bonuses, or a combination of the two (Kellough and Nigro 2002, 146). According to Kellough (2006),

> Presumably, such a policy would prevent resentment or alienation of the best employees that could result when their superior contributions are not recognized, and they receive the same pay as their less-productive colleagues. At the same time, poorer performers are offered an incentive to improve their levels of productivity. (184)

The federal government tested performance-based pay systems from 1981 to 1993 (Kellough and Nigro 2002). However, government-wide attempts during this period, which relegated performance-based pay to individual agency-level decisions, proved unsuccessful. An inability to distinguish poor performance from other levels of performance, inadequate financial support, and insufficient evidence to confirm improved performance led to the demise of federal performance-based pay systems (Perry, Engbers, and Jun 2009; Perry, Patrakis, and Miller 1989). More recently, the Homeland Security Act of 2002 granted authority to DHS and DOD to implement performance-based pay systems. According to Brook and King (2008), approximately 90,000 of the total 2.7 million federal civilian employees were covered by performance-based pay systems by 2005 (10).

Despite its problematic history at the federal level, numerous jurisdictions at the state level have continued to pursue performance-based pay systems (Hays 2004). Hays and Sowa (2006) noted that more than half of the states they surveyed indicated either implementing or planning some form of pay reform. GeorgiaGain, the performance-based pay reform in the state of Georgia, has garnered significant attention from both practitioners and academics as a result of implementation problems (Kellough and Nigro 2002, 2006b). Like pay reform initiatives elsewhere, the Georgia reforms were politically popular, but they failed to achieve demonstrable evidence of success among state employees. Even though implementing GeorgiaGain has proven problematic, the state has continued to rely on performance-based pay for improving employee and agency productivity. In Georgia, as with in many states, this is often the result of the government's desire to demonstrate legitimacy to the public—that is, while the evidence for success is sparse, the continued pursuit of accountability policies in itself is attractive to a public that feels cynical about traditional government efficiency (Perry, Engbers, and Jun 2009). Thus, politicians are encouraged to continue advocating performance-based policies as long as citizens are convinced that government is broken.

Declassification

Civil service systems have typically employed hierarchical **step-in-grade** classification structures as a means for career management. Upon hire, public employees are typically ranked at a particular grade (and pay) level based on their qualifications, education, and experience. Through time-in-service, employees are promoted to higher steps within each grade, and eventually higher grade levels, receiving better pay as long as they perform satisfactorily. Grades are classified according to strict job descriptions in a career class category, and each step, grade, and corresponding pay level is listed in a matrix often called a "general schedule."

However, the view of many reformers is that traditional classification structures restrict hiring authorities' ability to attract applicants from outside the agency or the broader public sector. **Declassification** refers to the easing of the rules that define pay grades in terms of very specific job descriptions. Advocates argue that more open-ended job searches can exploit a larger, more talented pool of qualified applicants whose résumés do not necessarily match up exactly with the job description.

Broadbanding (or **paybanding**) classification structures—the collapsing or combining of a number of traditional grades into a single band—is often employed as a means for declassification. Managers then hire for jobs with broader descriptions and pay structures and have greater flexibility over pay rates both at hire and during the employee's tenure (Hays 2004; Whalen and Guy 2008). Broadbanding emerged as a result of Title VI of the Civil Service Reform Act of 1978, which authorized agencies to waive civil service rules in order to develop innovative new approaches to traditional PHRM functions (Shafritz et al. 2001). It has its roots in the demonstration projects—that is, limited rollouts of new initiatives on a small scale before implementing them on a wider basis—commissioned under Title VI, and it has since been used more widely in government. By compensating employees according to their unique skills, broadbanding was intended to promote egalitarianism by removing the distinctions accompanying traditional pay grades and by deemphasizing the centralized personnel system's insistence on titles and hierarchy.

Classification reform during the Clinton administration was part of NPR's mission to reinvent OPM and the human resources function (Shafritz et al. 2001). While the Clinton administration included language in civil service reform legislation that authorized agencies to pursue broadbanding, labor unions resisted these proposals, viewing declassification efforts as encroaching on union authority. As a result, the federal government continued to rely on authorization for such measures through Title VI (201). However, civil service reform legislation by the Bush administration post–September 11 included provisions for replacing the general schedule with paybanding systems for DHS and DOD (Thompson 2007). As suggested earlier, these efforts focus on enhancing manager discretion over compensation and employee performance, thereby moving away from central personnel authorization.

At the state level, there is a general trend toward fewer job classifications (Hays and Sowa 2006; Whalen and Guy 2008). In 2008, Whalen and Guy surveyed all fifty states in an effort to assess the extent of broadbanding. The authors found that civil service systems implemented broadbanding to reduce job classifications as well as promote pay for performance. While demonstrable evidence of the effectiveness of broadbanding is lacking, Whalen and Guy's work suggests that it is still part of the broader PHRM reform movement in the states. Among those states utilizing broad-banding, twelve implemented government-wide broadbanding, and four employed such measures on a limited scale (Whalen and Guy 2008, 1). Additionally, the authors found that eighteen states considered broadbanding but opted against it.

Deregulation

Over the last few decades, there has been a general trend in eliminating personnel rules and regulations—**deregulation**—in an effort to expedite PHRM decisions. Rules akin to the ten-thousand-page personnel manual regulating federal govern-ment staffing exist in jurisdictions throughout the country. Traditionally, civil ser-vice systems have afforded public employees the right to a hearing (the right to due process of law) as part of the grievance process. In the spirit of managerial flexibility, reformers have supported severe limitations to, or outright elimination of, employee procedural due process rights to promote greater efficiency and effectiveness in public management (Facer 1998). The elimination of the grievance process is seen as a critical component of streamlining and expediting the termination of poor-performing employees. The trend toward eliminating such rights altogether has led to what some have called "radical" civil service reform (Condrey and Battaglio 2007). These "radical" personnel systems operate under an employment-at-will (EAW) environment in which employees may be dismissed summarily, for any rea-son that does not violate employment law (Muhl 2001). Employees within EAW systems have no expectation of continued employment, as has traditionally been the case under the protections provided through civil service systems (Gertz 2007; Kellough and Nigro 2006b; Lindquist and Condrey 2006). Thus, many public employees now have no guarantee of procedural due process before discipline or removal (Kuykendall and Facer 2002).

EAW is seen as a means for increasing managerial efficiency because it removes what some view as the cumbersome grievance and appeals processes under tradi-tional civil service systems. Instead of following guidelines that might lead to a lengthy dismissal process—a process that reform proponents suggest is a waste of taxpayer dollars—managers under EAW need provide little or no notice before ter-minating an employee they perceive as performing poorly.

During the last decade, efforts at the federal level have sought to curb tradi-tional civil service system practices, especially through legislation promoted by the George W. Bush administration in the wake of September 11 (Kellough and Nigro 2005). Federal efforts have generally emanated from legislation permitting exemption from Title V, OPM demonstration projects, and legislative approval of performance-based polices (Woodard 2005, 110). At the state level, efforts to curb employee rights have occurred in Georgia, Florida, and, more recently, Colorado and Arizona (Hays and Sowa 2006; see also Bowman and West 2007; Condrey and Maranto 2001; Kellough and Nigro 2006a). EAW reforms in Georgia and Florida have been the most visible (Battaglio and Condrey 2006; Bowman and West 2006; Condrey and Battaglio 2007). Georgia has led the "radical" reform trend toward EAW by phasing out its merit system for all "unclassified" positions (i.e., those not granted protection by the State Civil Service Board) beginning in 1996. Approximately 80 percent of Georgia's state employees are now employed at will (Condrey 2002; Condrey and Battaglio 2007; Facer 1998). Florida followed in 2001 with Governor Jeb Bush's Service First initiative, which placed senior state government managers in at-will status (approximately 13 percent of total employees; Condrey and Battaglio 2007, 427). As will be detailed in later chapters, some research suggests that the increased use of EAW policies has had a negative effect on employee motivation and performance.

Privatization

A key component of public management reform, privatization is intended to improve accountability and quality of service (Kettl 2000; Savas 2000). According to Savas (2000) **privatization** entails increased reliance on private sector and nongovernmental (i.e., nonprofit) institutions—rather than government—for the delivery and production of public sector needs. Indeed, governments at all levels have increasingly looked to the private sector for the delivery of many HRM functions, such as payroll and benefits administration (Battaglio and Condrey 2006; Fernandez, Rainey, and Lowman 2006; Shafritz, Russell, and Borick 2007). Proponents of privatization insist that the inefficiency of rule-bound PHRM systems presents no alternative but to encourage the increased use of contractors who can hire new personnel quickly and dismiss poor performers (Maranto 2001, 75).

The rationale for opting out of in-house provision of HRM services mirrors more general reasons proffered for privatization within public management. HR privatization may allow public agencies to take advantage of larger firms' economies of scale or the quality advantage inherent in specializing in HRM (Fernandez, Rainey, and Lowman 2006, 220). Moreover, by unburdening current HR employees from more mundane tasks, privatization has the potential to provide greater flexibility to pursue core functions such as strategic planning (Fernandez, Rainey, and Lowman 2006, 220; Rainey 2005). The rationales for privatization may depend on the degree of difficulty associated with the tasks outsourced (Coggburn 2007, 317; Rainey 2005). PHRM services associated with more mundane tasks, such as payroll, are often outsourced as a way of saving money and freeing up personnel to focus on more strategic functions (Coggburn 2007, 317; Kellough and Nigro 2006a, 320; Rainey 2005, 706). Looking to the private sector to provide functions such as workforce planning and performance management, on the other hand, may be oriented not so much toward saving money as toward tapping expertise not readily available in the public sector (Coggburn 2007, 317; Rainey 2005, 706). This is especially true when functions are outsourced to consulting companies (e.g., Deloitte, PricewaterhouseCoopers, The Segal Company), which have entire divisions dedicated to workforce planning.

While the push for private sector involvement in the delivery of public services has received considerable attention in recent decades, the demonstrable evidence regarding public HRM privatization (or outsourcing) is scant. Although the public sector has experimented with outsourcing HRM functions such as payroll and benefits administration, consulting, wage and salary surveys, job analysis, and job evaluation, little is known about the perceived efficiency gains from such activities (Coggburn 2007, 316). More recently, the George W. Bush administration sought to rely more heavily on the private sector through privatization programs such as the Competitive Sourcing Initiative (CSI), which encouraged government agencies to consider outsourcing to private contractors. In fact, in 2004 the Bush administration outsourced the management of the federal government's workforce recruitment system, USAJOBS, to a private firm (Llorens and Kellough 2007; Shafritz, Russell, and Borick 2007, 423).

Governments have sought to outsource some, if not all, of the HR function as a means to tap private sector know-how and quality. For states, outsourced activities range from specific functions to agency HRM services to HR functions for the entire state. Indeed, state HR privatization activities have been much more pervasive than those at the federal level. For example, the firm Convergys, based in Cincinnati, Ohio, was awarded lucrative contracts to provide HR functions to the states of Florida and Texas (see Battaglio and Condrey 2006; Coggburn 2007; Condrey and Battaglio 2007). In the case of Florida, Convergys was awarded a $350 million, nine-year contract to perform transaction and process functions related to benefits, payroll, and staffing (Battaglio and Condrey 2006, 122–25). In Texas, Convergys was awarded an $85 million, five-year contract with the state's Health and Human Service Commission to provide many HR-related functions, such as performance management, recruitment and selection, benefits, payroll, and compensation and classification administration (Coggburn 2007, 319). Coggburn (2007) suggested that these efforts in Texas and Florida have motivated private sector interest in soliciting government business and public sector interest in outsourcing state functions. In both instances, however, the expenses associated with misuse of public funds, cost overruns, and monitoring proved detrimental to overall efficiency. Given the trend toward outsourcing to the private sector, there is a critical need for managers in the public sector who can effectively coordinate contractual relationships.

Implications for Public HRM

Each of these reforms has to some extent dramatically altered the traditional core functions of PHRM related to merit and equity (Thompson 2001), and they suggest the need for a significant reassessment of PHRM education. For example, as governments decentralize HR, moving it out of central personnel offices, HR professionals at the agency level are now burdened with more responsibilities. Without the expertise of central personnel staff, HR professionals need extensive training to cope with these new responsibilities. Moreover, these tasks may be particularly cumbersome for HR professionals in smaller agencies who lack the greater resources of larger organizations (Coggburn 2001; Hou et al. 2000). With performance-based pay systems, HR policy makers face difficulties in creating a government-wide standard given agency differences (Hays and Sowa 2006; Kellough and Nigro 2002). HR professionals need better training in designing and implementing an efficient performance appraisal system that accurately rewards the behaviors that contribute to success in the absence of clear standards. Criticism related to broadbanding often cites the potential for decentralized pay decisions to lead to increased costs, legal liability, problems with pay comparability, and a disconnection with the labor market (Hays and Sowa 2006; Shafritz et al. 2001; see also Whalen and Guy 2008). Thus, HR professionals need adequate training in competitive compensation practices, salary negotiations, performance appraisal, budgeting, and labor market analysis.

The push to further diminish public sector job security through EAW has the potential to exacerbate recruitment and retention problems. With job security no longer a viable incentive for public sector employment, HR professionals need to be skilled in novel methods for marketing to prospective employees, as well as motivating and retaining employees. For example, federal agencies have begun to use student loan repayment incentives to recruit younger employees who carry ever-increasing levels of educational debt (US Office of Personnel Management 2008). Guidelines for the student loan repayment program state that agencies may offer up to $10,000 in loan repayments per calendar year but are not to exceed $60,000 in total payments per employee. However, deciding the extent of payments to be offered and whether or not to pair payments with service requirements necessitates the use of skill sets not commonly covered in the traditional PHRM curriculum. Also, given the limited or outright removal of due process rights, HR professionals will also need to be aware of the legal environment of EAW systems (Kuykendall and Facer 2002; Lindquist and Condrey 2006). Last, privatization of HR functions requires more extensive knowledge of cost-benefit analysis and contract management, and HR professionals charged with contract management need tools to ensure accountability through monitoring, legal restrictions, competition, cost accounting, and overall evaluation (Siegel 1999, 2000).

Organization of the Book

The book is divided into three parts: *Foundations*, *Functions*, and *The Future*. In Part I of the text—*Foundations*—the material reviews the underpinnings of modern PHRM, beginning with this chapter's review of the trends in public service reform: decentralization, performance-based pay, declassification, deregulation, and privatization. In Chapter 2, "Evolution of the Public Service in the United States," the focus is the development on the modern civil service system. The chapter argues that public service as we know it in America would not exist without the foundation of civil service law and employee protections, buttressed by merit-based employment, neutral competence, an open and competitive examination process, equal pay, and protection against redress for disclosing malfeasance in government. Chapter 3, "Employment Law in the Public Sector," reviews current and previous precedents in statutory law and case law regulating public employment, as well as the legal implications of recent reforms at the federal and state levels. Public HR managers will need to be knowledgeable in this area if they hope to avoid significant costs associated with settling disputes in court. The final chapter in *Foundations*, "Equal Employment Opportunity, Affirmative Action, and Diversity Planning," details how PHRM functions have incorporated policies to promote and enforce equal employment opportunity (EEO), affirmative action, and diversity management. For many public employers, legal uncertainty and fiscal constraints require practical solutions for implementing diversity policies. The chapter reviews the research in this area and legal precedents for public employers, offering pragmatic advice for coping with the legal environment of diversity.

Part II—*Functions*—addresses routine activities of PHRM in light of the current era of reform. Chapter 5, "Recruitment and Selection," highlights the difficulties of recruiting and maintaining qualified personnel an in increasingly reform-oriented environment. Recruiting the future public service will be a challenge for HR directors in a declassified and deregulated climate. In Chapter 6, "Pay and Benefits," efforts at reforming public sector compensation have sought to institutionalize performance-based pay and broadbanding, despite evidence that these approaches may not be the most effective (Perry, Engbers, and Jun 2009). The chapter reviews these efforts along with the foundation of modern compensation in the public sector—job analysis. Chapter 7, "Performance Appraisal," examines PHRM reforms that have retooled the performance appraisal process. The chapter offers insight into how HR managers might use such approaches in their workplace. "Managing Motivation in the Public Service," Chapter 8, looks at efforts to get public employees to be more performance oriented. Performance-based pay and employment-at-will are frequently employed to improve motivation in the public service. However, recent research suggests that these tools are not as motivationally oriented as previously proposed. Chapter 9,

"Labor Relations in the Public Sector," reviews the challenges public sector unions and collective bargaining face at the state and local levels in the contemporary environment of PHRM reform.

In the third and final section of the text—*The Future*—the chapters focus on those issues that will influence future PHRM practices. Chapter 10, "Privatizing Human Resource Functions in the Public Sector," considers the increased reliance on both private and nonprofit firms to provide HR functions in a bid for greater efficiency. To be sure, outsourcing has proven to be productive in many instances. However, in a number of instances, public/private sector arrangements have not proven fruitful, resulting in both waste and legal complications. The chapter means to improve upon the best of what government and business have to offer the public service. In Chapter 11, "Human Resource Information Systems," the impact of information technology on PHRM is considered, especially in light of the trend toward knowledge management as a key component of successfully navigating the information age. HRIS has proven to be an important tool for public HR managers who are tasked with human capital management and workforce planning. Thus, HRIS has the potential to serve as a vital tool in public sector efforts to think strategically—the topic of Chapter 12, "Strategic Public Human Resource Management." While the literature on strategic human resource management (SHRM) is broad and expansive, this chapter seeks to provide an introductory overview of the potential contribution of a human capital management approach to the public sector. The chapter considers the merits of strategic planning, improving internal processes and employee capacity, workforce planning, and accountability—features now considered essential to the future of PHRM. Chapter 13, "Public Human Resource Management Education," considers the reevaluation of those subject areas and competencies that have long been considered the core of PHRM education. The chapter explores new HRM competencies and the extent to which contemporary academic and practitioner-based educational programs reflect the current landscape of public sector HR management. Finally, Chapter 14, "Conclusion: Challenges and Opportunities," assesses the potential challenges and opportunities public HR managers will face in the 21st century, tying together the analysis of PHRM reforms in each chapter into an overall assessment.

Often included in the broader discussion of public sector HRM are personnel activities in nonprofit organizations. The recurring "Nonprofits in Focus" boxes will provide insights into how the issues raised in each chapter affect nonprofits. While nonprofits are frequently included in the public affairs curriculum, they are also governed by a distinct set of legal guidelines. This is indeed the case for human resources in the nonprofit sector, where personnel rules and guidelines do not always mirror those of federal, state, and local PHRM.

References

Battaglio, R. Paul, Jr., and Stephen E. Condrey. 2006. "Civil Service Reform: Examining State and Local Cases." *Review of Public Personnel Administration* 26:118–38.

Bowman, James S., and Jonathan P. West. 2006. "Ending Civil Service Protections in Florida Government: Experiences in State Agencies." *Review of Public Personnel Administration* 26:139–57.

Bowman, James S., and Jonathan P. West, eds. 2007. *American Public Service: Radical Reform and the Merit System.* Boca Raton, FL: Taylor & Francis.

Brook, Douglas A., and Cynthia L. King. 2008. "Federal Personnel Management Reform: From Civil Service Reform Act to National Security Reforms." *Review of Public Personnel Administration* 28:205–21.

Brudney, Jeffrey L., F. Ted Hebert, and Deil S. Wright. 1999. "Reinventing Government in the American States: Measuring and Explaining Administrative Reform." *Public Administration Review* 59:19–30.

Coggburn, Jerrell D. 2001. "Is Deregulation the Answer for Public Personnel Management? Revisiting a Familiar Question: Introduction." *Review of Public Personnel Administration* 20:5–8.

Coggburn, Jerrell D. 2007. "Outsourcing Human Resources: The Case of Texas Health and Human Services Commission." *Review of Public Personnel Administration* 27:315–35.

Condrey, Stephen E. 2002. "Reinventing State Civil Service Systems: The Georgia Experience." *Review of Public Personnel Administration* 22:114–24.

Condrey, Stephen E., and R. Paul Battaglio Jr. 2007. "A Return to Spoils? Revisiting Radical Civil Service Reform in the United States." *Public Administration Review* 67:424–36.

Condrey, Stephen E., and Robert Maranto, eds. 2001. *Radical Reform of the Civil Service.* Lanham, MD: Lexington Books.

Elling, Richard C., and T. Lyke Thompson. 2007. "Dissin' the Deadwood or Coddling the Incompetents? Patterns and Issues in Employee Discipline and Dismissal in the States." In *American Public Service: Radical Reform and the Merit System,* edited by James S. Bowman and Jonathan P. West, 195–217. Boca Raton, FL: Taylor and Francis.

Facer, Rex L., II. 1998. "Reinventing Public Administration: Reform in the Georgia Civil Service." *Public Administration Quarterly* 22:58–72.

Fernandez, Sergio, Hal G. Rainey, and Carol E. Lowman. 2006. "Privatization and Its Implications for Human Resources Management." In *Public Personnel Management: Current Concerns, Future Challenges,* 4th ed., edited by Norma M. Riccucci, 204–24. New York: Longman.

Gertz, Sally C. 2007. "At-Will Employment: Origins, Applications, Exceptions, and Expansions in Public Service." In *American Public Service: Radical Reform and the Merit System,* edited by James S. Bowman and Jonathan P. West, 47–74. Boca Raton, FL: Taylor and Francis.

Gore, Al. 1993. *Creating a Government That Works Better and Costs Less: The Report of the National Performance Review.* New York: Plume.

Hays, Steven W. 2004. "Trends and Best Practices in State and Local Human Resource Management: Lessons to Be Learned?" *Review of Public Personnel Administration* 24:256–75.

Hays, Steven W., and Jessica E. Sowa. 2006. "A Broader Look at the 'Accountability' Movement: Some Grim Realities." *Review of Public Personnel Administration* 26:102–17.

Hou, Yilin, Patricia Ingraham, Stuart Bretschneider, and Sally Coleman Selden. 2000. "Decentralization of Human Resource Management: Driving Forces and Implications." *Review of Public Personnel Administration* 20:9–22.

Kellough, J. Edward. 2006. "Employee Performance Appraisal in the Public Sector: Uses and Limitations." In *Public Personnel Management: Current Concerns, Future Challenges,* 4th ed., edited by Norma M. Riccucci, 177–89. New York: Longman.

Kellough, J. Edward, and Lloyd G. Nigro. 2002. "Pay for Performance in Georgia State Government: Employee Perspectives on GeorgiaGain after 5 Years." *Review of Public Personnel Administration* 22:146–66.

Kellough, J. Edward, and Lloyd G. Nigro. 2005. "Radical Civil Service Reform: Ideology, Politics, and Policy." In *Handbook of Human Resource Management in Government,* 2nd ed., edited by Stephen E. Condrey, 58–75. San Francisco, CA: Jossey-Bass.

Kellough, J. Edward, and Lloyd G. Nigro, eds. 2006a. *Civil Service Reform in the States: Personnel Policy and Politics at the Subnational Level.* Albany: SUNY Press.

Kellough, J. Edward, and Lloyd G. Nigro. 2006b. "Dramatic Reform in the Public Service: At-Will Employment and the Creation of a New Public Workforce." *Journal of Public Administration Research and Theory* 16:447–66.

Kettl, Donald F. 2000. *The Global Management Revolution: A Report on the Transformation of Governance.* Washington, DC: Brookings Institution.

Kettl, Donald F., Patricia W. Ingraham, Ronald P. Sanders, and Constance Horner. 1996. *Civil Service Reform: Building a Government That Works.* Washington, DC: The Brookings Institute.

Kuykendall, Christine L., and Rex L. Facer II. 2002. "Public Employment in Georgia Agencies: The Elimination of the Merit System." *Review of Public Personnel Administration* 22:133–45.

Lindquist, Stefanie A., and Stephen E. Condrey. 2006. "Public Employment Reforms and Constitutional Due Process." In *Civil Service Reform in the States: Personnel Policy and Politics at the Subnational Level,* edited by J. Edward Kellough and Lloyd G. Nigro, 95–114. Albany: SUNY Press.

Llorens, Jared J., and R. Paul Battaglio Jr. 2010. "Human Resources Management in a Changing World: Reassessing Public Human Resources Management Education." *Review of Public Personnel Administration* 30:112–32.

Llorens, Jared J., and J. Edward Kellough. 2007. "A Revolution in Public Personnel Administration: The Growth of Web-Based Recruitment and Selection Processes in the Federal Service." *Public Personnel Management* 36:207–21.

Maranto, Robert. 2001. "Thinking the Unthinkable in Public Administration: A Case for Spoils in the Federal Bureaucracy." In *Radical Reform of the Civil Service,* edited by Stephen E. Condrey and Robert Maranto, 69–86. Lanham, MD: Lexington Books.

Mesch, Debra J., James L. Perry, and Lois Recascino Wise. 1995. "Bureaucratic and Strategic Human Resource Management: An Empirical Comparison in the Federal Government." *Journal of Public Administration Research and Theory* 5:385–402.

Muhl, Charles J. 2001. "The Employment-at-Will Doctrine: Three Major Exceptions." *Monthly Labor Review* 124:3–11.

Naff, Katherine C., and Meredith A. Newman. 2004. "Symposium: Federal Civil Service Reform; Another Legacy of 9/11?" *Review of Public Personnel Administration* 24:191–201.

Perry, James L., Trent A. Engbers, and So Yun Jun. 2009. "Back to the Future? Performance-Related Pay, Empirical Research, and the Perils of Persistence." *Public Administration Review* 69:39–51.

Perry, James L., Beth Ann Petrakis, and Theodore K. Miller. 1989. "Federal Merit Pay, Round II: An Analysis of the Performance Management and Recognition System." *Public Administration Review* 49:29–37

Rainey, Glen W. 2005. "Human Resources Consultants and Outsourcing: Focusing on Local Government." In *Handbook of Human Resource Management in Government,* 2nd ed., edited by Stephen E. Condrey, 701–34. San Francisco, CA: Jossey-Bass.

Savas, E. S. 2000. *Privatization and Public-Private Partnerships.* New York: Chatham House.

Selden, Sally Coleman. 2006. "The Impact of Discipline on the Use and Rapidity of Dismissal in State Governments." *Review of Public Personnel Administration* 26:335–55.

Selden, Sally Coleman, Patricia W. Ingraham, and Willow Jacobson. 2001. "Human Resource Practices in State Government: Findings from a National Survey." *Public Administration Review,* 61:598–607.

Shafritz, Jay M., David H. Rosenbloom, Norma A. Riccucci, Katherine C. Naff, and Al C. Hyde. 2001. *Personnel Management in Government: Politics and Process.* New York: Marcel Dekker.

Shafritz, Jay M., E. W. Russell, and Christopher P. Borick. 2007. *Introducing Public Administration.* 5th ed. New York: Pearson Longman.

Siegel, Gilbert B. 1999. "Where Are We on Local Government Contracting?" *Public Productivity & Management Review* 22:365–88.

Siegel, Gilbert B. 2000. "Outsourcing Personnel Functions." *Public Personnel Management* 29:225–36.

Thompson, James R. 2001. "The Civil Service under Clinton: The Institutional Consequences of Disaggregation." *Review of Public Personnel Administration* 21:87–113.

Thompson, James R. 2007. "Federal Labor-Management Relations Reforms under Bush: Enlightened Management or Quest for Control?" *Review of Public Personnel Administration* 27:105–24.

US Office of Personnel Management (USOPM). 2008. "Pay & Leave: Student Loan Repayment." Accessed March 23, 2014. http://www.opm.gov/policy-data-oversight/pay-leave/student-loan-repayment/.

Whalen, Cortney, and Mary E. Guy. 2008. "Broadbanding Trends in the States." *Review of Public Personnel Administration* 28:349–66.

Woodard, Colleen A. (2005). "Merit by Any Other Name—Reframing the Civil Service First Principle." *Public Administration Review* 65:109–16.

2

Evolution of the Public Service in the United States

Upon completion of the chapter, you will be able to do the following:

- Describe and list the characteristics of each of the periods of public service as delineated by Frederick Mosher.
- Explain how the current US civil service system has evolved since the country's founding.
- List the key principles of the merit system.

This chapter will discuss how public employment in the United States has evolved since our nation's founding in 1789, focusing on how the **civil service system** was a key element in its development. Public service as we now know it in America would not exist without the underpinning of civil service law and employee protections set forth with the passage of the Pendleton Act in 1883. Early development of civil service began with this landmark piece of legislation. It established the initial principles of civil service employment in the US federal personnel system, which were later diffused to and adopted by state and local governments. The principles outlined in the Pendleton Act, discussed more fully later in this chapter, still serve as the foundation of the laws governing our civil service system today.

While the focus of the chapter is the current era of reform, beginning in the late 1970s and continuing through the present day, the first six sections of the chapter will provide historical background on the evolution of public employment. The remainder of the chapter will cover the current era and delve more deeply into the reforms discussed in Chapter 1, as well as provide analysis of these modern PHRM reforms.

Using Mosher's (1982) typology as a foundation, we can trace the evolution of public sector employment in the United States. Mosher's historical overview is useful for providing context to the key events and legislation that shaped the development of public employment. Beginning with the founding of the United States in 1789, Americans have wrestled with how to govern public employment, as can be seen by the numerous phases that have characterized public service over the years. Politicians, practitioners, and academics continue to debate the extent of autonomy afforded public servants and the degree of administrative control provided to politicians and managers over public employment. Table 2.1 presents significant periods in United States history that proved formative in the development of public employment broadly and civil service more specifically. While the first few periods reflect public employment as a work in progress, the First Reform Period shows the beginning of civil service reform in earnest.

Government by Gentlemen: The Guardian Period (1789–1829)

During the initial public employment period—Government by Gentlemen—the newly formed country required very little in the way of public servants. The fledgling republic had limited public policy capacities—the exceptions being the military and foreign affairs—so public services were managed and staffed by a select few. Vital public services—such as public works—were often left up to municipalities and the

Table 2.1	Timeline of Public Employment in the United States	
Date	**Period**	**Benchmark**
1789–1829	Government by Gentlemen: The Guardian Period	Inauguration of Washington
1830–1883	Government by the Common Man: The Spoils Period	Inauguration of Jackson
1884–1906	Government by the Good: The First Reform Period	Passage of the Pendleton Act
1907–1937	Government by the Efficient: The Scientific Management Period	Founding of the New York Bureau of Municipal Research
1938–1964	Government by Individuals: The Behavioralism Period	Establishment of the President's Committee on Administrative Management
1965–1978	Government by Equality: The Civil Rights Period	Passage of the Civil Rights Act of 1964
1979–Present	Government by Reform: The Managerialist Period	Passage of the Civil Service Reform Act of 1978

Source: Adapted from Mosher (1982).

states. The founders in many ways espoused a general hostility toward bureaucracy and elites. This is not surprising given the antigovernment sentiment toward their British colonial masters before and during the Revolutionary War. Accordingly, early presidential administrations based appointment to the ranks of government by "fitness of character." As such, a prospective government employee was judged by his standing in the community, educational attainment, and record of supporting the American Revolution (Mosher 1982). Those chosen for public service were seen as men of integrity, as "guardians" to be trusted with carrying out the public interest. Lacking a formal or uniform selection process, the government had only strength of character, determined by the criteria above, as a guide to choosing candidates for employment until the 1820s.

Government by the Common Man: The Spoils Period (1829–1883)

The inauguration of Andrew Jackson (1829–1837) marked a new era in public service characterized by a more egalitarian view of government. The lack of rotation among public servants led to an increasing awareness of elitism among the echelons of government—antithetical to the original mistrust of those in power. In response to such fears, Andrew Jackson sought to democratize the public service (Mosher 1982). The Jackson presidency encouraged greater participation in the electoral process and public service by the mass populace, regardless of status or educational attainment. During the era of Jacksonian Democracy, universal white male suffrage attracted a greater plebian constituency to the political process (i.e., *Government by the Common Man*). For Jackson, public service was a necessary and effortlessly agreeable vocation. Indeed, Jackson famously quipped,

> The duties of public office are so plain and simple that men of intelligence may readily qualify themselves for their performance; and I cannot but believe that more is lost by the long continuance of men in office than is generally to be gained by their experience. (Riccucci and Naff 2006, 6)

Jackson feared that persons in public office risked attenuating the public interest by extending their incumbency (White 1954). Thus, the rotation of those in office with each election cycle was seen as a move toward a more democratic system of public employment.

The notion of the **spoils system**[1] is typically attributed to Andrew Jackson, but in reality, his commitment to an egalitarian public service was equivocal. During the

---

[1]The phrase can be attributed to Sen. William L. Marcy (NY), who, in an 1832 debate with Sen. Henry Clay (KY), stated that the politicians in the United States "see nothing wrong in the rule, that to the victor belong the spoils of the enemy" (White 1954, 320).

spoils period of public employment, hiring, removal, and related personnel decisions increasingly relied upon the employee's partisan affiliation, specifically whether he supported the political goals of the party in power. Indeed, many state and local jurisdictions had been practicing the spoils system well before the Jackson era. However, even at the height of Jackson's power, there existed career public servants who retained their tenure through several administrations. Indeed, even Jackson recognized the importance of ensuring capable appointments to the public service (Mosher 1982). The overriding legacy of the era, though, was an intellectual and political rationale for effectively staffing the bureaucracy by the doctrine of rotation in office (Shafritz et al. 2001). Presidents following Jackson continued this practice, which had numerous negative consequences.

Reflecting on the spoils era, Mosher (1982) suggested that its mark on the federal government, as well as state and local jurisdictions, has been indelible.

- Increasingly, public servants were chosen because of their political affiliation instead of their competence. The only qualification for public employment was often political support for a particular candidate.
- Every time a new executive was elected, there was a new wave of government employees because the spoils system rewarded those who were sympathetic to the party in power. This process proved ever more chaotic for subsequent administrations.
- Everybody wanted a political appointment since it was available to the "common man," and people went to great lengths to attain such appointments—including unethical means. Those with political connections—patronage—had an advantage.
- Further compounding the Spoils Period was infighting between the executive and legislative branches over control of the appointment process (66).

Arguably, the most notable spoils abuses were the attempts of William "Boss" Tweed to garner greater influence over the Democratic Party machine in New York politics. Boss Tweed used his spoils system—commonly referred to as Tammany Hall—in a strategic effort to control New York State politics at the judicial and legislative levels. His machine was not above rigging the ballot box by use of fraud, money laundering, profit sharing, and racketeering (Ackerman 2005). According to Mosher, the end result was not a more representative government but a more political government. While the Jackson era opened up public service to the common man, the common man did not ultimately benefit. A new American elite consisting of office seekers who successfully won appointments through political machinations was created. This exclusive group was dominated by politicians more interested in increasing their political capital than in serving the public. Instead of creating a more egalitarian public service, the spoils era was just as irresponsible and unrepresentative as the system Jacksonian reformers had intended to fix. By the 1880s, the public service was again due for reform.

Government by the Good: The First Reform Period (1883–1906)

Toward the end of the 19th century, the overwhelming sentiment was that the public service was broken and in need of reform. Abuses of power, like those of Boss Tweed in New York, rendered rooting out the rampant, endemic corruption in government a moral imperative. As in the previous era of Jacksonian Democracy, reformers of this era, deemed **Progressives**, sought a more egalitarian and democratic public service, but they pursued their objective by different means (Mosher 1982).

A confluence of factors set in motion the Progressive reforms, which would usher in the modern civil service system. Rapid industrialization meant a need for increased government presence to deal with economic growth, as government was the only viable entity capable of building and maintaining the necessary infrastructure for promoting industry. Shaping industrial growth in urban areas necessitated the expertise of engineers, planners, and architects. Moreover, media reports regarding abuses in industry created a public outcry for greater regulation of the mass production of goods. For example, Upton Sinclair's exposure of conditions in the meatpacking industry in *The Jungle* (1906) is often credited with passage of the Pure Food and Drug Act of 1906, which authorized government regulation of such activities. The public service, such as it was in the mid- to late 1800s, was staffed by opportunistic office seekers and was not professionally equipped to meet the public demand for expertise related to industrialization and regulation.

Immigration also changed the demographic reality of 19th-century America. Immigrants looking for work to provide for their families sought the promise of economic prosperity and democratic government in the United States. Their presence, however, upset the socioeconomic order dominated by political elites of the spoils system. The many immigrants, seeking access to the political system but continually rebuffed by the old gentry and their connections to industry, viewed political action as a necessity. Moreover, immigrants holding political office sought expanded political opportunities for the groups they represented. Again, the imperative for political reform was seen as a social and moral right for the governed. A public service based on merit, instead of political affiliations or connections, was viewed as a means for increasing the economic, political, and moral development of the country (Mosher 1982; Van Riper 1958).

Initially, the push for merit reform in the United States began in the 1860s. Some politicians, notably Rep. Thomas A. Jenckes (RI), sought an end to corruption in the public service through the creation of a **merit-based system** modeled after that of Great Britain, which had reformed its public service a decade earlier. The British government advocated a public service that clearly separated support staff and their more routine clerical work from a professional class engaged in policy formulation and implementation. Selection into the professional public service would rely on **open recruitment**, meaning that anyone was welcome to apply, and appointment would be based on merit, as demonstrated by performance on examinations. Based on the recommendations of the Northcote-Trevelyan Report, commissioned by the British Parliament to review public service in 1854, a civil service commission was established in 1855 to administer this selection process, ending the long-standing system of patronage (Mosher 1982; Van Riper 1958).

Influenced by the British reform efforts, Jenckes, along with like-minded reformers of his time, looked to examinations and open recruitment as a means for ending patronage run amok in the public service. Bureaus of municipal research (e.g., the New York Civil Service Reform Association and the National Civil Service Reform League) aided these reformers in championing a civil service system as a means for reforming government (Van Riper 1958, 78). These early efforts paved the way for the eventual establishment of a civil service commission. However, not until the unfortunate events resulting in the 1881 assassination of President James A. Garfield by a disgruntled office seeker, Charles J. Guiteau, would public service reform actually be achieved.

For many, the spoils system was unfair and biased, and Garfield's assassination demonstrated just how severe the consequences could be, impressing "upon the public and the politicians the realities of the spoils system" (Van Riper 1958, 89). The groundwork laid by Jenckes and other reformers in the 1860s proved instrumental in the creation of the civil service system. Their efforts resulted in passage of the Pendleton Act in 1883. The **Pendleton Civil Service Reform Act** (Ch. 27, 22 Stat. 403) established the US **Civil Service Commission**, ending the spoils era and transforming public service hiring to a merit system. The Pendleton Act had three primary functions, based on the precedent established in Great Britain decades earlier (Van Riper 1958, 98–100). First, it established competitive examinations for entrance into the public service. Second, the act guaranteed relative security of tenure for employees. Under the Pendleton Act, the appointing authority would not be able to discharge employees from the competitive examination process for any political reason. To reinforce this idea, the third tenet of neutrality forbid the coercion of employees in the public service to participate in political activities—such as those infamously exemplified by Boss Tweed. Penalties for violation of the neutrality clause of the Pendleton Act included criminal sanctions.

Though based on the British system, the Pendleton Act "Americanized" the British idea of merit-based public service to fit the political landscape of the United

States (Van Riper 1958). Unlike the British and European models, the American civil service was more open to appointing citizens from a broader spectrum of society at all levels of government. It did so by means of competitive examinations that tested practical skills and expertise required by employment. The notion of tenure in public employment was not absolute in the American model; property rights to one's position would be debated at a much later date. Moreover, the act applied only to federal jobs instead of to all levels of government. Any expansion or retraction of the act's coverage was subject to presidential discretion.

The civil service system laid out by the Pendleton Act was a direct response to the chaos and arbitrary nature of the spoils system, and it ushered in a transparent and uniform hiring process. Competitive exams meant that hiring was based on ability, not political connections. Security of tenure gave a public service job stability, so employees would not be let go every time a new administration came into power. And neutrality meant that a person's political affiliation could not be used against him or her in the professional environment. While the act initially covered only a small number of civilian jobs in the federal government, over time, more federal jobs came under civil service protections. The act was integral to promoting a paradigm in public administration that demarcated politics and administration (Shafritz et al. 2001). The civil service system became seen as a guarantor of democracy and egalitarianism—any person who was qualified for a government position, regardless of social status or political affiliation, was eligible to serve.

Nonprofits in Focus	A *Brief* History of Nonprofit Organizations in the United States

Long before the founding of the United States of America, philanthropic, volunteer, and fraternal associations played a vital role among colonial citizens (Arnsberger et al. 2008; Boorstin 1958). In fact, many of these associations provided crucial services to people in the form of hospitals, fire departments, and orphanages, to name a few. Fraternal organizations, such as the Freemasons, counted members of the founding fathers—including Benjamin Franklin and George Washington—among their ranks. For many Americans wary of a return to monarchy or tyranny, charitable associations represented a viable alternative for serving the public interest (Salamon 1992). The American proclivity for charitable organizations was noted by Alexis de Tocqueville during his travels through the country in the early 1800s. De Tocqueville marveled at the extent of such associations for providing for the public good (de Tocqueville 2003).

So, how might we describe nonprofit organizations (NPOs) in the United States? Salamon's typology defines nonprofit organizations according to the following criteria (1999, 10–11; see also Hammack 2002):

- They are formal organizations operating under relevant law, legally distinct from their officers, capable of holding property, engaging in contracts, and persisting over time.

(Continued)

(Continued)

- They are "private," institutionally separate from government (though government officials may appoint some members of their governing boards).
- They do not share profits with owners or shareholders (though they may sell services, pay high salaries, and accumulate surpluses).
- They are self-governing (though they must obey relevant general laws).
- They are voluntary in the sense that participating on their boards or supporting them is not required by law.
- They serve some "public benefit."

The nonprofit and public sectors are often discussed in tandem because they both serve the public interest, although they are organized differently, operate under different laws, and are accountable to different stakeholders. The special relationship between nonprofits and the American public sector is due in no small part to the 501(3)(c) tax-exempt status afforded such organizations. Section 501(c) of the US Internal Revenue Code (26 U.S.C. § 501[c]) specifies 28 different types of nonprofit organizations that are afforded federal tax-exempt status (IRS 2011). Subsequent sections of the Code outline the guidelines for attaining tax-exempt status. In addition, states may afford such exemptions. Nonprofits' tax-exempt status dates back to the Tariff Act of 1894, which provided for exemption from taxes for certain charitable organizations (Arnsberger et al. 2008). Since then, legislation enacted by Congress over the last century has allowed for corporate tax deductions for charitable giving (1936), granted NPOs the ability to earn tax-free income (1950), and raised deduction limitations for donations (1964) (Arnsberger et al. 2008, 106–7). Congress has also placed limitations on NPOs, specifically their revenue-generating arms, to make them more accountable.

The two IRS-deemed classes of NPOs—public charities and private foundations—have had a remarkable record over the last 30 years. Public charities focus on philanthropic activities that are charitable, educational, and religious in nature and whose sources of revenue accrue from the general public and government entities (e.g., the American Cancer Society). According to Arnsberger et al. (2008, 110), by 2004 public charities held more than $2.0 trillion in assets and reported nearly $1.2 trillion in revenue, 70 percent of which was attributable to program services. Private foundations are NPOs established by individuals for charitable (e.g., the Bill and Melinda Gates Foundation) and/or noncharitable endeavors (e.g., estate planning) and rarely, if ever, solicit funds from the general public. For the period of 1985–2004, private foundations' total charitable expenses (including grants and operating and administrative expenses) increased from $9.7 billion, in constant dollars, to $32.1 billion (115).

According to the latest data from the National Center for Charitable Statistics (NCCS 2013), 1,537,465 organizations hold tax-exempt status in the United States. This number includes 955,817 public charities and 97,792 private foundations. Chambers of commerce, fraternal organizations, and civic leagues comprise another 483,856 NPOs. The economic recession that began in 2008 does not appear to have had a significant impact on the growth of charitable organizations, perhaps in part due to increased reliance upon the generosity of NPOs by those hardest hit financially (Blackwood and Roeger 2013). Perhaps more telling has been the impact of the elimination of the advance ruling by the IRS that permitted NPOs to be treated as "publicly supported organizations" for their first five years—a crucial period for building public support (1). This ruling allows NPOs to enjoy the benefits of charity status for the first five years, without having to provide proof of support until year six. No doubt NPOs will continue to fill the gap for services not afforded by the public or private sector well into the future.

Government by the Efficient: The Scientific Management Period (1906–1937)

The period immediately following the passage of the Pendleton Act adhered to the depoliticization of the public service. Buttressing these efforts was a revolution in thinking about organizing for work. Advances in scientific inquiry during the turn of the last century had ushered in new technologies that greatly enhanced the daily lives of individuals. Likewise, scientific inquiry was viewed as a means for improving the operations of the public service. Empirical observation was viewed as an indispensable tool for improving merit-based, nonpartisan public service. This sentiment was best articulated by the writings of Frederick W. Taylor regarding the concept of scientific management.

According to Taylor, **scientific management** was predicated upon the principles of turn-of-the-century organization theory. The tenets assumed a "one best way" for organizing based on systematic scientific inquiry, with efficiency as the overarching criterion. Before the Industrial Revolution, work practices were based on apprenticeships and learning a trade by doing it. Scientific management took issue with these practices as inexact and based on estimation. In contrast, scientific management adopted factual, analytical approaches to back up intuitive reasoning with evidentiary support. The theory was that once experts in scientific management agreed upon the best approach to management—based upon thorough measurement and analysis of the physical aspects of the work—a perfect harmony would exist between labor and management. As such, workers would be happy and motivated to perform according to the results of scientific inquiry implemented by management. Thus, science was the solution to bringing the selection and training of workers together, effectively and efficiently organizing people. Taylor believed that his principles would optimally cause each person to achieve his or her greatest potential. In practice, laborers often resented Taylor's approach to management as condescending—suggesting that they were incapable of implementing efficient practices on their own. In some instances, the implementation of Taylor's vision was met with stiff resistance, as at the Watertown Arsenal where strikes resulted in a congressional hearing on the matter (Aitken 1960/1985).

While scientific management was originally intended for private sector consumption, public personnel systems would eventually evolve toward its tenets, which were notably embodied in the **Classification Act of 1923**. The act set about organizing and centralizing merit principles according to the wisdom of scientific management (Shafritz et al. 2001). Before the act's passage, job descriptions, career grades, and formal appraisals were largely nonexistent in the public sector. The law's result was the creation of modern position classification, establishing (1) broad occupational divisions or "services"; (2) "grades" as a means for distinguishing jobs by levels of importance, difficulty, responsibility, and value; (3) uniform compensation schedules; (4) a general appraisal system of the duties and responsibilities of office; (5) a policy of equal pay for equal work; (6) "classes" and "class specifications"; (7) a central classifying authority; and (8) finality of the classifying authority's decisions (Van Riper 1958, 299) (Chapter 6, "Pay and Benefits," includes a more detailed discussion of occupational and position classification.) The act effectively centralized authority over all the terms of employment, particularly by implementing job analysis and job descriptions under **position management**—a practice in effect to this day in many jurisdictions.

Government by Individuals: The Behavioralism Period (1937–1964)

The crises of the 1930s and 1940s—the Great Depression (1929–1939) and World War II (1939–1945)—severely tested the limits of the merit system. In the federal government, a relatively new and small professional cadre of public managers was tasked with pulling the United States through two of the most significant crises in its history. To meet the charge, a larger and better equipped bureaucracy was needed. Beginning in 1933, President Franklin Roosevelt passed sweeping legislation under the New Deal that greatly expanded government's capacity to grow and regulate the economy. The New Deal implemented a number of domestic economic policies and programs that sought to end the economic depression and to institute measures to prevent its recurrence. Additionally, the programs aimed to provide relief to the unemployed and indigent (Berkin et al. 2011, 629–32).

The growth in government arose from a coordinated effort to put millions of Americans back to work. However, federal expansion led to coordination problems; there were significant instances of agencies with overlapping jurisdiction and contradictory functionality (Van Riper 1958). Moreover, the "one best way" approach proved to be an overly simplistic solution in the face of such growth. Advances in industrial psychology suggested that organization charts alone were not enough to manage an expanded civil service.

Revolutionary research in **behavioralism** at this time advanced the understanding of human resource theory. Human resource theory shifted its focus from the employer and organization to labor and the individual within the workplace. Experiments during this period (e.g., the **Hawthorne experiments** conducted to assess human behavior in the workplace) demonstrated that the internal and external elements of the organization's environment were profoundly important to understanding human behaviors such as motivation and morale (Shafritz et al. 2001). Along with efficiency, employers' concerns now included employee well-being. Internally, a climate of openness and an appreciation of human interactions were critical to motivation and, in turn, morale. Externally, resources and the political process also played an important role in individual and organizational behavior. The sentiment of this behavioral research was that people were not just automatons who produce and perform in a linear, mechanical way; they are human beings influenced by factors such as career aspirations, values, ethics, and integrity. Such factors were deemed just as important—if not more important—as scientific principles in the performance of workers and the organization.

It became apparent to the president that his meager staff resources would not be enough to steer the country out of the Great Depression. To this end, Roosevelt commissioned the President's Committee on Administrative Management—the Brownlow Committee—in 1937 to deliberate and offer advice on how he might better manage the bureaucracy. Staffed by some prominent scholars of the time—Louis Brownlow, Charles E. Merriam, and Luther Gulick—the committee targeted personnel administration for purposes of reforming management and modernizing the executive office. Emphasizing the ideals of the era, the committee wrote that the "administrator should be concerned with human relations, values, deeper . . . needs of the human beings whose government he represents" (President's Committee on Administrative Management [Brownlow Committee] 1937, 34). The committee viewed the current state of the civil service as detrimental to the president's ability to serve the needs of the people. Specifically, the president was ill equipped to manage a growing bureaucracy given the lack of professional staff in the White House. The result was the creation of the Executive Office of the President with a strong executive leadership role over the civil service. The president would no longer take a role subordinate to that of Congress and the Civil Service Commission in the staffing of the government apparatus. The new framework advocated moving Congress into an oversight role so as not to constrain the president's ability to manage the bureaucracy. According to the committee, the establishment of

> a responsible and effective chief executive as the center of energy, direction, and administrative management; the systematic organization of all activities in the hands of a qualified personnel under the direction of the chief executive; and to aid him in this, the establishment of appropriate managerial and staff agencies. (Brownlow Committee 1937, 2)

Civil service reform continued through World War II and afterward. Dismantling the wartime buildup of military and civilian personnel in the public service was an overriding characteristic of the postwar period of the late 1940s. Beginning with President Harry S. Truman, the period saw the pursuit of a more decentralized and reorganized personnel system (Van Riper 1958, 417–20). Even with the exodus of World War II personnel, the public service in the 1950s was still much larger than before the Great Depression. Thus, while the president had greater powers over the bureaucracy, the sheer magnitude of government services meant that executive authority would need to be extended to presidential appointments to run federal agencies. So, presidential power was decentralized to political appointments while still beholden to a centralized personnel system under the

Civil Service Commission. This tension between the two—political appointees and career executives—would be an overarching theme throughout the Behavioralism Period. For example, the Civil Service Commission ceded some of its personnel authority to agencies, while striving to maintain some centralization through job classification. In fact, passage of the **Classification Act of 1949** strengthened the Civil Service Commission's control over position classification. Like the previous act of 1923, the 1949 act further regulated the federal pay system under step-and-grade classification. The result was the General Schedule (GS) pay system that is still in use today for white-collar positions.

The trend moving forward was to balance executive authority over the civil service, while expanding Civil Service Commission responsibility for position management. Unfortunately, the balancing act proved challenging, resulting in what Wallace Sayre (1948) termed "the triumph of techniques over purpose" (134). The focus on technical details (e.g., rigid pay grades) diverted public personnel from their responsibilities in the service of public policy and the public interest.

Government by Equality: The Civil Rights Period (1964–1978)

The Civil Rights Movement of the 1950s and 1960s brought about a new era of change. Like the preceding periods, the theme once again was egalitarianism in the public service, but this time focusing on a new set of criteria. Until the 1960s, disenfranchisement of African Americans and other minorities in the public service was widespread. The treatment of minorities in the public service was not taken seriously until the administration of President John F. Kennedy. President Kennedy's campaign challenged the norms of the time to promote a greater inclusion and equity in the political process. According to Hellriegel and Short (1972):

> By 1961 it was apparent that policies of nondiscrimination and enforcement provisions that responded primarily to acts of overt discrimination were insufficient to insure full equality of opportunity. The new policies, initiated by President Kennedy, began the period of proaction. Affirmative action programs were established to provide an atmosphere conducive to equal opportunity and to correct imbalances in employment and advancement of minority employees. (852)

President Kennedy's Executive Order 10925 prohibited discrimination in employment, as had previous orders, but it also included language for implementing affirmative action to right the wrongs in employment practices that had disenfranchised minorities. The Civil Rights Act of 1964 and Equal Employment Opportunity Act of 1972 would codify antidiscriminatory practices in employment into law for future generations. (Chapter 4 covers both of these topics in greater detail.)

For many public administration scholars during this era, government was seen as a part of the problem; it prevented effective bureaucratic action to combat discrimination in the workplace. They felt that the public service—being dominated by white males—was unrepresentative of the larger public and catered only to the "haves" (as opposed to the "have nots"). Moreover, they believed this composition did not reflect public sentiment or the public interest. Even by the late 1970s, white males held approximately 90 percent of top-level federal positions (Lewis 1991, 154). Advocates of personnel reform during the 1960s and 1970s sought a public service that embraced the political values of change (see Marini 1971; Waldo 1971). In contrast to the clear separation of politics from administration set forth in the Pendleton Act, these advocates felt that politics and administration could not be separated—in fact, administration was part of the political process, and administrators should embrace political values. Administrators could add to the political process, advocating on behalf of their agency's clientele. Selecting personnel for the public service who were more representative of the broader public could bring more diverse expertise to bear for the greater public good. Rather than emphasizing efficiency, as had reformers in the Scientific Management period, advocates of reform now held social equity to be the central concern of the public service.

In the mid- to late 1960s, President Lyndon B. Johnson's war on poverty put into practice this emphasis on social equity through Great Society legislation, such as the Food Stamp Act of 1964 and the Economic Opportunity Act of 1964, aimed at eliminating poverty and expanding educational opportunities for the poor. The focus of the public service included not only the charge of efficiency but also enhancement of social equity—working to redress the deprivation of minorities and enhance their political power and economic well-being (Frederickson 2010).

The move toward an emphasis on social equity refocused the public service on improving the institutional arrangements of government to deal with the difficult issues of poverty and discrimination. The challenge was to reorganize in a way that improved the quality of services for all. For those employed in the public service, there was a renewed emphasis on scientific understanding, but it was tempered by a consideration of how it could more effectively improve the lives of agency clientele— the poor and those disenfranchised by the political system (Frederickson 2010). Public servants, therefore, were not mere technocrats executing policy but advocates for the well-being of society—change agents for the greater good.

The emphasis on social equity and diversity that became prominent during this period had an impact on the civil service system. Along with the guiding principles in the Pendleton Act (merit-based employment, neutral competence, and an open and competitive examination process)—the principles of **representation**, equal pay, and protection against whistle-blowing would be introduced. Today, civil service employment is still governed by the foundational ideas originally set out in the Pendleton Act over 130 years ago, as well as the influence of the civil rights era of the 1960s and 1970s. **Title V of the US Code**, the primary law governing civil service, codified these guiding principles into law (Box 2.1).

Box 2.1	**Merit System Principles**

TITLE 5 (5 USC Sec. 2301)—GOVERNMENT ORGANIZATION AND EMPLOYEES

    PART III—EMPLOYEES

        Subpart A—General Provisions

            CHAPTER 23—MERIT SYSTEM PRINCIPLES

§ 2301. Merit system principles

(a) This section shall apply to—

    (1) an Executive agency; and

    (2) the Government Printing Office.

(b) Federal personnel management should be implemented consistent with the following merit system principles:

    (1) Recruitment should be from qualified individuals from appropriate sources in an endeavor to achieve a work force from all segments of society, and selection and advancement should be determined solely on the basis of relative ability, knowledge, and skills, after fair and open competition which assures that all receive equal opportunity.

    (2) All employees and applicants for employment should receive fair and equitable treatment in all aspects of personnel management without regard to political affiliation, race, color, religion, national origin, sex, marital status, age, or handicapping condition, and with proper regard for their privacy and constitutional rights.

    (3) Equal pay should be provided for work of equal value, with appropriate consideration of both national and local rates paid by employers in the private sector, and appropriate incentives and recognition should be provided for excellence in performance.

    (4) All employees should maintain high standards of integrity, conduct, and concern for the public interest.

    (5) The Federal work force should be used efficiently and effectively.

    (6) Employees should be retained on the basis of the adequacy of their performance, inadequate performance should be corrected, and employees should be separated who cannot or will not improve their performance to meet required standards.

    (7) Employees should be provided effective education and training in cases in which such education and training would result in better organizational and individual performance.

    (8) Employees should be—

(A) protected against arbitrary action, personal favoritism, or coercion for partisan political purposes, and

(B) prohibited from using their official authority or influence for the purpose of interfering with or affecting the result of an election or a nomination for election.

(9) Employees should be protected against reprisal for the lawful disclosure of information which the employees reasonably believe evidences—

(A) a violation of any law, rule, or regulation, or

(B) mismanagement, a gross waste of funds, an abuse of authority, or a substantial and specific danger to public health or safety.

(c) In administering the provisions of this chapter—

(1) with respect to any agency (as defined in section 2302(a)(2)(C) of this title), the President shall, pursuant to the authority otherwise available under this title, take any action, including the issuance of rules, regulations, or directives; and

(2) with respect to any entity in the executive branch which is not such an agency or part of such an agency, the head of such entity shall, pursuant to authority otherwise available, take an action, including the issuance of rules, regulations, or directives; which is consistent with the provisions of this title and which the President or the head, as the case may be, determines is necessary to ensure that personnel management is based on and embodies the merit system principles.

Sources: Added Pub. L. 95-454, Title I, Sec. 101(a), October 13, 1978, 92 Stat. 1113; amended Pub. L. 101-474, Sec. 5(c), October 30, 1990, 104 Stat. 1099.

The behavioral revolution of the previous era continued to influence developments in the 1960s (Golembiewski 1977). The behavioral movement emphasized the importance of people in the organization—their motivations, values, and commitment to the organization's mission. In particular, the literature of organizational development and change emphasized the importance of organizational flexibility and adaptability to changes in the environment. Modifying the bureaucracy to cope with the issues of civil rights and economic inequality meant that the public sector had to be more decentralized to facilitate interaction with the environment, especially to promote involvement with the people being served by agency personnel. Giving greater authority to those at the "street level" of public service was viewed as a means for putting policy decisions into the hands of public servants with a better appreciation for the interests of agency clientele.

As the public service moved into the 1970s, these challenges placed a great deal of pressure on civil service systems to comply with values that were at times incompatible. Emphasizing efficiency could be to the detriment of social equity and democracy and vice versa. The Civil Service Commission increasingly found its dual approach of emphasizing productivity as well as policing the bureaucracy for abuse and malfeasance problematic. This strategy proved too difficult to manage, setting the stage for the largest civil service reform since the Pendleton Act.

Government by Reform:
The Managerialist Period (1978–present)

Experience at the Federal Level

In the wake of the sociopolitical turmoil of the 1960s, government once again came under criticism for ineffectively dealing with socioeconomic concerns such as poverty and urban economic development. Reformers of the 1970s assailed many of the Great Society programs of the previous decade, in particular taking issue with the government's inability to track and evaluate outcomes. Practitioners and scholars were only beginning to appreciate the complexity of policy implementation, and without an understanding of the finer details of putting policy into action, great ideas would fail to be translated from their enabling legislation. Many programs had noble aims but showed little measurable progress. Although government had pursued limited decentralization efforts, those efforts suffered from inconsistencies in their application across personnel. Requiring a relatively stable bureaucracy to be an agent of change was also unsettling for many. As was the case in precious decades, the strain of pursuing concepts sometimes in conflict with each other became too demanding. Pursuing efficiency often entailed hierarchy and rigid application of procedures, details that in the end proved detrimental to productivity. Moreover, the Civil Service Commission was criticized for failing to achieve a more representative civil service, and it ultimately failed to provide the executive office with the control necessary to manage a large bureaucracy. The 1972 Watergate scandal involving then president Richard Nixon and his staff further eroded the credibility of the public sector.

These criticisms led to the present era of government—*Government by Reform.* This era has provided practitioners and scholars with a great deal to mull over. The benchmark of the era—the **Civil Service Reform Act of 1978**—ushered in a new era of public personnel that emphasized the *management* of public service, placing a greater emphasis on accountability and performance. The act abolished the Civil Service Commission, replacing it with the Office of Personnel Management (OPM) and the Merit System Protection Board (MSPB). The managerial aspect of staffing and directing federal personnel was relegated to OPM, with lines of supervision going directly to the president. MSPB would serve as the policing arm of the personnel system, investigating and adjudicating employee grievances. Splitting the Civil Service Commission into two entities was viewed as a means for pursuing the often incompatible values of efficiency and representation. OPM would be headed by the president's appointed director and tasked with the efficiency directives previously under the Civil Service Commission—personnel management, appraisal and evaluation, and executive authority over the bureaucracy (Shafritz et al 2001).

The MSPB would be a bipartisan "watchdog" of the federal civil service system, ensuring that the public service was run on a merit basis. Within the MSPB, the Office of Special Counsel was authorized to investigate abuses such as engaging in politics, discrimination, and suppression of information (Shafritz et al. 2001). Moreover, the MSPB would be responsible for investigating "whistle-blowing," protecting informants and investigating abuses.

Additionally, the act created an independent body for regulating labor issues in the federal service—the Federal Labor Relations Authority.

While the Civil Service Reform Act contained a number of additional provisions, three in particular support the reform arguments espoused in Chapter 1 and continue to be influential.

1. Decentralization of personnel decision making to agency-level managers, eschewing central personnel agencies in favor of more fluid managerial practices

2. Creation of the Senior Executive Service (SES), a cadre of exceptional personnel positions, to bridge the gap between political appointees and career civil servants. Agency managers are given greater flexibility regarding compensation of the SES personnel.

3. Establishment of a performance-based pay system (merit pay) for mid-level managers and supervisors (Mosher 1982).

It should be clear to the reader at this point that "reform" is not a recent phenomenon in the history of civil service in America. On the contrary, reforms have taken place periodically since passage of the Pendleton Act in 1883. What sets the 1978 act apart from previous reforms is the systemic change it represented for the civil service system. Previous reforms (e.g., the Classification Acts of 1923 and 1949) represented piecemeal efforts to enhance the civil service system, often with an aim to tweak efficiency. The reforms of the 1978 act represent a turning point in that they were aimed at enhancing efficiency along with representation in the civil service system-wide. Moreover, the 1978 reforms emulated private sector practices, ceding greater control of managerial functions to agencies and their managers (especially to the SES) and implementing a performance-based pay system for improving productivity. Decentralization was never fully achieved under previous reforms because position management was still vested in the central personnel office—the Civil Service Commission. Beginning with the 1978 reforms, however, greater authority would be given to agencies to handle their own staffing needs. Moreover, this practice was emulated at the state and local levels. Performance-based pay systems not only represented a shift from rewarding seniority but also provided agency managers with greater flexibility over reward decisions. Since the passage of the 1978 act, reform efforts have generally concentrated on providing both politicians and managers with greater latitude over personnel decisions. As discussed in the first chapter, five reform themes characterize the era: decentralization, performance-based pay, declassification, deregulation, and privatization. These efforts directly attack the long-standing model of specialized, hierarchical, and relatively closed bureaucracies that are governed by rules, paperwork, and official procedures (Condrey and Maranto 2001). As an alternative, the aforementioned concepts emphasize productivity, marketization, service orientation, decentralization, improved capacity to devise and track policy, and accountability for results (Kettl 2000). However, this penchant to "let managers manage" has also occasionally resulted in the diminution or outright demolition of job security in the public sector in favor of at-will employment arrangements.

At the federal level, these reform efforts were part of President Bill Clinton's **National Performance Review (NPR)** in 1993. Chaired by then vice president Al Gore, the task force was spurred by David Osborne and Ted Gaebler's *Reinventing Government.* This practitioner-based text advocated a more entrepreneurial take on public management (Osborne and Gaebler 1992). At issue was the rigid adherence to personnel rules and procedures (e.g., the infamous ten-thousand-page personnel manual). The interagency task force was charged with studying the contemporary managerial practices (in particular those of the private sector) that might streamline public personnel procedures and reduce the size of a "bloated" federal bureaucracy. The NPR targeted the mechanisms of federal government, arguing that the system was broken, and ultimately backed "reinventing government" by means of a system that "works better and costs less" (Gore 1993). The problem, NPR contended, was not people but the red tape and regulation that stifled innovation and creativity. The report argued that the federal government was too focused on standards, procedures, and hierarchy, all of which created an inefficient bureaucracy. NPR embraced four key tenets in an effort to create a more efficient public sector: (1) cutting red tape, (2) putting customers first, (3) empowering employees to get results, and (4) producing better government for less (Gore 1993, xxxviii–xl). The report's authors were particularly interested in targeting the bureaucratic inefficiencies of the federal personnel system. The intent of the NPR reforms was to transfer greater authority over the machinery of government from Congress to the executive branch. The chief executive and his or her appointments were viewed as an indispensable means for empowering civil servants, particularly through the executive-controlled OPM. If political considerations were removed and civil servants were freed from congressional red tape and oversight, it was argued, service provision would greatly improve.

Unfortunately, the reality of politics set in with the election of a Republican majority, which controlled both houses of Congress by 1995. The rivalry between the Republican Congress and President Clinton limited the extent to which NPR reforms were implemented. Indeed, the **reductions in force (RIF)** championed during the period were mostly due to the post–Cold War drawdown of both civilian and military personnel (Kettl 2002, 202). However, the Clinton-Gore reform efforts have drawn praise for their reduction of red tape. They succeeded in eliminating the *Federal Personnel Manual*, thereby removing a number of procedural requirements regarding the staffing of the bureaucracy. The Clinton-Gore initiative also made strides in budget reform and performance management (e.g., the Government Performance and Results Act of 1993). Critics of NPR have suggested that the initiative failed to consider the incompatibility of customer satisfaction and efficiency with constitutional values (e.g., equality, due process) (see Piotrowski and Rosenbloom 2002).

For the past decade, federal initiatives have continued to roll back traditional merit-based practices. The majority of these initiatives have resulted from demonstration projects and congressional approval exempting agencies from having to abide by Title V provisions (see Table 2.1) (Brook and King 2008; Woodard 2005, 110). Reform efforts under George W. Bush, dubbed the "Bush Management Agenda," have furthered these practices as part of larger national security legislation targeting the Department of Homeland Security (DHS) and Department of Defense (DOD). The Homeland Security Act of 2002 and the National Security Personnel System (part of the National Defense Authorization Act for Fiscal Year 2004) provided DHS and DOD greater discretion over agency personnel matters (Brook and King 2008), providing for increased use of performance-related pay systems, greater managerial flexibility vis-à-vis labor relations, and greater agency-specific authorization to design and operate personnel systems (Brook and King 2008, 215). Brook and King (2008) contended that personnel reform at DHS and DOD "represent[s] the largest and most visible granting of agency discretion to date" (215). While conclusive evidence about the success of these reforms is lacking, a number of studies suggest that the impact may have been detrimental to employee morale (see e.g., Bradbury, Battaglio, and Crum 2010).

Experiences at the State Level

The influence of market-based reforms was not limited to the federal level. In fact, the 1990s saw an unprecedented flurry of civil service reform targeting the perceived inefficiencies of state bureaucracy. The diffusion of deregulation and decentralization policies to state governments was catalogued by Hays and Sowa's (2006) survey of all fifty states. Their research illustrates the expansion of deregulation policies such as EAW and confirms the increasing decentralization of the human resource function in state governments. By 2006, employment at will (EAW) had diffused to a majority of state governments (28 states) (107–8). Of the 28 state governments reporting the expansion of EAW, 25 also indicated decentralization of their personnel systems as a key factor (107–8). It is clear from Hays and Sowa's findings that states are forgoing centralized personnel structures in favor of agency-specific, manager-centered PHRM. This would appear to be especially true for states with relatively weak employee unions and collective bargaining rights. Without the resources and procedures afforded labor in states with friendly union environments, public employees can do little to resist deregulation efforts. This was the case for the lightening rod of radical reform—the state of Georgia.

Citing a recalcitrant and unresponsive state personnel system, Georgia's then governor Zell Miller backed legislation in 1996, Act 816, that abolished job protections for newly hired state employees (see the Case Study section in this chapter for a detailed review of the Georgia reforms). Dubbed "radical reform" by scholars and practitioners, Georgia's actions provided researchers with a great deal of material to use to assess the efficiency promises of market-based initiatives. The "radical" overtures in Georgia were in response to perceived overly bureaucratic civil service practices, especially those that made difficult the dismissal of poor-performing employees. Instead of incremental reforms to the state personnel system, radical civil service reformers in the state sought to eliminate employee protections, making state employees at-will (i.e., serving without the guarantee of tenure or job security). As employees voluntarily or involuntarily left state employment, their open positions were then converted to unclassified status in the state personnel system, meaning that the new incumbents of these jobs were employees at will. In addition to abolishing civil service protections for newly hired employees, the Georgia reform legislation did so for those accepting promotions or transfers to other positions in state government. Moreover, Georgia embarked on a performance-based pay initiative known as GeorgiaGain. The aim of GeorgiaGain was to modernize the state's performance management system by implementing performance measurement and evaluation procedures (Kellough and Nigro 2002). In so doing, reformers hoped that the new performance management system would garner trust from management and employees alike by focusing on employee results rather than tenure in office.

Presently, the Georgia state workforce is over 80 percent employed at will. For states interested in pursuing reform of their personnel system, Georgia has presented a signal case study for emulation. Since passage of Act 816, several states have pursued similar EAW initiatives. As observed by Hays and Sowa (2006), the implementation of Georgia-like reforms in some fashion is observable in a number of other states. The cases of Texas and Florida in particular have drawn interest from practitioners and scholars who are eager to assess the successes and failures of PHRM reform initiatives.

Like Georgia, Texas and Florida have been at the forefront in the evolution (or revolution) of decentralization, deregulation, declassification, performance-based pay, and privatization policies. Since 1986, the state of Texas has operated in a decentralized, deregulated HR environment, with the law allowing local governments and agencies to opt in or out of civil service protections (Coggburn 2006). Interestingly, the state operates without a personnel authority office and retains only an adjudicatory body for grievances. The Texas PHRM structure has proven popular, because it avoids the wholesale cronyism that one might expect would result from the abolition of employment rights. In a recent survey of HR directors in the state, 97.4 percent of respondents agreed that "even though employment is at-will, most employee terminations are for good cause" (Coggburn 2006, 166).

In 2001, then Florida governor Jeb Bush proposed legislation similar to the deregulation policies in Georgia. Dubbed Florida's Service First program, the legislation placed a large number of senior state government managers—approximately 16,000 out of 120,000 plus state employees—in EAW status (Condrey and Battaglio 2007, 427). Additionally, through its People First initiative, Florida engaged in a very active privatization initiative, outsourcing much of the state's HR function. Florida's reform has been proven controversial. This is especially true of its pursuit of privatized PHRM, which some feel has led to an erosion of traditional public service provision (Bowman and West 2006). Convergys, the firm to which many routine HR-processing functions was outsourced, experienced delays and "significant problems . . . as they became operational," which included payroll and benefits errors (Office of Program Policy Analysis & Government Accountability [OPPAGA] 2006, 2). While savings to the state were touted as $24.7 million annually, by 2006—five years after the initial privatization—the state had yet to establish "a methodology to capture project cost savings" (OPPAGA 2006, 3).

Assessing the Impact of PHRM Reform

The proliferation of PHRM reform policies has heightened interest in the potential implications of these efforts for merit systems and public sector employment practices (Bowman 2002; Coggburn 2006; Hays and Sowa 2006; Kellough and Nigro 2006; Kuykendall and Facer 2002; Rainey 2006). The application and consequences of PHRM reform continue to pose challenging research questions. Of particular interest is the impact these reforms have had on trust and motivation among professionals in public human resources (Battaglio and Condrey 2009; Coggburn et al. 2010). The experience and status of HR professionals within agencies give them a unique and substantive capacity to shed light on the era of *Government by Reform*.

Since they see the effects of personnel actions across an agency or multiple agencies, these HR professionals can assess the implementation of specific PHRM reforms from an important vantage point. In particular, views of EAW and performance-based pay have proven to be significant for understanding organizational and managerial trust. Additionally, HR professionals may be more aware of agency HR policies than are other agency employees and be more capable of protecting themselves against adverse actions in the workplace. These employees are essentially the "canary in the coal mine," since they are more likely than others to have knowledge of the failures and successes of reform policies (Battaglio and Condrey 2009, 698).

Recent research on Georgia's reform efforts has found significant reservations among HR professionals in state government with regard to the impact these changes have had on motivation, trust, and morale—key factors in overall organizational productivity (Battaglio 2010; Battaglio and Condrey 2009). Indeed, initial research on the performance-based pay reforms coinciding with the implementation of EAW has found similar reservations among state employees regarding the merits of such pay systems in the public sector (Kellough and Nigro 2002; 2006). Findings suggest that past employee experience with spoils in the workplace is a significant predictor of the erosion of trust. Georgia HR professionals reported that they had on occasion witnessed first the firing of competent employees for political and/or non-job-related reasons and then their replacement with politically connected individuals (see Condrey and Battaglio 2007). The perception that EAW enables a spoils system adversely affects employee perceptions of organizational fairness, their trust in management, and their trust in the organization. The erosion of trust in the workplace can be a significant impediment to improving productivity—the initial goal of these reform efforts. With respect to deregulation efforts, initial optimism about reforms tends to wane as EAW systems are implemented. Research suggests that this may be the result of experience of perceived unfairness under EAW, which sours HR professionals' perceptions of improved productivity. Thus, EAW systems may have a fundamental flaw: familiarity may indeed breed contempt (Battaglio and Condrey 2009, 702–3). If this is so, EAW systems may, in fact, undermine the very public management systems they were intended to strengthen.

The loss of job security in EAW environments has also frayed trust in the workplace. In exchange for less job security, reformers promised better pay, leave, or other benefits (Bowman and West 2006). However, research suggests that job security has a positive impact on employee productivity and commitment to the organization (Coyle-Shapiro and Kessler 2003; Gossett 2003; Green et al. 2006; Hays and Sowa 2006; Hindera and Josephson 1998; Lewis and Frank 2002; Radin and Werhane 1996; Schwoerer and Rosen 1989). Unfortunately, employee perceptions of job security have dropped off precipitously as a result of EAW. These findings may prove problematic for long-term recruitment efforts and overall organization performance (Battaglio and Condrey 2009, 702–3). The impact on productivity and commitment also tends to be more pronounced in large bureaucratic settings (Battaglio and Condrey 2009).

HR professionals have similar reservations regarding the ability of reform efforts to motivate employee performance (Battaglio 2010; Battaglio and Condrey 2009). Erosion of traditional practices (e.g., job security) has contributed to a decline in motivation. Moreover, there are misgivings with regard to EAW as a policy that instills motivation, because it may discourage open dialogue among employees who fear reprisals if they speak their minds. In this regard, EAW may be sending a mixed message to employees. Doubtful of EAW's ability to encourage policy innovation, employees are also aware that their jobs are on the line if they don't produce results. Such a conflicting message may prove problematic for progress in an EAW environment. Perhaps EAW employees are interested only in getting the bottom line accomplished in order to keep their jobs instead of looking "outside the box" for policy solutions. If this is indeed the case, then EAW may have inadvertently created the exact opposite of what was intended. Instead of motivating employees to be innovative and performance oriented, EAW has potentially eroded traditional principles supporting job security and influenced employees to be less assertive and progress oriented (Battaglio and Condrey 2009, 702–3). Kellough and Nigro (2002, 2006) have found similar reservations among employees with regard to performance-based pay.

A particularly troubling finding from recent research is the negative attitudes of minorities regarding EAW (Battaglio 2010; Battaglio and Condrey 2009; Condrey and Battaglio 2007). African Americans, in particular, have expressed objections to EAW as a motivational tool. Traditionally, civil service systems have been associated with advancing the cause of a representative workforce, with the core principle of placing people in positions based on their professional abilities and not on the basis of race, gender, or ethnicity. Perhaps African Americans feel that an EAW environment does not foster representativeness in the makeup of the public service. Because EAW gives managers the upper hand in the employment relationship, African Americans may view it as a tool for discrimination in HR decisions (Wilson 2006). If discouraged by perceived erosion of equal opportunity, African Americans may not support a reform such as EAW.

Findings elsewhere have corroborated the evidence from the Georgia case (Coggburn et al. 2010). This research suggests that HR professionals' experience with EAW matters. If EAW is pursued for legitimate purposes (i.e., as a tool to promote effective management versus a spoils system), HR professionals may be inclined to support its success. However, once the specter of spoils is experienced, HR professionals are less inclined to see EAW succeed. In either instance, the perceptions HR professionals have of policy reforms matters. Jurisdictions considering EAW should know how at-will terminations will be viewed by personnel in general. Likewise, the success of reform depends on how HR professionals negotiate the learning curve

(Coggburn et al. 2010). HR professionals operating under the auspices of reform may have a greater appreciation of the constraints that EAW imposes on HR functions (Gertz 2007; Selden 2006). While on its face EAW may appear to sidestep lengthy grievance processes, in reality HR professionals will seldom make arbitrary decisions without guidance from HR offices and legal staff. Given the legal implications of establishing a set of grievance policies, EAW systems may avoid developing personnel manuals. HR personnel are subsequently given little or no guidance in disciplining employees in EAW jurisdictions.

Experience may also be a factor that contributes to success. Considering the aging workforce, a loss of workplace knowledge may be a factor in receptivity to reform: newer workers who lack the tacit knowledge of workforce veterans may be more willing to implement EAW-like reforms (Coggburn et al. 2010). Unfortunately, less-experienced employees' limited knowledge of civil service reforms and their consequences may provide an opportunity for private sector enthusiasts. Younger workers may also be less committed to the public service as a career (Light 1997), leading to sector switching during their working careers. Experience in both public and private sector work environments may also portend a greater receptivity to reforms like EAW (Coggburn et al. 2010, 203).

Conclusion

Supporters of PHRM have had a difficult time proving that reforms have fulfilled their promise of creating a more effective and efficient government. Different types of PHRM reform, individually or combined, have yet to yield the hoped-for effects on productivity. Coggburn's 2000 research suggests that deregulation policies have not produced the cost savings and efficiencies purported by their proponents. Additionally, Sanders (2004) and others (see Perry, Engbers, and Jun 2009) have little evidence that performance-based pay is a magic elixir for motivation and productivity in the public sector workplace. These findings are troubling, as jurisdictions continue to buy into the PHRM reform mantra.

Critical to the success of any measure, including reform efforts, are adequate resources. PHRM reforms have consistently been underfunded. They have also been enacted under stress from the difficulties of coordination within and among agencies. Decentralization and deregulation efforts have burdened agency HR managers who now have responsibilities that were once the domain of central personnel offices. Lacking a central personnel authority's expertise, HR managers in agencies will need extensive skill development and training to coordinate PHRM reform efforts—a task that may be particularly cumbersome for managers operating in smaller agencies that lack adequate resources (Hou et al. 2000; Coggburn 2000). Agency differences may also prove difficult to overcome. Governments do not lend themselves to a "one-size-fits-all" approach. Public organizations often differ in terms of their size, mission, goals, and culture (Longo 2008). Compounding these differences are the institutional arrangements of the United States, which include national, state, and local jurisdictions. Agencies in different jurisdictions may differ significantly in terms of their accountability and managerial arrangements. PHRM has yet to consider these differences in assessing the prospects for and outcomes of reform. This is especially true for performance-based pay systems; developing a government-wide appraisal system has proven impractical given agency differences (Hays and Sowa 2006; Kellough and Nigro 2002; Perry, Engbers, and Jun 2009).

Given the historical antecedents of discrimination against women and minorities in the public workplace, scholars have also been keen to explore the impact PHRM reforms have had on these groups (Battaglio 2010; Condrey and Battaglio 2007; Wilson 2006). Merit systems are predicated on the ideal of equal opportunity, an open public service, and equal treatment for all (Mosher 1982, 224). Efforts geared toward improving the status of women in the public sector have been praised for their notable advances (Moynihan and Landuyt 2008). Unfortunately, findings suggest that minorities are less than enthusiastic about the merits of PHRM reform (Battaglio 2010; Battaglio and Condrey 2009; Condrey and Battaglio 2007; Bradbury, Battaglio, and Crum 2010). With respect to deregulation reforms, the perception is that giving management and/or politicians greater discretion over HR decisions may be a means for encouraging "discrimination-induced job dismissals" (Wilson 2006, 178). The potential for PHRM reforms to erode years of progress toward diversity in the public sector is a continued concern.

References

Ackerman, Kenneth D. 2005. *Boss Tweed: The Rise and Fall of the Corrupt Pol Who Conceived the Soul of Modern New York.* New York: Carroll & Graf.

Aitken, Hugh G. J. 1985. *Scientific Management in Action: Taylorism at Watertown Arsenal, 1908–1915.* Princeton, NJ: Princeton University Press. Originally published 1960, Cambridge, MA: Harvard University Press.

Arnsberger, Paul, Melissa Ludlum, Margaret Riley, and Mark Stanton. 2008. "A History of the Tax Exempt Sector: An SOI Perspective," *Statistics of Income Bulletin*, Winter. http://www.irs.gov/pub/irs-soi/tehistory.pdf.

Battaglio, R. Paul, Jr. 2010. "Public Service Reform and Motivation: Evidence from an Employment-at-Will Environment." *Review of Public Personnel Administration* 30:341–63.

Battaglio, R. Paul, Jr., and Stephen E. Condrey. 2009. "Reforming Public Management: Analyzing the Impact of Public Service Reform on Organizational and Managerial Trust." *Journal of Public Administration Research & Theory* 19:689–707.

Berkin, Carol, Christopher L. Miller, Robert W. Cherney, and James L. Gormly. 2011. *Since 1865*. Vol. 2 of *Making America: A History of the United States*. Boston: Cengage Learning.

Blackwood, Amy S., and Katie L. Roeger. 2013. "Applications for 501(c)(3) Tax-Exempt Status Declining: Recession or Rule Change?" Washington, DC: Urban Institute. http://www.urban .org/UploadedPDF/412736-Applications-for-501-Tax-Exempt-Status-Declining-Recession- or-Rule-Change.pdf.

Boorstin, Daniel J. 1958. *The Americans: The Colonial Experience*. New York: Random House.

Bowman, James S. 2002. "At-Will Employment in Florida Government: A Naked Formula to Corrupt Public Service." *WorkingUSA* 6:90–102.

Bowman, James S., and Jonathan P. West. 2006. "Ending Civil Service Protections in Florida Government: Experiences in State Agencies," *Review of Public Personnel Administration* 26:139–57.

Bradbury, Mark D., R. Paul Battaglio Jr., and John L. Crum. 2010. "Continuity Amid Discontinuity? George W. Bush, Federal Employment Discrimination, and 'Big Government Conservatism.'" *Review of Public Personnel Administration* 30:445–66.

Brook, Douglas A., and Cynthia L. King. 2008. "Federal Personnel Management Reform: From Civil Service Reform Act to National Security Reforms." *Review of Public Personnel Administration* 28:205–21.

Coggburn, Jerrell D. 2006. "At-Will Employment in Government: Insights from the State of Texas." *Review of Public Personnel Administration* 26:158–77.

Coggburn, Jerrell D. 2000. "Personnel Deregulation: Exploring Differences in the American States." *Journal of Public Administration Research and Theory* 11: 223-244.

Coggburn, Jerrell D., R. Paul Battaglio Jr., James S. Bowman, Stephen E. Condrey, Doug Goodman, and Jonathan P. West. 2010. "State Government Human Resource Professionals' Commitment to Employment at Will." *American Review of Public Administration* 40:189–208.

Condrey, Stephen E., and R. Paul Battaglio Jr. 2007. "A Return to Spoils? Revisiting Radical Civil Service Reform in the United States." *Public Administration Review* 67:424–36.

Condrey, Stephen E., and Robert Maranto, eds. 2001. *Radical Reform of the Civil Service*. Lanham, MD: Lexington Books.

Coyle-Shapiro, Jacqueline A.-M., and Ian Kessler. 2003. "The Employment Relationship in the U.K. Public Sector: A Psychological Contract Perspective." *Journal of Public Administration Research and Theory* 13:213–30.

Frederickson, H. George. 2010. *Social Equity and Public Administration: Origins, Developments, and Applications*. Armonk, NY: M. E. Sharpe.

Gertz, Sally C. 2007. "At-Will Employment: Origins, Applications, Exceptions, and Expansions in Public Service." In *American Public Service: Radical Reform and the Merit System*, edited by James S. Bowman and Jonathan P. West, 47–74. Boca Raton, FL: Taylor & Francis.

Golembiewski, Robert T. 1977. *Public Administration as a Developing Discipline: Part 1, Perspectives on Past and Present.* New York: Marcel Dekker.

Gore, Al. 1993. *From Red Tape to Results: Creating a Government that Works Better and Costs Less; The Report of the National Performance Review.* Washington, DC: US Government Printing Office.

Gossett, Charles W. 2003. "The Changing Face of Georgia's Merit System: Results from an Employee Attitude Survey in the Georgia Department of Juvenile Justice." *Public Personnel Management* 32:267–78.

Green, Richard A., Robert Forbis, Anne Golden, Stephen L. Nelson, and Jennifer Robinson. 2006. "On the Ethics of At-Will Employment in the Public Sector." *Public Integrity* 8:305–27.

Hammack, David C. 2002. "Nonprofit Organizations in American History: Research Opportunities and Sources." *American Behavioral Scientist* 45:1638–74.

Hays, Steven W., and Jessica E. Sowa. 2006. "A Broader Look at the 'Accountability' Movement: Some Grim Realities in State Civil Service Systems." *Review of Public Personnel Administration* 26:102–17.

Hellriegel, Don, and Larry Short. 1972. "Equal Employment Opportunity in the Federal Government: A Comparative Analysis." *Public Administration Review* 32:851–58.

Hindera, John L., and Jyl J. Josephson. 1998. "Reinventing the Public Employer-Employee Relationship: The Just Cause Standard." *Public Administration Quarterly* 22:98–113.

Hou, Yilin, Patricia Ingraham, Stuart Bretschneider, and Sally Coleman Selden. 2000. "Decentralization of Human Resource Management: Driving Forces and Implications." *Review of Public Personnel Administration* 20:9–22.

Internal Revenue Service (IRS). 2011. "Tax-Exempt Status for Your Organization." Publication 557. http://www.irs.gov/pub/irs-pdf/p557.pdf.

Kellough, J. Edward, and Lloyd G. Nigro. 2002. "Pay for Performance in Georgia State Government: Employee Perspectives on GeorgiaGain After 5 Years." *Review of Public Personnel Administration* 22:146–66.

Kellough, J. Edward, and Lloyd G. Nigro. 2006. "Dramatic Reform in the Public Service: At-Will Employment and the Creation of a New Public Workforce." *Journal of Public Administration Research and Theory* 16:447–66.

Kettl, Donald F. 2000. *The Global Public Management Revolution: A Report on the Transformation of Governance.* Washington, DC: The Brookings Institution Press.

Kettl, Donald F. 2002. *The Transformation of Governance: Public Administration for Twenty-First Century America.* Baltimore: Johns Hopkins University Press.

Kuykendall, Christine L., and Rex L. Facer. 2002. "Public Employment in Georgia State Agencies: The Elimination of the Merit System." *Review of Public Personnel Administration* 22:133–45.

Lewis, Gregory B. 1991. "Turnover and the Quiet Crisis in the Federal Civil Service." *Public Administration Review* 51:145–55.

Lewis, Gregory B., and Sue A. Frank. 2002. "Who Wants to Work for the Government?" *Public Administration Review* 62:395–404.

Light, Paul C. 1997. *The Tides of Reform: Making Government Work, 1945–1995*. New Haven, CT: Yale University Press.

Longo, Francesco. 2008. "Managing Public Reforms Effectively: A Strategic Change Management Approach." In *Strategic Change Management in the Public Sector*, edited by Francesco Longo and Daniela Cristofoli, 1–20. Hoboken, NJ: Wiley.

Marini, Frank. 1971. *Toward a New Public Administration: The Minnowbrook Perspective*. Scranton, PA: Chandler.

Mosher, Frederick C. 1982. *Democracy and the Public Service*. 2nd ed. Oxford, England: Oxford University Press.

Moynihan, Donald P., and Noel Landuyt. 2008. "Explaining Turnover Intention in State Government: Explaining the Roles of Gender, Life Cycle, and Loyalty." *Review of Public Personnel Administration* 28:120–43.

National Center for Charitable Statistics (NCCS). 2013. "Quick Facts about Nonprofits." http://nccs.urban.org/statistics/quickfacts.cfm.

Office of Program Policy Analysis & Government Accountability (OPPAGA) [Florida]. 2006. "While Improving, People First Still Lacks Intended Functionality, Limitations Increase State Agency Workload and Costs." Report No. 06–39. http://www.oppaga.state.fl.us/MonitorDocs/Reports/pdf/0639rpt.pdf.

Osborne, David, and Ted Gaebler. 1992. *Reinventing Government: How the Entrepreneurial Spirit Is Transforming the Public Sector*. Reading, MA: Addison-Wesley.

Perry, James L., Trent A. Engbers, and So Yun Jun. 2009. "Back to the Future? Performance-Related Pay, Empirical Research, and the Perils of Persistence." *Public Administration Review* 69:39–51.

Piotrowski, Suzanne J., and David H. Rosenbloom. 2002. "Nonmission-Based Values in Results-Oriented Public Management: The Case of Freedom of Information." *Public Administration Review* 62:643–57.

President's Committee on Administrative Management (Brownlow Committee). 1937. *Report with Special Studies*. Washington, DC: Government Printing Office.

Radin, Tara J., and Patricia H. Werhane. 1996. "The Public/Private Distinction and the Political Status of Employment." *American Business Law Journal* 34:245–60.

Rainey, Hal G. 2006. "Reform Trends at the Federal Level with Implications for the States: The Pursuit of Flexibility and the Human Capital Movement." In *Civil Service Reform in the States: Personnel Policy and Politics at the Subnational Level*, edited by J. Edward Kellough and Lloyd G. Nigro, 33–58. Albany: SUNY Press.

Riccucci, Norma M., and Katherine C. Naff. 2006. *Personnel Management in Government: Politics and Process*. Boca Raton, FL: CRC Press.

Salamon, Lester M. 1992. *America's Nonprofit Sector: A Primer*. New York: Foundation Center.

Salamon, Lester M. 1999. *America's Nonprofit Sector: A Primer.* 2nd ed. New York: Foundation Center.

Sanders, Robert M. 2004. "GeorgiaGain or GeorgiaLoss? The Great Experiment in State Civil Service Reform." *Public Personnel Management* 33:151–64.

Sayre, Wallace S. 1948. "The Triumph of Techniques over Purpose." *Public Administration Review* 8:134–37.

Schwoerer, Catherine, and Benson Rosen. 1989. "Effects of Employment-at-Will Policies and Compensation Policies on Corporate Image and Job Pursuit Intentions." *Journal of Applied Psychology* 74:653–56.

Selden, Sally Coleman. 2006. "The Impact of Discipline on the Use and Rapidity of Dismissal in State Governments." *Review of Public Personnel Administration* 26:335–55.

Shafritz, Jay M., David H. Rosenbloom, Norma A. Riccucci, Katherine C. Naff, and Albert C. Hyde. 2001. *Personnel Management in Government: Politics and Process.* 5th ed. New York: Marcel Dekker.

Sinclair, Upton. 1906. *The Jungle.* New York: Doubleday, Page.

Tocqueville, Alexis de. 2003. *Democracy in America.* London: Penguin Books. Originally published 1835/1840.

Van Riper, Paul P. 1958. *History of the United States Civil Service.* Evanston, IL: Row, Peterson.

Waldo, Dwight. 1971. *Public Administration in a Time of Turbulence.* Scranton, PA: Chandler.

White, Leonard D. 1954. *The Jacksonians: A Study in Administrative History, 1829–1861.* New York: Macmillan.

Wilson, George. 2006. "The Rise of At-Will Employment and Race Inequality in the Public Sector." *Review of Public Personnel Administration* 26:178–87.

Woodard, Colleen A. 2005. "Merit by Any Other Name—Reframing the Civil Service First Principle." *Public Administration Review* 65:109–16.

Employment Law
in the Public Sector

Upon completion of the chapter, you will be able to do the following:

- Explain the incorporation doctrine.
- Discuss the role of ethics in public human resource management (PHRM).
- Explain the public service model as a legal framework for PHRM.
- Discuss the constitutional rights of public employees with regard to

  o freedom of expression,
  o freedom of association,
  o privacy in the information age,
  o liberty and off-duty conduct,
  o equal protection and strict scrutiny, and
  o due process and human resource functions.

- Explain the implications of constitutional torts in PHRM.
- Discuss the legal implications of PHRM reform.

Many recent public human resource management (PHRM) reforms have considerably changed the legal environment of HR in the public service. This chapter will first review the tradition of the law and PHRM in a civil service system. The sections that follow address the statutory law and case law regulating public employment and discuss the legal implications of reform for PHRM, providing further guidance for HR managers navigating the new landscape of public service. The chapter also includes an appendix summarizing employment law cases relevant to the public sector.

The Legal Landscape of PHRM

Employment law in the public sector can be difficult to navigate for those not prepared for the complexities of codified law (legislation and statutes) and case law. This is especially true of the courts' interpretation of constitutional law and its application to public employment. The dilemma for many public HR managers is how to efficiently coordinate HR functions while adhering to the legal precedents set forth by case law, statutes, and legislation. Legal precedents have set forth a framework that is intended to protect public employees from maltreatment, discrimination, and exploitation by members of the political establishment or other public employees (Shafritz et al. 2001).

The sections below are organized to assist public HR managers in navigating the legal landscape of PHRM. The sections cover relevant codified laws and noteworthy case law that has had an impact on the practice of PHRM. To be sure, this chapter is in no way exhaustive, as case law is in continual development. Indeed, there are cases now in the US court system that might have important implications for the future of PHRM practices. Thus, it is vital that public HR managers have up-to-date knowledge of the law and/or consult with agency or jurisdictional legal counsel when questions arise.

Codified Law in the United States and PHRM

Recall from the discussion in Chapter 2 that the desire for a civil service system of employment led to the passage of the Pendleton Act in 1883. This act codified into law the principles of a merit-based, politically neutral personnel system based on competitive examinations. The purpose was to mandate the hiring of persons based on their professional abilities rather than political patronage. Subsequent legislation has also provided public employees with protection from wrongful termination. These laws were intended to prevent maltreatment of public employees by superiors or political officials; as long as public employees performed satisfactorily in their positions, they could expect some degree of job security.

Title V of the US Code and the Civil Service Reform Act of 1978

As you will recall from Chapter 2, Title V of the US Code governs employment in the federal government. Originally enacted in 1966 and subsequently amended in 1978 and 1979, Title V outlines civil service functions and responsibilities. Box 2.1 of Chapter 2 outlines the specific functions and responsibilities of the civil service system with respect to the principles contained in in Chapter 23 of Title V, which mandates that recruitment and selection to the civil service occur in an equitable manner. Applicants must be considered without regard to "political affiliation, race, color, religion, national origin, sex, marital status, age, or handicapping conditions, and with proper regard for privacy and constitutional rights." The intended goal of Chapter 23 is to recruit and maintain a public sector workforce that is representative of the population at large.

Section 3 of Chapter 23, Title V, ensures proper remuneration for work in the public sector, mandating equal pay for equal work (see also Equal Pay Act of 1963, Chapter 6) as well as stipulating appropriate incentives and mechanisms for recognition, including performance-based pay. Section 6 covers performance evaluation and employee discipline—essentially the tools for holding employees accountable.

Sections 4, 5, and 8 ensure that public employees are treated ethically. Title V emphasizes the efficient maintenance of a civil service system that has a high regard for integrity, conduct, and the public interest. Drawing from the earlier foundation of the Pendleton Act, Section 8 of Title V and the Civil Service Reform Act of 1978 protect employees from "arbitrary action, personal favoritism, and coercion for partisan political purposes" (5 U.S.C. § 2301). In addition, Section 8 includes whistleblower provisions that protect public employees who choose to disclose malfeasance in office.

The Civil Service Reform Act of 1978 (§ 2301) also mandates protection from discrimination based on marital status; the use of information other than personal knowledge or materials in the employee's or applicant's record to make a personnel decision (e.g., acting on a political recommendation); obstruction of the right to compete for employment; the exercise of influence to secure an advantage for one candidate over another (e.g., **"wiring"** or undercutting competition); nepotism; reprisal for exercising appeal rights; and adverse judgment based on an employee's private conduct that does not affect the individual's or the organization's performance (e.g., conduct of an employee outside the workplace) (Shafriz et al. 2001, 102).

Civil Rights Law

We will discuss the civil rights movement and equal employment opportunity in greater detail in Chapter 4, but the equitable administration of civil service practices requires consideration of relevant civil rights legislation. The **Civil Rights Act of 1964**, the landmark civil rights legislation of the 1960s, mandates equality in the application of the law and political empowerment and guarantees equality of employment opportunity. Specifically, Title VII of the Civil Rights Act prohibits discriminatory employment practices based on race, color, religion, sex, national origin, or protected activity (US Equal Employment Opportunity Commission [EEOC] 2012). The act also created the EEOC to enforce the mandates of the legislation.

Passage of the **Equal Employment Opportunity Act** by Congress in 1972 was meant to give the EEOC greater power to enforce the mandates of the Civil Rights Act of 1964. Under the 1964 act, the EEOC served more as an investigatory body than an enforcer of the law, relegating litigation to the Department of Justice (EEOC 2012). However, the 1972 Equal Employment Opportunity Act provided the EEOC with a framework by which individuals could actually seek redress for discriminatory practices in their places of employment. The 1972 act enhanced the EEOC's power to enforce and litigate instances of discriminatory practices. As a result of the 1972 legislation, the EEOC is able to provide judicial interpretation of key elements of civil rights legislation and policy relevant to public employment practices. In particular, the 1972 act governs the practice of **affirmative action**—actionable legal remedies aimed at addressing intentional discriminatory practices in employment. The courts have confirmed the constitutionality of affirmative action plans as a remedy to address previous instances of discrimination (Rosenbloom 2007). Affirmative action, largely an involuntary practice, is typically the result of a court order, a negotiated settlement, or government regulation.

The **Civil Rights Act of 1991** and the **No FEAR Act of 2002** have provided clarification of the policies regarding intentional discrimination and remedies in such cases. With respect to equal employment opportunity, the Civil Rights Act of 1991 gives claimants seeking redress for intentional discrimination in public and private sector employment the right to a trial by jury, and it allows them to seek **punitive** and **compensatory damage awards**. However, punitive damages against government agencies and their subdivisions are restricted under the 1991 act (EEOC 2012).

The No FEAR (Notification and Federal Employee Antidiscrimination and Retaliation) Act of 2002 places additional responsibilities upon federal agencies to provide a workplace free of discrimination and retaliation for the reporting of discriminatory practices. The act requires federal agencies to pay for damage judgments out of the agency's budget, provide personnel with annual notice of their rights with respect to discrimination and whistle-blower protection, administer training every two years that covers the obligations under the act, provide annual compliance reports to relevant federal agencies, and post relevant statistical data quarterly on the agency's website (EEOC 2012). Unlike previous legislation, which was more reactive in nature, the No FEAR Act directs federal agencies to take several proactive measures toward creating a workplace climate free of discrimination.

Navigating the current climate of equal employment opportunity can be challenging. Recent legislation and court cases have added to the already daunting quantity of information public HR managers must know with respect to the promotion of equal employment opportunity. For many public managers, understanding equal employment opportunity can be exacting, especially in terms of the legality of affirmative action plans and diversity initiatives. Chapter 4, "Equal Employment Opportunity, Affirmative Action, and Diversity Planning," reviews these concepts in greater detail and addresses the primary EEO concerns of the last few decades (sexual harassment, age discrimination, and disability discrimination).

Ethics Law

Public employment practices are also concerned with creating a workplace that espouses integrity, honesty, and generally ethical conduct in the carrying out of the public interest. Consequently, states and local governments have passed a number of ethics-related laws, primarily to ensure the political neutrality of public employees in the execution of public policy. While the Pendleton Act and executive orders forbade the involvement of public employees in political activities, what constituted such activities was not clarified until the 1930s. The Hatch Act of 1939 restricted public employees' partisan speech, electioneering, and campaign involvement, and it safeguarded employees and the public from partisan influence. The objectives of the 1939 Act were as follows:

- To ensure the political neutrality of government workers by making partisan political activity by federal and other government workers illegal
- To restrict partisan elected officials from using government employees for political purposes
- To prevent the public employee from being loyal to the political party of a public official
- To protect public employees from politically motivated job actions (Bowman and West 2009, 21)

The Hatch Act was amended in 1940 to cover state and local government employees in jurisdictions that received federal aid. The act was further amended in 1993 to allow federal employees greater latitude to participate in the political process during their off-duty time, removing the prohibition on participation in "political management or political campaigns." Permitted activities include distributing literature, making phone calls, stuffing envelopes, making speeches, and holding offices in political parties (Shafritz et al. 2001, 115). However, federal employees are still forbidden from using their authority to affect the results of elections or campaigns, running for office in partisan elections, and soliciting or receiving political contributions. The 1993 reforms do not cover members of the SES, administrative law judges, law enforcement positions, defense or intelligence agencies, and other agencies such as Merit System Protection Board and the Federal Election Commission (115). Any of these employees must abide by the restrictions in the original 1939 act.

States and local jurisdictions maintain ethics laws similar to the Hatch Act, and they have also forbidden political activity in the public sector workplace. However, these laws vary widely from state to state and tend to focus only on managers and supervisors, rather than on rank-and-file workers (Cozzetto, Pedeliski, and Tompkins 2004, 190). Moreover, certain activities may be subject to 5 U.S.C. § 1502, which specifically governs the activities of state and local officials in elections and political campaigns. Section 1502 prohibits said officials from doing the following:

- Using official authority or influence to interfere with or affect the result of an election or a nomination for office
- Directly or indirectly coercing, attempting to coerce, commanding, or advising a state or local officer or employee to pay, lend, or contribute anything of value to a party, committee, organization, agency, or person for political purposes
- Running for elective office (5 U.S.C., Chapter 15, § 1502)

Exempted from the sections' prohibitions are certain elected officials, such the governor, lieutenant governor, mayor, other elected officials (e.g., duly elected head of an executive department), and individuals holding office (5 U.S.C., Chapter 15, § 1501–1508).

The reform themes raised at the outset of the book—decentralization, performance-based pay, declassification, deregulation, and privatization—have many scholars fearful of a return to the days of patronage in public service decisions (Condrey and Battaglio 2007). This is especially true of deregulation and privatization efforts. Under employment at will (EAW), employees may fear reprisals for not supporting a particular candidate. Privatization also has the potential to further patronage by awarding lucrative government contracts to political supporters. According to a recent survey, state officials indicated concern over a lack of oversight that would protect civil servants from potential partisan activity (Bowman and West 2009). While the authors find no widespread evidence of patronage in the public service, state officials did voice reservations regarding the impartial application of the law. Although they lauded the attributes of a merit-based system, state officials also indicated a desire for continued enactment of Hatch-like laws to regulate the public service so that patronage could not creep back in.

Labor Law

Codified law also prohibits unfair labor practices in the public sector. The extent and coverage of such laws vary according to the level of government (federal law versus state law) and from state to state. Some states have been more progressive than others in terms of advancing labor rights. Generally, labor laws related to public employment cover labor-management relations, bargaining rights of both negotiating parties, and codes of unfair labor practices for both management and labor. Chapter 9, "Labor Relations in the Public Sector," covers the relevant laws affecting labor and management in greater detail.

The Constitutional Rights of Public Employees

In addition to codified law, public employment is also governed by portions of the Bill of Rights of the US Constitution through case law (i.e., through decisions of the Supreme Court and federal court system regarding the constitutional rights of individuals in the workplace). The first application of the Bill of Rights occurred in 1925 with the Supreme Court decision in *Gitlow v. New York* (268 U.S. 652) (Meese 1985). Benjamin Gitlow, a member of the Socialist Party of America, was charged with criminal anarchy in the state of New York for publishing a communist manifesto. In this case, the Supreme Court ruled that the Fourteenth Amendment of the US Constitution governing due process and equal protection of the laws prohibited states from infringing upon the free speech rights of citizens. The decision further defined the scope of the First Amendment's protection of free speech and established the standard to which a state or the federal government would be held accountable in instances of criminalizing speech. It was the first instance in which the Supreme Court applied the Bill of Rights to public employment. Since then, constitutional adjudication has aimed at extending the scope of the **doctrine of incorporation**— the process by which the federal courts have applied portions of the Bill of Rights to states and localities. This process has had a profound impact on public employment, especially in terms of the relationship between employee and employer. In many instances, case law has expanded the rights of individuals in the workplace and challenged HR managers, who must apply new court decisions to HR policy.

Before the application of the Bill of Rights, public employment was treated as a privilege. Much like private sector employmentat this time, public employment was largely unregulated and subject to the "will" of the employer. The **doctrine of privilege** maintained that there was no constitutional right to public employment, deeming service in government a privilege (Shafritz et al. 2001, 106). Public employment was viewed as a voluntary arrangement, and this treatment allowed employers to skirt the rights of employees in HR practices such as selection and termination.

However, as government experienced exponential growth in the 1930s, managing public sector employment proved increasingly difficult for managers seeking to address the rights of employees while focusing on efficiency. Although court cases were affirming the rights of individuals in their capacity as citizens, the rights of public employees were largely being ignored. Tension existed between restraining government practices with regard to citizen rights, on the one hand, and allowing the government to infringe upon those same rights of its employess, on the other.

After the Supreme Court decision in *Gitlow,* the Court broadened the applicability of constitutional protections afforded by the Bill of Rights. The civil rights movement of the 1950s and 1960s, led by the NAACP's Legal Defense Fund, put the question of guaranteed constitutional rights to the federal judiciary. The result was a more active judiciary that was eager to protect the rights of citizens and employees in the public sector. The Court's reasoning was based on a firm belief that constitutional guarantees afforded individuals as citizens should also pertain to their status as public employees (Shafritz et al. 2001, 109). The Court rejected the "doctrine of privilege" in the 1970s, replacing it with the **doctrine of substantial interest** as Court decisions broadened the scope of rights afforded public employees and supported their ability to challenge the decisions of management.

Unfortunately, the use of "substantial interest" in court decisions led to ambiguities and inconsistencies in the application of constitutional doctrines (Shafritz et al. 2001, 109). During this period, the courts wrestled with the use of subjective criteria (e.g., dress, personality) as a pretext for discrimination against members of a protected class. For example, employers seeking to exclude minorities from positions might claim that certain candidates did not perform well during an interview as a justification for not hiring them. These cases were ultimately concerned with potential adverse impact on protected classes; however, establishing a clear framework proved elusive. This lack of clarity in the constitutional framework created a litigious atmosphere, and public HR managers had no clear guidelines on what constituted public employee rights under the doctrine of substantial interest.

By the late 1970s, the courts began to put in place a clearer legal framework for assessing constitutional rights vis-à-vis public employment—the **public service model**. According to Rosenbloom (2003), the public service model balances three factors:

- The interest of the employee in exercising his or her constitutional rights, that is, in being free of governmental controls
- The government's interest in achieving some important purpose as an employer
- The public's interest in the way government and public administration operate (44)

The public service model makes a distinction between the role government plays as a regulator of the conduct of citizens and its role as an employer. When adjudicating matters of public employment, the courts must weigh the importance of efficiency in managing a public office against the freedom of employees to exercise their constitutional rights. Thus, the public service model attempts to balance the sometimes competing claims of government employers (efficient and effective operation), public employees (retention of constitutional guarantees), and the public interest (efficient and effective management of the public's money). Of course, this balancing act does not always lead to greater clarity for public HR managers or public employees. Because case law is determined by previous precedents, one cannot simply refer to the authorizing language of a statute or legislation. As Rosenbloom and Bailey (2003) noted, the Court considers each decision depending on the context and circumstances surrounding that specific case, so it is difficult for public HR managers to make a general application of constitutional principles to any particular HR activity (31). Public HR managers must rely on the advice of agency or jurisdictional attorneys. Below, we will examine some of the most common constitutional rights or freedoms that are at issue in public employment.

Freedom of Expression

Over the last four decades, the courts have carefully reviewed the rights afforded public employees to express their opinions under the First Amendment protection for freedom of speech. The issue of First Amendment protections is particularly salient for public employees speaking to matters of public concern. What designates a matter of public concern is not entirely clear given that case law decisions tend to be specific to the circumstance of the particular case. The Supreme Court's decision in *Pickering v. Board of Education* (1968) initially provided a legal framework for public employees' freedom of expression. In this case, the Supreme Court weighed the merits of the termination of a schoolteacher who had voiced criticism of the school board in a local periodical. The Court ruled that public employees had a First Amendment right to speak out on matters of public concern (including whistle-blowing) (Roberts 2012; Rosenbloom 2003; Shafritz et al. 2001). The ruling deemed that Pickering's actions did not represent a blatant disregard for the truth and did not interfere with workplace productivity. However, the Court went on to conclude that such a right can be abridged in specific situations, including when speech would impair discipline and harmony in the workplace, would breach confidentiality, would impede job performance, or would jeopardize close personal loyalty (Rosenbloom 2003, 45). Any disruptive speech falling into one of these categories was not fully protected by the First Amendment and could be subject to restrictions.

The Court went on to further outline the legal framework for determining issues with respect to public employees' freedom of speech; this framework is referred to as the **Pickering Test**. Like the framework of the public service model, the Pickering Test balances the interests of the employee, who as a citizen may wish to comment on matters of public concern, and the interests of the state, which as an employer seeks to promote workplace efficiency (*Pickering v. Board of Education* 1968, 568). In the *Pickering* case, the Supreme Court determined that the interest of the employee in speaking out on a matter outweighed the productivity concerns of the employer, and the Court decided that such speech was protected under the First Amendment. Subsequent to the ruling in *Pickering,* the courts have vacillated on the extent of rights to freedom of expression afforded public employees. The Court granted greater rights to freedom of speech in *Givhan v. Western Line Consolidated School District* (1979), but then it scaled back the scope of that freedom on matters of day-to-day management practices (see *Connick v. Myers* 1983).

The Supreme Court ruling in *Rankin v. McPherson* (1987) reexamined the right of public employees to freedom of speech in the case of a deputy constable in Harris County, Texas, who commented on the assassination attempt on then President Ronald Reagan to a co-worker. (To read excerpts from the Supreme Court decision in *Rankin v. McPherson,* see Case Study 3.1.) Regarding the attempt on President Reagan's life, deputy constable Ardith McPherson stated that "If they go for him again, I hope they get him" (379). The Court's ruling protected the employee's freedom of speech to comment on matters of public concern, declaring that while the plaintiff's comment may have been considered by some to be extreme, it did not—given her position and duties within the law enforcement office, which were mostly clerical in nature—unduly disrupt the efficient operation of the agency (Roberts 2012, 47). The *Rankin* decision added criteria to those given by *Pickering,* suggesting that "manner, time, and place of the employee's expression are relevant, as is the context in which the dispute arose" (*Rankin* 1987, 88).

Over the last two decades, the Supreme Court has addressed freedom of speech matters for public employees in two landmark cases: *Waters v. Churchill* (1994) and *Garcetti v. Ceballos* (2006). In *Waters v. Churchill* (1994), the Court permitted public employers to discipline public employees for perceived disruptive speech that was not covered by the First Amendment (Roberts 2012, 47). Cheryl Churchill, a nurse, was discussing personnel matters, and some of her opinions were critical of policy established by her supervisor, Cindy Waters. A nurse who overheard the discussion informed Waters of it and expressed concern that the discussion was harmful to the workplace policy governing department transfers. Churchill was subsequently fired without a hearing. The caveat to the *Waters* decision is that, before carrying out discipline, the employer needs to follow through on an investigation of the purported disruptive speech.

In *Garcetti v. Ceballos* (2006), the Court ruled to impose further restrictions on the constitutional rights afforded public employees to freedom of speech (Roberts 2007, 171–84; Roberts 2012, 47). Los Angeles assistant district attorney Richard Ceballos was critical of a search warrant and supporting affidavit emanating from district attorney Gil Garcetti's office with respect to a pending criminal case. Ceballos investigated the matter and communicated his misgivings to his supervisors. He also submitted a memorandum recommending that the case be dismissed. Due to his criticism of the search warrant and affidavit, Ceballos testified on behalf of the defense in the respective criminal case. Ceballos claimed that the district attorney's office undertook a number of retaliatory measures against him, which led him to initiate a grievance. The grievance was denied, and findings suggested there was no retaliation on the part of the district attorney's office. In the same vein as the *Waters* decision, the Court in *Garcetti* continued to favor the rights of employers to properly manage and discipline employees, granting them greater discretion over matters of speech in the workplace on grounds of efficiency. The Court ruled that "official communications have official consequences, creating a need for substantive consistency and clarity. Supervisors must ensure that their employees' official communications are accurate, demonstrate sound judgment and promote the employer's mission" (*Garcetti* 2006, 434).

For public HR managers, the court rulings suggest a need to balance the competing claims of freedom of speech afforded public employees on matters of public concern with the efficiency of public services. As a practical matter, public HR managers must fine-tune their ability to determine which matters are of public concern and the potential for speech to disrupt workplace efficiency. Matters voiced to employers by employees in private are most certainly protected. However, based on recent Court rulings, speech that promotes disharmony and discord in the workplace and/or deters the employee from performing his or her job is more than likely to be deemed unconstitutional.

Freedom of Association

Freedom of association cases have primarily addressed public employee membership in partisan or labor activities. In *Elfbrandt v. Russell* (1966), *Elrod v. Burns* (1976), *Branti v. Finkel* (1980), and *Rutan v. Republican Party of Illinois* (1990), the Supreme Court expanded the ability of public employees to seek redress for their right to freedom of association (Roberts 2008, 9). Each of these cases built upon the previous one in establishing the unconstitutionality of considering patronage (partisan affiliation) when making staffing decisions in the public sector. In *Elrod v. Burns*, the Supreme Court took up the issue of partisan affiliation as a cause for dismissal. In this case, Republican public employees of Cook County, Illinois, alleged they were dismissed because of their political affiliation after the election of a Democratic sheriff. In its ruling, the Court weighed the constitutional rights of the employee against the public service metric of efficiency, stating, "The cost of the practice of patronage is the restraint it places on freedom of belief and association. . . . The benefit gained [from patronage] must outweigh the loss of constitutionally protected rights." While the

Court recognized the merits of patronage—that elected officials should be able to appoint the individuals they want to serve in their administrations—such merits were not enough to warrant abridging the First Amendment rights of public employees (Shafritz et al. 2001, 94–95).

Branti v. Finkel (1980) furthered the sentiment in *Elrod*, requiring public hiring authorities to "demonstrate that party affiliation is an appropriate requirement for the effective performance of the public office involved" (Branti 518; Roberts 2008, 10). In this case, Republicans working for the Rockland County public defender's office in New York were discharged by the newly appointed Democratic public defender. The Supreme Court's decision required the employer to show that a particular party affiliation was necessary for an employee to perform a job effectively. The respondents demonstrated that they had been effectively performing their jobs and hence argued that termination had been based solely on party affiliation; the Supreme Court concurred.

Rutan v. Republican Party of Illinois (1990) extended the unconstitutionality of patronage in *Elrod* and *Branti* to other HR functions such as hiring, promotion, or transfer (Rosenbloom 2003, 46). In the *Rutan* case, respondents argued that the Illinois governor based staffing decisions during a hiring freeze on whether or not applicants had voted in the Republican primary. Ruling in favor of the aggrieved party, the Supreme Court ruled, "Unless . . . patronage practices are narrowly tailored to further vital government interests, we must conclude that they impermissibly encroach on First Amendment freedoms" (*Rutan* 1990).

The public service model has also guided Court decisions with respect to public employee membership in labor unions. In these decisions, the Supreme Court has protected a public employee's freedom to identify primarily with his or her government employer and not be coerced into joining or supporting union activities (Shafritz et al. 2001, 116). However, it should be noted that the Court has also upheld the constitutionality of garnishing wages to pay union membership dues when this has been negotiated with the union, as long as dues do not go toward political or social endeavors. Furthermore, unions are required to explain the activities financed by membership dues (see *Chicago Teachers Union v. Hudson* 1986).

While these Court rulings have supported the rights of public employees to join labor unions and political parties (and even antisocial or subversive groups, as long as the employees do not support or participate in subversive actions), legislation passed in the wake of the terrorist acts of September 11 has raised some unanswered questions. The USA Patriot Act of 2001 regulated the authority of government agencies to gather intelligence and monitor subversive (specifically terrorist) groups. **Title VII and Title VIII of the Patriot Act** allow the federal government to label associations "terrorist groups" according to their activities (e.g., cyberterrorism). The ramifications for public employees who are members of a group labeled a "terrorist group" are not yet clear. In previous rulings, the Court has generally upheld that membership alone does not constitute questionable actions. The Patriot Act may constrain public employees from associating with groups deemed suspect under Title VIII.

Privacy in the Workplace

Issues of privacy in the public sector workplace involve primarily the Fourth Amendment, which specifically protects individuals against unreasonable searches and seizures, and at times the Fifth Amendment, which protects against self-incrimination.

The Supreme Court took up the issue of workplace privacy in 1987 with *O'Connor v. Ortega.* The case examined public employees' reasonable expectation of privacy with regard to personal objects they bring to work. In the case, during an investigation for misconduct, an employer had conducted a search of an employee's work area while the employee (Magno Ortega) was on administrative leave. Applying the public service model, the Court weighed such privacy interests against the obligation of the employer to obtain a search warrant (*O'Connor v. Ortega* 1987, 721). In that landmark case, the Supreme Court recognized the Fourth Amendment right of public employees to privacy in their public offices (Roberts 2008, 9). However, the Court limited the expectation of privacy in instances in which public employers are conducting warrantless searches of public offices as part of an investigation of misconduct in office (*O'Connor v. Ortega* 1987). The notion of a reasonable expectation of privacy, as expounded upon in this case, is predicated upon two elements: whether the employee has such an expectation and whether such an expectation is one that society would accept as reasonable (Rosenbloom 2003, 47). The reasonable expectation standard is different from that used in law enforcement activities, in which the government is required to have a warrant or probable cause before conducting a search. In fact, if the government can prove that "both the inception and scope of the intrusion . . . [were] reasonable," the public employer would be constitutionally permitted to carry out said search (*O'Connor v. Ortega* 1987; Shafritz et al. 2001, 123).

The Supreme Court revisited the issues raised in *O'Connor* in light of the information age, which has brought office-issued mobile devices into the workplace, in *Ontario v. Quon* (2010). In this case, a law enforcement officer was issued a mobile phone by the city, which had an electronic communications policy that applied to all employees. The policy outlined the permitted usage of issued devices and explained how usage would be monitored. The law enforcement officer took issue with the city's monitoring of text messages; the city deemed text messages to be the same as emails under the policy. Many of this employee's messages were of a sexually explicit nature, resulting in disciplinary action. The Court, citing the precedent set in *O'Connor,* ruled in favor of the city's audit of the officer's phone records. Because the search was motivated by a legitimate work-related purpose, and because it was not excessive in scope, the search was reasonable (*Ontario v. Quon,* 2010)

As *Ontario v. Quon* (2010) indicates, technology in the workplace complicates the issue of privacy. Many public sector agencies employ **human resource information systems (HRIS)** as a means to collect and store personal, payroll, and benefits data. Moreover, agencies continuously use electronic means of communication (e.g., email, Internet, Facebook, Twitter, etc.) which may create ambiguity around the expectation of privacy. Clearly, security systems that keep electronic communications and records confidential, as well as how employers monitor employees' electronic activities, are important legal issues. Due to the relatively public nature of electronic communication via email, the Internet, and social media, demonstrating that the employee has a reasonable expectation of privacy may be difficult (Cozzetto, Pedeliski, and Tompkins 2004, 186–89).

From a practical standpoint, public HR managers would be wise to limit access to all confidential information, regardless of how it is stored, and to take necessary precautions against its disclosure without the affected employee's consent (187). The monitoring of employee usage of technology and communication, while yet to be clearly settled, also revolves around the reasonable expectation standard. Based on the inception and scope standard established under *Ortega,* the courts generally review whether the employer gave prior notice of the monitoring activity, whether there is a compelling interest for such activity (e.g., efficiency), and whether monitoring such communication is relevant to the job. For example, agency policies dictating that electronic communication as well as software and hardware usage might reflect a legitimate government interest in decreasing the possibility of sexual harassment claims or discrimination suits, as when they bar employees from surfing pornographic material or hate material on the Internet. Such policies might also reflect a legitimate interest in improving efficiency, as when they proscribe spending too much time on non-work-related websites.

Since passage of the Patriot Act in 2001, public employees now have a lower expectation of privacy with regard to email. The **Electronic Communications Privacy Act (ECPA),** enacted in 1986, originally established protection of email privacy; a warrant was required to access email accounts. However, the Patriot Act weakened this protection on the grounds that surveillance of email is necessary for national security. Further, emails lose protection after 180 days under the ECPA, at which time a warrant is no longer required to access any public employee's work email account. Additionally, the rights to public documents afforded citizens under the **Freedom of Information Act (FOIA)** mean that public employees have a reduced expectation of email privacy.

Search and seizure protections under the Fourth Amendment also pertain to tests for human immunodeficiency virus (HIV) and drugs. In *National Treasury Employees Union v. Von Raab* (1989), the Supreme Court ruled that drug testing is permissible for public employees engaged in public safety, transit, and other safety-related occupations (Rosenbloom and Bailey 2003, 36). In this case, the Court considered the US Customs

Service's drug-testing program for "employees seeking transfer or promotion to positions having direct involvement in drug interdiction" as well as those who carry firearms or have access to classified information. The Supreme Court affirmed the appeals court's decision to permit drug testing of employees in positions involving drug interdiction and firearms (*National Treasury Employees Union v. Von Raab* 1989). While the Court did not approve of random drug testing for all public employees, Rosenbloom (2003) suggested that employees have a "reasonable expectation of privacy in their body fluids, but suspicionless drug testing is constitutionally permissible when it reasonably promotes national security, law enforcement, or public safety" (47).

Nonprofits in Focus	Employee Privacy and Nonprofit Organizations: The Age of Social Media

As in all workplaces, advances in technology raise questions regarding employee privacy. Employers (public, private, and nonprofit) seek to create a work environment that balances employee privacy with a productive work environment. The advent of social media has complicated this balance. Knowing when and where accessing social media is appropriate is an important question for nonprofit HR professionals to consider. The recent outrage over a photo posted by a nonprofit employee that showed her using an inappropriate gesture at the Tomb of the Unknown Soldier in Arlington National Cemetery, Virginia, led to the dismissal of two employees, and it prompted nonprofits everywhere to consider the relevance of their social media policies (Grovum, 2012).

So, when is it appropriate to discipline an employee for violating social media policies? First, employees are protected by a number of laws that relate to privacy. Those include federal and state whistle-blower laws, antiretaliation laws, and off-duty conduct laws (Tenenbaum, 2012). In *Hispanics United of Buffalo*, 359 NLRB No. 37 (2012), the National Labor Relations Board (NLRB) recognized the right of employees to discuss protected concerted activity on social media (e.g., Facebook) under Section 7 of the National Labor Relations Act. Such discussions could include wages, hours, benefits, and other terms and conditions of their employment.

According to Jeffrey S. Tenenbaum and Lisa M. Hix of Venable LLP in Washington, D.C., employees have no absolute constitutional right to privacy in the workplace. However, nonprofits should have a social media policy and consider including the following in it:

- Specific disclaimers waiving employees' right to privacy
  - ○ Inform employees that email should not be considered private.
  - ○ Passwords, even if "personalized," are on loan and are the property of the organization.

- Blanket disclaimers in employee handbooks, etc.
  - ○ Company property is for company use.
  - ○ Using company property for private use may be cause for discipline.

- Notification of corporate testing, monitoring, and surveillance policies

In addition, nonprofit employers should proceed with caution before taking any disciplinary action against employees for violations of social media or Internet use policies (especially if the employee's use was personal) (NonProfitTimes 2012; Tenenbaum 2012)

Procedural Due Process

Procedural due process concerns the rights afforded public employees to "due process of law" and "fundamental procedural fairness" under the Fifth and Fourteenth Amendments, respectively. Such rights are generally triggered during employer or employee **grievance** issues, as they provide public employees with a right to a hearing when being disciplined and a right to be informed of the grounds for the hearing. Under the US Constitution, the government cannot deprive citizens of life, liberty, or property without due process (Kuykendall and Facer 2002, 138–39). Accordingly, governments as employers are subject to this constitutional requirement.

Tangible or real property is not the only protected interest. The Supreme Court has also included an employee's right to continued public employment (**property interest**) as a protected interest under the Constitution. In *Barnett v. Housing Authority of City of Atlanta* (1983), the Court ruled that employees with a property interest could not be deprived of this interest without procedural safeguards (138–39) (i.e., procedural due process). **Procedural due process** requires that any person deprived of property (i.e., his or her job) be given adequate notice and be given the right to respond (usually in the form of a hearing). Therefore, a public employee cannot be summarily dismissed from a job due to a disciplinary action without first being given the opportunity to make his or her case at a hearing. Supreme Court rulings have held that employment is a constitutionally protectable property interest so long as there are "rules or mutually explicit understandings that support . . . (a) claim of entitlement" (*Perry v. Sindermann*, 408 U.S. 593, S. Ct. 1972). Further, in *Board of Regents v. Roth* (1976), the Supreme Court declared that "property interests are not created by the Constitution; they are created and their dimensions are defined by existing rules or understandings that stem from an independent source such as state law" (*Board of Regents v. Roth* 1976). By extension, the Court's ruling in favor of property interest applies to state legislation as well as agency rules or regulations that create a property right to continued employment (Kuykendall and Facer 2002, 139).

The Court's rulings have provided a framework for determining both when procedural due process applies to public employment and, if it applies, what this procedural due process consists of. There are a few different ways to determine whether property interest is established. Civil service statutes that establish property rights to continued employment typically trigger procedural safeguards. A property interest may also be established when an employer and employee enter into a binding and legally enforceable employment agreement or contract, whether it is written, oral, or even implied (Buford and Lindner 2002, 61). Once such an interest is established, a public employee may expect continued employment, and any termination proceeding must abide by constitutional due process (*Cleveland Board of Education v. Loudermill* 1985). Moreover, the *Loudermill* decision gives a public employee the right to oral or written notice of the charges against him or her, an explanation of the evidence, and an opportunity to present his or her side of the issue (*Cleveland Board of Education v. Loudermill* 1985). Threats to an employee's liberty and harm to his or her professional/personal reputation—especially as it relates to future employability—may also trigger procedural due process (*Board of Regents v. Roth* 1976). Indeed, employees may be entitled to a hearing even when they do not enjoy civil service protections, for example, if they are on probationary employment status (*Rankin v. McPherson* 1987).

Once property interest is established, three factors determine what constitutes procedural due process:

- The employee's interests that will be affected by the government's actions
- The risk that the procedure will result in error and the probability that alternative procedures might reduce that risk
- The government's interest in using the proposed procedure, including the administrative and financial burdens of alternatives (Shafritz et al. 2001, 121; see also *Mathews v. Eldridge* 1976; *Cleveland Board of Education v. Loudermill* 1985)

The recent move by many state government reformers toward a deregulated, EAW environment raises a number of legal due process questions. The state of Georgia eliminated civil service protections for newly hired employees in 1996, potentially challenging Court precedent that had established procedural safeguards. By focusing the legislation solely on new hires, the state sought to avoid the procedural due process implications of civil service protections. However, procedural safeguards established by federal and state judicial decisions may not be so easy to disregard (Kuykendall and Facer 2002, 133). Kuykendall and Facer (2002) argued that the by establishing agency policy and procedural manuals, the state may have unknowingly or unwillingly promulgated expectations of a property right in continued employment (133). In fact, then governor Zell Miller's request for internal grievance procedures within agencies further supported an implied right to due process protections (144). While there have been no legal challenges to the Georgia reforms, jurisdictions embarking on deregulation should take great care to recognize the potential legal ramifications of abridging employee procedural due process rights. As a matter of good policy, public HR managers should allow employees facing discipline or termination to voice their concerns, even when a constitutional right to do so is not clear.

Substantive Due Process

Substantive due process focuses specifically on the issue of liberty in the Fifth Amendment protections of life, liberty, and property. **Substantive due process** protects individuals by affording them due process of law against restrictions of their personal liberties, and it is frequently triggered by issues such as mandatory maternity leave, dress codes and grooming standards, and residency requirements. Typically, liberty concerns the protection of fundamental rights not specifically articulated elsewhere in the Constitution (Rosenbloom 2003, 48). The result, according to Rosenbloom (2003), is that substantive due process is an open-ended and sometimes controversial issue. Further clouding the discussion is the lack of a framework under the public service model that would guide judicial rulings; cases tend to be adjudicated on a case-by-case basis on the merits of the specific circumstances before the court. On matters of marriage and family life, the Supreme Court has allowed for a great deal of personal freedom. For example, in *Cleveland Board of Education v. LaFleur* (1974), the Court reflected on the issue of maternity leave. In the case, pregnant public schoolteachers challenged the constitutionality of mandatory maternity leave rules of the Cleveland, Ohio, and Chesterfield County, Virginia, school boards. The Cleveland maternity leave policy required pregnant schoolteachers to take unpaid maternity leave starting five months before the baby's due date. The employee was allowed to return to work in the next regular semester after the child had reached three months of age. The Supreme Court held that policies based solely on elapsed time rather than on the individual's capacity to continue work were constitutionally unacceptable, though making an exception for forced leave that starts a few weeks before the expected date of birth (*Cleveland Board of Education v. LaFleur* 1974).

Regarding dress codes and grooming standards, the courts have tended to uphold such policies promulgated by employers, placing the burden of proof on employees, who must "demonstrate that there is no rational connection between the regulation . . . and the promotion of safety of persons and property" (*Kelley v. Johnson* 1976). The courts are inclined to favor the employer as long as such policies are not arbitrary, capricious, or unfairly enforced (Buford and Lindner 2002, 64).

The courts have also ruled in favor of employers when residency requirements are at issue. In *McCarthy v. Philadelphia Civil Service Commission* (1976), the Court ruled that residency requirements do not violate due process or equal protection. In the case, the plaintiff (McCarthy) had been terminated after sixteen years of service because he had moved outside the city of Philadelphia, thus violating the city's residency requirement for employment in the fire department. The courts tend weigh the needs of the government more heavily than any hardship imposed on the employee when considering residency requirements.

Another issue raised under substantive due process concerns is the off-duty conduct of public employees. The regulation of off-duty conduct varies from state to state and among jurisdictions. Typically, such conduct is concerned with not only potential offenses an employee might commit while off duty but another job the employee may hold outside of work hours ("moonlighting"). The MSPB ruled in *Curtis Douglas v. Veterans Administration* (1981), which concerned the termination of federal employees for off-duty misconduct, that the legitimacy of discipline or termination for an employee's conduct outside the workplace depends on twelve factors. Hoping to avoid future legal entanglements, the MSPB established the twelve **Douglas Factors** based on the 1981 case (see Box 3.1).

Box 3.1	**The Douglas Factors**

1. The nature and seriousness of the offense, and its relation to the employee's duties, position, and responsibilities, including whether the offense was intentional or technical or inadvertent, or was committed maliciously or for gain, or was frequently repeated

2. The employee's job level and type of employment, including supervisory or fiduciary role, contacts with the public, and prominence of the position

3. The employee's past disciplinary record

4. The employee's past work record, including length of service, performance on the job, ability to get along with fellow workers, and dependability

5. The effect of the offense upon the employee's ability to perform at a satisfactory level and its effect upon supervisors' confidence in the employee's ability to perform assigned duties

6. Consistency of the penalty with those imposed upon other employees for the same or similar offenses

7. Consistency of the penalty with any applicable agency table of penalties

8. The notoriety of the offense or its impact upon the reputation of the agency

9. The clarity with which the employee was on notice of any rules that were violated in committing the offense, or had been warned about the conduct in question

10. Potential for the employee's rehabilitation

11. Mitigating circumstances surrounding the offense such as unusual job tensions; personality problems; mental impairment; harassment; or bad faith, malice, or provocation on the part of others involved in the matter

12. The adequacy and effectiveness of alternative sanctions to deter such conduct in the future by the employee or others (US MSPB 2009)

With respect to holding job outside the workplace, most jurisdictions maintain that the public employment position is the individual's primary occupation. Generally speaking, as long as there is no conflict of interest between the two employers, and the government employer does not have regulatory authority over the other place of employment, then such employment is acceptable. Typically, agencies have ethics manuals or specific policies that offer guidelines with regard to outside employment.

Equal Protection

After passage of historic civil rights legislation in the 1960s and 1970s, the courts took up the issue of **classification of persons**. While the Civil Rights Act of 1964 and the Equal Employment Opportunity Act of 1972 laid the foundation for equal protection under the law, subsequent court rulings fine-tuned this legislation's intent and meaning. Specifically, the question is whether or not a law, regulation, rule, policy, or government practice explicitly or implicitly classifies people into different classes along race, age, gender, and so forth (Shafritz et al. 2001, 119) and whether that classification is permissible.

Certain classifications—such as age, residency, and wealth—are subject to a lower standard of court scrutiny known as "ordinary scrutiny." **Ordinary scrutiny** places the burden of proof on the challenger (the employee) in such cases to demonstrate that the classification is not rationally related to the achievement of a legitimate governmental purpose (DiNome, Yaklin, and Rosenbloom 2004, 149). For example, government tax rates based on a person's income or wealth are deemed a legitimate classification for government purposes. If not rationally related to a legitimate governmental purpose, then restrictions based on age, residency, and education in job classifications are nonetheless acceptable so long as they do not violate any fundamental constitutional rights. For example, when an organization enforces a mandatory retirement age, age could be a **bona fide occupational qualification (BFOQ)**, if, for example, the job were physically demanding, and so could be a legitimate classification for a particular job.

Gender-based classification generally faces tougher legal standards; such classification must be substantially related to the achievement of important governmental purposes (Rosenbloom 2003, 48). However, **intermediate scrutiny** (sometimes referred to as **heightened scrutiny**) might be triggered in instances of sex-based or sexual orientation classification. If the circumstances involve a compelling government interest, then strict scrutiny (discussed below) is used; if they involve merely an important government interest, then the intermediate standard, which is generally less rigorous than the strict scrutiny standard, is applied. In instances of sex-based classification (see, e.g., *Glenn v. Brumby et al.*, in which the US Court of Appeals held that Georgia's general assembly had erred in firing a legislative staffer based on her transgender status), the courts will weigh the merits of the case to determine whether the policy is substantially related to furthering an important government interest. In the case of sexual orientation, policies such as "don't ask, don't tell" (DADT) "must advance an important governmental interest, the intrusion must significantly further that interest, and the intrusion must be necessary to further that interest" (*Witt v. Department of the Air Force,* 2008).

On the other hand, cases involving classification by race; ethnicity; and, for non-federal governments, alienage are subject to a higher and more demanding level of scrutiny called **strict scrutiny**. Strict scrutiny places the burden of proof for such cases on the government imposing the classification. The public employer must prove that the classification protects a compelling government interest and the policy is narrowly tailored so as not to interfere with individuals' constitutional rights. The development of strict scrutiny and its components—compelling government interest and narrow tailoring—has evolved over time (DiNome, Yaklin, and Rosenbloom 2004, 149). A compelling government interest might be in redressing a previous instance of unconstitutional discrimination by a public agency. In *U.S v. Paradise* (1987), for example, the Supreme Court upheld an Alabama Department of Public Safety promotion scheme that disproportionately appointed qualified African Americans due to the "department's long and shameful record of delay and resistance" in complying with judicial requirements (see also the Chapter 4 case study, "The Courts and PHRM Reform—The Jefferson County Alabama Personnel Board"). If a classification is considered to be narrowly tailored, the policy should include (1) a review of the efficacy of alternative remedies, (2) the duration of the remedy, (3) the relevant labor pool of minority group members in the population or workforce, (4) waiver provisions in case of a lack of qualified minority applicants, (5) an assessment that the remedy will have limited harmful effects on innocent third parties, and (6) an individualized consideration of each candidate (DiNome, Yaklin, and Rosenbloom 2004, 149). Affirmative action and diversity policies often consider the ramifications of tailoring. Chapter 4 will take up this issue in greater detail.

Recently, the Supreme Court addressed the issue of equal protection in *Ricci v. DeStefano* (2009), which involved promotion tests administered at the New Haven, Connecticut, fire department; firefighters needed to not only pass this test but also achieve more than a certain score in order to be promoted. The African Americans who passed the test failed to score high enough to warrant promotion, so the department dismissed the promotion test results of everyone who had taken the test, hoping to avoid legal consequences. The department was concerned that the African Americans who had failed to qualify for promotion would sue, alleging racial discrimination in the promotion and employment process. Justice Anthony Kennedy argued that a justification for disparate treatment (see Chapter 5) must be grounded in the **strong-basis-in-evidence standard**, a standard whose definition remains ambiguous in case law precedent, concluding that

> once [a] process has been established and employers have made clear their selection criteria, they may not then invalidate the test results, thus upsetting

an employee's legitimate expectation not to be judged on the basis of race. Doing so, absent a strong basis in evidence of an impermissible disparate impact, amounts to the sort of racial preference that Congress has disclaimed, §2000e-2(j), and is antithetical to the notion of a workplace where individuals are guaranteed equal opportunity regardless of race. (*Ricci v. DeStefano,* 2009)

The Court ultimately ruled that the promotion test results could not be dismissed because they did not represent an intentional act of discrimination. Thus, public HR managers pursuing intentional discrimination or classification for the purpose of avoiding or remedying unintentional discrimination, as was the case in this matter, must take care to have strong-basis-in-evidence for doing so.

Refusal to Engage in Unconstitutional Actions

Public employees also have a right to refuse to engage in activities that they perceive to be unconstitutional. In *Harley v. Schuylkill County* (1979), a prison guard refused to perform an action that he deemed violated inmates' Eighth Amendment protections from cruel and unusual punishment. The guard was discharged and subsequently filed suit against his government employer for wrongful termination on the grounds that his firing had deprived him of due process, and his refusal to act was protected by the First Amendment. The district court ruled that the right to refuse to perform an unconstitutional action was indeed safeguarded by the Constitution. The ruling also held that the county government involved was liable for the action of its employees who had ordered the unconstitutional act. Since the ruling in *Harley v. Schuylkill,* government employees alleging a right to disobey an order must sincerely believe that the proposed action is unconstitutional (Shafritz et al. 2001).

Public Employees and Constitutional Torts

Lawsuits involving employment law may be filed against governments and individual public employees. The accountability of government and its personnel depends on the branch in which the alleged malfeasance occurred, the circumstances around the action at issue, and the alleged violation's consequences (French 2009). The federal government enjoys **sovereign immunity**, a legal doctrine that says a sovereign nation cannot be sued by its citizens for a legal wrong committed against those citizens since it is in effect the legal embodiment of its citizenry. The federal government is protected from potential civil suits unless immunity is waived or the government has consented to the suit on the basis of a civil wrong on the part of the government. Likewise, states are protected by the Eleventh Amendment to the Constitution, which also grants sovereign immunity. Local governments, unfortunately, are not afforded the same protections; the Supreme Court has ruled that only states can be granted immunity from suits authorized by federal law (Durchslag 2002). By this ruling, the political subdivisions of states (e.g., counties, municipalities, school districts) are not entitled to the safeguards afforded under the Eleventh Amendment (French 2009).

While once immune to such civil suits, public employees are potentially liable for damages as a result of a constitutional tort. **Torts** are "acts committed by public officials or employees within the frameworks of their jobs that violate individuals' constitutional rights in ways that can be appropriately remedied by civil suits for money damages" (Rosenbloom and Bailey 2006, 127). Prior to the 1970s, public employees were fully protected from civil suits brought forth as a result of a tort; however, in 1982 the Supreme Court instituted **qualified immunity** standards for public employees, which provided only limited protection from civil suits. In *Harlow v. Fitzgerald* (1982), the Supreme Court ruled that immunity was qualified due to expectations that public officials would act in good faith. This case stemmed from the conspiracies perpetrated by the administration of then president Richard Nixon in the early 1970s. Two aides to President Nixon who were being sued in civil court for their actions claimed immunity under the executive authority of the president. The Court concluded:

> Where an official could be expected to know that certain conduct would violate statutory or constitutional rights, he should be made to hesitate; and a person who suffers injury caused by such conduct may have a cause of action. But where an official's duties legitimately require action in which clearly established rights are not implicated, the public interest may be better served by action taken "with independence and without fear of consequences." (*Harlow v. Fitzgerald* 1982)

Thus, public employees were held to a certain expectation of reasonable and good-faith behavior. It was therefore possible for them to be held personally liable in a civil lawsuit and to have to pay damages if they had violated this expectation. When damages are awarded in civil suits, those damages can be both compensatory and punitive in nature. While **compensatory damages** are awarded to compensate the plaintiff for expenses incurred as a result of the tortious action, **punitive damages** are awarded to send a message that such actions will not be tolerated. To merit the infliction of punitive damages, the public employee would have to act with "malice" and a "callous disregard of, or indifference to, the rights or safety of others" (*Smith v. Wade* 1983, 37). In addition, according to French (2009), if a state or local government employee violates the federally protected rights of an individual (e.g., First Amendment, Fourteenth Amendment), civil action for the deprivation of rights can be initiated and redress sought through the court system (93).

Qualified immunity has raised a number of questions, primarily as to how public HR managers and public administrators, who can be held personally liable, should balance the sometimes competing interests of employee constitutional rights and managerial prerogatives. The Court has made it clear that public managers are expected to be knowledgeable about constitutional matters. Indeed, the courts have proven quite interested in using potential liability as a tool for enforcing constitutional rights and exercising discretion over public agencies (Rosenbloom and Bailey 2006). Countless civil suits have been brought against public employees, yet little is known about the majority of resolutions since many are settled out of court (French 2009; Rosenbloom and Bailey 2006). The cost to public administration is born out in insurance premiums and legal fees. For public HR managers, careful consideration of constitutional rights is essential to avoid lawsuits. In fact, if a local government fails to take appropriate steps to train all employees in the appropriate law, the government and the HR professionals responsible for implementing training can be held liable (*City of Canton v. Harris* 1989). Thus, employment law education may be an important cost prevention measure. Rosenbloom and Bailey (2006) argued that training HR professionals to assess constitutional compliance can be a strategic measure that helps jurisdictions reduce the risk and cost of legal liability (140).

The Legal Environment of PHRM in an Era of Reform

Effectively practicing PHRM requires an appreciation of public sector employment laws and, in fact, any laws that are relevant to public sector employment. Employment law in the public sector is unique and affects every aspect of the day-to-day operations of human resources. Understanding the law is even more essential in the 21st century given the legal implications of many recent reforms, especially decentralization, deregulation, and privatization efforts.

Decentralization and deregulation reforms have diminished (or outright eliminated) a number of public employment rules and procedures meant to ensure due process and equal protection. While such efforts at the federal level have been challenged in the courts to some degree, efforts at the state and local levels continue to be weighed in the court of public opinion. A public HR manager in an EAW environment should take great care to recognize potential risks to due process and procedural fairness. By issuing agency policies and procedural manuals, jurisdictions may unknowingly or unwillingly promulgate employee regulations leading to the expectation of a property right in continued employment (Kuykendall and Facer, 2002).

In the case of privatization, the relationship between the government and the contractor can open up the hiring agency to potential lawsuits when sovereign immunity has been waived. In the federal government, the Federal Tort Claims Act (1948) and the Tucker Act (1887) waive immunity over claims arising out of contracts to which the federal government is a party and opens up both the employer and employee to potential liability for actions of the contractor. As we will see in Chapter 10, privatization also complicates due process, because contractors receiving federal funding may be obligated to afford their employees the same rights and protections given public employees. Moreover, legislation passed in the post–September 11 environment lessens the privacy expectations of public and private employees alike.

Official HR policies should be effectively communicated regularly to personnel. Advances in information technology allow HR managers to continuously impart to public employees the latest in legal information and requirements. Communicating what is expected of employees should not be relegated to new-hire orientation but be part of the ongoing training and development of the public service. To ignore the Constitution's relevance to public employment practices could be costly.

Conclusion

For HR managers, the importance of knowing employment law cannot be understated. Agency- and division-level managers are increasingly responsible for staffing decisions and thus should be well versed in the legal consequences of termination, transfer, and demotion. Indeed, recent reform trends necessitate that all public employees have a greater knowledge of the legal environment of PHRM. PHRM systems may include a mixture of classified and unclassified personnel or an EAW environment. Additionally, privatization of government activities may require HR mangers to be cognizant of contract law. Such a variety of contexts taxes the ability of HR managers to be equipped for all circumstances. When questions arise as to the correct course of action, HR managers should not hesitate to contact their agencies' legal departments.

References

Barnett v. Housing Authority of City of Atlanta, 707 F.2d 1571 (11th Cir. 1983).

Board of Regents v. Roth, 408 U.S. 564 (S. Ct. 1976).

Bowman, James S., and Jonathan P. West. 2009. "State Government 'Little Hatch Acts' in an Era of Civil Service Reform: The State of the Nation." *Review of Public Personnel Administration* 29:20–40.

Branti v. Finkel, 445 U.S. 507 (1980).

Buford, James A., Jr., and James R. Lindner. 2002. Human Resource Management in Local Government: Concepts and Applications for HRM Students and Practitioners. Cincinnati, OH: South-Western.

Chicago Teachers Union v. Hudson, 475 U.S. 292 (1986).

City of Canton v. Harris, 489 U.S. 378 (1989).

Cleveland Board of Education v. La Fleur, 414 U.S. 632 (1974).

Cleveland Board of Education v. Loudermill, 470 U.S. 532 (S. Ct. 1985).

Condrey, Stephen E., and R. Paul Battaglio Jr. 2007. "A Return to Spoils? Revisiting Radical Civil Service Reform in the United States." *Public Administration Review* 67:425–36.

Connick v. Myers, 461 U.S. 138 (1983).

Cozzetto, Don A., Theodore B. Pedeliski, and Jonathan Tompkins. 2004. "Employee Responsibilities: Setting Expectations." In *Human Resource Management in Local Government: An Essential Guide,* edited by Siegrun Fox Freyss, 179–200. Washington, DC: International City/Council Management Association.

Curtis Douglas v. Veterans Administration (5 Merit Systems Protection Board [MSPB]), 313 (1981).

DiNome, John A., Saundra M. Yaklin, and David H. Rosenbloom. 2004. "Employee Rights: Avoiding Legal Liability." In *Human Resource Management in Local Government: An Essential Guide,* edited by Siegrun Fox Freyss, 109–52. Washington, DC: ICMA Press.

Durchslag, Melvyn R. 2002. State Sovereign Immunity: A Reference Guide to the United States Constitution. Westport, CT: Praeger.

Electronic Communications Privacy Act of 1986 (ECPA), Pub.L. 99-508, 100 Stat. 1848, 18 U.S.C. §§ 2510–22.

Elfbrandt v. Russell, 384 U.S. 1 (1966).

Elrod v. Burns, 427 U.S. 347 (1976).

Federal Tort Claims Act (1948). Ch. 646, Title IV, 62 Stat. 982, 28 U.S.C. Pt.VI Ch.171 and 28 U.S.C. § 1346(b).

French, P. Edward. 2009. "Employment Laws and the Public Sector Employer: Lessons to Be Learned from a Review of Lawsuits Filed against Local Governments." *Public Administration Review* 69:92–103.

Garcetti v. Ceballos, 547 U.S. 410 (2006).

Gitlow v. New York, 268 U.S. 652 (1925).

Givhan v. Western Line Consolidated School District, 439 U.S. 410 (1979).

Glenn v. Brumby et al., 724 F. Supp. 2d 1284 (N.D. Ga. 2010), aff'd, 663 F.3d 1312 (11th Cir. 2011).

Grovum, Emma Carew. 2012. "Nonprofit Fires Employees After Facebook Photo Causes Controversy." *The Chronicle of Philanthropy,* November 21. http://philanthropy.com/blogs/social-philanthropy/nonprofit-employee-causes-furor-over-facebook-photo/31962.

Harley v. Schuylkill County, 476 F.Supp. 191 (1979).

Harlow v. Fitzgerald, 457 U.S. 800 (1982).

Hispanics United of Buffalo, Inc., 359 NLRB No. 37 (2012). http://www.nlrb.gov/case/ 03-CA-027872.

Kelley v. Johnson, 425 U.S. 238 (1976).

Kuykendall, Christine L., and Rex L. Facer II. 2002. "Public Employment in Georgia State Agencies: The Elimination of the Merit System." *Review of Public Personnel Administration* 22:133–45.

Mathews v. Eldridge, 424 U.S. 319 (1976).

McCarthy v. Philadelphia Civil Service Commission, 424 US 645 (1976).

Meese, Edwin, III. 1985. "The Attorney General's View of the Supreme Court: Toward a Jurisprudence of Original Intention." *Public Administration Review* 45:701–4.

National Treasury Employees Union v. Von Raab, 489 U.S. 656 (1989).

NonProfitTimes. 2012. *8 Elements of Employee Online Privacy.* January 9. http://www.thenon-profittimes.com/management-tips/8-elements-of-employee-online-privacy/.

O'Connor v. Ortega, 480 U.S. 709 (1987).

Ontario v. Quon, 560 U.S. 130 (S. Ct. 2619 2010).

Perry v. Sindermann, 408 U.S. 593 (S. Ct. 1972).

Pickering v. Board of Education, 391 U.S. 563 (1968).

Rankin v. McPherson, 483 U.S. 378 (1987).

Ricci v. DeStefano, 129 S. Ct. 2658, 2671, 174 L. Ed. 2d 490 (2009).

Roberts, Robert N. 2007. "The Supreme Court and the Deconstitutionalization of the Freedom of Speech Rights of Public Employees." *Review of Public Personnel Administration* 27:171–84.

Roberts, Robert N. 2008. "The Supreme Court and the Continuing Deconstitutionalization of Public Personnel Management." *Review of Public Personnel Administration* 29:3–19.

Roberts, Robert N. 2012. "The Deconstitutionalization of Academic Freedom After *Garcetti v. Ceballos?*" *Review of Public Personnel Administration* 32:45–61.

Rosenbloom, David H. 2003. *Administrative Law for Public Managers.* Boulder, CO: Westview Press.

Rosenbloom, David H. 2007. "The Public Employment Relationship and the Supreme Court in the 1980s." In *Public Personnel Administration and Labor Relations,* edited by Norma Riccucci, 201–16. New York: M. E. Sharpe.

Rosenbloom, David H., and Margo Bailey. 2003. "What Every Public Personnel Manager Should Know About the Constitution." In *Public Personnel Administration: Problems and Prospects,* 4th ed., edited by Steven Hays and Richard C. Kearney, 29–45. Upper Saddle River, NJ: Prentice Hall.

Rosenbloom, David H., and Margo Bailey. 2006. "Public Employees' Liability for 'Constitutional Torts.'" In *Public Personnel Management: Current Concerns, Future Challenges,* 4th ed., edited by Norma M. Riccucci, 126–43. New York: Longman.

Rutan v. Republican Party of Illinois, 497 U.S. 62 (1990).

Shafritz, Jay M., David H. Rosenbloom, Norma A. Riccucci, Katherine C. Naff, and Albert C. Hyde. 2001. *Personnel Management in Government: Politics and Process.* 5th ed. New York: Marcel Dekker.

Smith v. Wade, 461 U.S. 31 (1983).

Tenenbaum, Jeffrey S. 2012. *"Big Brother" in the Office: Helping Nonprofits Manage Employee Privacy in the Modern Workplace.* Washington, DC: Venable LLP. http://www.venable.com/files/Publication/14af77d3-4893-4ad5-817d-569fc4a788ef/Presentation/Publication Attachment/18e656ad-1315-415c-9951-5f3061cc9df6/Big_Brother_handout.pdf.

Tucker Act (1887). Ch. 359, 24 Stat. 505, 28 U.S.C. § 1491.

US Equal Employment Opportunity Commission (EEOC). 2012. "Laws, Regulations & Guidance." http://www.eeoc.gov/laws/index.cfm.

US Merit System Protection Board (MSPB). 2009. "Addressing Poor Performers and the Law." http://www.mspb.gov/netsearch/viewdocs.aspx?docnumber=445841&version=446988.

U.S. v. Paradise, 480 U.S. 149 (1987).

USA Patriot Act, 115 Stat. 272 (2001).

Waters v. Churchill, 511 U.S. 661 (1994).

Witt v. Department of the Air Force, 527 F.3d 806 (9th Cir. 2008).

Additional Resources

American Bar Association, Section of Administrative Law and Regulatory Practice—http://apps.americanbar.org/adminlaw/news/

Cornell University Law School, Cornell Legal Information Institute (LII)—http://www.law.cornell.edu

FindLaw—http://www.findlaw.com

The Oyez Project, Illinois Institute of Technology, Chicago-Kent College of Law—http://www.oyez.org

Appendix: Important Public Sector Employment Law Cases[1]

[1]The chapter appendix is by no means an exhaustive listing of all employment law cases relevant to the public sector. It merely provides a concise overview of the relevant cases discussed here in Chapter 3. For a more thorough account of the appropriate employment law, public HR managers should review the cases in their entirety and consult with their respective legal representatives for the jurisdiction.

Freedom of Expression	
Pickering v. Board of Education (1968)	Provided an initial legal framework for public employees' freedom of expression. Supreme Court ruled that public employees had a First Amendment right to speak out on matters of public concern (including whistle-blowing). Court went on to conclude that such a right can be abridged in specific situations, including speech that would impair discipline and harmony in the workplace, breach confidentiality, impede job performance, or jeopardize close personal loyalty.
Givhan v. Western Line Consolidated School District (1979)	A public employee does not forfeit First Amendment protection against governmental abridgment of freedom of speech when he or she arranges to communicate privately with the employer rather than to express views publicly.
Connick v. Myers (1983)	The Court held that the First Amendment protects a government employee's speech if it is on a matter of public concern and the employee's interest in expressing him- or herself on this matter is not outweighed by any injury the speech could cause to the government's interest, as an employer, in promoting the efficiency of the public services it performs through its employees.
Rankin v. McPherson (1987)	The Supreme Court's ruling protected the employee's freedom of speech to comment on matters of public concern, declaring that the plaintiff's position and duties within the law enforcement office—mostly clerical in nature—did not unduly disrupt the operations of the agency. The *Rankin* decision suggests that "manner, time, and place of the employee's expression are relevant, as is the context in which the dispute arose."
Waters v. Churchill (1994)	The Supreme Court permitted public employers to discipline public employees for perceived disruptive speech that was not covered by the First Amendment. The caveat to the *Waters* decision is that in order to carry out said discipline, the employer must follow through on an investigation of the purported disruptive speech.
Garcetti v. Ceballos (2006)	The Court ruled that official communications have official consequences, creating a need for substantive consistency and clarity. Supervisors must ensure that their employees' official communications are accurate, demonstrate sound judgment, and promote the employer's mission.
Freedom of Association	
Elfbrandt v. Russell (1966)	Political groups may embrace both legal and illegal aims, and one may join such groups without embracing the latter. Those who join an organization without sharing in its unlawful purposes pose no threat to constitutional government, either as citizens or as public employees.

(Continued)

(Continued)

Elrod v. Burns (1976)	The cost of the practice of patronage is the restraint it places on freedom of belief and association. The benefit gained from patronage must outweigh the loss of constitutionally protected rights. The Court recognized the merits of patronage, but such merits were not enough to warrant abridging the rights of public employees
Branti v. Finkel (1980)	The First and Fourteenth Amendments protect respondents from discharge solely because of their political beliefs.
Chicago Teachers Union v. Hudson (1986)	Required unions to explain the grounds for union dues and the activities financed by them. The fact that nonunion employees' rights are protected by the First Amendment requires that the procedure be carefully tailored to minimize an agency shop's infringement on those rights. The nonunion employee must also have a fair opportunity to identify the impact on those rights and to assert a meritorious First Amendment claim.
Rutan v. Republican Party of Illinois (1990)	Extended the unconstitutionality of patronage-associated actions to HR functions such as hiring, promotion, or transfer. The Supreme Court ruled that "unless . . . patronage practices are narrowly tailored to further vital government interests, we must conclude that they impermissibly encroach on First Amendment freedoms."
Privacy in the Workplace	
O'Connor v. Ortega (1987)	The Supreme Court recognized the Fourth Amendment right of public employees to an expectation of privacy in their public offices. The Court limited that expectation in instances where public employers were conducting warrantless searches of public offices as part of an investigation of misconduct in office. A reasonable expectation of privacy is predicated upon two elements: whether the employee has such an expectation and whether such an expectation is one that society would accept as reasonable.
National Treasury Employees Union v. Von Raab (1989)	Allowed for the testing of employees who apply for promotion to positions directly involving sensitive materials—in this case the interdiction of illegal drugs or carrying of firearms—despite the absence of a requirement of probable cause or some level of individualized suspicion. Drug testing is permitted for public employees engaged in public safety, transit, and other safety-related occupations.
Ontario v. Quon (2010)	The Court, citing the precedent set in *O'Connor*, ruled in favor of the city's audit of employees' phone records, finding that the search was motivated by a legitimate work-related purpose and, because it was not excessive in scope, the search was reasonable.

Procedural Due Process	
Perry v. Sindermann (1972)	The Supreme Court supported the application of procedural safeguards in public employment, noting that a job is a constitutionally protectable property interest so long as there are "rules or mutually explicit understandings that support . . . [a] claim of entitlement."
Board of Regents v. Roth (1976)	The Supreme Court declared, "Property interests are not created by the Constitution, they are created and their dimensions are defined by existing rules or understandings that stem from an independent source such as state law." By extension, the Court's ruling in favor of property interest applies to state legislation as well as agency rules or regulations that create a property right to continued employment. Threats to an employee's liberty and harm to his or her professional/personal reputation—especially as to future employability—may also trigger procedural due process.
Mathews v. Eldridge (1976)	Requiring an evidentiary hearing upon demand in all cases involving termination of disability benefits would entail fiscal and administrative burdens out of proportion to any countervailing benefits.
Cleveland Board of Education v. Loudermill (1985)	Once a property interest is established, a public employee may expect continued employment, and any termination proceeding must abide by constitutional due process. This Court ruling provides for the right of an employee to oral or written notice of the charges against him or her, an explanation of the evidence, and an opportunity to present his or her side of the issue.
Substantive Due Process	
Cleveland Board of Education v. LaFleur (1974)	The mandatory termination provisions of maternity rules violate the Due Process Clause of the Fourteenth Amendment.
Kelley v. Johnson (1976)	Upheld the constitutionality of dress codes and grooming standards promulgated by employers, placing the burden of proof on employees, who must "demonstrate that there is no rational connection between the regulation . . . and the promotion of safety of persons and property."
McCarthy v. Philadelphia Civil Service Commission (1976)	The Court ruled that residency requirements do not violate due process or equal protection. When considering residency requirements, the courts tend to weigh the needs of the government more heavily than any undue hardship to the employee.
Equal Protection	
U.S. v. Paradise (1987)	Outlined the argument for a "compelling government interest" in redressing a previous instance of unconstitutional discrimination by a public agency. In *U.S. v. Paradise* (1987), the Supreme Court upheld the constitutionality of an

(Continued)

(Continued)

	Alabama Department of Public Safety promotion scheme that disproportionately appointed qualified African Americans due to the "department's long and shameful record of delay and resistance" in complying with judicial requirements.
Ricci v. DeStefano (2009)	Once a selection process has been established and employers have made clear their selection criteria, they may not then invalidate test results, thus upsetting an employee's legitimate expectation not to be judged on the basis of race. Doing so, absent a strong basis in evidence of an impermissible disparate impact, amounts to the sort of racial preference that Congress has disclaimed, and it is antithetical to the notion of a workplace where individuals are guaranteed equal opportunity regardless of race.
Refusal to Engage in Unconstitutional Actions	
Harley v. Schuylkill County (1976)	The right to refuse to perform an unconstitutional action is safeguarded by the Constitution. This ruling also held that the county government involved was liable for the actions of its employees. Government employees who disobey an order must sincerely believe the order and the proposed action to be unconstitutional.

Sources: Findlaw.com; Roberts 2007, 2008, 2012; Rosenbloom 2003, 2007; Rosenbloom and Bailey 2003, 2006

Case 3.1   Freedom of Speech and Public Employment Law

Rankin v. McPherson

CERTIORARI TO THE UNITED STATES COURT
OF APPEALS FOR THE FIFTH CIRCUIT

No. 85–2068 Argued: March 23, 1987—Decided: June 24, 1987

Ardith McPherson, a deputy constable employed by Texas's Harris County Constable's Office, was discharged for remarking to one of her coworkers upon learning of the attempt on President Ronald Reagan's life in 1981, "If they go for him again, I hope they get him." According to the facts of the case, Ms. McPherson was a clerical employee whose responsibilities to the Constable's Office were limited to civil process functions. She was not a deputized peace officer, did not wear a uniform, and was not authorized to carry a firearm nor make arrests on behalf of the Constable's Office. The circumstances surrounding the conversation were made during a private discussion and did not involve a greater public audience. The Constable's Office subsequently fired Ms. McPherson for the incendiary remarks.

Ms. McPherson challenged her firing by filing suit in federal district court alleging her termination violated her First Amendment right to free speech. While the district court disagreed with Ms. McPherson's challenge, subsequent appeals led to the conclusion by the U.S. Court of Appeals that the circumstances surrounding the case addressed a matter of public concern and thus necessitated further remediation. The issue in question: Does the government's interest in maintaining an efficient workplace through proper discipline outweigh the worker's right to free speech under the First Amendment of the Constitution?

The U.S. Supreme Court took up the case and weighed in on the side of Ms. McPherson, maintaining that her termination violated her First Amendment right to free speech. Delivering the Court's opinion, Justice Thurgood Marshal asserted:

> (a) The content, form, and context of respondent's statement, as revealed by the record, support the threshold conclusion that the statement constitutes speech on a matter of public concern. The statement was made in the course of a conversation addressing the policies of the President's administration, and came on the heels of a news bulletin regarding a matter of heightened public attention: an attempt on the President's life. Although a statement amounting to a threat to kill the President would not be protected by the First Amendment, the lower courts correctly concluded that respondent's remark could not properly be criminalized. Moreover, the inappropriate or controversial character of a statement is irrelevant to the question whether it deals with a matter of public concern. (384–87)

> (b) Petitioners have not met their burden of demonstrating a state interest justifying respondent's discharge that outweighs her First Amendment rights, given the functions of the Constable's office, respondent's position therein, and the nature of her statement. Although that statement was made at the workplace, there is no evidence that it interfered with the efficient functioning of the office. Nor was there any danger that respondent had discredited the office by making the statement in public. Her discharge was not based on any assessment that her remark demonstrated a character trait that made her unfit to perform her work, which involved

no confidential or policy-making role. Furthermore, there was no danger that the statement would have a detrimental impact on her working relationship with the Constable, since their employment-related interaction was apparently negligible. (388–92)

Source: The case can be read in its entirety through FindLaw: http://caselaw.lp.findlaw.com/scripts/getcase.pl?court=US&vol=483&invol=378.

Discussion Questions

Based on your review of the facts of the case and the Supreme Court decision, please answer the following questions:

1. In your opinion, does the speech in question in *Rankin* constitute a matter of public concern? The dissent in the case (see excerpt below), articulated by Chief Justice Rehnquist, argued that the speech in question was not a comment on President Reagan's policy and, thus, was not a matter of public concern. Do you agree or disagree with the majority opinion in the case?

2. Suppose the employee's comments regarding President Reagan had sowed discord and disharmony in the workplace. Had the defendant been able to demonstrate this, would the ruling have changed based on the Supreme Court's legal framework for freedom of expression cases?

3. What if the employee in question had been attached to the president's local security detail in Washington, D.C., during the time of the assassination attempt. Might this have affected the opinion of the Court?

Chief Justice William Rehnquist penned the dissenting opinion, arguing that the expansion of free speech in this case was problematic and potentially harmful to workplace efficiency. Chief Justice Rehnquist concluded that

the Court, applying the two-prong analysis of *Connick v. Myers*, 461 U.S. 138 (1983), holds that McPherson's statement was protected by the First Amendment because (1) it "addressed a matter of public concern," and (2) McPherson's interest in making the statement outweighs Rankin's interest in suppressing it. In so doing, the Court significantly and irrationally expands the definition of "public concern"; it also carves out a new and very large class of employees—i.e., those in "non-policy-making" positions—who, if today's decision is to be believed, can never be disciplined for statements that fall within the Court's expanded definition. Because I believe the Court's conclusions rest upon a distortion of both the record and the Court's prior decisions, I dissent.

Exercise

Examining Social Media Policy in the Workplace

Advances in technology have presented a host of opportunities and challenges for public employers and employees alike. For public employers, technology has provided an unprecedented means for collaborating with employees in real time. Likewise, employees have instant access to the information necessary to perform their job duties. However, access to technology, especially social media outlets like Facebook and Twitter, presents a number of challenges as well. Information posted on such sites may remain there in perpetuity for all to see, including one's supervisors. Posting your innermost thoughts and the first thought that enters your head may not always be a wise decision. Access to social media is often blocked by employers, who see it as a distraction to workplace productivity. But what about posts after work—do these constitute a threat to workplace efficiency? What about the First Amendment right to free speech? To meet the demands of a workplace environment increasingly dominated by technology, the White House issued a memorandum on "Guidance for Agency Use of Third-Party Websites and Applications": http://www.whitehouse.gov/sites/default/files/omb/assets/memoranda_2010/m10-23.pdf.

Review and critique the elements of a local organization's (public, nonprofit, or for-profit) social media policy and report your analysis to the class. What are the strong points of the social media policy? What elements, if any, are missing from the policy? For more information on the federal government's guidelines, visit the HowTo.gov site at http://www.howto.gov/social-media/using-social-media-in-government/.

4

Equal Employment Opportunity, Affirmative Action, and Diversity Planning

LEARNING OBJECTIVES

Upon completion of the chapter, you will able to do the following:

- Define representative bureaucracy as a paradigm for organizing government.
- Describe the history and development of equal employment opportunity (EEO) in the United States.
- Discuss the legal environment of affirmative action.
- Explain emotional labor, comparable worth, and pay equity in the public sector.
- Define the types of sexual harassment and their legal consequences.
- Discuss age discrimination in the workplace.
- Discuss accommodating persons with disabilities in the workplace.
- Discuss the development and management of diversity plans.
- Discuss the impact PHRM reforms have had on diversity in the workplace.

Diversity in the workplace has been increasingly discussed in public human resource management (PHRM) literature and practice over the last two decades. It is precisely for this reason that while Chapter 3, "Employment Law in the Public Sector," offers robust coverage of the employment laws that govern HR practices in the public sector, this chapter focuses on the main pieces of legislation that govern diversity policies—specifically equal employment opportunity (EEO), affirmative action, and diversity management—and the managerial implications of such policies. For many public employers, legal uncertainty and fiscal constraints require a pragmatic approach to implementing the many diversity policies mandated by various laws and statutes. The sections below review research into this area and the legal precedents that can guide public employers in coping with the legal environment of diversity.

Representative Bureaucracy as Administrative Theory

Why has diversity in the workplace become so important? The notion of a representative workforce (i.e., a public sector comprising employees who are demographically similar to the citizens they serve) is not new. Rooted in the civil rights movement and related scholarship of the 1960s, **representative bureaucracy** has proven to be a valuable organizing principle for both scholars and practitioners. A representative workforce has been seen as an asset for guiding the many interests of a diverse citizenry (Krislov 1974). This stood in contrast to the makeup of the public sector workforce through the 1960s, which was overwhelmingly white and male. For practitioners and academics alike, the advantage of a representative bureaucracy was that it could draw from the many skills and abilities of the entire spectrum of the population, enabling the public sector to address a broader set of policy problems (see also Kingsley 1944). Indeed, research has highlighted the performance gains attributable to a representative workforce, noting boosts to productivity among minorities and nonminorities (Meier, Wrinkle, and Polinard 1999). A representative bureaucracy was also seen as a means for establishing greater legitimacy in the public service, a view expressed in the Civil Service Reform Act of 1978 (see Chapter 2).

There are two important forms of representative bureaucracy that consider the assessment and measurement of diversity in the workplace (Mosher 1982). First, **passive representation** considers to what degree the workforce has the same characteristics as the overall population. An assessment of passive representation entails a demographic analysis of the population based on available data (such as data from the US Census Bureau or the Bureau of Labor Statistics) and the extent to which the public sector workforce reflects that data. For example, if the population of a jurisdiction was 60 percent white, 30 percent African American, 8 percent Asian-American, and 2 percent Native American, the public service would strive to mirror this demographic breakdown. Ideally, this mirror image of the population would be present at both the supervisory and subordinate levels of the organization.

Secondly, and more important to Mosher (1982), such an assessment was useless unless the public service pursued an "active" form of representation. **Active representation** calls for an active civil service, one that works as an advocate for its respective constituencies. For Mosher, active representation resulted in the manifestation of the theory of representative bureaucracy. Active representation was realized to a large extent during the civil rights era, when the legislation discussed below actively sought to include a broader segment of society in the work of government and the pursuit of policies that would assist the poor.

The legislation that has implemented equal employment opportunity as well proactive diversity initiatives serves as the basis for employment law in the public sector and has given rise to a long history of case law. The section below discusses the landmark pieces of legislation that came out of the civil rights movement and their continued influence on employment in the public sector.

The Civil Rights Movement

The civil rights movement of the 1950s and 1960s brought a greater appreciation for the disenfranchisement of African Americans in American society. Emphasizing equality in the application of the law and political empowerment, the movement quickly turned to the unfair and discriminatory treatment of minorities in employment. In many jurisdictions, African Americans, minorities, and women were barred from seeking employment, especially supervisory-level positions.

Landmark court decisions in the 1950s (e.g., *Brown v. Board of Education* 1954) led to more substantial legislation and executive orders at the federal level guaranteeing equality of opportunity. In *Brown*, the Supreme Court pronounced that the doctrine of "separate but equal" was unconstitutional. The case specifically dealt with school segregation in Topeka, Kansas, where there were separate but equal schools for African American students; the decision found that having separate schools was inherently unequal, paving the way for the notion of equal opportunity.

During the early 1960s, the movement reached a turning point when the administration of President John F. Kennedy sought sweeping civil rights legislation. Signed into law on July 2, 1964, by President Lyndon B. Johnson, the **Civil Rights Act of 1964** solidified the early efforts of civil rights pioneers and paved the way to eliminate discriminatory HR practices in both public and private organizations (US Equal Employment Opportunity Commission [EEOC] 2013). To be sure, precursors to the Civil Rights Act of 1964—such as President Franklin Roosevelt's Executive Order 8802 in 1941, which prohibited discrimination in employment among defense-related industries—had been earnest attempts to stamp out discriminatory practices. However, none of these early efforts had the necessary statutory grounding to effect fundamental change, and they were often narrow in focus. Executive orders, for example, can be rescinded by future administrations. In contrast, the 1964 act established a solid legal framework to ensure equality of employment opportunity. Title VII of the act specifically governs employment practices; it prohibits discriminatory employment practices by covered employers (i.e., those with 15 or more employees) based on race, color, religion, sex, national origin, or protected activity (EEOC n.d.b). The act also created the Equal Employment Opportunity Commission as the agency responsible for enforcing its provisions.

In practice, however, the EEOC proved to be ill-equipped for enforcing equal employment opportunity. The 1964 act did not really give the EEOC the authority to enforce the law. The agency could investigate claims of discrimination or denial of equal opportunity, but it lacked the power to sue employers that violated these laws or otherwise implement any proactive measures against discrimination; litigation of discrimination claims was as a practical matter relegated to the Department of Justice (EEOC n.d.b).

This lack of enforcement power led to passage of the **Equal Employment Opportunity Act** by Congress in 1972. The 1972 act enhanced the EEOC's power, giving it the authority to enforce and litigate instances of discriminatory practices in employment. The EEOC was now able to provide legally binding interpretations of key elements of civil rights legislation and policy—an authority still in use today to interpret policies regarding sexual orientation in the workplace (discussed in the next section). The EEOC also developed a framework that lays out specific procedures individuals can follow to seek redress for discriminatory practices in the workplace. In this way, individuals can take affirmative steps toward improving equality of opportunity in the workplace

Equal Employment Opportunity, Affirmative Action, and Diversity

Navigating the current climate of equal employment opportunity can be challenging for scholars and practitioners alike. Since the passage of the 1964 Civil Rights Act, numerous court decisions and legislative changes have complicated employer efforts to promote diversity in the workplace. While the evolving law has solidified the importance of equal employment opportunity in the public sector, it has also added to the already voluminous information with which HR personnel must be familiar. For many public managers, understanding equal employment opportunity can be exacting, especially in the context of affirmative action plans and diversity initiatives. The differences among these three concepts—equal employment opportunity, affirmative action, and diversity—can be nuanced, but the distinctions are important. Table 4.1 provides an overview of the three approaches.

While equal employment opportunity and affirmative action have a firmer grounding in law, diversity plans have become popular among employers as a means of promoting a diverse workplace without the controversy surrounding the other two approaches (particularly affirmative action). Diversity plans are seen as a means to implement proactive solutions to workforce diversity without the red tape often associated with legal proceedings. The managerial approach of diversity plans differs significantly from the policing aspects of equal employment opportunity and affirmative action. The sections below review each of the three policies in greater detail. Given the legal challenges many of these policies face, it is important

Table 4.1	**Equal Employment Opportunity, Affirmative Action, and Diversity**		
Function	**Equal Employment Opportunity**	**Affirmative Action**	**Diversity Initiatives**
Key Legislation	Civil Rights Act of 1964 as amended by the Equal Employment Opportunity Act of 1972 as amended by the Civil Rights Act of 1991; No FEAR Act of 2002	Civil Rights Act of 1964 as amended by the Equal Employment Opportunity Act of 1973 as amended by the Civil Rights Act of 1991	Title VII of the Civil Rights Act of 1964 permits diversity initiatives to address a manifest imbalance. However, the courts have not ruled on the legality of an "operational need" rationale for diversity.
Objective	Prohibits discriminatory employment practices based on Title VII classifications of race, color, national origin, sex, and religion and prevents retaliation against individuals for exercising Title VII rights.	Provides actionable legal remedy for intentional discriminatory practices in employment. Requires strategic planning, recruiting, goal setting, training and development, and monitoring.	Proactive managerial tool aims to capitalize on diversity, that is, to derive benefits from the skills and abilities that come with a more diverse workforce.
Coverage	Employers with 15 or more employees	Employers with 15 or more employees; employers with federal contracts and their subcontractors	Voluntary effort
Action	Investigation is triggered by current or past instances of discrimination.	May be the result of a court order, negotiated settlement, government regulation, or voluntary action.	Management seeks to enhance employment opportunities for Title VII groups, capitalize on diversity, and avoid legal action.
Enforcement Agency	EEOC	EEOC, OFCCP, courts, state policy, city policy	No enforcement agency
Intended Outcome	Equal employment opportunity is achieved for all employees and potential employees, and workplaces are free of discrimination.	Prior discriminatory practices are redressed.	Improved organizational performance results from a workplace that supports equity and from leveraging the abilities of all qualified workers.

Sources: Adapted from Shafritz et al. (2001) and Klingner and Nalbandian (2003).

for HR managers to always consult with their legal departments when a question arises about their implementation.

EEO Compliance and Enforcement

Equal employment opportunity today is firmly grounded in the Civil Rights Act of 1964. The essence of EEO is that no citizen can be discriminated against in the workplace on the basis of race, color, religion, sex, national origin, or protected activity (e.g., whistle-blowing). Equal employment conveys an expectation that one will not, for example, be denied a job based on race, get paid less than a co-worker because of the color of one's skin, or be denied a religious holiday. The EEOC is the agency responsible for enforcing EEO legislation.

EEO is not a static concept, however. It has been amended and/or clarified by subsequent pieces of civil rights legislation through the years (e.g., the Equal Employment Opportunity Act of 1972, discussed earlier). Two pieces of legislation— the **Civil Rights Act of 1991** and the **No FEAR Act of 2002**—have provided additional clarification about **intentional discrimination** or disparate treatment (a topic we discuss further in Chapter 5, "Recruitment and Selection"). With respect to equal employment opportunity, the Civil Rights Act of 1991 detailed the punitive and compensatory damages that plaintiffs can seek and the right to a trial by jury for claimants seeking redress for intentional discrimination. Before the 1991 act, jury trials could be held only in cases brought under the Equal Pay Act (EPA) and Age Discrimination in Employment Act (ADEA). The 1991 act also caps compensatory and punitive damages against government agencies and their subdivisions at a combined amount of $300,000 (EEOC n.d.b).

The No FEAR Act (Notification and Federal Employee Antidiscrimination and Retaliation) of 2002 places additional responsibilities upon federal agencies to provide a workplace free of discrimination and retaliation for the reporting of discriminatory practices (i.e.,whistle-blowing). The consequences of not doing so can be severe; the No FEAR Act requires the infringing federal agency to pay for damage judgments out of its own budget. Federal agencies must also provide personnel with annual notice of their rights with respect to discrimination and whistle-blower protection, administer training every two years covering the obligations under the act, provide annual compliance reports to relevant federal agencies such as the Department of Justice, and post relevant statistical data quarterly on the agency's website (EEOC n.d.b). Unlike previous legislation, which was more reactive in nature, the No FEAR Act directs federal agencies to take proactive steps toward creating workplaces free of discrimination.

Affirmative Action

Affirmative Action refers to actionable legal remedies aimed at addressing intentional discriminatory practices in employment. Affirmative action plans may be the result of a court order intended to redress violations of civil rights legislation (as in the case study for this chapter), negotiated settlement between two parties (e.g., employer and employee), or government regulation. Affirmative action plans may also be voluntary in nature (e.g., diversity plans), incorporated into HR practices to address perceived imbalances in certain job categories. **Occupational segregation** often occurs on the basis of gender, because women are often disproportionately represented in jobs traditionally held by women (e.g., teacher, nurse).

To be sure, controversy has surrounded affirmative action, but much of the controversy stems from a lack of understanding regarding such policies and their goals. As previously discussed, the 1964 Civil Rights Act lacked actionable enforcement powers. A series of landmark court cases between 1964 and 1971 created a greater awareness of this deficiency. Beginning with *Griggs v. Duke Power Company* (1971), the Supreme Court paved the way for affirmative action policies. During the 1950s and 1960s, one of the Duke Power Company plants in North Carolina had hired African Americans only into a specific division, and the company required a high school diploma for advancement. Given the practice of school segregation in the South at the time, the plaintiffs filing suit argued that the promotion policy indirectly excluded African Americans from higher-paying jobs. In its ruling, the Supreme Court deemed that such practices, while not intentionally discriminatory, had an adverse impact on African Americans. Promotion should be based on one's ability to perform the job, not on attributes tangential to productivity (*Griggs v. Duke Power Co.* 1971). Since *Griggs*, the Court has upheld that remedial efforts to address instances of intentional discrimination are constitutional (Rosenbloom 2006). However, since the 1980s, a more judicially conservative Court has tended to restrict the application of affirmative action in practice, placing a greater burden on plaintiffs. Those seeking redress for discrimination must demonstrate that the employer carried out discriminatory actions; the burden is not on the employer to justify its employment practices.

Table 4.2 highlights key findings from recent court cases reviewing affirmative action. *Gratz v. Bollinger* (2003) and *Grutter v. Bollinger* (2003) suggest that the courts are firm in their commitment to uphold strict scrutiny in their evaluations. As described in Chapter 3, strict scrutiny is a higher standard whereby, when a government agency or entity classifies employees according to race or ethnicity, that agency must prove that it has a compelling interest in doing so and is applying the categories to achieve narrowly tailored purposes. In other words, for jurisdictions considering affirmative action programs, there must be a compelling government interest in pursuing such policies (i.e., remedying past discriminatory practices), and these efforts should consider race as only one of many factors. The Court's recent ruling in *Fisher v. University of Texas* (US Supreme Court 2012) held that the lower court had not applied strict scrutiny as established in *Regents of the University of California v. Bakke* (1978) and more recently in the *Grutter* (2003) decision. The *Fisher* case involved the affirmative action admission policy of the University of Texas at Austin. Plaintiffs alleged that their admission was denied because of their race (white). Although the Court did not directly review the constitutionality of affirmative action in the *Fisher* case, the ruling does affirm the standard of strict scrutiny as outlined in *Grutter* and *Bakke*—specifically that racial equity may be an appropriate admissions goal but should play a limited role in the admissions criteria.

Practically speaking, it is often difficult for managers to make sense of the legal arguments surrounding affirmative action. HR managers must interpret the requirements of civil rights laws in light of specific instances in their workplace that might trigger a lawsuit. Managers should always consult with a jurisdiction's legal counsel if questions arise.

Table 4.2	**Recent Affirmative Action Cases**	
Case	**Jurisdiction**	**Finding**
Taxman v. Board of Education of Piscataway Township (1996)	3rd US Circuit Court of Appeals	Use of race to maintain racial diversity is impermissible. Upheld district court ruling that school board's consideration of race did not fall within the parameters of legally permissible affirmative action. At issue was remedying a manifest racial imbalance versus maintaining specific balance.
Hopwood v. State of Texas (1996)	5th US Circuit Court of Appeals	Use of race is impermissible as a factor in deciding admissions to the University of Texas School of Law in order to achieve a diverse student body, to combat the perceived effects of a hostile environment at the law school, to alleviate the law school's poor reputation in the minority community, or to eliminate any present effects of past discrimination by actors other than the law school.
Smith v. University of Washington Law School (2000)	9th US Circuit Court of Appeals	Fourteenth Amendment permits university admissions programs to consider race for other than remedial purposes. Educational diversity is a compelling governmental interest that meets the demands of strict scrutiny of race-conscious measures.
Johnson v. Board of Regents of the University of Georgia (2001)	11th US Circuit Court of Appeals	Court rejected university diversity admissions policy as not representing a compelling government interest under strict scrutiny and as violating the Equal Protection Clause of the Fourteenth Amendment. Court ruled university diversity policy was arbitrary in its application of "diversity bonuses" to nonwhites and failed to consider other factors relevant to diversity.

Case	Jurisdiction	Finding
Grutter v. Bollinger (2001)	US Supreme Court	Court ruled that the University of Michigan Law School admissions policy demonstrated a compelling interest in promoting class diversity. Race-conscious admissions processes may favor "underrepresented minority groups," as long as race is one of various criteria for admissions that are applied on an individual basis.
Gratz v. Bollinger (2001)	US Supreme Court	Court ruled that University of Michigan undergraduate admissions policy, which awarded racial minorities automatic points rather than assessing individual merit, violated the Equal Protection Clause of the Fourteenth Amendment.
Fisher v. University of Texas (2012)	US Supreme Court	While not directly affirming the issue of constitutionality, the Court decision held to the strict scrutiny standards established in *Grutter* and *Bakke*.

Sources: Kellough 2006 and US Supreme Court 2012.

Despite the numerous court cases, affirmative action is still largely a voluntary effort. Instances in which affirmative action has been mandated are usually tied to violations of Title VII of the Civil Rights Act of 1964. In such cases, the courts have required implementation of affirmative action programs as a remedy when they find that an employer has violated the law (Kellough 2006, 148; see this chapter's case study concerning Jefferson County, Alabama). According to Kellough (2006), court-mandated affirmative action in response to violations of Title VII is the law under which employers are forced to implement remedial measures. When employers seek consent agreements to settle discrimination lawsuits, the measure is a voluntary policy act. Government entities—including federal, state, and local agencies and public colleges and universities—that incorporate affirmative action policies in civil service systems are also voluntarily establishing programs (148). The same can be said of contractual relationships with government agencies in which the parties are not forced to contract with government (148). Kellough continued:

> All other affirmative action programs that exist in the private sector also result from voluntary efforts. In other words, government has voluntarily (without the pressure of litigation) established affirmative action programs within the public workforce, in public colleges and universities with respect to student admissions, and as a condition placed upon firms with whom government enters into contracts. In addition, whether affirmative action is

voluntary or nonvoluntary, it may take the form of recruitment and outreach efforts, goals and timetables, or other preferential strategies. (148–49)

Thus, affirmative action is really a proactive measure designed to address a history of intentionally discriminatory practices in the workplace. Whereas EEO policy focuses on investigating instances of discrimination, affirmative action is a tool used to implement a long-term plan to rectify discriminatory practices. Affirmative action plans should be a strategic effort that sets relevant goals, monitors progress toward those goals, and incorporates HR functions such as recruitment and training in meeting the goals.

Managing Diversity

Given the legal complications that might arise with affirmative action plans, many organizations—both public and private—have pursued voluntary efforts to create a climate of diversity. Why might an organization pursue diversity policies when not required to do so by a court or government order? For many organizations, diversity plans serve as proactive managerial tools that capitalize on the skills and abilities of a workforce drawn from a broader segment of society. Moreover, organizations may seek to avoid legal action by implementing plans that promote equal opportunity for all rather than pursuing explicitly race-based initiatives like affirmative action. For example, organizations might recruit at historically black colleges and universities or establish relationships with Hispanic chambers of commerce. Diversity plans also offer organizations an opportunity to address occupational segregation by sex, for example by hiring and promoting more women into management positions or increasing women's representation in traditionally male occupations such as truck driver or construction worker.

While the courts have suggested that voluntary efforts like diversity plans may be a permissible means of improving access to employment for all in certain circumstances, case law has not established whether such plans are constitutional or not (Rosenbloom 2006). Without a definitive legal decision, employers—public and private—must weigh the merits of voluntary diversity efforts against potential drawbacks. Managers and legal departments need to consider such plans in light of Title VII and the **Equal Protection Clause** of the Constitution (EEOC n.d.b). While the EEOC encourages voluntary diversity efforts, such efforts must be implemented with great deference to the law. In their legal analysis of court cases considering voluntary affirmative action efforts, Klein and Papas (2006, 2) offered the following questions employers should ask:

- Is the plan intended to break down old patterns of segregation and hierarchy in occupations that have been traditionally closed to women or minorities?

- Is the plan premised on an understanding of what the Supreme Court meant by "traditionally segregated job categories"?
- Does the plan avoid unnecessarily trammeling the interests of white or male employees by ensuring that opportunities continue to be available to them?
- Does the plan envision an end point when the plan will no longer be necessary. That is, is it a temporary measure, intended simply to eliminate a manifest racial or gender imbalance, not to maintain racial or gender balance?
- Is the plan based upon statistics demonstrating a manifest imbalance between the number of women or minorities in the relevant labor market who are qualified for the positions and the number of women and minorities in the workforce?
- Is the plan predicated on a level of disparity sufficient to constitute a manifest imbalance worthy of a remedy by affirmative action?

These guidelines suggest that diversity initiatives are meant to be finite in duration and aimed at correcting imbalances in race and gender. They are not to be a relatively permanent instrument for maintaining racial and gender balance. The imbalances to be corrected must also be corroborated by statistical evidence about the relevant labor market.

Does Diversity Matter?

Proponents of diversity plans have touted their many benefits, including greater awareness of cultural differences, improved communication, and even enhanced productivity (see Meier, Wrinkle, and Polinard 1999). However, diversity also has potential drawbacks. When there is little or no planning, diversity initiatives can introduce conflict into the workplace. While communication may be improved over time, in the short-term, communication among employees may be inhibited. Research has turned an inquisitive eye toward the assertion that diversity initiatives bring about performance gains.

In their review of economic research on affirmative action in the workplace, Holzer and Neumark (2000) found that affirmative action programs were not necessarily harmful to efficiency and that they do "offer significant redistribution toward women and minorities" (559). In fact, the authors found that, in many cases, affirmative action programs had been devised in such a fashion that they were not harmful to organizational productivity. For example, the authors suggested that a focus on recruitment and training efforts is important to generating qualified minority applicant pools. Maintaining validity and fairness in evaluation and selection procedures can broaden standards without necessarily lowering them (544). Holzer and

Neumark (2000) cautioned that affirmative action programs incur significant costs (e.g., personnel and administrative costs to operate the program), but there is scant evidence of losses to efficiency that would make a plausible case against such programs. While Holzer and Neumark included education institutions in their assessment, further analysis of affirmative action in the public sector is warranted.

More recently, Pitts and Wise (2010) assessed the state of research into public sector diversity initiatives, focusing on empirical evidence, diversity management, and organizational outputs and outcomes. The authors' findings suggest that while much research has been done over the last decade, evidence-based knowledge for practitioners is limited. More importantly, their efforts suggest that what research is being conducted lacks the empirical rigor to justify any conclusions regarding diversity and organizational results.

Nevertheless, workplace diversity remains a priority for many governments seeking to create a climate that values differences. Governments pursuing diversity initiatives often do so to transform the organizational culture for the better, irrespective of any efficiency gains. Their focus might be on improving morale or openness in the workplace. Affirmative action programs do not always improve workplace diversity (see Rice 2001; Shin and Mesch 1996; Thomas 1991–92). Moreover, affirmative action may leave employees with feelings of resentment at the outcome. As such, diversity plans may be a viable alternative to affirmative action. For public agencies considering diversity plans, Rice and White (2005) suggested that the key is to embrace a comprehensive approach that reflects (1) conversion from a singular to a multicultural organization, (2) adoption of a participatory approach to leadership, (3) vigilant pursuit of diversity objectives, and (4) promotion of the plan to employees and other stakeholders to ensure proper design and execution (230). Table 4.3

Table 4.3	Diversity Objectives and Actions
Objective	**Action**
Evaluation of the commitment of leadership/management to diversity	Include diversity criteria in succession planning. Train management in effective communication and feedback.
Effective recruitment and retention of a diverse workforce	Develop recruitment efforts that reach out to underrepresented groups. Develop selection criteria that emphasize unbiased, job-related qualifications. Conduct timely job analysis.

Objective	Action
Development of an innovative, creative, and people-oriented work environment	Include diversity criteria in organizational mission, values, and goals. Implement rotational assignments and empowerment programs.
Evaluation of the commitment of employees to diversity	Develop internal advocacy groups. Include diversity awareness in performance appraisal. Include diversity criteria in promotion decisions.
Continuous emphasis on valuing, understanding, and managing diversity	Diversity training is delivered to all employees.
Implementing management approaches that support a diverse workforce	Poor performance or transgressions against work rules are addressed with training. Management is trained in effective communication and feedback.
Enabling employees to balance career and personal needs	Clear career ladders are developed. Diversity criteria are considered in promotion decisions. Quality of work life programs are developed and implemented.
Incorporation of training and development in the diversity initiative	Diversity training is delivered to all employees.
Accountability for management of the diversity plan	Include diversity awareness in performance appraisal. Consider diversity criteria when making promotion decisions. Consider diversity criteria in succession planning.
Clearly defined goals and timetables, preferably long-term	Include diversity criteria in workforce planning. Consider diversity criteria in succession planning.
Recognition of individuals who have contributed to diversity accomplishments	Employees recognized for diversity achievement should be involved in internal advocacy groups and training efforts as "idea champions."

Source: Adapted from Rice and White (2005).

offers specific objectives and actionable items that might be included in a public sector diversity plan.

Additional EEO Concerns

Comparable Worth and Pay Equity

While the Equal Pay Act of 1963 and case law strictly prohibits intentional pay discrimination on the basis of gender, the same cannot be said with certainty for gender pay inequities among different job titles that have the same value to their employer (Buford and Lindner 2002, 316). Pay inequity is at the heart of the **comparable worth** debate. For instance, public waste management departments might employ women in administrative roles at one pay level while employing men as truck drivers at a higher rate of pay. Both positions are equally important to the function of the agency, but they are not remunerated as such. These differences are real for many men and women in the public service, and comparable worth research strives to effectively measure the intrinsic worth of jobs. However, case law remains unclear as to the liability employers may bear for gender-based pay disparities in their organizations.

This compensatory bias against women is the subject of much debate among scholars and practitioners alike (Guy and Newman 2004; Guy, Newman, and Mastracci 2008). The pay gap has women in all sectors of the economy earning 80 percent of what men are paid (US Department of Labor 2005). The gap is even greater in the public sector than in the private and nonprofit workforces (US Department of Labor 2005). Many believe that the pay gap between men and women is due to freely made career choices and free-market forces.

Guy, Newman, and Mastracci (2008) suggested that this explanation alone is insufficient and that pay inequity by gender deserves greater reflection. Cultural beliefs—that men perform productive work while women play a nurture role— remain a force in explaining occupational sex segregation, despite the advances women have made in the workforce over the last few decades (139). The concept of **emotional labor** offers a richer explanation for differences in occupations for men and women. Emotional labor entails face-to-face or voice-to-voice contact with the public, a common feature of the work that public servants do as they interact with citizens on a daily basis (Hochschild 1983). Such work requires eliciting an emotional response from people and training in order to exercise one's control over emotional responses. Such skills are crucial for street-level bureaucrats (e.g., nurses, teachers, police officers) on the front line of public service, where emotional labor plays a critical role in policy decisions and communication. While such skills are critical, they are nonetheless often undervalued in the workplace. Given the greater propensity for women to occupy positions requiring such skills, female employees are often underremunerated. The literature on emotional labor offers a framework for a more robust dialogue on inequity in the workforce.

Fortunately, comprehensive classification and compensation systems in the public sector allow public employees to use job analysis—a topic explored in the next chapter—to evaluate all jobs in the organization relative to one another. Focusing on the job requirements, rather than market determinants, provides public HR managers with a means to reduce any gender-based pay gap. When job evaluations reveal gender pay differentials, public employers should remedy these inequities. The research on emotional labor may prove useful to public HR managers as they revise job descriptions and performance appraisals to incorporate and value all the skills used to perform work.

Sexual Harassment

Sexual harassment includes unwelcome sexual advances, requests for sexual favors, or other verbal or physical conduct of a sexual nature (DiNome et al. 2004, 112). The EEOC and the courts have defined two types of sexual harassment in the workplace: quid pro quo and hostile work environment. Instances of **quid pro quo** (from the Latin meaning "this for that") occur when the terms or an offer of employment is accompanied by an unwelcome sexual advance, a request for sexual favors, or some other verbal or physical conduct of a sexual nature. Such conduct may be explicit or implicit in nature. When untoward conduct is purposeful or impacts an individual's ability to perform his or her duties, the result is a **hostile work environment**. The intimidating environment may be the result of verbal, written, or electronic communication of gender-based slurs, jokes, or derogatory comments (see *Meritor Savings Bank v. Vinson* 1986). Retaliating against an employee for bringing forth a claim of sexual harassment is also covered under the adverse action protections of the Civil Rights Act of 1964 (see *Burlington Northern & Santa Fe [BNSF] Railway Co. v. White* 2006).

In *Oncale v. Sundowner Offshore Services* (1998), the Supreme Court applied the same legal framework to defining same-sex sexual harassment. In other words, sexual harassment can be male to female, female to male, male to male, or female to female.

It is imperative that employers clearly state in their equal employment opportunity guidelines a description of sexual harassment, reporting mechanisms, and corrective actions. Failure to establish such guidelines may result in employers being held vicariously liable for failing to sanction actions that might lead to a hostile work environment (*Faragher v. City of Boca Raton* 1998). Even with an official sexual harassment policy, employers may be liable when employees suffer a tangible employment action (e.g., not being hired or promoted, being fired or demoted) as the result of sexual harassment committed by a supervisor (*Burlington Industries, Inc. v. Ellerth* 1998).

Age Discrimination

Discrimination in employment based on age is illegal under the **Age Discrimination in Employment Act (ADEA) of 1967**. The act initially made it illegal for private businesses to refuse to hire, discharge, or otherwise discriminate against an individual 40 years of age or older (EEOC n.d.b). The act was subsequently amended in 1974 to cover federal, state, and local governments as well. Further amendments to the ADEA have raised the minimum mandatory age for retirement to 70 and banned forced retirement in the federal government at any age. Claims of age discrimination are brought before the EEOC, which then investigates and enforces the provisions of the ADEA. Any employment conditions based on age must be justified under the bona fide occupational qualification (BFOQ) standard, meaning that employers must demonstrate that being below a certain age is necessary to carry out particular job duties.

The Supreme Court decision in *Gomez-Perez v. Potter* (2008) held that § 633a of the ADEA affords federal employees the same protection as private sector employees in all aspects of employment covered by the law, including the ability to file lawsuits in response to being retaliated against for complaining (Mitchell 2009). Prior to this decision, such lawsuits had to be filed under civil rights legislation (e.g., the Civil Rights Act of 1964). In the case, a postal employee (Myrna Gomez-Perez) alleged that her request for a transfer had been denied based on her age. She also stated that, subsequent to her initial complaint, she had been subjected to a number of retaliatory measures. Earlier rulings by lower courts argued that the ADEA did not cover retaliatory actions. However, the Supreme Court overruled the lower courts, using the same logic as in earlier Court decisions that had affirmed protection from adverse action under other antidiscrimination legislation.

Under EEOC guidelines, a charging party (i.e., the plaintiff) is protected from retaliation for opposing discriminatory practices based on a reasonable belief that the practices are unlawful. According to the EEOC, such a claim may be warranted when

- the employee engaged in protected activity, as by communicating opposition to discrimination or participating in the statutory complaint process (protected activity);
- the employer then subjected the charging party to adverse action; and
- there is direct evidence that the employer's adverse action was in retaliation for the protected activity (EEOC 1998).

The finding in *Gomez-Perez* (2008) is important because an increasing number of government employees are 40 or older (Mitchell 2009). Age-related claims are expected to rise. In 2007, EEOC statistics showed age-related retaliation complaints were second only to race claims among all charges received in both the public and private sectors (Mitchell 2009, 94). Federal employers would be wise to consider the implications of *Gomez-Perez* when handling complaints of discrimination or retaliation under the ADEA.

Disability Discrimination

Protections against employment discrimination based on disability were first introduced under the **Vocational Rehabilitation Act of 1973**. The act as amended prohibits employment discrimination against disabled persons in federal government;

the act does not apply to state and local jurisdictions. Sections 503 and 504 of the Vocational Rehabilitation Act prohibit disability discrimination in programs receiving federal financial assistance and federal contractors and subcontractors, respectively.

The act served as a foundation for expansion of protections against employment discrimination for disabled persons under the **Americans with Disabilities Act (ADA) of 1990**. The ADA includes protections against employment discrimination as well as other forms of discrimination, such as unequal access to public accommodations and services. Title I of the ADA extends coverage to employers, employment agencies, labor unions, and joint labor-management committees with 15 or more employees. Title II covers state and local governments ("public entities") excluding federal employers, who are covered by the Rehabilitation Act of 1973 (EEOC n.d.b). Under the ADA, disabled people are protected from discriminatory employment practices in selection, promotion, compensation, transfer and recruitment, advertising, hiring and termination, and other terms and conditions of employment. The EEOC defines a person with a disability as someone with

- a physical or mental impairment that substantially limits one or more major life activities;
- a record of such an impairment; or
- being regarded as having such an impairment (EEOC n.d.b).

The standard for remedying a claim under the ADA is whether a reasonable accommodation could be made to employ a person with a disability that would not impose undue hardship on the employer. The EEOC considers four factors in determining whether an accommodation would constitute an undue hardship:

- The nature and cost of the accommodation needed
- The overall financial resources of the employer, the number of persons employed, the effect the accommodation would have on expenses and resources, and any other impact the accommodation would have on the operation of the facility
- The type of operation or operations of the employer, including the composition, structure, and functions of the workforce and the geographic, administrative, or fiscal relationship of the facility in question to the employer (EEOC n.d.b)

In 2008, Congress amended the ADA in response to Supreme Court decisions that had arguably changed the original intent of the act. The ADA Amendments Act of 2008 (ADAAA) placed a more significant burden on the employer and, as a result,

HR managers. Before the ADAAA, federal law required employers to focus their efforts on reasonable accommodation. Now employers had to assume the validity of a claimed disability, whether or not they believed the disability limited a major life activity (Rush 2012). To clarify implementation of the amendments, the EEOC suggested that the term "substantially limits" be interpreted as a "lower threshold" than the precedents established by Supreme Court cases and previous EEOC guidelines ("Regulations to Implement," 2011, 16981).

Public employers at the state and local levels are subject to higher standards than are private employers with regard to the ADA; HR managers in agencies with 50 or more employees are required to designate a coordinator for ADA compliance and develop a grievance process for ADA claims under Title II of the act (Rush 2012). Public employers are also required to continuously monitor and evaluate their ADA plan and grievance practices.

While federal employers are covered by the Rehabilitation Act, the extent to which ADA covers state and local governments is unclear. The result has been legal uncertainty and fiscal stress for state and local governments attempting to apply ADA (Rush 2012). The Supreme Court's decision in *Board of Trustees of the University of Alabama v. Garrett* (2001) limited state governments' liability for claims under ADA, citing state sovereign immunity under the Eleventh Amendment. However, this decision does not relieve state employers from ADA requirements entirely. In demonstrated instances of discrimination, state employees may be able to gain injunctive relief and hold persons responsible for personal liability damages (Kuykendall and Lindquist 2001; Rush 2012). Although local governments are not specifically defined in Title I of the ADA, which discusses employment, they are covered under the public services provision of Title II, which prohibits discrimination on the basis of a disability. Moreover, local governments receiving financial assistance are required to abide by the guidelines established by the Rehabilitation Act.

Needless to say, public HR managers need practical advice for wrestling with the legal and fiscal uncertainty imposed by the ADA. Rozalski et al. (2010) suggested that public HR managers should know the law as well as foster an organizational culture based on acceptance of individuals with different abilities and openness to making reasonable accommodations (see also Rush 2012). Public employers should also develop a team of HR professionals who are responsible for examining current ADA practices and implementing new policies.

Sexual Orientation and Gender Identity

Federal legislation governing discrimination against persons who are lesbian, gay, bisexual, or transgender (LGBT) does not currently exist. However the Employment Non-Discrimination Act (ENDA)—intended to protect workers from discriminatory hiring, firing, promotion, or compensation practices, as well as retaliation for report-ing such practices—has been proposed several times in Congress since 1974, most recently in 2011 (American Civil Liberties Union n.d.a; National Gay and Lesbian Task Force 2013). Also, in 2011 the EEOC ruled that discrimination based on an indi-vidual's sexual orientation (gay, lesbian, or bisexual) or "sex-stereotyping" constituted a form of sex discrimination protected by Title VII of the Civil Rights Act of 1964. In 2013, the EEOC extended this ruling to cover discrimination against transgender persons (referred to as "gender identity discrimination") (EEOC n.d.a).

At the state level, legislation prohibiting discrimination on the basis of sexual orientation and gender identity varies from jurisdiction to jurisdiction. According to the American Civil Liberties Union (ACLU), 16 states (California, Colorado, Connecticut, Hawaii, Illinois, Iowa, Maine, Massachusetts, Minnesota, Nevada, New Jersey, New Mexico, Oregon, Rhode Island, Vermont, and Washington) prohibit dis-crimination based on sexual orientation and gender identity by all employers (ACLU n.d.b). Indiana, Kansas, Kentucky, Michigan, Ohio, and Pennsylvania prohibit dis-crimination based on sexual orientation or gender identity in public employment. Arizona, Missouri, and Montana prohibit discrimination based on sexual orientation in public employment. Delaware, Maryland, New Hampshire, New York, and Wisconsin prohibit discrimination based on sexual orientation. The remaining 20 states lack any nondiscrimination laws based on sexual orientation or gender identity.

Nonprofits in Focus	Diversity, Sexual Orientation, and NPOs

At its 2013 annual meeting in Grapevine, Texas, the Boy Scouts of America (BSA) voted to allow openly gay youths to join scouting, effective January 1, 2014. The resolution reads, "No youth may be denied membership in the Boy Scouts of America on the basis of sexual orientation or preference alone." Sixty percent of the national council's 1,400 members made this historic decision to move past "a single, divisive, and unresolved societal issue" (Gast, Botelho, and Sayers 2013). This decision stands in contrast to the BSA's successful legal challenge 13 years earlier, *Boy Scouts of America v. Dale* (2000), in which the BSA claimed a right to expression under the First Amendment. In that case, the Supreme Court ruled in favor of BSA, affirming its right as a private organization to determine membership criteria, regardless of its status as a "public accommodation" with "open membership" (Pynes 2009, 103). While the BSA will continue its policy of banning gay adult leaders, its recent decision to open membership to gay youths raises a number of questions regarding sexual orientation and HR policies for nonprofits.

Changing public opinion regarding sexual orientation was a factor in the BSA's decision. Furthermore, a recent *Washington Post*–ABC News poll showed that 63 percent of Americans said they would support allowing gay youths to join the Boy Scouts (Gast, Botelho, and Sayers 2013). Public opinion and local interests are key factors to consider when crafting a practical policy toward sexual orientation in the nonprofit workplace. Pynes (2009) suggested that national

(Continued)

(Continued)

nonprofit organizations would be wise to allow such policy development to occur in local units of their organizations, which can take into account a specific community's interests (103).

Moreover, HR managers should be aware of penalties and triggers for recourse under state law. According to the Center for American Progress Action Fund, gay and transgender workers may be protected from discrimination in the workplace in 32 states, but only 21 of these states afford these workers legal recourse. The 10 states that do not have legislation provide protection only through executive policies that can be rescinded and do not provide any legal recourse (Hunt 2012, 8).

Below is an example of a nondiscrimination statement and policy for nonprofits provided by the Denver Foundation Inclusiveness Project:

Adopted by the Board of Directors on [DATE]

[NONPROFIT] does not and shall not discriminate on the basis of race, color, religion (creed), gender, gender expression, age, national origin (ancestry), disability, marital status, sexual orientation, or military status, in any of its activities or operations. These activities include, but are not limited to, hiring and firing of staff, selection of volunteers and vendors, and provision of services. We are committed to providing an inclusive and welcoming environment for all members of our staff, volunteers, subcontractors, vendors, and clients.

[NONPROFIT] is an equal opportunity employer. We will not discriminate and will take affirmative action measures to ensure against discrimination in employment, recruitment, advertisements for employment, compensation, termination, upgrading, promotions, and other conditions of employment against any employee or job applicant on the bases of race, color, gender, national origin, age, religion, creed, disability, veteran's status, sexual orientation, gender identity or gender expression. (Denver Foundation, n.d.)

Equal Employment, Diversity, and PHRM Reform

The last two decades of PHRM reform has generated considerable research regarding the impact that personnel restructuring has had on racial equity and disparity (Battaglio 2010; Battaglio and Condrey 2009; Bradbury, Battaglio and Crum 2010; Condrey and Battaglio 2007; Daley, Vasu, and Weinstein 2002; Kellough and Nigro 2002, 2006; Kim 2010; Nigro and Kellough 2000; Schulz and Tanguay 2006). Given the historical roots of discrimination against women and minorities in the workplace, scholars have been eager to assess the impact of recent reforms on Title VII–protected classes in the public service (Battaglio 2010; Condrey and Battaglio 2007; Wilson 2006).

With respect to deregulation, the increasing prevalence of EAW has heightened fears that reform will peel back years of progress toward a more diverse workforce (Battaglio 2010; Battaglio and Condrey 2009; Wilson 2006). In Georgia, African American respondents to a survey of state personnel were more likely than white respondents to perceive the reforms as detrimental to motivation—a primary component of EAW's quest for improved productivity (see Battaglio 2010). Research elsewhere has found similar negative attitudes toward the deregulated environment of Georgia (Kellough and Nigro 2002). While research has not produced evidence of systematic discrimination as a result of deregulation, minorities' skeptical views of reform efforts are noteworthy. Perhaps African Americans feel that the public service is incapable of achieving or maintaining a representative workplace in a deregulated environment.

Basing civil service staffing practices on merit has long been seen as a basis for implementing the ideals of equal opportunity and an open public service (Mosher 1982, 224). In fact, merit-system principles have been lauded for improving the status of women in the public workforce (Bernhardt and Dresser 2002; Moynihan and Landuyt 2008). Research findings suggest that minorities, however, are pessimistic about the merits of public service reform (Battaglio 2010; Battaglio and Condrey 2009; Bradbury, Battaglio and Crum 2010; Condrey and Battaglio 2007). With respect to EAW, the perception is that giving management and/or politicians greater discretion over PHRM functions may be a means for encouraging "discrimination-induced job dismissals" (Wilson 2006, 178), that is, enabling discrimination under the guise of an EAW policy. The potential for public service reforms to erode years of progress in the promotion of diversity in the public sector should be a continued concern for scholars and practitioners. Practitioners considering reform efforts such as deregulation would be wise to take into account the impact such reforms might have on minorities.

Privatization also represents a potential threat to equal employment opportunity in public employment. Government often opts to outsource HR functions to circumvent staffing procedures, increase the number of political appointees (i.e., non–civil service hires), and provide greater flexibility to managers over the ability to develop outsourcing personnel options. Hays (1996) suggested that the collective effect of privatization and other PHRM reforms (e.g., decentralization) may be to enable abuse in the civil service,

> increasing such age-old risks of politicization, discrimination, and/or incompetency. . . . To the extent that line managers internalize the values of a merit system, the risks may not be very great. However, to the extent that their new-found freedoms over the public personnel system permit managers to engage their biases, to trade political favors or to reward their friends, then the professional public service suffers grievous harm. (289)

Although there is no evidence to suggest that a new era of spoils has reared its ugly head, the fear that such a culture will arise in a deregulated HR environment is tangible among HR and non-HR employees. Such fears may pose a threat to building a positive workplace and productivity (see, e.g., Battaglio 2010; Battaglio and Condrey 2009; Condrey and Battaglio 2007).

Conclusion

For HR managers operating in a reform environment, greater flexibility in the staffing process comes with greater responsibility. In particular, public HR managers have a responsibility to staff the bureaucracy in a way that embraces the constitutional right to equal employment opportunity. HR managers in decentralized and deregulated environments may face political pressure to staff the bureaucracy with unqualified applicants (see, e.g., Haraway and Kunselman 2006) or select contractors based on their political ties (Condrey and Battaglio 2007). The moral and ethical dilemmas for HR managers are apparent. Practicing accountable HR practices in a reform environment is imperative in order to ensure public trust. Fundamental to this practice is a moral obligation on the part of public HR managers to act ethically and responsibility so as to "not take actions that violate the fundamental constitutional rights of those they serve" (Roberts 1999, 21).

References

ADA Amendments Act (ADAAA). 2008. Pub. L. 110-325.

Age Discrimination in Employment Act (ADEA). 1967. Pub. L. 90-202, 29 U.S.C. § 621–34.

American Civil Liberties Union (ACLU). n.d.a. "Employment Non-Discrimination Act." Accessed July 3, 2013. http://www.aclu.org/hiv-aids_lgbt-rights/employment-non-discrimination-act/.

American Civil Liberties Union (ACLU). n.d.b. "Non-Discrimination Laws: State by State Information—Map." Accessed July 3, 2013. http://www.aclu.org/maps/non-discrimination-laws-state-state-information-map/.

Americans with Disabilities Act (ADA). 1990. Pub. L. 101-336, 104 Stat. 327.

Battaglio, R. Paul, Jr. 2010. "Public Service Reform and Motivation: Evidence from an Employment At-Will Environment." *Review of Public Personnel Administration* 30:341–63.

Battaglio, R. Paul, Jr., and Stephen E. Condrey. 2006. "Civil Service Reform: Examining State and Local Government Cases." *Review of Public Personnel Administration* 26:118–38.

Battaglio, R. Paul, Jr., and Stephen E. Condrey. 2009. "Reforming Public Management: Analyzing the Impact of Public Service Reform on Organizational and Managerial Trust." *Journal of Public Administration Research & Theory* 19:689–707.

Bernhardt, Annette, and Laura Dresser. 2002. "Why Privatizing Government Services Would Hurt Women Workers." Institute for Women's Policy Research. http://www.european-services-strategy.org.uk/outsourcing-ppp-library/equalities-and-social-justice-impacts/why-privatizing-government-services-would-hurt/women-impact-privatisation-us.pdf.

Board of Trustees of the University of Alabama v. Garrett, 531 U.S. 356 (2001).

Boy Scouts of America v. Dale, 530 U.S. 640 (2000).

Bradbury, Mark D., R. Paul Battaglio Jr., and John L. Crum. 2010. "Continuity Amid Discontinuity? George W. Bush, Federal Employment Discrimination, and 'Big Government Conservatism.'" *Review of Public Personnel Administration* 30:445–66.

Brown v. Board of Education, 347 U.S. 483 (1954).

Buford, James A., and James R. Lindner. 2002. *Human Resource Management in Local Government: Concepts and Applications for HRM Students and Practitioners.* Cincinnati, OH: South-Western.

Burlington Industries, Inc. v. Ellerth, 118 S. Ct. 2257 (1998).

Burlington Northern & Santa Fe (BNSF) Railway Co. v. White, 548 U.S. 53 (2006)

Civil Rights Act. 1964. Pub. L. 88-352, 78 Stat. 241.

Condrey, Stephen E., and R. Paul Battaglio Jr. 2007. "A Return to Spoils? Revisiting Radical Civil Service Reform in the United States." *Public Administration Review* 67:425–36.

Daley, Dennis M., Michael L. Vasu, and Meredith Blackwell Weinstein. 2002. "Strategic Human Resource Management: Perceptions among North Carolina County Social Service Professionals." *Public Personnel Management* 31:359–75.

Denver Foundation. n.d. "Inclusiveness Project: Example of Non-discrimination Statement and Policy." Accessed June 18, 2013. http://www.nonprofitinclusiveness.org/example-non-discrimination-statement-and-policy/.

DiNome, John A., Saundra M. Yaklin, and David H. Rosenbloom. 2004. "Employee Rights: Avoiding Legal Liability." In *Human Resource Management in Local Government: An Essential Guide,* edited by Siegrun Fox Freyss, 109–52. Washington, DC: International City/Council Management Association.

Faragher v. City of Boca Raton, 524 U.S. 775, 118 S. Ct. 2275 (1998).

Gast, Phil, Greg Botelho, and Devon M. Sayers. 2013. "Boy Scouts to Allow Gay Youths to Join." CNN.com, May 24. http://www.cnn.com/2013/05/23/us/boy-scouts-sexual-orientation/.

Gomez-Perez v. Potter, 553 U.S. 474 (2008).

Gratz v. Bollinger, 539 U.S. 244 (2003).

Griggs v. Duke Power Company, 401 U.S. 424 (1972).

Grutter v. Bollinger, 539 U.S. 306 (2003).

Guy, Mary E., and Meredith A. Newman. 2004. "Women's Jobs, Men's Jobs: Sex Segregation and Emotional Labor." *Public Administration Review* 64:289–98.

Guy, Mary E., Meredith A. Newman, and Sharon H. Mastracci. 2008. *Emotional Labor: Putting the Service in Public Service.* Armonk, NY: M. E. Sharpe.

Haraway, William M., III, and Julie C. Kunselman. 2006. "Ethical Leadership and Administrative Discretion: The Fire Chief's Hiring Dilemma." *Public Personnel Management* 35:1–14.

Hays, Steven W. 1996. "The 'State of the Discipline' in Public Personnel Administration." *Public Administration Quarterly* 20:285–304.

Hochschild, Arlie R. 1983. *The Managed Heart: Commercialization of Human Feeling.* Berkeley: University of California Press.

Holzer, Harry J., and David Neumark. 2000. "What Does Affirmative Action Do?" *Industrial and Labor Relations Review* 53:240–71.

Howell, V. "Repairer Talks to Mayors about Costs." 2003. *The Birmingham News,* January 17.

Hopwood v. State of Texas, 78 F.3d 932 (5th Cir. 1996).

Hunt, Jerome. 2012. "A State-by-State Examination of Nondiscrimination Laws and Policies." Center for American Progress Action Fund. http://www.americanprogress.org/issues/2012/06/pdf/state_nondiscrimination.pdf.

Johnson v. Board of Regents of the University of Georgia, 263 F.3d 1234, 11th Cir. (2001).

Kellough, J. Edward. 2006. *Understanding Affirmative Action: Politics, Discrimination, and the Search for Justice.* Washington, DC: Georgetown University Press.

Kellough, J. Edward, and Lloyd G. Nigro. 2002. "Pay for Performance in Georgia State Government: Employee Perspectives on GeorgiaGain After 5 Years." *Review of Public Personnel Administration* 22:146–66.

Kellough, J. Edward, and Lloyd G. Nigro. 2006. "Dramatic Reform in the Public Service: At-Will Employment and the Creation of a New Public Workforce." *Journal of Public Administration Research and Theory* 16:447–66.

Kim, Jungin. 2010. "Strategic Human Resource Practices: Introducing Alternatives for Organizational Performance Improvement in the Public Sector." *Public Administration Review* 70:38–49.

Kingsley, J. Donald. 1944. *Representative Bureaucracy: An Interpretation of the British CivilService.* Yellow Springs, OH: Antioch Press.

Klein, Jeffrey S., and Nicholas J. Pappas. 2006. "Legality of Voluntary Affirmative Action Plans." *New York Law Journal* 236:1–2.

Klingner, Donald E., and John Nalbandian. 2003. *Public Personnel Management: Contexts and Strategies,* 5th ed. Upper Saddle River, NJ: Prentice Hall.

Krislov, Samuel. 1974. *Representative Bureaucracy.* Englewood Cliffs, NJ: Prentice Hall.

Kuykendall, Christine L., and Stefanie A. Lindquist. 2001. "Board of Trustees of the University of Alabama v. Garrett: Implications for Public Personnel Management." *Review of Public Personnel Administration* 21:65–69.

Meier, Kenneth J., Robert D. Wrinkle, and J. L. Polinard. 1999. "Representative Bureaucracy and Distributional Equity: Addressing the Hard Question." *The Journal of Politics* 61:1025–39.

Meritor Savings Bank v. Vinson, 477 U.S. 57 (1986).

Mitchell, Charles E. 2009. "Retaliation Lawsuits Held Applicable for Federal Employees Under the Age Discrimination in Employment Act: A Victory for Older Federal Workers; The Supreme Court's Decision in Gomez-Perez vs. Potter, Postmaster General." *Review of Public Personnel Administration* 29:89–94.

Mosher, Frederick C. 1982. *Democracy and the Public Service.* 2nd ed. Oxford, England: Oxford University Press.

Moynihan, Donald P., and Noel Landuyt. 2008. "Explaining Turnover Intention in State Government: Explaining the Roles of Gender, Life Cycle, and Loyalty." *Review of Public Personnel Administration* 28:120–43.

National Gay and Lesbian Task Force. 2013. "History of Nondiscrimination Bills in Congress." Accessed July 3, 2013. http://www.thetaskforce.org/issues/nondiscrimination/timeline/.

Nigro, Lloyd G., and J. Edward Kellough. 2000. "Civil Service Reform in Georgia: Going to the Edge?" *Review of Public Personnel Administration* 20:41–54.

Notification and Federal Employee Antidiscrimination and Retaliation Act (No FEAR Act). 2002. Pub. L. 107-174, 116 Stat. 566.

Oncale v. Sundowner Offshore Services, 523 U.S. 75 (1998).

Pitts, David W., and Lois Recascino Wise. 2010. "Workforce Diversity in the New Millennium: Prospects for Research." *Review of Public Personnel Administration* 30:44–69.

Pynes, Joan E. 2009. *Human Resource Management for Public and Nonprofit Organizations.* San Francisco: Jossey-Bass. 103.

Regents of the University of California v. Bakke, 438 U.S. 265 (1978).

Regulations to Implement the Equal Employment Provisions of the Americans with Disabilities Act, as Amended. 2011. 76 FR 16977–17017, 29 CFR 1630. https://www.federal-register.gov/articles/2011/03/25/2011-6056/regulations-to-implement-the-equal-employment-provisions-of-the-americans-with-disabilities-act-as/. Rehabilitation Act. 1973. Pub. L. 93-112, 87 Stat. 355.

Rice, Mitchell F. 2001. "The Need for Teaching Diversity and Representativeness in University Public Administration Education and Professional Public Service Training Programmes in Sub-Saharan Africa." In *Managing Diversity in the Civil Service,* 99–110. Amsterdam, Netherlands: IOS Press.

Rice, Mitchell F., and Harvey L. White. 2005. "Embracing Workplace Diversity in Public Organizations: Some Further Considerations." In *Diversity and Public Administration: Theory, Issues, and Perspectives,* edited by Mitchell F. Rice, 230–6. Armonk, NY: M. E. Sharpe.

Roberts, Robert N. 1999. "The Supreme Court and the Law of Public Service Ethics." *Public Integrity* 1:20–40.

Rosenbloom, David H. 2006. "The Public Employment Relationship and the Supreme Court in the 1980s." In *Public Personnel Administration and Labor Relations,* edited by Norma Riccucci, 201–16. New York: M. E. Sharpe.

Rozalski, Michael, Antonis Katsiyannis, Joseph Ryan, Terri Collins, and Angela Stewart. 2010. "Americans with Disabilities Act of 2008." *Journal of Disability Policy Studies* 21:22–28.

Rush, Christine Ledvinka. 2012. "Amending the Americans with Disabilities Act: Shifting Equal Employment Opportunity Obligations in Public Human Resource Management." *Review of Public Personnel Administration* 32:75–86.

Schulz, Eric R., and Denise Marie Tanguay. 2006. "Merit Pay in a Public Higher Education Institution: Questions of Impact and Attitudes." *Public Personnel Management* 35:71–88.

Shafritz, Jay M., David H. Rosenbloom, Norma A. Riccucci, Katherine C. Naff, and Al C. Hyde. 2001. *Personnel Management in Government: Politics and Process.* New York: Marcel Dekker.

Shin, Roy W., and Debra J. Mesch. 1996. "The Changing Workforce: Issues and Challenges." *International Journal of Public Administration* 19:291–98.

Sims, Ronald D. 2003a. "Fixing Jefferson County Personnel Board Underway." *The Birmingham News,* February 2.

Sims, Ronald D. 2003b. "Personnel Board Can't Take a Break at Halfway Point." *The Birmingham News,* July 6.

Sims, Ronald D. 2009. "Civil Service Reform in Action: The Case of the Personnel Board of Jefferson County, Alabama." *Review of Public Personnel Administration* 29:382–401.

Smith v. University of Washington Law School, 233 F.3d 1188, 9th Cir. (2000).

Taxman v. Board of Education of Piscataway Township, 91 F.3d 1547, 3rd Cir. (1996).

Thomas, R. Roosevelt, Jr. 1991-1992. "The Concept of Managing Diversity." *The Bureaucrat* (Winter): 19–22.

United States of America v. Jefferson County, Alabama, et al., Civil Action No. CV-75-S-666-S (2002).

University and Community College System of Nevada v. Farmer, 930 P2d 730 (Nev. 1997).

US Department of Labor. 2005. *Women in the Labor Force: A Databook.* Report 985. http://www.bls.gov/cps/wlf-databook-2005.pdf.

US Equal Employment Opportunity Commission (EEOC). n.d.a. "Facts about Discrimination in Federal Government Employment Based on Marital Status, Political Affiliation, Status as a Parent, Sexual Orientation, or Transgender (Gender Identity) Status." Accessed July 3, 2013. http://www.eeoc.gov/federal/otherprotections.cfm.

US Equal Employment Opportunity Commission (EEOC). n.d.b. "Laws & Guidance." Accessed July 3, 2012. http://www.eeoc.gov/laws/.

US Equal Employment Opportunity Commission (EEOC). 1998. "Directives Transmittal No. 915.003." http://www.eeoc.gov/policy/docs/retal.html.

US Supreme Court. 2012 *Fisher v. University of Texas at Austin et al.* Slip opinion. October term. http://www.supremecourt.gov/opinions/12pdf/11-345_15gm.pdf.

Walton, Val. 2003. "1 Year Down, More Time Given." *The Birmingham News,* July 27.

Wilson, George. 2006. "The Rise of At-Will Employment and Race Inequality in the Public Sector." *Review of Public Personnel Administration* 26:178–87.

Additional Resources

American Association for Affirmative Action—http://www.affirmativeaction.org

American Association of Colleges and Universities, Diversity Web—http://www.diversityweb.org

American Civil Liberties Union (ACLU)—http://www.aclu.org

Office of Federal Contract Compliance Programs (OFCCP)—http://www.dol.gov/ofccp/

Office of Federal Contract Compliance Programs (OFCCP). 2002. "Facts on Executive Order 11246—Affirmative Action." http://www.dol.gov/ofccp/regs/compliance/aa.htm.

US Department of Labor, "Hiring: Affirmative Action"—http://www.dol.gov/dol/topic/hiring/affirmativeact.htm#lawregs

Case 4.1 The Courts and PHRM Reform—The Jefferson County, Alabama, Personnel Board

In July 2002, Judge Lynwood Smith Jr. of the US District Court, Northern District of Alabama, Southern Division, ruled the Personnel Board of Jefferson County, Birmingham, Alabama, to be in contempt of court for violating the terms of a December 1995 court order to reform the personnel practices of the county. At issue were alleged discriminatory practices against African Americans in job selection and hiring. As a result, the National Association for the Advancement of Colored People (NAACP) had initiated litigation against the Personnel Board of Jefferson County in 1974 (Sims 2009). This lawsuit resulted in a consent decree in 1981 that ordered the development of "nondiscriminatory tests" and establishment of "fair job selection procedures and hiring tests" for the personnel system (*United States of America vs. Jefferson County, Alabama, et al.* 2002). Due to Jefferson County's inaction over the past two decades since that ruling, Judge Smith extended and modified the 1981 consent decree. What follows is an account of the remedial actions taken by the court-appointed receiver, Dr. Ronald R. Sims.

As part of the remedy, the federal judge appointed a receiver to function as the "sole board member" to implement the changes necessary to eliminate discriminatory practices. According to ruling, the receiver was granted "all powers state law assigns to the three-member board, its executive director and the Citizen Supervisory Commission" with respect to personnel decisions. The personnel board is responsible for hiring and promotion in Jefferson County and most county municipalities, including the city of Birmingham. The court appointed Dr. Ronald R. Sims, senior professor in the Graduate School of Business at the College of William and Mary, to serve as the receiver at the pleasure of the federal district court. Dr. Sims's duties were to "manage and control property and employees, and perform contractual, financial, legal and personnel duties" of the personnel board (*United States of America vs. Jefferson County, Alabama, et al.* 2002).

In compliance with the court's decision, Dr. Sims began a full reorganization of the Personnel Board of Jefferson County. His efforts included

- conducting a five-year survey of all job classifications and pay of civil servants;
- assessing the basic skills and abilities of board employees and creating appropriate job-training/professional-development programs to build more in-house competency;
- recruiting a qualified consultant to quickly develop new selection procedures for police and sheriff's deputies and to develop similar procedures for nineteen of the thirty-three job classifications remaining in the consent decree;
- developing plans to build an information technology (IT) infrastructure that would modernize and streamline job selection and promotion procedures;
- and rewriting the board's rules and regulations for greater clarity, uniformity, and compliance with state and federal requirements (Sims 2003a; Howell 2003).

During the first year of reorganization, an interim job selection mechanism was not put into place. This was particularly problematic for personnel in public safety. However, Dr. Sims's initial findings reported to the federal judge were that most board employees were not qualified to do their jobs; in fact, they ignored board rules and regulations or made them up as they went along. Furthermore, Dr. Sims's initial report found that the county's IT system could not handle the thousands of civil servant records it needed to process (Sims 2003a; Howell 2003). Consequently, Dr. Sims attempted to improve the Personnel Board's operations, specifically in hiring competent managers and staff, establishing professional development training for staff, and formulating new rules and regulations.

The court order also gave the receiver power over the financial resources needed to enact the stipulated changes (*United States of America vs. Jefferson County, Alabama, et al.* 2002). After an initial infusion of $8.5 million "for staff development, professional services, legal fees and computer equipment," an additional $7 million was deemed necessary to carry out the consent decree (Howell 2003). In accordance with state law, the additional revenue had to come from both city and county sources. Participating governments in Jefferson County were instructed to pay a percentage of the Personnel Board's operating costs based on their number of employees.

Dr. Sims's efforts to establish a modern and professional examination process within the Personnel Board led to the addition of sixteen new testing professionals, selected after a nationwide search. Additionally, Dr. Sims created three teams oriented toward recruitment, training, and performance to ensure quality practices (Sims 2003b). Sims asserted that these actions, along with developments in IT infrastructure, enabled the board to enhance its five-year classification and compensation survey.

While the courts and persons involved in the case were eager to see a quick resolution to the court decree, Dr. Sims's efforts took longer than expected due to insufficient funding. In an effort to bolster support for his efforts, Dr. Sims opened the lines of communication with mayors and county commissioners to explain the progress thus far and what had to be done to ensure that the Personnel Board would develop and implement lawful job-selection procedures (Walton 2003). In July 2003, Judge Smith extended the appointment of Dr. Sims to oversee the implementation of personnel reforms and the recruitment of a permanent director for the Personnel Board (Battaglio and Condrey 2006). Dr. Sims's appointment as receiver ended on August 26, 2005, just over three years after the date of the consent decree.

The Personnel Board of Jefferson County, Alabama, illustrates a unique chapter in the history of civil service reform in the United States. The federal court's consent decree to reform county personnel practices is the only known instance of judicially initiated PHRM reform. Legal action has been an important aspect in this case, especially with respect to eliminating discriminatory practices in personnel decisions. For further reference, see Sims's 2009 assessment of the case in the *Review of Public Personnel Administration*.

Discussion Questions

1. How might the Jefferson County Personnel Board have avoided court-ordered reform of its selection process?

2. What laws apply to the issues surrounding the Jefferson County case?

3. What losses were incurred monetarily and in terms of accountability as a result of the Personnel Board's failures?

4. Would you have approached reform differently than did Dr. Sims?

5. What lessons might be drawn from the Jefferson County case?

Exercise

Examining Diversity Plans in the Local Community

As we have discussed throughout this chapter, organizations—public, nonprofit, and for-profit—are acutely aware of the advantages of attracting and retaining a diverse workforce. A diverse, harmonious work environment can bring out the best in people and lead to greater productivity. To evaluate their efforts, many organizations have crafted diversity plans. These plans come in a variety of forms. This exercise entails reviewing diversity plans in your local community. Review and critique the elements of a local organization's (public, nonprofit, or for-profit) diversity plan and report the results to the class. What are the strong points of the diversity plan? What elements, if any, are missing? Below are some examples of diversity plans developed by federal, state, and local authorities:

City of Longview, Texas—http://hr.longviewtexas.gov/sites/default/files/files/human-resources/diversity_plan_12-10.pdf

Missouri Department of Labor—http://labor.mo.gov/documents/2011WDP.pdf

National Aeronautical and Space Administration (NASA)—http://diversity.gsfc.nasa.gov/DCPrivate/Diversity_StrategicPlan.pdf

Functions

Recruitment and Selection

LEARNING OBJECTIVES

Upon completion of the chapter, you will be able to do the following:

- Discuss the legal environment of recruitment and selection in the public sector.
- Explain the difference between disparate treatment and disparate impact.
- Outline the key components of the staffing process in the public sector.
- Explain the importance of reliability and validity in selection methods.
- Discuss the role of e-recruitment in the future public service workforce.
- Evaluate the challenges to recruitment and selection in an era of PHRM reform.

Recruiting and maintaining qualified personnel are important and challenging tasks for public human resource managers in the 21st century. As discussed in Chapters 3 and 4, the legal environment of public human resource management (PHRM) can be complex: Legislation and court rulings necessary for ensuring non-discrimination in the workplace can also make hiring in a timely manner a challenge. Economic downturns, budget cutbacks, and an aging workforce have also strained the capacity of governments to recruit a qualified workforce. In addition, many jurisdictions have embraced decentralized and deregulated elements of reform in their staffing processes to improve efficiency and responsiveness in government. As previously noted, decentralization gives managers more flexibility in recruitment and selection, with the aim of replacing the centralized, rule-bound systems that exemplified traditional PHRM practices with a more agency-specific, manager-centered system.

Diminishing public employee access to traditional dismissal-rights procedures is considered a key feature of deregulation reform efforts. Most notably, deregulation has taken the form of employment-at-will (EAW), which is seen as a means for increasing managerial efficiency by removing the cumbersome grievance and appeals processes characteristic of traditional civil service systems. Efforts to curb employee rights have increased in a number of governments (Hays and Sowa 2006; see also Bowman and West 2007; Condrey and Maranto 2001; Kellough and Nigro 2006). However, these changes have not gone unnoticed by employees, who appear to be less than enthusiastic about them. In fact, reform has had a dramatic impact on the attitudes and motivations of public sector personnel. Given these changes, it becomes apparent that recruiting the future public service will be a challenge for HR directors.

This chapter begins with an assessment of the legal climate of recruitment and selection and introduces the basics of staffing in the public sector—methods of recruitment and selection procedures. The chapter will then turn to efforts at both the federal and state levels to remove traditional merit practices and the impact these reforms have had on recruitment and selection.

The Legal Climate Regulating Selection and Hiring Practices

Navigating the legal environment of employment in the public sector can be difficult, warranting an appreciation of both past and current legislation and case law. The discussion in Chapter 3 highlighted the legal environment of PHRM, including the selection process in the public sector. In contrast to hiring in the private or even nonprofit sector, where managers may simply hire whomever they deem fit, hiring in the government is less straightforward. Public HR managers are more constrained in hiring decisions and practices, and applying for government jobs can be a lengthy process due to the time it takes to authorize a new position. Steps include securing budgetary approval, ensuring an open and fair selection process, and ensuring conformance to public employment law. When hiring a potential employee, public HR managers must be cognizant not only of general practices but also of the court decisions regarding review and selection of candidates. In particular, a key defining aspect of American public employment is the merit system and its emphasis on equal employment opportunity in the selection process.

Disparate Treatment and Disparate Impact

Ever since the Civil Rights Era, careful consideration has been given to upholding equal employment opportunity in the selection process. Years of discrimination against minorities and women in the staffing of the public sector led to the passage of sweeping civil rights legislation. Title VII of the Civil Rights Act of 1964 prohibits discrimination in selection based on race, color, religion, sex, national origin, or protected activity (42 U.S.C. §2000e et seq.). Title VII specifically deals with what the courts have termed **disparate treatment**—intentional discrimination or maltreatment of groups and protected classes. Not all instances of disparate treatment are necessarily illegal. For example, there are bona fide occupational qualifications (e.g., gender, age) that are acceptable in specific circumstances, reviewed below. However, instances of disparate treatment might provoke the following questions:

- Were people of one race, color, religion, sex, or national origin treated differently than people of another category?
- Is there any evidence of bias, such as discriminatory statements?
- What is the employer's reason for the difference in treatment?
- Does the evidence show that the employer's reason for the difference in treatment is untrue and that the real reason for the different treatment is race, color, religion, sex, or national origin? (US Equal Employment Opportunity Commission [EEOC] 2010).

The answers to these questions will provide guidance in determining whether disparate treatment has occurred and an EEOC inquiry is warranted. Disparate treatment is suspected when the evidence suggests intentional discrimination on the part of the employer. For example, if a minority job applicant was more qualified than a white candidate but was denied employment because the hiring manager disliked people of that ethnic group, or a minority employee was passed over for a promotion despite being more qualified than a white employee, then that person has suffered from disparate treatment. He or she has been intentionally discriminated against because of race, a protected class under Title VII. Such treatment is illegal.

Toward the end of the 1960s, however, it became apparent that the persistence of discrimination in the workplace was more pervasive than evidence of intentional discrimination would indicate. Recall our discussion in Chapter 4 of the landmark Supreme Court decision in *Griggs v. Duke Power Co.* (1971), which took up the issue of pervasive discrimination in selection practices. At issue in the case was the promotion policy at Duke Power Company in North Carolina, which required a high school diploma for job advancement. Given the practice of school segregation in the South at the time, a disproportionate number of African Americans did not complete high school. The plaintiffs argued that the promotion policy indirectly excluded African Americans from higher-paying jobs since they disproportionately lacked the required education. In the *Griggs* ruling, the Court said that Title VII prohibited employers from using selection procedures that disproportionately excluded protected classes, where such procedures are not "job-related and consistent with business necessity" (EEOC 2010). Thus, selection procedures that might appear to be neutral (e.g., requiring a high school diploma) are not necessarily legal; unequal or disproportionate consequences of such procedures may have an adverse or **disparate impact** on protected groups. An unintentional consequence of requiring a high school diploma at Duke Power Company was the disproportionate exclusion of African Americans from promotion. The EEOC has offered some selection procedure questions that might lead one to conclude an employment practice has a disparate impact:

- Does the employer use a particular employment practice that has a disparate impact on individuals of a certain race, color, religion, sex, or national origin? For example, if an employer requires that all applicants pass a physical agility test, does the test disproportionately screen out women? Determining whether a test or other selection procedure has a disparate impact on a particular group ordinarily requires a statistical analysis.
- If the selection procedure has a disparate impact based on race, color, religion, sex, or national origin, can the employer show that the selection procedure is job-related and consistent with business necessity? An employer can meet this standard by showing that meeting the selection criterion is necessary to perform the job safely and efficiently. The challenged policy or practice must evaluate an individual's skills as they relate to the job in question.
- If the employer shows that the selection procedure is job related and consistent with business necessity, can the person challenging the selection procedure demonstrate that a less discriminatory alternative is available? For example, would another test be equally effective in predicting job performance but not disproportionately exclude the protected group? (EEOC 2010)

While not due to a malicious intent to discriminate, disparate impact still results in discrimination and is therefore undesirable and illegal.

Applying Strict Scrutiny

Unfortunately, the *Griggs* decision did not settle all of the legal issues surrounding selection procedures, and by the 1980s, several cases that challenged *Griggs* came before the Supreme Court. In *Wards Cove v. Antonio* (1989) and *City of Richmond v. J. A. Croson Co.* (1989), the Court contradicted the decision laid out in *Griggs*, specifying that selection procedures would be subject to strict scrutiny. In *Wards Cove,* the Court looked at alleged discriminatory hiring practices in a salmon cannery operation where a large proportion of the skilled jobs were held by whites and a large share of the unskilled jobs were held by nonwhites. A lower court sided with the company, but then the US Appeals Court ruled that the plaintiffs had demonstrated statistical evidence of discriminatory hiring practices. However, the Supreme Court overruled the appeals court, citing an error in the statistical methodology used. The Court determined that to establish discrimination, plaintiffs must do more than show the proportion of whites and nonwhites in the relevant jobs. Instead, evidence must include a comparison of the racial composition of the workforce in the jobs at issue to the composition of the qualified and relevant labor pool (*Wards Cove* 1989). In other words, just because there are more whites than nonwhites in a job does not indicate discrimination; it must be demonstrated using established methodologies.

In the *Richmond* case, the Supreme Court ruled that minority set-aside programs (a form of affirmative action) established by the city of Richmond, Virginia, were unconstitutional. Under the programs, the city showed preference to minority-owned businesses when awarding contracts. The Court ruled that such programs must demonstrate a need for remedial action and that no other, nondiscriminatory remedies are applicable (*City of Richmond* 1989). These rulings were further refined by the strict scrutiny standard in *Adarand Contractors Inc. v. Peña* (1995), which entails more rigorous assessment of selection procedures implemented under affirmation action programs. There must be a "compelling government interest" in remedying prior discriminatory practices, and the remedy must be "narrowly tailored" so as not to infringe upon the rights of nonprotected groups.

While several of the cases cited here deal explicitly with affirmative action efforts (see Chapter 4), they also bear on selection procedures in general. Specifically, examinations and other selection procedures should be properly validated for the positions and purposes for which they are used (EEOC 2010). This point was reinforced in the decision in *Ricci v. DeStefano* (2009), a case involving the New Haven, Connecticut, fire department's promotion tests. In an effort to avoid legal action, the department disregarded the results of the examination because African Americans who passed the test did not score high enough to warrant promotion. The Supreme Court ruled that concern about potential litigation alone is not sufficient grounds to avoid disparate impact.

The lesson for public HR managers is to know the law applicable to recruitment and selection. The courts give careful consideration to equal employment when considering cases where disparate treatment and/or disparate impact are alleged. Selection procedures must be job related and necessary for the proper function of government.

Recruitment for Public Service

Today's PHRM climate means that employers must use novel methods to successfully recruit employees. Economic downturns, budget cutbacks, demographic changes, and baby boomer retirements have necessitated greater attention to efficient and effective recruitment and selection processes that promote a performance-driven and productive public service (Choudhury 2007; Llorens and Battaglio 2010; National Academy of Public Administration 2001; Partnership for Public Service and Grant Thornton 2007; US Merit Systems Protection Board 2006; Voinovich 2000). The baby boomer generation is nearing retirement age, so a large portion of government staff will soon exit public service, leaving many positions empty. Thus, public HR managers must use as many innovative recruitment techniques as possible to ensure a large pool of high-quality applicants. Reforms such as decentralization and deregulation have been implemented to improve the efficiency of this recruitment and selection.

Move to Decentralized Recruitment

Traditionally, recruitment was carried out by a central personnel office that was the sole authority for determining and meeting workforce needs. For example, a personnel office in a state capital might decide how and where to recruit for a regional office or some other division or location across the state. Decentralization efforts in the 1990s, however, challenged the conventional wisdom of using central personnel offices in recruitment. Critics of a centralized approach cited the additional time, effort, and paperwork needed to overcome the distances between a central office and the locations it managed. These inefficiencies were seen as detrimental to managerial prerogatives to hire the best and brightest. Allowing agency managers at the street level to handle recruitment and selection was deemed more efficient, since those managers were more familiar with the staffing situations in their own divisions or offices and could better evaluate their personnel needs; distant personnel offices overseeing recruitment for thousands of applicants government-wide were ill-equipped to make such assessments. Thus, over the last two decades, agency-level HR directors have been given greater leeway and control over personnel decisions (e.g., selection) and have become the primary points of contact for recruitment efforts.

Recruitment Methods

Recruitment methods have also changed over the last few decades. Traditional methods have included sending recruiters to job fairs or colleges, posting job vacancies in agency hallways, buying advertisements at local media outlets (newspapers or radio), establishing relationships with college career placement offices, and relying on word of mouth (Llorens 2011, 412).

However Llorens (2011) noted that many jurisdictions are increasingly pursuing recruitment strategies that take advantage of advances in information technology—a tool vital for meeting workforce needs as the population becomes increasingly technologically savvy. Such **e-recruitment** efforts involve the use of various online or electronic resources. A number of governments have gone a step further by adopting **Web 2.0** technologies and using third-party e-recruitment networks. Web 2.0 technology includes blogs, where users compose personal posts on various interests; wikis (e.g., Wikipedia), where groups compose and edit knowledge on a variety of subjects in a structured manner; social networking sites (e.g., Facebook and LinkedIn), where people create and update personal and professional profiles; social bookmarking applications (e.g., del.icio.us), where people identify websites of interest or "favorites"; and microblogs (e.g., Twitter), where people post brief, public messages (Dixon 2010, 423).

The most common examples of e-recruitment tactics are posting job vacancies on agency or government websites and advertising vacancy information on sites such as Facebook and Twitter. For example, the website USAJOBS.gov is the official source for federal jobs; it is a central warehouse where individuals can access hundreds of federal job listings, as well as apply for those jobs directly online. Many states have similar websites listing available positions in the state government. USAJOBS.gov also has a YouTube channel that features dozens of videos of public employees working in their office environments and talking about what they do and how they serve the public, as well as practical videos on how the federal government's recruiting process works. Another example of e-recruiting is holding virtual job fairs over the Internet; candidates have the opportunity to interact with potential employers without leaving home (Llorens 2011, 413). Skype, which enables free video conference calls over the Internet, allows job candidates to be interviewed online instead of physically visiting an office.

These advances have fundamentally changed recruiting processes, as HR offices can now gather and disseminate information much more quickly, as well as reach many more potentially qualified applicants. Moreover, Internet-based selection methods offer significant cost savings.

Nonprofits in Focus	Recruiting Online Volunteers

Recruitment and selection in the information age has proven to be a powerful component of public sector employment (Llorens 2011; Llorens and Kellough 2007). Web-based applications are especially important for NPOs, which often have constrained budgets and can take advantage of the efficiencies the Internet provides. Although many NPOs rely heavily on volunteers, they must be as savvy in their selection of volunteers as of paid employees. NPOs have important objectives and need the right people to achieve them. Indeed, NPO recruiters have been quick to adopt web-based tools to recruit and select the next generation of volunteers (Dhebar and Stokes 2008).

So, how can on-governmental human resource managers utilize web-based applications to benefit their organizations? According to Dhebar and Stokes (2008), NGOs have begun to use the Internet to recruit a new cadre of volunteers who are eager to lend a hand from home as opposed to providing services on-site. Online volunteering allows those who may not have considered volunteering—perhaps due to remote geography or a physical disability—an avenue for contributing to NGO missions. Dhebar and Stokes suggested that careful planning, communicating,

(Continued)

(Continued)

monitoring, and giving feedback are the most important components of effective use of online volunteering. Here are several timely online volunteering lessons offered by Dhebar and Stokes (2008):

Lesson 1: Plan with Clarity

Clearly articulate your strategic basis for pursuing online volunteers.

Define assignments fully before beginning recruitment.

Keep assignments clear and product focused.

Limit assignments in duration and intensity.

Lesson 2: Communicate, Communicate, Communicate

Seek matching services that specialize in volunteers with profiles of interest to your organization.

Determine the screening mechanism at your matching service. If the service does not have an adequate screening mechanism, be prepared to introduce one yourself.

Phrase the assignment posting to clearly connect the work to its impact on your organization's goals and programs.

Date assignment requests so potential volunteers know how long the assignment has been posted.

Request that filled assignments be pulled (or marked as "filled") to reduce the number of late applications.

Timely communication is key. Be sure to check email daily and keep volunteers up to speed with new developments.

Be prepared to provide clear and specific feedback in a timely manner, informing volunteers of their assignments.

Lesson 3: Monitor and Learn from Results

Monitor volunteers' performance and provide regular, informal feedback, detailing how well volunteers performed.

Maintain data on assignment completion and retention rates and review the data periodically.

Prepare a standard evaluation form for all volunteers to respond to when they end their assignments.

Dhebar and Stokes also provide a number of useful electronic resources for facilitating online volunteering:

http://www.idealist.org—Idealist's volunteer board lists international volunteer opportunities.

http://www.mentornet.net—MentorNet's e-mentoring service connects students (undergraduate, graduate, doctoral) and faculty in science, technology, engineering, and mathematics careers with potential mentors.

http://www.onlinevolunteering.org—UN Volunteers, sponsored by the United Nations, promotes networking between development organizations and volunteers.

http://www.serviceleader.org/vv/—Sponsored by the Center for Philanthropy and Community Service at the University of Texas at Austin, ServiceLeader.org provides resources for organizations looking to use technology in volunteer management.

http://www.volunteermatch.org—VolunteerMatch.org encourages civic engagement among the nonprofit, volunteer, and business communities in the United States.

In an NPO setting, employees are often paid below market, and volunteers are not compensated. Therefore, these practices will help to ensure high morale and good performance. These suggestions can easily be applied in a public sector setting as well.

Preemployment Screening Practices

While the potential for e-recruitment efforts is limitless, the extent to which e-recruitment has effectively reached underrepresented groups (e.g., minorities) is still unclear (Cober et al. 2000; Kim and O'Connor 2009; Llorens and Kellough 2007; West and Berman 2001). Consequently, public HR managers, and everyone involved in the recruitment and selection processes, should be mindful of technology's potential to introduce disparate treatment and disparate impact into preemployment and employment. Public HR managers need a thorough understanding of what recruitment and selection practices are acceptable and what practices are illegal. Table 5.1 reviews considerations such as race, creed, and national origin, as well as information

Table 5.1	Acceptable and Illegal Employment-Screening Questions	
Subject	**Acceptable Questions**	**Illegal Questions**
Name	What is your full name? Do you have relevant work experience while using another name?	What part of the world is your name from? Have you ever changed your name? Do you prefer to be called Mr., Ms., or Mrs?
Residence	What is your full address?	How long have you lived at your current address? If you have lived in a foreign country, what was your address there? With whom do you reside? Do you rent or own your home?
		(Exceptions may exist in jurisdictions that have residency requirements.)

(Continued)

(Continued)

Subject	Acceptable Questions	Illegal Questions
Race, creed, national origin	Are you legally able to work in the United States? Whom would you like to be notified in the event of an emergency? What languages do you speak or write fluently (if foreign language fluency is job related)? Are you a member of a trade organization that represents your profession?	What is your race? What political organizations do you belong to? What country does your family come from? Where are you a citizen? What is your previous foreign address? What is your birthplace? What is the name of a relative to be notified in case of emergency? What is your native language? (Exceptions: Information on race and national origin may be solicited on a form kept separate from the application. A bona fide occupational qualification [BFOQ] may apply to national origin, e.g., if a casting agent seeks an Italian to play an Italian character in a movie.)
Sex, marital status	Do you have relevant work experience you gained while using another name? Can you meet the work schedule for this job?	Are you male or female? What is your maiden name? Have you changed your name? What is your sexual orientation? Are you married? Are you pregnant? How many children do you have? Do you have child care? Do you plan on having any more children? (Exceptions: A person's sex may be requested on a form kept separate from the application. A BFOQ exception may apply to sex.
Age	Can you submit proof of legal age to work upon employment? Are you at least 18 years old?	What is your age? When were you born? (A BFOQ exception may apply.)
Health and physical characteristics	Is there any reason you would not be able to perform the responsibilities and	Do you have any disabilities? Have you had certain diseases? What is your

Subject	Acceptable Questions	Illegal Questions
	tasks of this position? Can you perform the essential job functions? Can you perform the job tasks with or without accommodations	height? What is your weight? Have you ever filed a workers' compensation claim?
Religion	Can you meet the work schedule for this job?	What is your religious affiliation? What religious holidays do you observe? Of what groups are you a member? (A BFOQ exception may apply for a religious organization, [e.g., religious nonprofit].)
Education	What academic, vocational, or professional institutions have you attended? What were your areas of study? Degrees earned? Diplomas or certificates awarded?	Is the college you attended a historically black college? What was your grade point average or class rank? What were your dates of enrollment (to elicit age)?
Financial status	What are your salary requirements?	What is your credit rating? Do you have any garnishments, debts, or other liabilities? What are your assets?
Criminal record	Have you been convicted of a crime related to the duties and responsibilities of this position?	Have you been arrested? Have you been convicted of any crime?
Military service	What was your occupation while in military service? Did you receive training related to this job? In what arm or branch of the military did you serve? When were you discharged? What was your rank?	Have you been dishonorably discharged from the military? What was the type of discharge? What were your years of service (to elicit age)?
Experience	What is your work experience, including names and addresses of previous employers and dates worked? What type of position did you hold? What was your reason for leaving? What is your salary history?	Inquiries that focus on experience not required for the job.

Sources: Adapted from Buford and Lindner 2002, 192–93; Witt and Patton 2004, 50.

that is often solicited by application forms, in terms of what an employer may legally ask an interviewee. For each factor, the table includes examples of both acceptable and illegal questions.

Employers may consider residence when the agency has a residency requirement (e.g., some public safety or law enforcement agencies require new hires to live within the city limits). Employers may also ask an applicant to provide information on race, creed, and national origin for purposes of record keeping, especially for EEOC purposes. However, the records with this information must be kept separate from the application process. While the employer can ask whether an applicant can work the job's scheduled hours, the employer may not ask the applicant for information about personal or family arrangements. Age and physical abilities may be considered only insofar as they bear on the applicant's ability to perform essential responsibilities and tasks of the position. Salary requirements are a permissible consideration, but an applicant's financial situation or history is not. Convictions for a crime related to the duties and responsibilities of the position are job related and may be inquired about, but other convictions may not.

The hiring manager may ask certain job-related questions about military service. Moreover, veterans may be entitled to preferences in appointments and exemptions from reductions in force in accordance with the Veterans' Preference Act of 1944 and Title V of the US Code (US Office of Personnel Management [OPM] 2013). These **veterans preferences** in hiring may vary from state to state, so HR managers in state or local governments should consult the hiring practices of their jurisdictions.

Needless to say, interviewing and recruiting candidates for jobs in public service can be challenging. Merit and nondiscrimination policies in public employment, while time-consuming, ensure an effective and fair selection process. The primary organizing purpose for setting out such specific parameters for what may and may not be considered in the hiring process is to ensure **job-relatedness** with respect to the position being advertised. Any inquiries that focus on a characteristic or an experience not relevant to the job are not permissible.

Bona fide occupational qualifications (BFOQ) are the exception. If an employer can demonstrate that a particular protected-class characteristic (e.g., being older) is a BFOQ for the job in question, the usually discriminatory practice (e.g., asking an applicant how old he or she is) is legal (Walsh 2007, 184). Many of the factors listed in Table 5.1 may fall under the BFOQ exception. For example, mandatory retirement ages for pilots or bus drivers are not considered to be age discrimination and are permissible for public safety purposes; good eyesight is necessary for these jobs, and eyesight deteriorates with age. An BFOQ may also be involved when an applicant's religious affiliation is reasonably necessary for an organization's function. For example, Catholic institutions or universities may require executive officers (i.e., presidents, chaplains, faculty members) be members of the Catholic Church. Such a religious requirement is generally not considered necessary for custodial or clerical positions, however. It should be noted that considering race and color is never permissible; there is no BFOQ for these characteristics (Walsh 2007, 184).

Selection Procedures

The goal of recruitment and selection is to fill the ranks of the public service with a qualified workforce—locating candidates and identifying the best person for the job. It is necessary for human resource managers to be apprised of future workforce needs so that they can make sound decisions about current staffing. While Chapter 12 covers the topic of HR strategy in detail, the topic deserves attention here, given its link with selection. Strategic HR planning should determine the appropriate knowledge, skills, and abilities required for each position. This discovery phase is crucial to job analysis—the crux of any classification system in the public sector—which is discussed further Chapter 6. A proper job description makes identifying potential candidates a much easier task.

There are several methods for reviewing candidate applications and winnowing down the group to a list of qualified applicants. Determining the appropriate method is crucial not only to select the best person for the job but, as noted above, to comply with Title VII of the Civil Rights Act. Therefore, a review of the range of potential screening tools, followed by a discussion of how to choose the most appropriate tools, will be useful.

Selection methods generally focus on one of three functional bases: the individual, simulation, and examination. Table 5.2 provides an overview of the three groupings of selection procedures and the advantages and disadvantages of each.

Table 5.2	**Types of Selection Procedures**		
Selection Type	**Method**	**Advantages**	**Disadvantages**
Biographical data	Individual-based	Easily administered and compiled; cost-effective; demonstrated validity	Subject to applicant inflation of credentials; not always sufficient for all job-related activity
Interview	Individual-based	Conventional; interpersonal exchange focus; demonstrated validity; cost-effective	Subject to rater error or bias; time-consuming; limited to the number of applicants; training required; Hawthorne effect

(Continued)

(Continued)

Selection Type	Method	Advantages	Disadvantages
Assessment centers	Simulation-based	Demonstrated validity with respect to organizational outcomes; favorably viewed by applicants; provides feedback; behavior focus; results less likely to differ by race and gender	Costly; labor and time intensive; not easily generalizable
Work sample	Simulation-based	Demonstrated validity with respect to performance; favorably viewed by applicants; less likely to produce false responses; provides feedback	Costly; lacks complex task assessment; does not test cognitive abilities; labor and time intensive
Physical ability tests	Simulation-based	Demonstrated validity with respect to physical performance; less likely to produce false responses	Costly; evidence of gender bias; medical-related exams not necessarily useful for job-related assessments; labor and time intensive
Job knowledge tests	Examination-based	Demonstrated validity with respect to organizational outcomes; results less likely to differ by race and gender; favorably viewed by applicants; less likely to produce false responses; provides feedback	Costly; labor and time intensive; inappropriate where knowledge can be easily learned through on-the-job training
Cognitive ability tests	Examination-based	Demonstrated validity with respect to organizational outcomes, especially for complex jobs; easily administered; cost-effective; less likely to produce false responses	Evidence of gender and race bias; time-consuming
Integrity tests	Examination-based	Demonstrated validity with respect to organizational outcomes; results less likely to differ by race and gender; easily administered; cost-effective; emphasizes organizational integrity	May result in false responses; not favored by applicants

Selection Type	Method	Advantages	Disadvantages
Personality tests	Examination-based	Demonstrated validity with respect to organizational outcomes; results less likely to differ by race and gender; easily administered; cost-effective; emphasizes organizational integrity	Questions may not be job related; may result in false responses

Source: Adapted from Society for Industrial and Organizational Psychology (SIOPb) 2012.

Individual-Based Selection Procedures

The most commonly employed selection methods are individual based, involving the evaluation of biographical data and the more formal interview (Society for Industrial and Organizational Psychology [SIOP] 2012b). Biographical data include a wide assortment of information, including the applicant's skills, leadership abilities, job-related knowledge (such as information technology expertise), and interpersonal skills. Biographical data may also include the candidate's education, job experience, and interests—items typically identified in a résumé or curriculum vitae. Interviews are used to gain greater insight into a candidate beyond what can be learned through biographical data alone. Interviews may take place face-to-face, over the telephone, or via video on the Internet (e.g., Skype, Adobe Connect, Google Hangouts). Job-specific questions should be developed with the goal of assessing candidate expertise. It is during the interview that an HR manager might ask about the factors listed in Table 5.1, as they relate to the job.

Simulation-Based Selection Procedures

Simulation-based selection procedures include assessment centers, work samples, and physical ability tests (SIOP 2012b). Assessment centers are generally designed to assess interpersonal skills, communication skills, planning and organizing skills, and analytical skills. The candidate is put through a series of "real-life" scenarios during which the hiring agency observes and assesses the person's ability to perform job-related tasks. Examples include coordinating a staff meeting, processing paperwork, dealing with a problem employee, or communicating with a client. Employers may either coordinate assessment center activities in-house or contract with a professional consultant. Typically, assessment centers are staffed by raters who are adept at analyzing candidate behaviors as well as skill sets.

Like assessment centers, work-sample exercises assess job-related requirements. However, they focus on more mundane organizational tasks such as writing a memo or entering data on a computer.

For jobs that demand more strenuous activity, physical ability tests may be used to ensure that the applicant is capable of performing the tasks of the job. Often utilized by law enforcement or other public safety organizations, physical tests might assess a candidate's ability to perform activities related to strength, dexterity, or endurance. Police officers and firefighters are often required to complete periodic physical exams so that their ability to carry out the demanding aspects of their jobs can be evaluated.

Examination-Based Selection Procedures

Examination-based selection methods use written tests to assess job-related knowledge, skills, and abilities. They include job knowledge tests, cognitive ability tests, integrity tests, and personality tests (SIOP 2012b). Job knowledge tests, the most straightforward of the examination-based tests, assess candidates' knowledge in a number of job-related areas such as computer programing or public budgeting. For example, you might be interested in whether or not a budgeting candidate is knowledgeable about specific accounting methods that can be used to put together a budget for the upcoming fiscal year.

Cognitive ability tests seek to establish a candidate's aptitude for the job based on a number of verbal, mathematical, and analytical questions. Such assessments test higher-order analytical skills and hope to determine a candidate's critical thinking and reading comprehension abilities.

Integrity tests are used to evaluate a candidate's ethical compass. Factors that might be evaluated include an individual's capacity for honesty, dependability, trustworthiness, reliability, and sociability. Such assessments are particularly useful for law enforcement and public safety agencies that require confidentiality and loyalty in certain jobs; for example, a district attorney must be able to handle sensitive and confidential information that is shared during a criminal case, or a police officer must be willing to report bribery or other wrongdoing.

Similarly, personality tests are employed to assess a person's proclivity toward assertiveness, ability to handle stress, emotional stability, and service orientation. Like the previous methods, personality tests aspire to predict a future candidate's success on the job.

Using Selection Procedures

Which method is appropriate for the organization may depend on the type of opening (supervisory or nonsupervisory), the number of openings, the potential applicant pool (labor market), and the factors raised in Table 5.2. Generally speaking, when assessing on-the-job skills, simulation-based methods are preferred, while assessing job knowledge requires an examination-based method. Individual-based methods are used to review biographical information (e.g., résumés). The public sector HR managers must consider some additional factors when deciding to implement any of the selection methods.

First, several of the selection methods may be vulnerable to race or gender bias. Recall from our review of the *Griggs* decision in Chapter 4 that education alone was not an adequate criterion for promotion, especially given the history of discrimination in education against African Americans in the South. Therefore, great care should be taken to remedy any issues that may result from race or gender bias embedded in the selection method. In fact, recent court decisions (e.g., *Ricci v. DeStefano* 2009) have stressed the importance of using empirical evidence to show that a selection procedure is not biased. In this regard, evaluating the *reliability* and *validity* of any method used is important to ensure that it is statistically sound (this will be discussed further in the next section).

Many of the selection methods are labor and time intensive, requiring resources to adequately implement. For financially strapped public sector agencies, cost-effectiveness may be an overriding criterion. Weighing the costs and benefits of the appropriate selection methods is difficult, especially when public HR managers must also take into account constitutional and public values. For example, while one method may be less time-consuming to administer, it may not stand up to legal scrutiny as well as an alternative method would. Finally, other aptitudes besides knowledge, skills, and abilities may also be useful to consider in the selection process. Recent scholarship (Guy and Newman 2004; Guy Newman, and Mastracci 2008) suggests that emotional capacity—caring, negotiating, empathizing, relationship building—may also be an important aspect of job performance. Personality tests, such as those that assess a person's emotional quotient, may be useful when hiring for nursing or social worker positions, for example, which require regular, sensitive contact with other people.

Assessing Reliability and Validity of Selection Procedures

As mentioned in the previous section, HR managers in the public sector need to ensure that a selection method shows validity and reliability.

Instrument **reliability** is more easily measured than validity, but it is by no means an acceptable substitute for validity. Reliability simply represents the stability and consistency of a selection procedure. For example, we would expect an individual's results on a reliable selection examination to be roughly the same each time that individual takes the test. However, validity—a much more statistically rigorous method—is a more important tool for assessing adverse impact and job-relatedness.

Validity is concerned with inferences or judgments that may be built into the instrument and its ability to predict performance on the job (OPM 2012a). Demonstrating validity is not only important for selecting qualified applicants but also for maintaining a selection process that protects against EEO liability (Shafritz et al. 2001).

An assertation that a selection instrument is valid must be based on solid empirical evidence. This point is made clear by the EEOC:

> Under no circumstances will the general reputation of a test or other selection procedures, its author or its publisher, or casual reports of its validity be accepted in lieu of evidence of validity. Specifically ruled out are: assumptions of validity based on a procedure's name or descriptive labels; all forms of promotional literature; data bearing on the frequency of a procedure's usage; testimonial statements and credentials of sellers, users, or consultants; and other non-empirical or anecdotal accounts of selection practices or selection outcomes. (Biddle Consulting Group 2012)

Evidence for the validity of selection procedures can come in several forms. **Content validity** demonstrates that a particular selection method (e.g., interview, biographical data such as education) measures the knowledge or skills that are critical to performance in a particular job.

Empirical validation (or **criterion-related validity**) goes a step further, demonstrating that selection tools are statistically significant predictors of performance on the job. For example, we would be interested in validating whether or not the selection metrics used to hire a new employee are predictive of their scores on annual performance evaluations. (If an applicant is successful in passing a test and then is hired, is she also successful in her performance on the job? If not, then the test may not be testing the right factors or criteria.) Such predictive validity of the selection procedure is desirable given its reliance on statistical analysis (Shafritz et al. 2001). Comparing the predictive power of one instrument to that of another leads to a higher predictive validity for a selection procedure (OPM 2012a). In other words, trial and error is a positive approach to building a more effective selection process.

Many jurisdictions have moved away from written tests as a method of selection. Cases concerning examinations, such as *Ricci* and the Luevano consent decree, have heightened fears that improperly used written tests will have adverse impact. The Luevano decree, which resolved a class-action suit that was filed in 1979, is now known as *Angel G. Luevano, et al., v. Janice R. Lachance, Director, Office of Personnel Management, et al.* The plaintiffs alleged that the Professional and Administrative Career Exam (PACE), which the government had been using to fill about 120 occupations at the GS-5 and GS-7 levels, had an adverse impact on the employment of

African Americans and Hispanics for reasons that were not job related (OPM 2012b). To avoid the courts, the federal government established a consent decree eliminating the PACE exam and promoting programs that would enhance diversity among underrepresented groups. As a result, **content validity**—measuring whether the content used in the selection procedure aligns with the content necessary for the doing the job—is a justifiable criterion for choosing a selection measure (SIOP 2012a). Examining a selection procedure's content validity requires demonstrating the relationship between the selection procedure and job-related work behaviors, critical tasks, requirements, or outcomes. When public sector HR selection practices emphasize knowledge, skills, and abilities (KSAs), content validation is important evidentiary support for the instrument being employed.

Showing that a particular selection procedure assesses critical job-related characteristics and predicts performance in that job is crucial to the validation process (Goldstein Zedeck, and Schneider 1993; SIOP 2012a). For public HR managers, sound practice is to measure both the reliability and validity of selection procedures.

Employee Recruitment and Selection in an Era of PHRM Reform

Recall from our discussion in Chapter 1 that decentralization of PHRM is a significant component of recent reform efforts (Coggburn 2000; Kettl 2000; Thompson 2001). In a move to enhance responsiveness and efficiency, decentralization efforts have transferred the responsibility for selection and recruitment functions within public agencies to frontline managers. The goal is to replace the perceived intractability of centralized, rule-bound systems and traditional PHRM practices with more agency-specific, manager-centered systems. During the 1990s, reforms in selection and recruitment spearheaded by the Clinton administration's efforts under the National Performance Review (NPR) led to the elimination of the *Federal Personnel Manual* and enactment of the Federal Workforce Restructuring Act in 1994 (Naff and Newman 2004). The personnel manual stipulated a lengthy centralized approach to selection that focused on following strict hiring guidelines. The Clinton administration's reform efforts provided agency managers with greater leeway in personnel decisions. The 1994 act provided federal agencies with greater authority not only over hiring but also over reductions in force. Advances in technology (e.g., e-recruitment) have also streamlined the recruitment and selection process over the last two decades.

Initiatives at the federal level have continued the impetus for deregulation and decentralization in recruitment and selection processes, especially by means of online tools. As noted earlier, federal agencies leverage USAJOBS to recruit a qualified applicant pool. Further, legislative exemption from Title V of the US Code has provided many agencies the ability to develop more flexible systems (Woodard

2005, 113). Instead of having to use the traditional methods of outlined in the *Federal Personnel Manual*, federal agencies may employ a variety of e-recruitment mechanisms specifically suited to their hiring needs. For example, the US Peace Corps has moved away from sending representatives to job fairs to leveraging social media (e.g., Facebook, Twitter), thereby reaching a new generation of candidates (Llorens 2011).

State governments have also decentralized decision making, investing it in agencies (Selden Ingraham, and Jacobson 2001). For example, many states have restructured their central personnel offices into consulting organizations that then aid agencies in their personnel decisions. The state of South Carolina did away with its central personnel office as part of a larger government reform effort in 1993 in order to afford state agencies greater authority over hiring, transfers, pay, and discipline. The former central personnel office was streamlined and remade as a consulting body for agency HR managers (Hays Byrd, and Wilkins 2006).

Hou et al. (2000) asserted that decentralization at the state level has increased the support, planning, and supervision responsibilities required of central state personnel offices due to the greater need for coordination among subdivisions. Thus, while decentralization may be more efficient at the agency level, Hou's research suggests that there are other consequences and that a better balance between centralization and decentralization may need to be found (see Selden and Wooters 2011).

In fact, over the last decade, decentralization has not proven an unmitigated success, and governments have had to find other solutions. **Shared services**, a blending of both centralized and decentralized approaches to PHRM, may be a viable alternative. Governments electing a shared service approach reap both the efficiencies of centralized rule making and the flexibility of agency-tailored recruitment and selection. For example, the state of Washington embarked on a shared services initiative in 2009 that established a human resource management system (HRMS) that allows employees to access personal data and request leave time (State of Washington, Department of Human Resources 2011).

Privatization has also influenced public sector recruitment and selection. At the federal level, the Competitive Sourcing Initiative (CSI), implemented in 2001 under the administration of George W. Bush, has encouraged greater reliance on the private sector. USAJOBS is one example of the federal government's outsourcing the operation and management of its workforce recruitment system to a private firm (Llorens and Kellough 2007; Shafritz Russell, and Borick 2007, 423). A variety of privatization initiatives at the state level have also influenced recruitment and selection functions. The firm Convergys, based in Cincinnati, Ohio, operates a number of personnel functions that have been awarded to the firm by the states of Florida and Texas (see Battaglio and Condrey 2006; Coggburn 2007; Condrey and Battaglio 2007). In the case of Florida, Convergys was awarded a $350 million, nine-year contract to administer many transaction and process functions related to HR, benefits, payroll, and staffing (Battaglio and Condrey 2006, 31–32). In Texas, Convergys was awarded an $85 million, five-year contract with the state Health and Human Service Commission to provide many HR-related functions such as performance management, recruitment and selection, benefits, payroll, and compensation and classification administration (Coggburn 2007, 319).

Like decentralization, privatization has not been the panacea proponents touted it as. In the case of Florida, HR privatization initiatives proved more costly and time-consuming than initially anticipated. Operational problems included employees failing to receive pay and being dropped from their health insurance. For public HR managers, the lesson is clear: before pursing privatization of personnel functions, the costs and benefits must be weighed very carefully.

Decentralization and privatization efforts, as well as other reforms such as EAW, have the potential to exacerbate recruitment and retention problems (Battaglio 2010; Battaglio and Condrey 2009; Coggburn et al. 2010; Condrey and Battaglio 2007). In an EAW setting, job security is no longer a viable recruitment incentive for public sector employment. Consequently, HR directors and public managers will need to learn novel methods for marketing public sector employment, as well as motivating and retaining employees. The federal government, for example, has authorized agencies to employ student loan repayment incentives to recruit younger employees carrying ever-increasing levels of educational debt (OPM 2008). Web 2.0 technologies will also be vital for reaching the next generation of public service employees.

Decentralization has caused friction because of its failure to provide uniform guidelines. This is especially true for smaller jurisdictions that lack the resources to embed HR functions within each agency. Shared service models that provide both uniformity and flexibility in the delivery of HR functions may be a viable alternative to decentralization alone. Privatization is clearly troublesome for maintaining morale, as the process entails replacing public employees with private contractors. (The issue of motivation in the public service is discussed at length in Chapter 8.) Declassification methods such as salary broadbanding have also been used as recruitment strategies; broad pay scales that allow hiring managers to offer higher starting salaries to potential employees are an attractive tool. Unfortunately, broadbanding has the potential to create pay inequities, because new employees may make more than senior staff. Performance-based pay, which promises bonuses to employees as a reward for productive behavior, has also been used as a recruitment strategy. Such bonus mechanisms, however, have often been underfunded and deficient (as discussed in greater detail in Chapter 6), thus thwarting the recruitment strategies behind them.

Conclusion

In the face of budget shortfalls and economic uncertainty, many governments have opted to reform their HR functions in a bid to make their jurisdictions leaner. Therefore, public HR directors must be adept at selecting the recruitment and selection procedures that garner the largest pool of qualified applicants for the respective job. HR directors face the challenge of balancing efficiency, cost, and fairness in their recruiting tactics. For example, some selection procedures may be more cost-effective but also carry a risk of race bias. The pursuit of firm legal footing is no small task, and HR managers need access to the right tools for recruitment and selection as well as a knowledge of the legal framework for implementing such procedures.

The *Ricci v. DeStefano* (2009) case raises a number of questions for both public and private sector employers to consider. According to Peffer (2009), employers in both sectors will be hard-pressed to prevail in Title VII disparate treatment lawsuits. Employers will need to demonstrate solid evidentiary support for any decision to remedy past discrimination or ameliorate disparate impact. Peffer concluded that the Supreme Court unfortunately provides little guidance to assist employers in assembling such evidence. Even when employers are able to demonstrate job-relatedness or business necessity for selection practices, plaintiffs may prevail if they are able to provide evidence of viable alternatives that would have diminished the impact on minorities (408). According to Peffer, the *Ricci* decision poses a dilemma for employers:

> When employers reject employment practices or procedures such as examinations as a result of reasonable doubts about their reliability (disparate impact), they can be held to have engaged in discrimination because of race (disparate treatment). Again, the employer is left with little direction in how to overcome this conundrum. (409)

The lesson for employers is that they must continually review and validate their selection procedures to ensure that they are fair and job related. Moreover, employers should make every effort to explore all alternatives to identify those that have the least impact on minority and other protected-class applicants.

In addition, given the expanded possibilities in the information age, public HR managers will be tasked with assessing which of the new recruitment mechanisms are most optimal for their particular organizations. Innovative IT recruitment methods tapping Web 2.0 technologies and third-party e-recruitment may be viable alternatives for HR directors who want to enhance their abilities to garner a larger pools of qualified applicants in a cost-effective manner.

According to Selden and Wooters (2011), a shared services model of PHRM creates a centralized service function that treats employees and agency-based HRM professionals as internal customers. This approach is designed to enable a government to better leverage existing resources; reduce duplication of HRM activities across state agencies; and provide more consistent, higher-quality services to internal customers by concentrating existing resources and streamlining processes.

References

Adarand Contractors Inc. v. Peña, 515 U.S. 200 (1995).

Battaglio, R. Paul, Jr. 2010. "Public Service Reform and Motivation: Evidence from an Employment At-Will Environment." *Review of Public Personnel Administration* 30:341–63.

Battaglio, R. Paul, Jr., and Stephen E. Condrey. 2006. "Civil Service Reform: Examining State and Local Government Cases." *Review of Public Personnel Administration* 26:118–38.

Battaglio, R. Paul, Jr., and Stephen E. Condrey. 2009. "Reforming Public Management: Analyzing the Impact of Public Service Reform on Organizational and Managerial Trust." *Journal of Public Administration Research & Theory* 19:689–707.

Biddle Consulting Group. 2012. *Uniform Guidelines on Employee Selection Procedures.* Section 5: General standards for validity studies. http://uniformguidelines.com/uniformguide lines.html#20.

Bowman, James S., and Jonathan P. West, eds. 2007. *American Public Service: Radical Reform and the Merit System.* Boca Raton, FL: Taylor & Francis.

Buford, James A., Jr., and James R. Lindner. 2002. *Human Resource Management in Local Government: Concepts and Applications for HRM Students and Practitioners.* Cincinnati, OH: South-Western.

Choudhury, Enamul H. 2007. "Workforce Planning in Small Local Governments." *Review of Public Personnel Administration* 27:264–80.

City of Richmond v. J. A. Croson Co., 488 U.S. 469 (1989).

Civil Rights Act of 1964 Title VII, as Amended through 1991, 42 U.S.C. §2000e et seq. (2009).

Cober, Richard T., Douglas J. Brown, Alana J. Blumental, Dennis Doverspike, and Paul E. Levy. 2000. "The Quest for the Qualified Job Surfer: It's Time the Public Sector Catches the Wave." *Public Personnel Management* 29:479–95.

Coggburn, Jerrell D. 2000. "Is Deregulation the Answer for Public Personnel Management? Revisiting a Familiar Question: Introduction." *Review of Public Personnel Administration* 20:5–8.

Coggburn, Jerrell D. 2007. "Outsourcing Human Resources: The Case of the Texas Health and Human Services Commission." *Review of Public Personnel Administration* 27:315–35.

Coggburn, Jerrell D., R. Paul Battaglio Jr., James S. Bowman, Stephen E. Condrey, Doug Goodman, and Jonathan P. West. 2010. "State Government Human Resource Professionals' Commitment to Employment at Will." *American Review of Public Administration* 40:189–208.

Condrey, Stephen E., and R. Paul Battaglio Jr. 2007. "A Return to Spoils? Revisiting Radical Civil Service Reform in the United States." *Public Administration Review* 67:424–36.

Condrey, Stephen E., and Robert Maranto, eds. 2001. *Radical Reform of the Civil Service.* Lanham, MD: Lexington Books, 2001.

Dhebar, Beatrice Bezmalinovic, and Benjamin Stokes. 2008 "A Nonprofit Manager's Guide to Online Volunteering." *Nonprofit Management & Leadership* 18:497–506.

Dixon, Brian E. 2010. "Towards E-Government 2.0: An Assessment of Where E-Government 2.0 Is and Where It Is Headed." *Public Administration & Management* 15:418–54.

Goldstein, Irwin L., Sheldon Zedeck, and Benjamin Schneider. 1993. "An Exploration of the Job Analysis-Content Validity Process." In *Personnel Selection in Organizations*, edited by Neal Schmitt and Walter C. Borman. San Francisco, CA: Jossey-Bass.

Griggs v. Duke Power Company, 401 U.S. 424 (1971).

Guy, Mary E., and Meredith A. Newman. 2004. "Women's Jobs, Men's Jobs: Sex Segregation and Emotional Labor." *Public Administration Review* 64:289–98.

Guy, Mary E., Meredith A. Newman, and Sharon H. Mastracci. 2008. *Emotional Labor: Putting the Service in Public Service.* Armonk, NY: M. E. Sharpe.

Hays, Steven W., Chris Byrd, and Samuel L. Wilkins. 2006. "South Carolina's Human Resource Management System: The Model for States with Decentralized Personnel Structures." In *Civil Service Reform in the States: Personnel Policy and Politics at the Subnational Level*, edited by J. Edward Kellough and Lloyd G. Nigro, 171–202. Albany: SUNY Press.

Hays, Steven W., and Jessica E. Sowa. 2006. "A Broader Look at the 'Accountability' Movement: Some Grim Realities in State Civil Service Systems." *Review of Public Personnel Administration* 26:102–17.

Hou, Yilin, Patricia Ingraham, Stuart Bretschneider, and Sally Coleman Selden. 2000. "Decentralization of Human Resource Management: Driving Forces and Implications." *Review of Public Personnel Administration* 20:9–22.

Kellough, J. Edward, and Lloyd G. Nigro, eds. 2006. *Civil Service Reform in the States: Personnel Policy and Politics at the Subnational Level.* Albany: SUNY Press.

Kettl, Donald F. 2000. *The Global Public Management Revolution: A Report on the Transformation of Governance.* Washington, DC: Brookings Institution Press.

Kim, Soonhee, and Jennifer G. O'Connor. 2009. "Assessing Electronic Recruitment Implementation in State Governments: Issues and Challenges." *Public Personnel Management* 38:47–66.

Llorens, Jared J. 2011. "A Model of Public Sector E-Recruitment Adoption in a Time of Hyper Technological Change." *Review of Public Personnel Administration* 31:410–23.

Llorens, Jared J., and R. Paul Battaglio Jr. 2010. "Human Resources Management in a Changing World: Reassessing Public Human Resources Management Education." *Review of Public Personnel Administration* 30:112–32.

Llorens, Jared J., and J. Edward Kellough. 2007. "A Revolution in Public Personnel Administration: The Growth of Web-Based Recruitment and Selection Processes in the Federal Service." *Public Personnel Management* 36:207–22.

Mesch, Debra J., James L. Perry, and Lois R. Wise. 1995. "Bureaucratic and Strategic Human Resource Management: An Empirical Comparison in the Federal Government." *Journal of Public Administration Research and Theory* 5:385–402.

Naff, Katherine C., and Meredith A. Newman. 2004. "Symposium: Federal Civil Service Reform; Another Legacy of 9/11?" *Review of Public Personnel Administration* 24:191–201.

National Academy of Public Administration. 2001. *The Quest for Talent: Recruitment Strategies for Federal Agencies.* Washington, DC: National Academy of Public Administration.

New York State Department of Civil Service (NYDCS). 1998. *Quality Standards/Innovative Applications: Award-Winning Performance from New York State's New Civil Service.* Albany: State of New York, Department of Civil Service.

Partnership for Public Service and Grant Thornton. 2007. "Federal Human Capital: The Perfect Storm; A Survey of Chief Human Capital Officers." http://ourpublicservice.org/OPS/publications/viewcontentdetails.php?id=119.

Peffer, Shelly L. 2009. "Title VII and Disparate-Treatment Discrimination versus Disparate-Impact Discrimination: The Supreme Court's Decision in Ricci v. DeStefano." *Review of Public Personnel Administration* 29:402–10.

Ricci v. DeStefano, 557 U.S. 557 (2009).

Riccucci, Norma M. 2006. "Civil Service Reform in New York: A Quiet Revolution." In *Civil Service Reform in the States: Personnel Policy and Politics at the Subnational Level,* edited by J. Edward Kellough and Lloyd G. Nigro, 303–14. Albany: SUNY Press.

Selden, Sally Coleman, Patricia Wallace Ingraham, and Willow Jacobson. 2001. "Human Resource Practices in State Government: Findings from a National Survey." *Public Administration Review* 61:598–607.

Selden, Sally Coleman, and Robert Wooters. 2011. "Structures in Public Human Resource Management: Shared Services in State Government." *Review of Public Personnel Administration* 31:349–68.

Shafritz, Jay M., David H. Rosenbloom, Norma A. Riccucci, Katherine C. Naff, and Al C. Hyde. 2001. *Personnel Management in Government: Politics and Process.* 5th ed. New York: Marcel Dekker.

Shafritz, Jay M., E. W. Russell, and Christopher P. Borick. 2007. *Introducing Public Administration.* 5th ed. New York: Pearson Longman.

Sinnott, George C. 1998. "Civil Service—Bully, Bully." Albany: New York State Department of Civil Service. http://www2.sunysuffolk.edu/formans/CivilServiceBully.htm.

Society for Industrial and Organizational Psychology (SIOP). 2012a. *Sources of Validity Evidence.* http://www.siop.org/_Principles/pages13to26.pdf.

Society for Industrial and Organizational Psychology (SIOP). 2012b. "Types of Employment Tests." http://www.siop.org/workplace/employment%20testing/testtypes.aspx.

State of Washington, Department of Human Resources, HR Leadership & Shared Services. 2011. "HR Shared Services Update: 2/2/2011." http://www.dop.wa.gov/SiteCollection Documents/Strategic%20HR/SharedServices/SharedServicesUpdate.pdf.

Thompson, Frank, and Michael J. Malbin. 1999. "Reforming Personnel Systems in New York State: Interview with George C. Sinnott." *Rockefeller Institute Bulletin*, New York. http://www .cs.state.ny.us/pio/rockefellerbulletin.htm (no longer online).

Thompson, James R. 2001. "The Civil Service under Clinton: The Institutional Consequences of Disaggregation." *Review of Public Personnel Administration* 21:87–113.

US Equal Employment Opportunity Commission (EEOC). 2010. "EEOC Fact Sheet." http:// www.eeoc.gov/policy/docs/factemployment_procedures.html.

US Merit Systems Protection Board (MSPB). 2006. *Designing an Effective Pay for Performance Compensation System.* http://www.mspb.gov/netsearch/viewdocs.aspx?docnumber=224104& version=224323.

US Office of Personnel Management (OPM). 2008. "Pay & Leave: Student Loan Repayment." http://www.opm.gov/policy-data-oversight/pay-leave/student-loan-repayment/.

US Office of Personnel Management (OPM). 2012a. "Attracting the Best Talent: Assessment; Assessment Strategy Design." http://www.opm.gov/hr/employ/products/assessments/ considerations.asp.

US Office of Personnel Management (OPM). 2012b. "Outstanding Scholar and Outstanding Bilingual/Bicultural Programs (Luevano Consent Decree)." http://www.opm.gov/luevano_ archive/luevano-archive.asp.

US Office of Personnel Management (OPM). 2013. "Veterans Services: Vet Guide." http:// www.opm.gov/policy-data-oversight/veterans-services/vet-guide/#2/.

Voinovich, George V. 2000. *Report to the President: The Crisis in Human Capital.* Washington, DC: Subcommittee on Oversight of Government Management, Restructuring, and the District of Columbia, Committee on Governmental Affairs, United States Senate.

Vonnegut, Michi. 1999. "New York State's New Civil Service." Paper prepared for nomination for the Eugene H. Rooney Jr. Innovative State Human Resource Management Award, National Association of State Personnel Executives, Lexington, KY.

Walsh, David J. 2007. Employment Law for Human Resource Practice. 2nd ed. St. Paul, MN: Thomson West.

Walters, Jonathan. 2002. *Life after Civil Service Reform: The Texas, Georgia, and Florida Experiences.* Armonk, NY: IBM Endowment for the Business of Government.

Wards Cove Packing Co. v. Antonio, 490 U.S. 642 (1989).

West, Jonathan P., and Evan Berman. 2001. "From Traditional to Virtual HR: Is the Transition Occurring in Local Government?" *Review of Public Personnel Administration* 21:38–64.

Witt, Stephanie L., and W. David Patton. 2004. "Recruiting for a High-Performance Workforce." In *Human Resource Management in Local Government: An Essential Guide*, edited by Siegrun Fox Freyss, 33–58. Washington, DC: International City/Council Management Association.

Woodard, Colleen A. 2005. "Merit by Any Other Name—Reframing the Civil Service First Principle." *Public Administration Review* 65:109–16.

Additional Resources

Office of Personnel Management (OPM)—http://www.opm.gov

Society for Industrial & Organizational Psychology (SIOP)—http://www.siop.org

US Equal Employment Opportunity Commission (EEOC)—http://www.eeoc.gov

USAJobs—http://www.usajobs.gov

Case 5.1 — Decentralization, Declassification, and Efficiency: Recruitment and Selection Reform in the State of New York Civil Service

In September of 1995, New York governor George Pataki set out to improve the state's civil service system, widely deemed antiquated, by implementing decentralization and declassification methods for streamlining the lengthy HR process. To do so, he instructed Civil Service Commissioner George Sinnott to head up a task force, which included directors of state operations and representatives from the Governor's Office of Employee Relations and Budget and sought input from the public employee unions, to carry out a comprehensive overview of New York's civil service system (Sinnott 1998). The joint labor-management task force's efforts produced New York's *New* Civil Service reform initiative, the first successful personnel reform in the state in over a century.

Past reform efforts had failed as a result of insurmountable political, legal, organizational, and procedural obstacles (Vonnegut 1999). For over 100 years, no significant changes had been made to the state civil service laws. Attempts at reform were often rebuffed by political opponents and public employee labor unions. One of the main reasons these efforts did not succeed was that reformers failed to consider the interests of the 70-plus state agencies, nine employee labor organizations, the legislature, the budget, and the courts. Emphasizing incremental changes to administrative reform efforts instead of more drastic change, the *New* Civil Service succeeded where previous efforts failed by championing a collaborative approach that elicited the feedback and cooperation of all of the stakeholders in the system— the unions, agency-level HR reps, and members of the legislature.

From the beginning of the civil service reform initiative, the administration worked extensively with the employee unions. Commissioner Sinnott's close involvement of the unions in the process gave them a "seat at the negotiating table," and successfully allayed any misgivings labor might have had. This approach enabled the state of New York to move forward with the *New* Civil Service (Thompson and Malbin 1999). The collaborative process was reinforced by establishing the reform policy as part of sunset legislation; in other words, if after the reform was implemented there was evidence of abuse, the legislation could be terminated.

The labor-management partnership successfully lobbied a joint legislative committee for passage of the reform package. The key elements of the *New* Civil Service reform initiative were legislation allowing for the transfer of employees from one agency to another, improvements to testing and test-reporting procedures, more detailed applicant lists that gave managers more flexibility, a new public management internship program, a reduction in and consolidation of the number of state position titles, IT improvements, and more open communication between state and local agencies regarding personnel changes (New York Department of Civil Service [NYDCS] 1998; Riccucci 2006; Vonnegut 1999; Walters 2002). These initiatives dramatically shifted a civil service system that had been rooted in tradition and mired in gridlock.

On March 29, 1996, the proposals agreed upon by the joint labor-management task force were adopted by the state legislature. The reform legislation authorized the Department of Civil Service (DCS) to transfer employees between agencies when budget shortfalls necessitated reductions in force. Instead of dismissing public employees outright, the DCS could institute a strict hiring freeze but then provisionally transfer the affected employees to open positions within the civil service. Additionally, early retirement incentives with multiple windows were implemented, giving senior employees the option to retire early instead of being laid off. These measures reduced the state workforce by 6,000 positions in fiscal year 1996, with the number of involuntary separations limited to just 235 employees. These numbers were especially significant when compared with the layoffs that had occurred under the previous retirement system (NYDCS 1998; Sinnott 1998). New York's reforms have been recognized nationally as a model for state HR management (Riccucci 2006); such publicity can be a powerful recruitment tool.

With respect to recruitment and selection, the *New* Civil Service legislation drastically changed the status quo. Improved testing methods allowing for more frequent testing provided employees with the opportunity to compete for permanent status, a right that was required by law. Relying entirely on internal resources, the DCS also developed and administered test batteries using rigorous state-of-the-art selection methodologies. Updated recruitment and selection procedures took advantage of technology to benefit both employees and managers by providing them with a more timely and efficient method of promotion and movement from provisional to permanent status (NYDCS 1998; Sinnott 1998). Following implementation of reforms, managers were much better able to plan for agency recruitment needs, and state employees were able to optimize their chances for promotion.

Provisional employees—employees holding a nine-month appointment while awaiting testing—were not considered to be in permanent status and thus were unable to receive the same benefits as permanent employees; however, they had the right to pursue and attain permanent status and could do so by passing the state civil service examination. Under the previous program, the selection system was inadequately monitored, and there was a backlog of over 600 open positions for which no promotion tests had been scheduled. This led to many competent provisional employees being unable to take the state exam and effectively denied the right to gain permanent civil service status. Moreover, as they languished in provisional status, questionable provisional appointments were allowed to circumvent the law. An advantage of promoting from within is that provisional employees already have the experience of working in the state agency, so they form an ideal and ready talent pool from which to hire; they can transition more smoothly to permanent status than someone who is new to the agency. By December 1998, two years after passage of the reform legislation, of the 140,672 Competitive Class employees in state service, only 0.7 percent remained in provisional status—a 79 percent reduction from previous years (NYDCS 1998; Riccucci 2006; Sinnott 1998).

Another technological improvement is a civil service website that gives candidates prompt results from their exams. The new website provides applicants with "employee test profiles," giving candidates a summary of their exam performance for each subject area, and provides state offices with up-to-date lists of candidates eligible for appointment. These improvements to recruitment and selection technologies help the DCS improve efficiency and to hire and promote based on merit, one of the fundamental principles and best practices of civil service (NYDCS 1998; Sinnott 1998).

Civil service rules in the state of New York apply not only to state agencies but also to local counties and municipalities, which are frequently audited by the state DCS to ensure compliance. For example, Onondaga County (Syracuse), New York, has reported that the *New* Civil Service's comprehensive reforms in testing and scoring and technological improvements have streamlined the hiring process, facilitating more timely and predictable notice to potential new hires about the status of their applications (Battaglio and Condrey 2006). The streamlined process has eliminated many of the provisional hires not only at the state level but also at the local level. A more efficient testing process has allowed exam results to be posted in as few as 60 days; employees used to wait for results for nine months. Moreover, efficient testing has positively impacted recruitment at the local level. In many cases, competency exams were held only on certain scheduled dates—and sometimes only once a year. Local HR directors are now able to administer these tests on demand and provide potential employees with more timely results. This development has been particularly helpful for local authorities in the competitive recruitment market for information technology jobs, as qualified candidates may accept jobs offers from the private sector rather than wait for a slow-moving government decision.

Additionally, the use of broadbanding with regard to test scores has given local authorities a great deal of flexibility. With broadbanding, hiring managers can select from applicants who have earned a wide range of scores rather than only from applicants who have earned scores within a narrow range, and managers can consider factors besides test scores.

Local authorities have also seen a significant impact from improved outreach by the state civil service system. Commissioner Sinnott appointed outreach units at the state level to serve as liaisons to local offices, supplying the local offices with training and other needs. This outreach has increased communication between local and state authorities.

Reform efforts in New York have brought this state's civil service into parity with other states' civil service systems. This is a considerable achievement given the long history of impediments to reform in the state (Riccucci 2006). This case stands in stark contrast to the antimerit values emphasized in more radical reform efforts, such as those in the states of Georgia and Florida. Additionally, scholarship (Mesch Perry, and Wise 1995) suggests that local HR managers in New York have appreciated the paring down of excessive rules and regulations that has accompanied implementation of the *New* Civil Service. This has enabled local managers to function more efficiently and to focus on achieving their organizational mission within a competitive environment.

Since passage of the reform, the state still experiences fragmentation in its ability to carry out HR functions, although not nearly to the extent as under the prior system. Overall, the reforms have been viewed positively by both those within the New York civil service system (employees, unions, politicians) and national recognition bodies (e.g., the Society for Human Resource Management and the American Society for Public Administration) (Riccucci 2006).

For HR managers involved in reform, communicating with affected stakeholders is key. Keeping employees, politicians, and the public informed is critical to avoiding costly obstacles (e.g., protests, work stoppages) to positive reforms.

Discussion Questions

1. Why was the state of New York able to pass comprehensive legislation in 1996 but unable to do so over the previous 100 years?

2. With regard to recruitment and selection, what changes were made? What was the impact of these changes? Do you believe these changes improved recruitment and selection for the state?

3. What changes might you have recommended? Whom might you have involved or excluded from the reform discussion? Is it better to compromise in order to achieve reform or better to maintain purity of vision? Did the players in the New York reforms sacrifice efficiency in order to appeal to a broader audience?

4. What role, if any, did state leaders have in passage of the civil service reform legislation?

5. Regarding the characteristics of reform discussed at the outset of the text (see Table 1.1), how might you characterize the reforms discussed in the state of New York? Did the New York reforms go far enough? Are there any drawbacks to increased managerial flexibility at the agency level?

Exercise

Using Web 2.0 Technology in the Recruitment and Selection Process

Assume you are a newly hired HR manager in the city of Washitonia. The city manager has asked you to review different approaches to implementing an updated recruitment and selection tool that taps online efficiencies. Having recently earned your master's of public administration (MPA), you are eager to approach the task based on your knowledge of PHRM. With that in mind, what might an updated candidate recruitment and selection process look like? What technologies might be involved in such an approach? In your opinion, are Web 2.0 technologies a good means of recruiting qualified candidates? Why or why not?

6

Pay and Benefits

HR managers are increasingly tasked with finding novel solutions to the challenges of the contemporary pay and benefits environment. Economic constraints over the last decade have made paramount the ability of public HR managers to recruit a qualified public workforce with limited resources. Compounding this dilemma are the many public human resource management (PHRM) reforms aimed at using compensation as a means to improve productivity. Compensation reforms in the public sector over the last few decades have targeted allegedly recalcitrant pay systems that have emphasized seniority over productivity. Many of these reforms have sought to tap productivity through arrangements such as performance-based pay and broadbanding. Although the evidence supporting their benefits is limited, performance-based pay schemes and other alternative compensation systems remain an attractive alternative to traditional compensation systems (Perry Engbers, and Jun 2009). This chapter will begin by reviewing the foundations of modern compensation in the public sector, specifically covering the concept of job analysis as the building block of any classification system. It will then discuss alternative compensation structures like performance-based pay and broadbanding, considering their advantages and disadvantages.

Laws Affecting Compensation
Policy and Practice in the Public Sector

While Chapter 3 provides an assessment of the legal environment of PHRM, a number of federal statutory laws apply specifically to compensation; therefore, this section will review these laws specifically. No single law governs compensation. Instead, policy draws upon several pieces of federal legislation, including the Fair Labor Standards Act (FLSA), the Equal Pay Act (EPA), Title VII of the Civil Rights Act of 1964, the Civil Rights Act of 1991, the Age Discrimination in Employment Act (ADEA), the Americans with Disabilities Act (ADA), and the Family and Medical Leave Act (FMLA). These laws subject public sector agencies and their employees to potential legal scrutiny; jury trials; and compensatory and punitive damages as a result of tort law rulings regarding defamation, misrepresentation, and negligence (French 2009). For example, a civil rights violation might prompt a suit against a local government, which can be held liable for the actions of its employees, and against those employees as individuals acting on behalf of the jurisdiction (see *Monell v. Department of Social Services of the State of New York* 436 U.S. 658 [1978]).

The federal government has long taken a keen interest in matters of pay. The first federal legislation that regulated compensation was the **Fair Labor Standards Act of 1938**, which required a minimum wage to be paid by all employers, established policy on overtime pay, and mandated record-keeping requirements for employers. The Supreme Court decision in *Garcia v. San Antonio Metropolitan Transit Authority* (1985) subjected state and local governments to the same regulations outlined in the 1938 Act, with very few exceptions (e.g., overtime pay policies may not necessarily apply to political appointees, executives, and administrative and professional employees) (Buford and Lindner 2002, 307–8). Further, the **Equal Pay Act of 1963** and Title VII of the Civil Rights Act of 1964 regulate potential civil rights violations in compensation. The EPA prohibits disparities in pay on the basis of gender, and Title VII extends this prohibition to race, color, age, sex, religion, national origin, handicap, or veteran status when jobs of equal duties and responsibilities are compared (Tompkins and Stapczynksi 2004, 24).

Pay equality between men and women who perform similar or equal work is strictly regulated under the EPA. However, the issue of comparable worth, which is distinct from "equal pay," remains unclear. The idea behind the comparable worth standard is that women and men may have different or dissimilar jobs, but the work done in those jobs is of comparable value to an employer. Therefore, pay of men and women in jobs of comparable worth should be adjusted so that it is equitable. According to Zeigler (2006), instances of discrimination occur when "employers offer a higher rate of compensation to those in jobs traditionally dominated by men" (212), despite the fact that jobs held by women may be just as important. For example, jobs traditionally associated with women in the workforce (e.g., nursing, teaching, social work) have tended to be "undervalued and undercompensated." Such valuative discrimination has proven difficult to document, let alone prohibit, without clear guidance from the courts.

Federal law also prohibits discrimination in compensation with regard to age and disability. Under the Age Discrimination in Employment Act of 1967 as amended, it is illegal to refuse to hire, discharge, or otherwise discriminate against an individual over the age of 40 in compensation or privileges of employment. The **Older Workers Protection Act of 1990** extended coverage of the ADEA to employee benefits (French 2009, 95). Distinctions made with respect to age and job requirements that impact pay or benefits must hold up to bona fide occupational qualification (BFOQ) standards established by the courts. Employers must demonstrate that age requirements for a specific job are defensible as necessary for the performance of that job. For example, jobs in public safety (e.g., police officers, firefighters) often involve a certain level of physical activity that may preclude candidates of a certain age from being able to perform work-related duties. Just as the ADEA extends pay equity under Title VII to workers over 40, the Americans with Disabilities Act of 1990 extends pay equity to those with disabilities.

Finally, the **Family and Medical Leave Act (1993)** was established to keep up with the changing dynamics of work and family life. Under the act, eligible persons can receive up to 12 weeks of unpaid leave per year for specified medical purposes (French 2009, 95). Qualifying medical events include pregnancy or the birth of a child, adoption or foster care of a newly placed child, personal or family illness, family military leave (US Department of Labor [DOL] 2013a). Upon completion of leave, covered employees are entitled to return to their "same position or another position that has equal pay, benefits, and working conditions." Employers may not punish an employee who takes family or medical leave by reducing that worker's salary once he or she has returned to work.

Job Analysis: The Foundation of Public Sector Compensation

The public HR manager must take many considerations into account when determining the appropriate pay and benefits for public employees. Generally, the government strives to provide reasonably competitive pay rates compared with those earned in similar jobs and maintain pay consistency within a government agency office. The primary factor that determines pay rates for a given job is the skills and knowledge required or needed for that job; a job requiring more skills and knowledge will be compensated at a higher rate than a position that requires fewer skills and less knowledge.

The process by which each employee's position is analyzed to determine what skills are required to perform the job is **job analysis**. This is the crux of building a dynamic and strategic HR system. An accurately constructed job analysis leads to accurate **job descriptions** (outlines of the duties and responsibilities of a job and the skills required), another critical HR component. Without precise job analysis methods, public organizations would find it difficult to maintain not only competitive compensation but also workforce planning, recruitment, and performance appraisal. Furthermore, job analysis is obligatory given the legal requirements for systematic analysis of alternative selection criteria (see Chapter 5).

Job analysis entails the collection of job-related information by observing and interacting with employees as they carry out required duties and tasks. Ultimately, job analysis assesses the content (responsibilities, tasks) of the employee's position and the conditions (work environment) under which such duties are undertaken (Buford and Lindner 2002). Increasingly, job analysis is also tied to effective workforce planning, as public organizations seek to prepare for future HR needs (Selden 2009). Table 6.1 reviews HR activities that depend on accurate and timely job analysis.

Reviewing Table 6.1, we see the crucial role that job analysis plays within the organization. Job analysis assists organizations in identifying and establishing the job-related knowledge, skills, abilities, and other characteristics (KSAOs) necessary for job performance. Identification of KSAOs is a necessary component of building accurate job descriptions, the comprehensive written statements of duties and responsibilities for each position. Identifying the skill sets necessary for each job allows the organization to systematically analyze compensation for similar jobs in the relevant labor market. Job analysis is critical for establishing internal and external consistency in classification and compensation systems, that is, ensuring that pay rates are in line with those of comparable jobs within the agency (internal) and with what other organizations or companies are offering for similar positions (external).

Workforce planning also relies on accurate job analysis to delineate relevant job information and qualifications for future workforce needs. Such efforts assist the organization in making strategic HR management plans by identifying the job-related KSAOs necessary for organizational performance. Likewise, recruitment efforts would be impossible without the identification of critical job-related KSAOs. Advertising an accurate job description is crucial to recruiting a qualified applicant pool and in selecting potential candidates for the job. Job analysis efforts aid managers in making selection decisions through validated mechanisms based on job-relatedness—an important legal aspect of staffing. Once a selection has been made, organizations rely on timely job analysis to orient new hires to their jobs and identify training and development needs and methods.

Finally, the establishment of job-related KSAOs through job analysis aids in accurate performance appraisal. Job analysis specifies performance standards by identifying

Table 6.1	Job Analysis and Human Resource Activities

Human Resource Activity	Information Provided by Job Analysis
Job Descriptions	Establishes job duties and responsibilities.
	Establishes the critical job-related knowledge, skills, abilities, and other characteristics (KSAOs) necessary for job performance.
Compensation	Maintains internal and external consistency in pay rates.
	Uses labor market analysis tools, such as wage and salary surveys, to systematically establish compensation for similar jobs.
	Determines minimum, maximum, and market-rate pay for jobs.
Workforce Planning	Delineates relevant job qualifications that define future workforce needs.
	Assists in strategic planning efforts.
	Identifies KSAOs necessary for organizational performance.
Recruitment	Identifies critical KSAOs of open and future positions.
	Assists in differentiating potential applicants based on requisite KSAOs.
Selection	Validates job-relatedness of selection procedures for legal purposes.
	Provides feedback to the process of establishing competitive pay, mitigating legal concerns about internal and external pay equity.
	Identifies KSAOs to validate the selection process.
Training and Development	Identifies job-related KSAOs necessary for organizational performance.
	Identifies training and development needs and delivery methods for new and veteran employees.
Performance Appraisal	Establishes the KSAOs necessary for job performance as a basis for performance evaluation.
	Establishes performance standards (critical work behaviors).
	Identifies performance criteria for determining the transfer, demotion, or termination of poor-performing employees and the promotion and reward of exceptional employees.

Source: Buford and Lindner 2002.

critical work behaviors. The appropriate benchmarks for employee performance are established, allowing managers to make sound decisions about the transfer, demotion, or termination of poor-performing employees and the promotion and reward of exceptional employees.

Using the labor market for information technology (IT) positions as an example, we can put the essentials of job analysis into practice. When hiring for an entry-level IT position, HR must make sure that the job description is up-to-date and accurate regarding the required KSAOs for performing the job. For example, the job might require knowledge of a specific software package or programming language. HR must also determine what market-rate pay is for an entry-level IT position (external consistency) and ensure that the rate offered is similar to pay levels for other entry-level IT positions within the organization or jurisdiction (internal consistency). Finally, in a strategic workforce-planning context, job analysis allows HR to update position descriptions to anticipate future workforce needs as the organization's mission statement or job requirements may change.

Objectives, Strategies, and Structures of Public Sector Compensation

Compensation in the public sector has a special responsibility to taxpaying citizens to maintain a system that is both cost-effective and internally and externally consistent. These two goals are sometimes at odds with each other. In terms of cost-effectiveness, PHRM reforms have encouraged public sector organizations to be more demanding of their workers while eroding costly benefits traditionally afforded public employees. Hard economic times and the pressure to increase efficiency have pressed governments to be more strategic, pursuing alternative pay schemes, such as performance-based pay, to promote productivity and performance in the workplace. Such mechanisms may test the public sector's ability to maintain internal and external consistency in pay structures. For example, performance-based pay schemes may vary by agency, or governments may be unable to meet bonus expectations when budgets are cut. When authority over compensation is decentralized to the agency level, pay disparities may arise for similar jobs across agencies, resulting in equal protection challenges (Rainey 2006, 54). At the same time, the legal framework established by the courts demands that employees be rewarded for their contributions equitably.

This section will first discuss the methods used to maintain internal and external consistency in pay structures, including the classification system that has traditionally been used to set compensation rates in the public sector. It will then discuss the alternative compensation methods, performance-based pay and broadbanding, that have been implemented in the last few decades as part of PHRM reform.

Traditional Classification Systems and Internal Consistency

Traditional classification systems offer the most reliable scheme for ensuring internal consistency among agency employees. Table 6.1 presents part of the General Schedule (GS), which is the compensation plan (also referred to as a career ladder) in place for most federal employees in the civil service. Upon entering public employment, an employee is assigned to a certain grade, or level. An employee ranked at grade 4, as an example, would commonly be referred to as being at a grade of "GS-4." Each of the fifteen grades is associated with a certain range of pay; there are ten fixed salary steps within each grade, with step 1 representing the minimum pay rate and step 10 representing the maximum pay rate for that grade. These rates may be adjusted annually. The pay structure is transparent and available to the public.

The grade that an employee qualifies for is based on his or her education, work experience, and other skills. An employee entering public employment at grade 2 might need just a high school education and three months of work experience, while someone at grade 5 might be required to have a college degree and three years of work experience. Employees may advance through the ten steps based on seniority or longevity, the acquisition of new skills, annual performance evaluation ratings, or a combination of factors determined by the jurisdiction. The amounts of the **within-grade or step increases**—such as the ones shown in the last column of Table 6.2— reflect years of trial and error with the aim of establishing an equitable compensation system. The salaries for each step may be calculated according to a variety of methods for determining the worth of positions, the most trustworthy of which is covered in the next section on external consistency.

Yet, within-grade tables, such as Table 6.2, do not provide us with all of the information necessary for making compensation decisions. Two additional schedules, the **class series** and job descriptions, provide a more robust picture of a government agency's comprehensive compensation scheme. Tables 6.3 and 6.4 detail a sample classification plan showing class series and job descriptions for a public agency's administrative/clerical positions. The classification plan illustrated in Table 6.3 lists the different occupations or class series in the administrative/clerical category, the full range of jobs in each class, and each job's corresponding grade level. The plan distinguishes each job by the type of work performed and the task difficulty and responsibilities required of each grade (the specifics of which are noted in Table 6.4, which shows job descriptions). Note that Table 6.3 only reviews one group of occupational categories (administrative). Public sector agencies generally have classification plans for a number of other occupational categories, including executive, professional, service, and public safety.

Each of the administrative positions is categorized by duties and responsibilities that differ depending on the occupation in each column. Organized in ascending

Table 6.2	General Schedule: Within-Grade and Step Increases, in Annual Salary (effective January 1, 2014)									
Grade	Step 1	Step 2	Step 3	Step 4	Step 5	Step 6	Step 7	Step 8	Step 9	Step 10	Within-Grade Amounts
GS-1	$17,981	$18,582	$19,180	$19,775	$20,373	$20,724	$21,315	$21,911	$21,934	$22,494	VARIES
GS-2	20,217	20,698	21,367	21,934	22,179	22,831	23,483	24,135	24,787	25,439	VARIES
GS-3	22,058	22,793	23,528	24,263	24,998	25,733	26,468	26,468	27,938	28,673	735
GS-4	24,763	25,588	26,413	27,238	28,063	29,713	29,713	30,538	31,363	32,188	825

Source: US Office of Personnel Management (OPM) 2012

order of relative value to the agency, each job in the class series is assigned a salary in accordance with the general schedule. Pay determination is then based on the criteria set forth by the organizations with regard to pay and promotion (e.g., longevity, training and development, performance evaluation, etc.). So, a Clerk Assistant IV, at a GS-4, would have a minimum starting salary of $24,763 (from Table 6.2).

What the plan shows is that in each class, there is a progression from the entry-level position to the highest or most senior position, which an employee would presumably attain as he or she gained more work experience. The plan also shows how the different classes rank in relation to one another. The Clerk Assistant IV is the most senior position attainable in that class, but the GS-4 grade level (and therefore pay rate) is equivalent to that of the lowest grade and pay in the Supervisor class, for a Supervisor I position.

Each job in the class series is differentiated by the composition of its job description. Table 6.4 provides the job description for each position in the Administrative Assistant class series. The job descriptions for each of these positions is distinct based on the skills the job requires and the responsibilities of the job. As one moves up from Administrative Assistant I to Administrative Assistant IV, more skills and responsibilities are required, as reflected in the lengthier job descriptions. This distinction informs staffing as well as promotion decisions. The General Schedule in Table 6.2 is used to determine the compensation for each of the job descriptions in the class series in Table 6.4, and each job description for the class series corresponds to a grade and job title in Table 6.3. Recall from the discussion earlier that proper job analysis generates the KSAOs that make up the building blocks of job descriptions.

Table 6.3	**Classification Plan for Administrative/Clerical Positions within a Public Agency**			
	Class Series			
Grade	**Clerk Assistant**	**Administrative Assistant**	**Administrative Coordinator**	**Supervisory**
GS-1	Clerk Assistant I			
GS-2	Clerk Assistant II	Administrative Assistant I		
GS-3	Clerk Assistant III	Administrative Assistant II	Administrative Coordinator I	
GS-4	Clerk Assistant IV	Administrative Assistant III	Administrative Coordinator II	Supervisor I
GS-5		Administrative Assistant IV	Administrative Coordinator III	Supervisor II
GS-6			Administrative Coordinator IV	Supervisor III
GS-7				Supervisor IV

Source: Adapted from Buford and Lindner 2002.

Table 6.4	**Job Descriptions for the Administrative Assistant Class Series**

Grade	Description
GS-2	Administrative Assistant I. Job entails somewhat difficult work in performing clerical tasks and responsibilities. Employees in this class perform a variety of clerical services to executives, professionals, and staff, such as schedule appointments, give information to callers, provide office management and otherwise relieve officials of clerical work and minor administrative and business detail.
GS-3	Administrative Assistant II. Job entails moderately difficult work in performing clerical tasks and responsibilities. Employees in this class perform a variety of clerical services to executives, professionals, and staff, such as arrange meetings, compose and circulate memoranda, compose correspondence, provide office management and otherwise relieve officials of clerical work and minor administrative and business detail. Knowledge of word processing software required.
GS-4	Administrative Assistant III. Job entails difficult work in performing clerical tasks and responsibilities. Employees in this class perform a variety of advanced clerical services to executives, professionals, and staff, such as bookkeeping, spreadsheets, graphs, providing office management and otherwise relieving officials of clerical work and minor administrative and business detail. Knowledge of word processing, decision-making, and business software required.

(Continued)

(Continued)

Grade	Description
GS-5	Administrative Assistant IV. Job entails difficult work in performing clerical tasks and responsibilities. Employees in this class perform a variety of advanced clerical services to executives, professionals, and staff, such as bookkeeping, web-design and layout, providing office management and otherwise relieving officials of clerical work and minor administrative and business detail. Knowledge of word processing, decision-making, image editing, telecommunications, and business software required.

Source: Adapted from Buford and Lindner (2002).

Point-Factor Method

Traditional classification—although the most frequently employed in government—is by no means the only classification and compensation method available to public HR managers. More sophisticated techniques for comparing and rating jobs can be used to establish the relative value of each position. The **point (or point-factor) method** is one such technique that offers enhanced rigor and sophistication. The point method uses a predetermined set of factors (e.g., skills, duties, working conditions) to evaluate each job. Each position is then assigned points based on the weighting of factors in the job description. The more points a job is assigned, the higher the salary. Tables 6.5 and 6.6 use the administrative positions detailed above to illustrate the components of point method job evaluation. Skills and duties are often given greater weight in the evaluation process than are other criteria because they relate more directly to the requirements of the job; for example, as seen in Table 6.5, skills account for up to 180 points, while working conditions can only contribute 100 points.

As a further distinction, specific criteria are used to award designated numbers of points for each factor. These criteria are organized by degrees. Table 6.6, again using the administrative assistant positions as an example, provides the definitions for each degree of the experience subfactor (under skills). Other subfactors, like stressful working conditions or technical difficulty of work, would have their own definitions for what is required at each degree. A higher degree requires a greater skill set and thus merits more points. Once degrees are established, the level of each position within a job hierarchy can be determined by totalling the points for each subfactor. In our example in Table 6.5, the total number of points that can be awarded is 520. Evaluating the position of administrative assistant would entail calculating points in a range from 0 to 520, and that total would determine the job's classification and, thus, compensation level.

| Table 6.5 | **Point Method of Job Evaluation** | | | |

Factor	Degrees and Points			
	1	**2**	**3**	**4**
Skills (180 points)				
Education	25	50	75	100
Experience	20	40	60	80
Duties (140 points)				
Data	20	40	60	80
Contacts	15	30	45	60
Difficulty of Work (100 points)				
Technical	15	30	45	60
Independence	10	20	30	40
Working Conditions				
(100 points)				
Physical	15	30	45	60
Stress	10	20	30	40
Maximum Total	130	260	390	520

Source: Adapted from Buford and Lindner 2002.

| Table 6.6 | **Point Method Degree Parameters for Skills (Experience)** |

1st Degree (20 points). Employees in this class perform a variety of clerical services to executives, professionals, and staff, such as schedule appointment, give information to callers, provide office management and otherwise relieve officials of clerical work and minor administrative and business detail.

2nd Degree (40 points). Employees in this class perform a variety of clerical services to executives, professionals, and staff, such as arrange meetings, compose and circulate memoranda, compose correspondence, provide office management and otherwise relieve officials of clerical work and minor administrative and business detail. Knowledge of word processing software required.

3rd Degree (60 points). Employees in this class perform a variety of advanced clerical services to executives, professionals, and staff, such as bookkeeping, spreadsheets, graphs, provide office management and otherwise relieve officials of clerical work and minor administrative and business detail. Knowledge of word processing, decision-making, and business software required.

(Continued)

(Continued)

4th Degree (80 points). Employees in this class perform a variety of advanced clerical services to executives, professionals, and staff, such as bookkeeping, web-design and layout, provide office management and otherwise relieve officials of clerical work and minor administrative and business detail. Knowledge of word processing, decision-making, image-editing, telecommunications, and business software required.

Source: Adapted from Buford and Lindner 2002.

To be sure, the information provided in Tables 6.2 to 6.6 overly simplifies the classification and compensation process. Which classification and compensation process is appropriate depends partly on jurisdictional preferences and is often determined by time and cost constraints. Whatever system is used, however, must be both structured and transparent so that compensation is equitable and is perceived as such. The systems presented here embody the principle of rewarding merit—the idea that all public employees should be treated fairly, based on their qualifications alone and that they should not be discriminated against for any reason. Equitable job evaluation systems evolve out of a great deal of trial and error and involve not only internal job evaluations but also a thorough assessment of the external job market for each position.

External Consistency

Establishing an equitable classification system is not the only essential task for public HR managers. A competitive compensation plan, along with other public sector benefits such as job security, is an indispensable recruitment tool for attracting qualified applicants to the public service. An important aspect of competitive compensation is external consistency, that is, pay comparable to that offered in not only similar public sector organizations but also the private sector (Llorens 2008, 308).

Certainly, competitive benefits packages (e.g., retirement, savings, health, medical, etc.) are also part of public sector recruitment. Nonwage forms of compensation include both monetary and nonmonetary tools used to recruit, retain, motivate, and reward employees "above and beyond traditional wage and salary payments" (Budd 2004, 597). Monetary nonwage compensation includes profit-sharing or group-sharing payments, lump-sum bonuses, stock options, and other forms of contingent compensation, although these are much more common in the private sector. Nonmonetary nonwage forms of compensation (sometimes referred to as "fringe" benefits) include employer-provided health insurance and pension plans, vacation and sick days, life and disability insurance, supplemental unemployment benefits, paid holidays, dental insurance, and educational and legal assistance (Budd 2004, 597). However, given the rising costs associated with many of these nonwage forms of compensation, the importance of competitive wages cannot be overstated (Ellickson and Logsdon 2001; Lee and Whitford 2008; Moynihan and Landuyt 2008).

In the past, the discussion of public sector compensation often focused on the legal issues associated with equitable pay—equal pay for comparable work within agencies. More recently, however, many public employers have focused on the disadvantages of traditional compensation in the public sector, specifically their inability to attract qualified applicants due to deflated wage rates relative to private sector employers (Kellough and Lu 1993; Kellough and Nigro 2002; Nigro and Kellough 2008).

To establish external consistency, HR management has drawn heavily from labor economics research. Many studies have examined the competitiveness of public and private sector wages (Belman and Heywood 1988; 1995; Belman, Heywood, and Lund 1997; Borjas 2003; Miller 1996; Smith 1976; 1977). The extent to which a public-private wage gap exists is debatable, and study results depend upon methodology as well data aggregation across employment sectors. However, we can say that in some occupations, people often make more money working in the private sector than in the public sector (Llorens 2008, 314). For example, white-collar employees in the public sector (e.g., attorneys) often make considerably less than their counterparts in the private sector. Thus, public HR managers require tools to support the mission of maintaining external consistency. **Labor market analysis** tools such as wage and salary surveys allow HR managers to determine market pay rates and set corresponding minimum and maximum pay rates for each job in the organization.

In labor market analysis, the HR manager identifies key characteristics of the relevant labor markets (e.g., local, regional, national, public, private, nonprofit), such as sources of qualified workers, unemployment rates, demographics, and wage differentials (Buford and Lindner 2002). Public employers often conduct compensation surveys to obtain information on the relevant labor market. Such surveys allow public sector agencies to determine applicable pay rates for similar jobs across the public, private, and nonprofits sectors. Typically, a public sector agency will develop a questionnaire that asks about pay rates, benefits, and position descriptions for jobs similar to those at the agency. The survey instrument can be delivered via email or post to a sample of employers in the relevant job market. The survey often addresses information beyond pay rates—such as job descriptions and nonwage compensation—so that public sector employers can use the information obtained from potential competitors in the labor market to update position descriptions for job analysis purposes.

Once the surveys have been returned, public sector HR directors can analyze the data to assess current labor market trends. Figure 6.1 illustrates a comprehensive salary survey analysis completed by the Washington State Department of Personnel in 2010. The salary survey provides a wealth of information relevant to competitive compensation in the public sector. In this case, the survey was categorized by occupation (e.g., accounting, administration, engineering, legal) so that similar jobs could be compared. For example, compensation for equivalent accounting jobs could be compared across other state agencies, other public entities (e.g., county or municipal

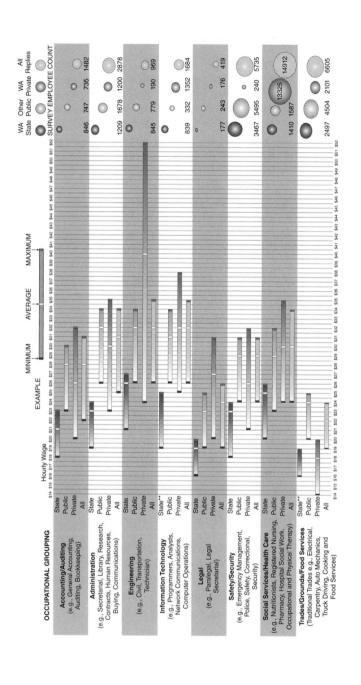

Figure 6.1   Washington State 2010 Salary Survey at a Glance

jobs), and private sector employers. The survey data is used to determine pay ranges for each occupational category, establishing minimum, average, and maximum rates.

For example, as demonstrated by the hourly wages in Figure 6.1, public information technology workers in Washington State earn between $19 and $25 per hour. To more effectively recruit for information technology positions, the state may want to offer an hourly rate closer to $31, which would be more in line with the average rate for similar positions in other public agencies. Salary surveys may also be beneficial for legislative committees or city councils seeking evidence that pay increases for public employees are necessary so that the governmental unit can compete in the labor market. Public HR managers should become familiar with the methods for establishing external consistency in their compensation plans so that they can implement initiatives to keep their agencies competitive.

Nonprofits in Focus	**Executive Pay in Nonprofit Organizations: A Comparison**

Compensation packages for executives in the public, private, and nonprofit sectors have become increasingly controversial. As some executives have been implicated in major financial scandals that have wreaked havoc on the lives of American citizens, the question has persisted: Do the CEOs of large corporations or organizations deserve the salaries they are paid? Citizens, customers, and donors are more vigilantly examining executive compensation in all three sectors.

How do nonprofit CEOs compare with their counterparts in the public and private sectors? According to Charity Navigator's 2012 CEO Compensation Study, the average charity CEO earns approximately $130,000 per year. That average varies by geographic region, with CEOs in the Northeast and Mid-Atlantic averaging about $150,000 and those in the Mountain West and South earning $111,920 and $118,636, respectively. Moreover, CEO pay varies by the size of the organization and charitable mission. Not surprisingly, larger nonprofits (as defined by total expenses) pay their CEOs better on average. Nonprofits with educational missions also tend to pay their CEOs higher on average ($177,734).

In comparison, members of the Senior Executive Service (leaders in the federal civil service system) earn a minimum salary of $119,554 (January 2012). SES maximum pay levels depend upon whether the federal agency uses a "certified" SES performance appraisal system. For those in agencies with a certified performance appraisal system, the maximum pay level is $179,900; for others, it is $165,300. The maximum total aggregate pay is limited to the salary of the vice president of the United States ($230,700 for 2010).

A 2009 survey conducted by the International City/County Management Association (ICMA) reviewed the average salaries of full-time municipal employees and found that the average city manager earns $106,408. ICMA reported that local government salaries are impacted by factors such as population, city size, employee expertise and education, form of government, metro status (urban, suburban, or rural), and the variety of services offered. Geography also plays a role, as managers in the West tend to earn higher salaries than managers elsewhere (Waters and Powell 2010).

The private sector, perhaps unsurprisingly, is a much different (and more lucrative) story. According to a 2012 analysis by the Associated Press, the average CEO of a large, publicly traded company earns $9.7 million, a 6.5 percent

(Continued)

(Continued)

increase from the previous year (Rexrode 2013). In contrast, some top nonprofit CEOs make much less: Wildlife Conservation Society ($787,747), Council on Foreign Relations ($879,591), Prostate Cancer Foundation ($1,204,968), and Salk Institute for Biological Studies ($841,193). The average NPO CEO salary is just $130,000. According to Charity Navigator, only six charities (of the 3,786 surveyed) paid their top executives over $1 million.

So, how do nonprofits determine compensation and compete for talent in the labor market? Just as do their counterparts in the public sector, nonprofits use salary surveys of the relevant labor market to determine what similar organizations are paying executives (Albert 2000; Pynes 2009; Stene 1980). According to Frumkin and Keating (2010), nonprofit CEO pay is largely based on what managers in similar-sized organizations receive. Interestingly, the authors found that CEO performance, as measured by either improved fund-raising results or better administrative efficiency, had very little bearing on executive compensation. Nonetheless, nonprofits wanting to attract the best and brightest should heed Pynes's (2009) warning that "paying low salaries can be self-defeating. After two or three years, employees leave, and agencies need to recruit and train new staff incurring significant costs" (271). This is a sentiment that the public sector has also begun to heed.

Alternative Compensation Systems

Use of the traditional compensation system in the public sector has many benefits: it is transparent, and it is less costly and time-consuming than other systems. Also, total compensation packages in the public sector often include many benefits that are not offered in the private sector. However, there are also perceived drawbacks, including the fact that salaries determined this way may not be competitive. Some posit that public employees should not receive pay increases merely because of their length of service; they believe that employees who outperform others should be duly rewarded. The classification plan, while straightforward, is also perceived by some as being too rigid and bureaucratic. As result, two alternative compensation systems—performance-based pay and broadbanding—have been promoted over the last few decades as means for bridging the pay gap, encouraging better performance, and increasing flexibility in recruitment.

Performance-Based Pay

Since the 1980s, performance-based or merit-pay schemes have been an attractive alternative to traditional compensation practices in the public sector. According to Kellough (2006, 184), the presumption is that recognizing the "superior contributions" of employees with performance-based pay averts the resentment they may feel if they receive similar pay as do less productive individuals. Additionally, the possibility of a "bonus" serves as an inducement for poor performers to improve. A number of performance-based pay schemes link individual, team, and/or organizational performance measurements to financial incentives. Financial incentives can be distributed as increases to base pay (i.e., **merit pay**), one-time bonuses, or a combination of the two

(Kellough and Nigro 2002, 146). Proponents of compensation reform suggest that performance-based pay systems, as compared to traditional pay systems that reward longevity, may increase employee performance and organizational productivity.

Performance-based pay is theoretically grounded in two theories of organizations and individuals: **expectancy theory** and **reinforcement theory**. Expectancy theory proposes that employees will exert additional effort in exchange for monetary reward. Thus, expectancy theory is tied to an individual's conviction that increased effort will result in valued results (Pearce and Perry 1983; Rainey 2009; Van Eerde and Thierry 1996). Reinforcement theory posits that the incidence of a desired behavior (e.g., job performance) is subject to its consequences (e.g., pay) (Perry Engbers, and Jun 2009, 41). Reinforcement theory therefore supports the idea that performance-based pay is a behavior-reinforcing mechanism for improved performance (Perry, Mesch, and Paarlberg 2006). Based on these theories, the expectation is that better performance will lead to the reward of increased pay and, moreover, that attaining this reward will be a positive reinforcing factor, compelling the employee to continue the improved performance so as to continue receiving the incentive.

Between 1981 and 1993, the federal government tested performance-based pay and decentralization on a system-wide basis, moving compensation decisions to the agency level (Kellough and Nigro 2002). The results of the federal experience were less than promising. Increasing antigovernment rhetoric and the failure to create a unified performance-based pay system for all jobs led to its demise. The National Research Council (NRC), under the auspices of the Office of Personnel Management (OPM), concluded that for individual incentive schemes to succeed, simplicity of the program and an atmosphere of trust are essential—neither of which were present during this failed effort, according to the council (Perry Engbers, and Jun 2009).

Yet by 2005, approximately 90,000 of the total 2.7 million federal civilian employees were covered by performance-based pay systems (Brook and King 2008, 10). How did this happen? Despite the problematic history of performance-based pay, a strong desire to rid the bureaucracy of inefficiencies proved to be a compelling enough reason to pursue alternative pay systems (Hays 2004). Hays and Sowa (2006) noted that more than half the states they surveyed were either implementing or planning some form of classification and pay reform. GeorgiaGain, the performance-based pay reform in the state of Georgia, has garnered the most attention (Kellough and Nigro 2002; 2006). While GeorgiaGain has had mixed results (see the case study in this chapter), the state has continued to rely on performance-based pay for improving employee and agency productivity.

Recently, Perry and colleagues (2009) assessed the state of research into performance-based pay. Their assessment suggested that while favorable research exists (see Milkovich and Wigdor, 1991, for an account of the NCR's report on performance-based pay), the preponderance of evidence refutes the effectiveness of performance-based pay (Ingraham 1993; Kellough and Lu 1993; Perry 1986; Perry, Mesch, and Paarlberg 2006). Perry, Engbers, and Jun (2009, 43–47) offered the following lessons for organizations considering performance-based pay:

- Performance-based pay has often failed to trigger the changes in employee behavior and motivation necessary to improve productivity.
- A variety of contextual factors (e.g., trust, adequate rewards, effective performance appraisal, and close geographic proximity) appear to moderate the effectiveness of performance-based pay systems. Especially significant is the type of public service industry involved (i.e., evidence suggests that such schemes have worked in health care fields but not in financial and regulatory sectors).
- Performance-based pay may have a greater effect at lower organizational levels, where job responsibilities are less ambiguous. This finding contradicts assumptions that contingent pay plans will be more effective at higher levels of organizations.
- Implementation breakdowns account for some failures of performance-based pay, but they are not the only reasons for failure. Institutional differences between the public and private sectors (e.g., political, legal, and value differences) may be more fundamental constraints on success. Consider them in shaping any performance-based pay approach in public organizations.
- Public service motivation theory and self-determination theory may be more applicable levers for improving performance in public agencies than expectancy and reinforcement theory.
- Do not adopt performance-based pay systems simply because everyone else is doing it. Consider your contextual contingencies and adapt your compensation strategy accordingly.

Discussed more thoroughly in Chapter 8, public service motivation theory offers a promising framework for those considering performance-based pay schemes. Public service motivation theory posits that public servants are motivated by notions of commitment, compassion, and self-sacrifice with regard to public policy and the public interest (Perry 1996; Perry and Hondeghem 2008). The theory has garnered considerable empirical support from a variety of social science disciplines (Perry and Hondeghem 2008). Motivation-based perspectives suggest that imposing performance-based pay systems on employees might actually be detrimental to performance. More nuanced research suggests that employees may feel pessimism toward performance-based pay because they react negatively to external control, not because they oppose change in general (Brehm and Gates 1997). Such negative perceptions may be exacerbated in an environment in which many HR reforms are being implemented or are anticipated. If these concerns can be addressed, performance-based pay schemes may be a viable alternative.

Broadbanding

In an effort to simplify the rigid structure of traditional job classification systems, which consist of grades and steps, many jurisdictions have implemented **broadbanding**. Broadbanding collapses multiple traditional pay grades (with relatively narrow pay ranges) into a single but broader band, giving managers greater flexibility over pay rates in hiring and promotion (Hays 2004; Whalen and Guy 2008). Broadbanding has been touted as a mechanism for promoting egalitarianism because it removes the distinctions accompanying traditional pay grades. By emphasizing compensation for employees' skills, broadbanding moves away from traditional job analysis.

Table 6.7 compares traditional within-grade step-increase pay systems with broadbanding as implemented in the state of Virginia. Virginia implemented broadbanding throughout state government in 2000 (Whalen and Guy 2008, 5). The table illustrates the flexibility afforded managers by broadbanding in contrast to more structured and confining traditional pay structures. Whereas previously, an employee entering public service at grade 6 could attain a maximum salary of $30,929, with broadbanding, she might enter at band 3 and be able to earn $40,659 while remaining in the same band. In addition, broadbanding allows for more flexibility in hiring. If an HR manager needs to fill an open position with grade 8 but can only find a very promising candidate who is qualified at grade 6, a broader set of job qualifications accompanying a band 8 position may allow the manager to hire the grade 6 employee for the job. Thus, the position is filled by someone who does not have the required qualifications on paper but who is capable of doing the job.

Research suggests, however, that states have had considerable difficulties with the implementation of broadbanding. Whalen and Guy's (2008) assessment of the status of broadbanding in the states, based on their survey of compensation reform in Florida, South Carolina, and Virginia, suggests that many managers are dubious of broadbanding's benefits. Among the issues cited in the survey are a lack of funding to pay higher salaries and performance-based pay, an inability to elicit accurate performance evaluations, a lack of guidance and direction during implementation, and additional work assignments and organizational changes (13).

Contemporary Benefits in the Public Sector

Most of this chapter's discussion has focused on pay, but each employee's total compensation package includes more than just salary. Benefits, many examples of which

Table 6.7	Comparison of Within-Grade/Step-Increase Pay Grade System with Broadbanding in Virginia (November 25, 1999)				
	Current			**New**	
	Range			**Range**	
Grades	**Minimum**	**Maximum**	**Bands**	**Minimum**	**Maximum**
1	$ 12,689	$ 19,811	1	$ 12,689	$ 26,042
2	$ 13,871	$ 21,657			
3	$ 15,164	$ 23,675			
4	$ 16,577	$ 25,881	2	$ 16,577	$ 34,021
5	$ 18,122	$ 28,292			
6	$ 19,811	$ 30,929	3	$ 19,811	$ 40,659
7	$ 21,657	$ 33,811			
8	$ 23,675	$ 36,962			
9	$ 25,881	$ 40,406	4	$ 25,881	$ 53,116
10	$ 28,292	$ 44,171			
11	$ 30,929	$ 48,287			
12	$ 33,811	$ 52,787	5	$ 33,811	$ 69,391
13	$ 36,962	$ 57,706			
14	$ 40,406	$ 63,083			
15	$ 44,171	$ 68,961	6	$ 44,171	$ 90,653
16	$ 48,287	$ 75,387			
17	$ 52,787	$ 82,412			
18	$ 57,706	$ 90,092	7	$ 57,706	$ 118,432
19	$ 63,083	$ 98,487			
20	$ 68,961	$ 107,665			
21	$ 75,387	$ 117,697	8	$ 75,387	$ 154,719
22	$ 82,412	$ 128,665			
23	$ 90,092	$ 140,654			
Over 23	No Current Range		9	$ 98,486 MARKET	

Source: State of Virginia Department of Human Resources 2000

have been mentioned, are also part of the compensation package. In public and non-profit sectors, where salaries may not be as high as those in the private sector, benefits have traditionally been more generous. Workplaces may also offer greater flexibility, perhaps affording employees the ability to telecommute or to take more vacation days. Benefits may not involve monetary payouts to employees, but they are still a cost that the government agency incurs when hiring someone. For example, health insurance premiums are typically paid to an insurance company, and generous time-off policies may require higher staffing levels to accomplish the work,

Benefit offerings in the public sector vary. Reform-minded politicians have sought to shed many of the generous public sector entitlements traditionally offered in favor of a leaner, more efficient public service. Benefit changes have also been mandated by fiscally strapped states and localities struggling to remain solvent during economic downturns. In addition, public disenchantment with government and reporting changes issued by the Governmental Accounting Standards Board (GASB) have forced jurisdictions to begin disclosing financial information regarding the amount of their unfunded pension and health care liabilities (Coggburn and Kearney 2010). **Unfunded liabilities** refer to the gap between outstanding obligations (e.g., retirement benefits) relative to funds available to pay them. For example, a local government may owe monthly retirement benefits to all of its retired employees but simply many not have enough money to make good on these promised benefits. The increased amount of unfunded liabilities resulting from the recession that began in 2008 has led to a greater demand for fiscal austerity, further taxing governments' ability to provide entitlements to citizens, such as education and Medicaid. Governments need to make hard choices about whose needs and expectations to meet.

Because generous public sector benefits have often been tapped as a recruitment tool, the erosion of traditional benefit offerings may adversely impact the ability to recruit new hires to enter the public sector workforce, as well as to promote motivation, job satisfaction, and tenure among current employees (Bergmann, Bergmann, and Grahn 1994; Center for State and Local Government Excellence 2007; Ellickson and Logsdon 2001; Roberts 2001; 2004). This is especially problematic in an era of PHRM reform that has eroded job security through deregulation, decentralization, and privatization efforts. Finally, furloughs, a recent economic necessity for some government offices, have represented one of the worst-case scenarios of working for the government—being forced to take days off work without pay.

As baby boomers retire from the public sector, positions will need to be filled. Finding the right person for the job will become increasingly difficult, as public employers will be competing with for-profit and nonprofit employers for qualified applicants with fewer traditional enticements to offer. Jurisdictions will need to be savvy in designing competitive benefit packages that emphasize the strategic goals of the agency. Such designs must consider current employee's expectations as well as what elements will attract potential applicants. Typically, public sector compensation packages include legal entitlements as well as a range of discretionary (or optional) benefits.

Legal Entitlements

Legal entitlements are benefits that an employer (public or private) is obligated to offer by law. Entitled benefits include **Social Security**, workers' compensation, and unemployment compensation. Social Security is a retirement plan administered by the federal government since 1935 (state and local jurisdictions were allowed to contribute in 1950). The Social Security fund is financed through the collection of payroll taxes. The idea is that employees contribute (pay in) to the fund as they work, through taxes, and when they retire, they will receive payments. The plan is meant to supplement discretionary retirement benefits offered by the employer (e.g., a pension or retirement savings plan) and individual retirement savings by the employee. The amount of benefits received upon retirement is determined by the amount and duration of the employee's earnings and the age at which the employee begins to collect benefits.

Social Security also provides disability, death, and survivor benefits (for widows or widowers), as well as the health insurance benefit program Medicare. The management of Social Security has been broadly criticized by those who believe the fund will run out of money as the large baby boom generation begins to retire. Also, the federal government has at times dipped into the Social Security fund to pay for things besides Social Security. This has led to proposals for privatization of the program. Privatization would entail mandating individual retirement accounts. Using these, individuals would save and invest for their own retirement instead of paying mandated taxes, which are then invested by the government (Devroye 2003, 316). The advantages of a privatized system include greater individual discretion over retirement investments and limits on the ability of government to tap Social Security for other spending (Feldstein 1998). However, with greater discretion comes greater risk; a volatile stock market could lead to rapid depreciation of one's retirement savings if such savings were not diversified (Diamond 1999).

Unlike Social Security, which is a federal program, laws governing **workers' compensation** are administered by state governments. Workers' compensation is financed by employers and provides payments to employees who are unable to work because of a job-related injury or illness. Typically, eligible employees are offered a percentage of wages lost on the job and reimbursement for medical and rehabilitation expenses.

Unemployed persons are eligible to receive **unemployment compensation** equivalent to a percentage of lost wages. To be eligible, employees must not have been terminated for misconduct, and they must be actively looking for work. Since welfare reform legislation in the 1990s, with the **Personal Responsibility and Work Opportunity Reconciliation Act (PRWORA)**, eligibility requirements have varied by state.

Discretionary Benefits

Employers also offer a variety of discretionary benefits that are not statutory entitlements. Public sector employers may offer retirement and savings options, health care plans, and a variety of fringe benefits as part of the compensation package. Employees may also be given a choice in the types of benefits they want through flexible benefit programs, also called cafeteria plans. Flexible benefit plans may be attractive to employees seeking a better value for their dollar amount; these plans allow employees to divert some of their pretax income to pay for some medical expenses, thereby lowering their taxable income and the amount of income tax they must pay.

Retirement Plans

Retirement plans in the public sector are generally of two types: defined benefit or defined contribution. Traditionally, **defined benefit plans** (pension plans) have been a staple of public sector employment, offering employees a predetermined level of retirement income determined by a formula (e.g., a percentage of the average of employee's five highest annual salaries). The benefit is funded by the government jurisdiction and possibly also the employee. Pension plans are generally operated by an independent body made up of public employees and political officials, with an administrative staff that monitors contributions and manages investments. These plans typically have detailed requirements regarding "vesting" in the program. Employees are required to work a specified number of years for the jurisdiction before they are eligible to receive retirement benefits. If they leave the employer before that specified period of time, they are not vested and they will not receive a pension upon reaching retirement age.

Unlike defined benefit plans, investment choices under **defined contribution plans** are at the discretion of the individual; money is not allocated to various investments by a pension plan manager. Also, jurisdictions are required to contribute a specific amount to the employee's account but not to pay out a specific amount upon retirement. Therefore, an employee's final retirement benefits are not predetermined as with a traditional pension or defined benefit plan, and they depend on the performance of the employee's chosen investments (e.g., stocks, bonds, etc.). Defined contribution plans are attractive to governments looking to place the burden of managing investments on employees and avoid the uncertain funding liabilities and high administrative costs of defined benefit plans (Buford and Linder 2002, 328).

Typically, employees are immediately vested in their contributions to defined contribution plans, though they often need to put in some years of service before being vested in any employer contributions. This vesting schedule makes these plans portable; that is, employees keep their retirement savings if they leave the employer.

Public sector employers increasingly offer **401(k) plans**, a specific type of defined contribution plan in which employees invest a percentage of their pretax income along with, often, a matching amount from the employer, into a financial portfolio that often includes index and mutual funds as well as individual stock investments. Along with a defined contribution plan, public sector employers may offer a variety of voluntary savings plans such as deferred compensation programs, tax-sheltered annuity programs, and Roth 403(b) plans. Such plans offer tax employees tax incentives to save for retirement (see the IRS website under "Additional Resources" at the end of this chapter for a full description of investment types).

It is important to note that there are no federal statutes regulating voluntary retirement programs in terms of disclosure, conduct, and remedial measures. While the **Employee Retirement Income Security Act of 1974 (ERISA)** protects the pension and health plans of private sector employees, no such omnibus plan exists for state and local governments.

Health and Medical Benefits

Along with retirement options, health care benefits are a significant factor in employee recruitment (Center for State and Local Government Excellence 2007). Medical benefits have typically been very generous in the public sector; in the past, employees could choose from many types of health coverage, and they typically received more comprehensive coverage than that offered in the private sector. Unfortunately, the value and variety traditionally offered is now untenable because of rising costs, longer life spans, and more retirees (Miller 2008). Many employees are presented with fewer options and must pay higher premiums. Public sector employees may have options such as traditional coverage, managed care networks, and preferred provider organizations.

Traditionally, health care coverage in the public sector allowed employees to choose their providers for a variety of diagnostic, medical, and hospitalization expenses. This type of plan often has a deductible, or an amount the covered person must pay out before the plan begins to reimburse expenses. As a practical matter, therefore, such plans to not cover routine exams and preventive tests, while they do pay for major medical expenses. They are thus suspected of discouraging employees and their families from getting care before medical situations become severe and of encouraging unnecessary procedures; both effects contribute to rising health care costs (Buford and Lindner 2002; Cayer and Volk 2004).

Eventually, managed care programs, operated through **health maintenance organizations (HMOs)** and **preferred provider organizations (PPOs)**, have been implemented as alternatives to traditional programs. While the expenses associated with HMOs and PPOs tend to increase over time, the rate of increase is much less than for traditional programs (Cayer and Volk 2004, 155). Employers contract with HMOs and PPOs for specified health care coverage, allowing employees to choose among designated managed care networks (HMOs) or physicians contracted with the PPO. Whereas under traditional coverage, an employee could see any doctor, under a PPO, an employee generally must pay more to see a physician who is not a preferred provider. HMOs, on the other hand, limit care options to those medical professionals under contract to the managed care organization. Where PPO participants might pay somewhat more or have to pay up front and then be reimbursed for out-of-network coverage, an HMO participant may not have such an option.

Two important pieces of federal legislation regulate the specifics of health care benefits for public and private employees. The **Consolidated Omnibus Budget Reconciliation Act of 1985 (COBRA)** provides employees with the right, under certain circumstances and for specified periods of time, to continue health care coverage on their employer's plan when it would normally end. Qualifying events include (1) voluntary or involuntary termination of employment for reasons other than gross misconduct; (2) reduction in the number of hours of employment; (3) for spouses and dependent children, the covered employee becoming entitled to Medicare; (4) for spouses and dependent children, divorce or legal separation of the covered employee; (5) for spouses and dependent children, death of the covered employee; and (6) for dependent children only, loss of dependent child status under the plan rules (DOL 2013b). Additionally, the **Health Insurance Portability and Accountability Act of 1996 (HIPPA)** authorizes the Department of Labor to regulate employers, insurers, and health care providers with respect to the coordination of benefit changes, and it requires the maintenance of confidentiality of health information contained in employee records.

On March 23, 2010, President Barack Obama signed into law **The Patient Protection and Affordable Care Act (PPACA)**, the most significant reform of the US health care system in decades. Not since the enactment of Medicaid by the administration of President Lyndon Johnson had the federal government embarked on such an ambitious intervention in the health care market. The purpose of the Affordable Care Act, commonly known as "Obamacare," was to improve the availability and cost of health care in the United States through the expanded offering of public and private insurance coverage. Mandates set by the Affordable Care Act require insurance companies to offer coverage to all applicants, regardless of preexisting conditions. Also, all citizens are required to have health insurance; to make this feasible for lower-income people, subsidies are provided. The law is aimed at increasing competition in the insurance market as a means for lowering costs and improving health care. According to the Congressional Budget Office (CBO), the Affordable Care Act is projected to reduce budget deficits by an estimated $1,383 billion (net) over a 10-year period (2015–2024), including by bringing in $503 billion in revenues, mostly from new taxes and fees, and by saving $792 billion in outlays for Medicare and other federal health care programs (CBO 2014, 3). Elements of the Affordable Care Act that have proven controversial are the individual mandates, subsidies, and sometimes poor functioning of the insurance exchanges (online marketplaces where people can buy insurance). While the tenets of the bill continue to be challenged, the US Supreme Court upheld the individual mandate under Congress's power to tax in *National Federation of Independent Business v. Sebelius* (2012).

Additional Offerings

Employees in the public sector enjoy a variety of additional benefit offerings, including sick leave, paid vacation, federal holidays, and payment for time not worked. Time in service to the employer generally determines the amount of vacation and sick leave one may accrue. While some jurisdictions might offer unlimited accrual of leave, generally restrictions are imposed on the amount of leave available to employees. For example, an employer may set six weeks as the maximum amount of leave an employee can accrue; any accruals above that amount are simply lost. Upon separation or retirement, the employee is typically eligible to receive a monetary payout for any accumulated leave. Employers need to consider the costs of such offerings in addition to the impact that absence from employment may have on performance; managers should also be prudent in administering paid time off to check potential abuses. Clearly defining each type of leave offered and when it will and will not be approved, along with disciplinary action for abuses, is essential to ensure accountability and performance. Many governments also offer alternative work schedules; for example, employees might be allowed to work an additional hour a day but take every other Friday off.

Many jurisdictions offer tuition reimbursement for coursework applicable to the agency's mission. Often employees who take advantage of such programs must stay employed with the organization for a specified period of time after completing their education. In addition to reimbursing tuition, some jurisdictions may cover additional costs (e.g., books, software, parking) incurred while in school.

Increased attention to balancing family and work life has also prompted jurisdictions to offer a variety of care programs for children and the elderly. Although not specifically covered by the FMLA, child care (e.g., a day care center at the office), elder care, and long-term care for disabled family members are often seen as potential recruiting and retention tools (Caillier 2012; French and Goodman 2012).

Pay and Benefits in an Era of PHRM Reform

The contemporary pay and benefits environment is anything but simple. The increasing complexity of managing pay and benefits in the public sector is a product of political reform and economic stress. To meet the challenges, public HR managers are opting for more novel pay schemes (such as performance-based pay and broadbanding) and are reducing or eliminating many benefits entirely. So, what can public HR managers take away from this chapter? With respect to pay, linking compensation to performance is still a popular theme: despite the dubious ties between pay and performance in the public sector, governments at all levels continue to turn to such mechanisms because they offer managers flexibility and may induce employees to be more productive. Given the complex nature of performance measurement in the public sector, HR managers would be wise to implement performance-based pay systems only after careful consideration of situational factors. Testing a new compensation plan as a demonstration project, to study its real-world outcomes and identify any problems, rather than implementing straightaway a system-wide overhaul will at the least save taxpayers money that would be wasted on a program that does not work as expected. Testing a new plan will also help management avoid widespread negative effects on morale, retention, and recruitment. Finally, such experimentation may lead to better metrics and management practices for performance-based pay in the public sector.

With regard to benefits, the erosion of this traditional recruitment tool for public sector employers is problematic. To be sure, cash-strapped governments often have very little choice but to cap generous benefits packages. However, considering the erosion of job security—another draw for public employers—through deregulation schemes such as employment at will, governments risk further undermining their ability to recruit and retain a qualified workforce by eliminating traditional benefits.

Conclusion

In a 2006 survey of Georgia state HR professionals, nearly 78 percent of those surveyed expressed uncertainty with regard to job security in a deregulated, employment-at-will environment (Battaglio and Condrey 2009). Job security has been positively linked to employee productivity and commitment to the organization (Coyle-Shapiro and Kessler 2003; Gossett 2003; Green et al. 2006; Hays and Sowa 2006; Hindera and Josephson 1998; Lewis and Frank 2002; Radin and Werhane 1996; Schwoerer and Rosen 1989). Public sector reformers, eager to tap into private sector know-how, have promised better pay, leave, and other benefits in exchange for the uncertainty of the EAW environment (Bowman and West 2006). A failure to follow through on promises of better pay and benefits may prove problematic for long-term recruitment efforts and overall organizational performance.

Continued use of compensation reform—like performance-based pay and broadbanding—should take into account the potential pitfalls of trading traditional public service incentives for private sector practices. Research (Ritter, Maranto, and

Buck 2009) suggests that while such pay schemes have the potential to improve public sector performance, consideration must be given to public value. In particular, the authors suggest establishing transparency, ease of measurement, and control of personnel (264) as preconditions for the implement of compensation reform. Ultimately, HR managers considering compensation strategies should give deference to the individual rights of employees in any efficiency calculations. A robust research agenda awaits scholars interested in developing a more empirically grounded theory of public service motivation and performance. This agenda includes the relationship between performance and base pay, the value of group incentives, and the elements and context of successful programs.

References

Albert, Sheila. 2000. *Hiring the Chief Executive: A Practical Guide to the Search and Selection Process,* rev. ed. Washington, DC: National Center for Nonprofit Boards.

Battaglio, R. Paul Jr., and Stephen E. Condrey. 2009. "Reforming Public Management: Analyzing the Impact of Public Service Reform on Organizational and Managerial Trust." *Journal of Public Administration Research & Theory* 19:689–707.

Belman, Dale, and John S. Heywood. 1988. "Public Wage Differentials and the Public Administration 'Industry.'" *Industrial Relations: A Journal of Economy and Society* 27:385–93.

Belman, Dale, and John S. Heywood. 1995. "State and Local Government Wage Differentials: An Intrastate Analysis." *Journal of Labor Research* 16:187–201.

Belman, Dale, John S. Heywood, and John Lund. 1997. "Public Sector Earnings and the Extent of Unionization." *Industrial and Labor Relations Review* 50:610–28.

Bergmann, Thomas J., Marilyn A. Bergmann, and Joyce L. Grahn. 1994. "How Important Are Employee Benefits to Public Sector Employees?" *Public Personnel Management* 23:397–406.

Borjas, George J. 2003. "Wage Structures and the Sorting of Workers in the Public Sector." In *For the People: Can We Fix Public Service?* edited by John D. Donahue and Joseph S. Nye, 29–54. Cambridge, MA, and Washington, DC: Brookings Institution Press.

Bowman, James S., and Jonathan P. West. 2006. "Ending Civil Service Protections in Florida Government: Experiences in State Agencies." *Review of Public Personnel Administration* 26:139–57.

Brehm, John, and Scott Gates. 1997. *Working, Shirking, and Sabotage: Bureaucratic Response to a Democratic Public.* Ann Arbor: University of Michigan Press.

Brook, Douglas A., and Cynthia L. King. 2008. "Federal Personnel Management Reform: From Civil Service Reform Act to National Security Reforms." *Review of Public Personnel Administration* 28:205–21.

Budd, John W. 2004. "Non-wage Forms of Compensation." *Journal of Labor Research* 25:597–622.

Buford, James A., and James R. Lindner. 2002. *Human Resource Management in Local Government: Concepts and Applications for HRM Students and Practitioners.* Cincinnati, OH: South-Western.

Cailler, James Gerard. 2012. "Satisfaction with Work-Life Benefits and Organizational Commitment/Job Involvement: Is There a Connection?" *Review of Public Personnel Administration.* http://rop.sagepub.com/content/early/2012/05/04/0734371X12443266.full.pdf+html.

Cayer, N. Joseph, and Will Volk. 2004. "Employee Benefits: Creating an Environment of Excellence." In *Human Resource Management in Local Government: An Essential Guide,* edited by Siegrun Fox Freyss, 153–78. Washington, DC: International City/Council Management Association.

Center for State and Local Government Excellence. 2007. *Data Report: Security; What Americans Want from a Job.* Washington, DC: Center for State and Local Government Excellence.

Charity Navigator. 2012. *2012 CEO Compensation Study.* http://www.charitynavigator.org/__asset__/studies/2012_CEO_Compensation_Study_Final.pdf.

Coggburn, Jerrell D., and Richard C. Kearney. 2010. "Trouble Keeping Promises? An Analysis of Underfunding in State Retiree Benefits." *Public Administration Review* 70:97–108.

Congressional Budget Office (CBO). 2014. "Insurance Coverage Provisions of the Affordable Care Act—CBO's April 2014 Baseline." http://www.cbo.gov/sites/default/files/cbofiles/attachments/43900-2014-04-ACAtables2.pdf.

Coyle-Shapiro, Jacqueline A.-M., and Ian Kessler. 2003. "The Employment Relationship in the UK Public Sector: A Psychological Contract Perspective." *Journal of Public Administration Research and Theory* 13:213–30.

Devroye, Dan. 2003. "Who Wants to Privatize Social Security? Understanding Why the Poor Are Wary of Private Accounts." *Public Administration Review* 63:316–28.

Diamond, Peter A., ed. 1999. *Issues in Privatizing Social Security: Report of an Expert Panel of the National Academy of Social Insurance.* Cambridge, MA: MIT Press.

Ellickson, Mark C., and Kay Logsdon. 2001. "Determinants of Job Satisfaction of Municipal Government Employees." *State and Local Government Review* 33:173–84.

Feldstein, Martin, ed. 1998. *Privatizing Social Security.* Chicago: University of Chicago Press.

French, P. Edward. 2009. "Employment Laws and the Public Sector Employer: Lessons to Be Learned from a Review of Lawsuits Filed Against Local Governments." *Public Administration Review* 69:92–103.

French, P. Edward, and Doug Goodman. 2012. "An Assessment of the Current and Future State of Human Resource Management at the Local Government Level." *Review of Public Personnel Administration* 32:62–74.

Frumkin, Peter, and Elizabeth K. Keating. 2010. "The Price of Doing Good: Executive Compensation in Nonprofit Organizations." *Policy and Society* 29:269–82.

Garcia v. San Antonio Metropolitan Transit Authority, 469 U.S. 528 (1985).

Gossett, Charles W. 2003. "The Changing Face of Georgia's Merit System: Results from an Employee Attitude Survey in the Georgia Department of Juvenile Justice." *Public Personnel Management* 32:267–78.

Green, Richard, Robert Forbis, Anne Golden, Stephen L. Nelson, and Jennifer Robinson. 2006. "On the Ethics of At-Will Employment in the Public Sector." *Public Integrity* 8:305–27.

Hays, Steven W. 2004. "Trends and Best Practices in State and Local Human Resource Management Lessons to Be Learned?" *Review of Public Personnel Administration* 24:256–75.

Hays, Steven W., and Jessica E. Sowa. 2006. "A Broader Look at the 'Accountability' Movement: Some Grim Realities in State Civil Service Systems." *Review of Public Personnel Administration* 26:102–17.

Hindera, John L., and Jyl J. Josephson. 1998. "Reinventing the Public Employer-Employee Relationship: The Just Cause Standard." *Public Administration Quarterly* 22:98–113.

Ingraham, Patricia W. 1993. "Of Pigs in Pokes and Policy Diffusion: Another Look at Pay-for-Performance." *Public Administration Review* 53:348–56.

Kellough, J. Edward. 2006. "Employee Performance Appraisal in the Public Sector." In *Public Personnel Management*, edited by Norma M. Riccucci, 177–89. New York: Longman.

Kellough, J. Edward, and Haoran Lu. 1993. "The Paradox of Merit Pay in the Public Sector: Persistence of a Problematic Procedure." *Review of Public Personnel Administration* 13:45–64.

Kellough, J. Edward, and Lloyd G. Nigro. 2002. "Pay for Performance in Georgia State Government: Employee Perspectives on GeorgiaGain After 5 Years." *Review of Public Personnel Administration* 22:146–66.

Kellough, J. Edward and Lloyd G. Nigro. 2006. "Dramatic Reform in the Public Service: At-Will Employment and the Creation of a New Public Workforce." *Journal of Public Administration Research and Theory* 16:447–66.

Lee, Soo-Young, and Andrew B. Whitford. 2008. "Exit, Voice, Loyalty, and Pay: Evidence from the Public Workforce." *Journal of Public Administration Research and Theory* 18:647–71.

Lewis, Gregory B., and Sue A. Frank. 2002. "Who Wants to Work for the Government?" *Public Administration Review* 62:395–404.

Llorens, Jared J. 2008. "Uncovering the Determinants of Competitive State Government Wages." *Review of Public Personnel Administration* 28:308–26.

Milkovich, George T., and Alexandra K. Wigdor. 1991. *Pay for Performance: Evaluating Performance Appraisal and Merit Pay.* Washington, DC: National Academy Press.

Miller, Gerard. 2008. "OPEB Deficits: Where Are the Rating Agencies?" http://www.governing.com (no longer available online).

Miller, Michael A. 1996. "The Public Private Pay Debate: What Do the Data Show?" *Monthly Labor Review* 119:18–29.

Monell v. Department of Social Services of the State of New York, 436 U.S. 658 (1978).

Moynihan, Donald P., and Noel Landuyt. 2008. "Explaining Turnover Intention in State Government Examining the Roles of Gender, Life Cycle, and Loyalty." *Review of Public Personnel Administration* 28:120–43.

National Federation of Independent Business v. Sebelius 132 S.Ct 2566 (2012).

Nigro, Lloyd G., and J. Edward Kellough. 2008. "Personnel Reform in the States: A Look at Progress Fifteen Years after the Winter Commission." *Public Administration Review* 68:S50–S57.

Pearce, Jone L., and James L. Perry. 1983. "Federal Merit Pay: A Longitudinal Analysis." *Public Administration Review* 43:315–25.

Perry, James L. 1986. "Merit Pay in the Public Sector: The Case for a Failure of Theory." *Review of Public Personnel Administration* 7:57–69.

Perry, James L. 1996. "Measuring Public Service Motivation: An Assessment of Construct Reliability and Validity." *Journal of Public Administration Research and Theory* 6:5–22.

Perry, James L., Trent A. Engbers, and So Yun Jun. 2009. "Back to the Future? Performance-Related Pay, Empirical Research, and the Perils of Persistence." *Public Administration Review* 69:39–51.

Perry, James L., and Annie Hondeghem. 2008. *Motivation in Public Management: The Call of Public Service.* Oxford, England: Oxford University Press.

Perry, James L., Debra Mesch, and Laurie Paarlberg. 2006. "Motivating Employees in a New Governance Era: The Performance Paradigm Revisited." *Public Administration Review* 66:505–14.

Personal Responsibility and Work Opportunity Reconciliation Act (PRWORA). 1996. Pub. L. 104-193, 110 Stat. 2105.

Pynes, Joan E. 2009. *Human Resources Management for Public and Nonprofit Organizations.* 3rd ed. San Francisco, CA: Jossey-Bass.

Radin, Tara J., and Patricia H. Werhane. 1996. "The Public/Private Distinction and the Political Status of Employment." *American Business Law Journal* 34:245–60.

Rainey, Hal G. 2006. "Reform Trends at the Federal Level with Implications for the States: The Pursuit of Flexibility and the Human Capital Movement." In *Civil Service Reform in the States: Personnel Policy and Politics at the Subnational Level,* edited by J. Edward Kellough and Lloyd G. Nigro, 33–58. Albany: SUNY Press.

Rainey, Hal G. 2009. *Understanding and Managing Public Organizations.* 4th ed. San Francisco, CA: Jossey-Bass.

Rexrode, Christine. 2013. "Median CEO Pay Rises to $9.7 million in 2012." *The Huffington Post,* May 22. http://www.huffingtonpost.com/2013/05/22/ceo-pay-2012_n_3319508.html.

Ritter, Gary W., Robert Maranto, and Stuart Buck. 2009. "Harnessing Private Incentives in Public Education." *Review of Public Personnel Administration* 29:249–69.

Roberts, Gary E. 2001. "New Jersey Local Government Benefits Practices Survey." *Review of Public Personnel Administration* 21:284–307.

Roberts, Gary E. 2004. "Municipal Government Benefits Practices and Personnel Outcomes: Results from a National Survey." *Public Personnel Management* 33:1–22.

Schwoerer, Catherine, and Benson Rosen. 1989. "Effects of Employment-At-Will Policies and Compensation Policies on Corporate Image and Job Pursuit Intentions." *Journal of Applied Psychology* 74:653–56.

Selden, Sally Coleman. 2009. *Human Capital: Tools and Strategies for the Public Sector.* Washington, DC: CQ Press.

Smith, Sharon P. 1976. "Government Wage Differentials by Sex." *Journal of Human Resources* 11:185–99.

Smith, Sharon P. 1977. "Government Wage Differentials." *Journal of Urban Economics* 4:248–71.

State of Virginia Department of Human Resources. 2000. "Comparison of Current Pay Grades with New Pay Bands." http://www.dhrm.virginia.gov/compreform/grade_band_comparison .pdf.

Stene, Edwin O. 1980. *Selecting a Professional Administrator: A Guide for Municipal Councils.* 2nd ed. Washington, DC: International City Managers Association.

Tompkins, Jonathan, and Aleksandra Stapczynski. 2004. "Planning and Paying for Work Done." In *Human Resource Management in Local Government: An Essential Guide,* 2nd ed., edited by Siegrun Fox Freyss, 1–32. Washington, DC: International City/Council Management Association.

US Department of Labor (DOL), Wage and Hour Division. 2013a. *Family and Medical Leave Act.* http://www.dol.gov/whd/fmla/.

US Department of Labor (DOL). 2013b. *Frequently Asked Questions: COBRA Continuation Health Coverage.* http://www.dol.gov/ebsa/faqs/faq_compliance_cobra.html.

US Office of Personnel Management (OPM). 2012. "Executive Order 13655: Adjustments of Certain Rates of Pay." Schedule 1. http://www.opm.gov/policy-data-oversight/pay-leave/ salaries-wages/pay-executive-order-2014-adjustments-of-certain-rates-of-pay.pdf.

Van Eerde, Wendelien, and Henk Thierry. 1996. "Vroom's Expectancy Models and Work-Related Criteria: A Meta-Analysis," *Journal of Applied Psychology* 81:575–86.

Waters, Rollie O., and Joyce C. Powell. 2010. "Salaries of Municipal Officials, 2009." In *The Municipal Year Book 2010.* Washington, DC: International City/County Management Association.

Whalen, Cortney, and Mary E. Guy. 2008. "Broadbanding Trends in the States." *Review of Public Personnel Administration* 28:349–66.

Ziegler, Sara L. 2006. "Litigating Equality: The Limits of the Equal Pay Act." *Review of Public Personnel Administration* 26:199–215.

Additional Resources

Governmental Accounting Standards Board—http://www.gasb.org

Internal Revenue Service (IRS), Tax Topic Index—http://www.irs.gov/taxtopics/ (Includes descriptions of retirement plans such as 401(k)s and Roth IRAs.)

US Office of Personnel Management (OPM)—http://www.opm.gov

Washington State Human Resources—http://www.dop.wa.gov (See the salary survey for an in-depth analysis.)

Case 6.1   Rhode Island's Bid for Performance-Based Compensation Reform

In 2012, the state of Rhode Island embarked on an ambitious bid to overhaul the state's personnel system. The economic downturn that started in 2008 had taken a toll on the state's fiscal health. During these fiscally lean years, the Rhode Island government passed a number of stopgap measures, including across-the-board budget cuts, layoffs, elimination of longevity pay, and pension and benefits reform (Segal Group 2013). However, these measures were only temporary fixes; the state sought more comprehensive measures to streamline the personnel system and become more efficient. The state Department of Administration (DOA), reporting to the governor of Rhode Island, is tasked with managing the "state's financial, human and other resources in support of other state agencies carrying out their responsibilities to provide the citizens of the State of Rhode Island with the most responsive and cost effective services possible" (State of Rhode Island n.d.). To this end, the Rhode Island DOA has spearheaded the mandate for personnel reform.

An initial bid for a comprehensive review of the state personnel system was awarded to The Segal Group, a for-profit benefits, compensation, and human resources consulting firm based in New York. Its assessment concluded that the "State's current human resources structures, policies, and processes place a great burden on State agencies' ability to recruit, retain, motivate, and reward the kind of workforce needed to achieve their missions" (Segal Group 2013, 2). The Segal Group noted the following as being of particular concern:

- The structure, organization, and staffing of the state's Human Resources division was not sufficient to support the state's human capital needs.

- The current recruitment and selection processes were highly paper based, with outdated and cumbersome procedures often causing delays and impeding hiring managers' ability to hire qualified candidates.
- The job classification structure and job descriptions did not reflect the skills and qualifications required to deliver 21st-century government services.
- The compensation structures and pay delivery policies were non-competitive, rigid, and insufficient to attract and retain skilled employees (5).

With respect to the last item, reforms have focused on creating a more performance-based pay system. To this end, the DOA solicited bids from prospective vendors for the job of overhauling the state's classification and compensation system. Below is the DOA's request for proposals (State of Rhode Island 2013, 4):

> The Rhode Island Department of Administration (DOA) is requesting proposals for a vendor to work directly with the Director of Human Resources, to redesign the State's classification and compensation systems for the Executive Branch of state government, and to develop a communications plan to distribute this information to State employees, collective bargaining units and other stakeholders.
>
> The four goals of the work are:
>
> - To increase the State's ability to attract and maintain a high quality workforce;
> - To increase flexibility within the classification and compensation systems;
> - To increase human resources system efficiency and effectiveness; and
> - To provide the State with a system that is easy for all "stakeholders" to understand (RFP #7536366 2013).

Based on your assessment of the contemporary pay and benefits environment, answer the following questions regarding the Rhode Island call for reform. Background materials are available online; see "Sources" below.

Discussion Questions

1. RFP #7536366 includes a number of guidelines for bidders seeking the contract to redesign the compensation system (see pages 7–8 of the RFP), including specific key components that the successful bidder would need to manage. If you were a potential bidder, what might you include in your proposal that would address the concerns listed in point 3 to ensure internal and external equity?

2. Suppose your bid includes the development of a performance-based pay system for the state of Rhode Island. What elements might you include in such a compensation system?

3. If you were working in the Rhode Island Governor's Office or the state's Department of Administration, what criteria would you use to evaluate the RFPs submitted by bidders?

4. The last goal of the RFP asks bidders to make the document accessible to state "stakeholders." With respect to pay and benefits, who are the potential "stakeholders" in the state of Rhode Island?

Sources

Segal Group. 2013. "State of Rhode Island Comprehensive Personnel Study: Final Report of Detailed Findings, January." http://www.governor.ri.gov/personnel/012613study.pdf.

State of Rhode Island. n.d. "Department of Administration (DOA): Mission." Accessed January 27, 2014. http://www.admin.ri.gov.

State of Rhode Island. 2013. "Request for Proposals (RFP) #7536366, State Classification and Compensation System Redesign." November 8. https://s3.amazonaws.com/s3.doc umentcloud.org/documents/894635/7536366-rfp.pdf.

Exercises

1. The mayor of a local municipality is considering implementing a performance-based pay system in order to increase productivity in the workplace. What advice would you give the mayor regarding performance-based pay? Apply concepts and information from this chapter.

2. A municipality is in the midst of a financial crisis due to an economic downturn. As a remedial measure, the city is considering making drastic changes to the compensation and benefits packages offered to its employees. The city has hired you as a consultant to coordinate the process. What benefits, if any, would you suggest the city cut from its compensation package? What are the potential repercussions of offering a more limited compensation package? Are there any legal issues to consider?

3. The human resource director of a municipality is interested in reviewing that city's employee compensation. The city has asked you, as an expert in human resources, to construct a salary survey to assess pay levels in the relevant labor market. What items would you include in such a survey? Would you survey employees in private, nonprofit, and other public sectors? Why or why not? Would you include specific occupations in the survey? Why or why not? Once the survey data are compiled, what information might the HR director impart to employees, managers, and politicians, respectively?

7

Performance Appraisal

LEARNING OBJECTIVES

Upon completion of the chapter, you will be able to do the following:

- Explain the objectives of performance appraisal.
- Design effective appraisal tools.
- Apply behavior-based and outcome-based techniques to performance assessment.
- Explain alternatives to traditional performance appraisal.
- Discuss the appropriate use of assessment centers.
- Discuss the appropriate use of multisource appraisal.
- Describe sources of bias and error in the appraisal process.
- Explain the evidence-based linkages between performance-based pay and performance appraisal.

Public human resource management (PHRM) reform efforts over the past few decades have aimed to improve the efficiency of the public service. To this end, many reforms have retooled the performance appraisal process in the public sector, the means by which employees and, in turn, the organization are evaluated on overall productivity. While being performance oriented is surely a good thing, assessing performance in the public sector is no easy task. Unlike the "bottom lines" of profits and market share in the private sector, the various goals and objectives of public sector agencies are often not easily measured. Public sector agencies are often eager to pursue goals such as social equity, equality, and diversity—goals that are not always as easy to assess as dollar amounts. The difficult tasks of measuring and monitoring individual performance are often in the hands of HR managers. This chapter will outline the various methods used in performance appraisal, assess recent efforts aimed at improving performance appraisal in the public service, and offer insight into how HR managers might utilize such efforts.

Performance Appraisal: Purpose and Process

Accurately defining the performance appraisal process is critical to achieving organizational missions and objectives. Determining which performance appraisal is appropriate for the type of organization and the work being done depends on the objectives of management and employees alike and what messages agencies wish to send regarding how HR recognizes, rewards, and develops employees. Management and employees have distinct purposes for performance appraisal. The specific set of criteria for performance appraisal should align with management's priorities as outlined in the organization's mission or vision statement. Linking agency objectives to employees' job outcomes is fundamental not only to effective performance appraisal but also to successful strategic planning, which we will discuss in Chapter 12.

Performance appraisal serves two crucial functions in any organization: employee evaluation and performance feedback. Evaluating employees is necessary so that HR managers can fulfill some of their key job functions such as deciding whom to promote, transfer, and terminate and determining pay levels (Schermerhorn, Hunt, and Osborn 2004). For management, evaluation decisions communicate to employees the goals key to organizational success. By evaluating employee performance, management is seeking to motivate employees to accomplish mission-critical objectives. Clearly outlining evaluation criteria also establishes how rewards are to be distributed. It is important that pay increases be based on equitable standards that explicitly outline how they are determined so that employees are aware of the standards they should adhere to. With respect to promotion, performance appraisal also serves as a tool to identify potential leaders of the organization, a task integral to succession planning and strategic HR management. Management can also use the metrics from performance appraisal to conduct research; analyzing performance appraisal metrics provides management with the ability to accurately track over time whether or not it is using criteria that are both critical and relevant to good job performance.

From the perspective of the employee, it is important that evaluation be conducted in a manner that adheres to the requirements of Title VII of the Civil Rights Act of 1964—a key component of public sector employment. Recall from our discussion in Chapter 5 of recruitment and selection that employers must validate HR techniques that impact employment decisions. Thus, adequate and timely job analysis is critical to the success of performance appraisal.

Performance feedback—the second function of performance appraisal—is important for ensuring the organization's priorities are met. Performance appraisal provides feedback to employees regarding organizational expectations. Feedback affords supervisors the opportunity to have one-on-one exchanges with their subordinates to clarify their evaluations and to provide additional guidance. During these two-way conversations, employee feedback may inform adjustments to agency objectives. Feedback also draws employees' attention to areas in which their performance could be improved, as well as whether they are fulfilling their job responsibilities. To this end, feedback can be useful for identifying opportunities for developing employee skills. Development opportunities, such as work improvement plans (WIPs), are important so that employees can continue to improve their performance; development may also be helpful in preparing future leaders for managerial positions.

Ultimately, public HR professionals should keep in mind the following when developing performance appraisals:

- Specificity is integral to linking job criteria with performance metrics. The clearer performance expectations are, the more informed employees will be regarding their job duties and responsibilities.
- Performance appraisal is a powerful communication tool. Evaluation conveys to employees managerial beliefs about what work behaviors, skills, and attitudes will lead to quality outcomes.
- Performance appraisal plays an important part in documenting performance; such documentation may be necessary to support disciplinary measures and terminations.
- Performance appraisal allows management to distinguish high performers and underperformers from other employees and thereby make compensation, promotion, and termination decisions appropriately.
- Development is an important outcome of performance appraisal. Feedback from performance appraisal serves to identify skill deficiencies and modify dysfunctional work behavior.

In a public sector increasingly oriented toward improving productivity, performance appraisal is an indispensable tool. Using the most appropriate evaluation instrument for the work culture and the jobs being done allows management to accurately measure performance. Traditionally, performance evaluation has had a short-term focus, but the current emphasis on strategic HR management has prompted a need for more future-oriented evaluation methods. As we will see, such methods are not always easily identifiable in the public sector workplace, where priorities include not only efficiency but also constitutional concerns of equity. Moreover, a comprehensive appraisal process can be costly and time-consuming; HR managers need to weigh the merits of appraisal methods with cost and time considerations.

Criteria Used in Performance Appraisals

Given the move toward performance management in the public sector, the approach to performance appraisal has changed over the past few decades (Kellough 2006).

Decentralization efforts have sought to transfer responsibility for the performance appraisal process from a central personnel office to middle managers and line managers. This shift is thought to better reflect the productivity aims of managers as opposed to the rule-enforcing goals of traditional HR practice. Likewise, performance appraisal is an indispensable tool for performance-based pay, which seeks to align individual productivity with agency performance and reward productive behavior. Traditionally, performance appraisals in the public sector consisted of written reports prepared by the supervisor and described the employee's performance over a specific period (typically one year) (Shafritz et al. 2001). These traditional reports tended to include the following:

- An outline of specific duties and responsibilities
- Previously agreed-upon objectives or results to be produced by the employee over the specified time period
- Rating scales used to evaluate specific performance factors
- Supervisor's written narrative describing specific work accomplishments
- Supervisor's written report about or rating of the employee's potential for advancement
- Supervisor's overall score of the employee's performance (274).

However, the written approach has proven to be problematic, especially for supervisors and public HR managers seeking more objective approaches to performance appraisal. Composing a paragraph that simply explains the employee's performance over the previous year lacks the objective, quantifiable rigor necessary for making performance evaluations meaningful. Oftentimes, written evaluations tend to be vague and do not provide objective measures of outcomes (Shafritz et al. 2001). In particular, managers find it difficult to compare often contradictory written statements over the course of an employee's career. Moreover, the traditional approach's focus on the supervisor's observations and opinions may exclude insightful input from an employee's peers, or even the employee's self-assessment.

Therefore, the traditional approach has tended to fall out of favor among public HR professionals seeking a wider array of more objective criteria for assessing employee performance (Buford and Lindner 2002; French and Goodman 2012; Kellough 2006; Shafritz et al. 2001). Public HR managers now use written reports buttressed by a variety of criteria that are trait based, behavioral based, and/or performance based. Ideally, public HR managers would use a performance method that can be standardized across agencies to facilitate comparative evaluation. While many performance appraisals have generalizable metrics (e.g., key competencies), other sections of the evaluation typically have more department-specific criteria (e.g., development plans). As we shall see, developing a comprehensive appraisal process is no easy task—especially in the public sector where multiple goals exist. The process entails a great deal of trial and error, and methods may change as evaluation objectives change.

Trait-Based Criteria

Trait-based criteria focus on specific traits or personal attributes presumed necessary for performance. Traits such as dependability, cooperativeness, honesty, and diligence are assumed to be positively associated with job performance (Buford and Lindner 2002; Kellough 2006). The advantage of including trait-based criteria as a basis for evaluation is that evaluating them is usually easy and inexpensive. Traits such as dependability, cooperativeness, honesty, and diligence are universally acceptable and desirable, making it easy for HR managers and employees to agree upon their importance. As a result, trait-based criteria are widely used in performance appraisal methods across the public sector.

Unfortunately, the disadvantages of trait-based criteria are compelling, especially when they are used as the sole means for evaluating employees. The link between particular traits and job performance is sometimes tenuous (Caroll and Schneider 1982; Tompkins 1995). Just because an employee is honest does not necessarily mean that he or she will be productive; honesty may have little to do with the job. Moreover, such links may be subjective, as supervisors managing employees in the same position or at the same level might differ on the traits they associate with effective performance. In addition, many employees may view trait-based criteria as merely a personality test predicated upon their relationship with the supervisor (Clifford 1999). Therefore, when considering the use of trait-based criteria, public HR managers must evaluate the job-relatedness of the personal characteristics. For managerial or leadership positions, for example, trait-based criteria might be suitable (Buford and Lindner 2002, 248); we often look for leaders to be outgoing and gregarious. The usefulness of trait-based criteria is also limited by their ability to identify employee training and development needs. To provide individuals with a plan for developing skills and behaviors that might improve their job productivity, HR managers must use behavior-based and outcome-based criteria (Kellough 2006, 180).

Behavior-Based Criteria

Proponents of behavior-based criteria suggest that certain behaviors are conducive—or detrimental—to good job performance. Acceptable behaviors include timely completion of required paperwork or reports; efforts to assist co-workers; respectful, courteous, timely, and tactful interaction with agency stakeholders; and tolerance of direction and feedback from supervisors (Kellough 2006, 179).

Productive behaviors are more easily observable than traits, and such behaviors are likely to apply to more than one position within the organization (Kellough 2006; Shafritz et al. 2001). Thus, from the HR manager's standpoint, templates for behavior-based performance appraisal are more easily developed across job types, allowing for comparisons across the organization. Behavior-based rating instruments tend to incorporate **behaviorally anchored rating scales (BARS)** such as those reviewed in Figure 7.3. Incorporating elements of traditional appraisal methodology, BARS forces HR managers to judge employee behaviors as poor, moderate, or good and explain in a narrative statement how the employee exhibited such behaviors. Only an up-to-date job analysis can ensure that the measurable behaviors (or knowledge, skills, and abilities) most related to the duties of the position are included.

Unfortunately, documenting examples of productive behavior is not the same as measuring desirable outcomes of behavior. For example, behaviors that demonstrate courtesy and tact are not the same as political behaviors such as shrewdness—a skill necessary for navigating the public policy process. In other words, demonstrating all the "right" behaviors does not necessarily carry over to winning political support for a policy or successfully completing a project in a timely and cost-effective manner. Thus, like trait-based performance evaluation, behavior-based appraisal does not necessarily measure job performance.

Outcome-Based Criteria

Trait- and behavior-based criteria may have their place in the appraisal process, but public HR managers are keenly interested in using quantifiable, measurable work outcomes as a means for assessing individual job performance (i.e., Did the employee achieve his or her goals?). Such criteria can also be usefully applied to assessing the overall success or failure of an agency, since they provide concrete measures of performance. Systematic job analysis identifies the appropriate behavioral criteria for measuring worker production (Kellough 2006). As with trait- and beahvior-based appraisal methods, job analysis is essential to effective outcome-based performance appraisal.

Outcome-based measures might include rates of production (e.g., number of forms completed, cases closed, customers served) or customer satisfaction survey results (Battaglio and Legge 2009; Kellough 2006, 178). For example, schools implementing outcome-based criteria in evaluations of teachers and principals often assess individuals based on their students' progress, as measured by standardized test scores and improvement over past scores, rather than document relevant behaviors or traits, such as whether teachers show empathy toward students or discipline students effectively (Brown 2005).

To be effective, however, outcome-based measures need to make allowances for events that are outside the employee's control. For example, road crews may have to stop work due to inclement weather; in this case, their ostensible underperformance in terms of number of miles of road paved may be due to the weather, not to a lack of skill or effort, and a fair appraisal would take this into account. Moreover, differences in type and difficulty of job content across organizations make standardized performance-based measures difficult to identify. This is especially true in the public sector, where bottom lines differ from agency to agency, some services are intangible, and constitutional values such as equity and equality weigh in the balance (Berman et al. 2006; Friedman 2006; Kellough 2006). Thus, determining appropriate performance-based criteria is difficult and time-consuming and can be accomplished only after a methodical assessment of job-related content.

While there is no "silver bullet" for performance appraisal in the public sector, outcome-based methods are preferred. The more clearly HR managers can outline job performance expectations, the more easily employees can carry out their jobs accordingly. Moreover, the unambiguous identification of desirable outcomes facilitates more straightforward development planning when employees fail to achieve expected performance.

The Question of Reliability and Validity

Just as in recruitment and selection methods, reliability and validity are important in performance appraisal methods. In terms of performance appraisal, reliability and validity are concerned with the ability of the evaluation instrument to accurately reflect work-related achievements and shortcomings during the review period. Reliability is the ability of the performance appraisal instrument to demonstrate consistent ratings by the rater (e.g., supervisor, HR manager, peer, customer, client) over time. For example, reviews for the same employee doing the same job should exhibit similar scores and feedback over several performance evaluation periods. With performance appraisal, however, reliability can be difficult to establish, because the goal of evaluation is to provide feedback that the employee will use to improve productivity. As such, one would expect an employee to show improved performance, not the same level of performance, over subsequent evaluation periods. Further complicating the process is the use of multiple raters, such as different supervisors in different rating periods, whose evaluations may contradict each other, thus challenging the reliability of appraisal scores. A number of rater errors, discussed below, may also compound the difficulties of maintaining reliability.

Performance appraisal validity concerns whether the evaluation instrument accurately measures intended outcomes. Valid performance appraisals accurately measure desirable (or undesirable) traits, behaviors, and/or results. Chapter 5 discusses various types of validity for the recruitment and selection process, but for performance appraisal, content validity is the most important type (Buford and

Linder 2002, 247). Building content validity into the performance appraisal means measuring employees according to job-related criteria. In other words, an administrative assistant's productivity should be assessed according to his or her ability to produce documents or coordinate scheduling, key responsibilities of that job, instead of, say, the ability to write an accurate budget. To this end, job analysis is critical to maintaining the job-relatedness of the traits, behaviors, and/or results the evaluation measures. Job-relatedness is also the measure by which the courts judge the legality of performance appraisal methods. Thus, reliability and validity not only support the organization's productivity objectives but also ensure that appraisals are fair, complying with ethical and legal considerations.

Methods for Appraising Employee Performance in the Public Sector

Managers responsible for implementing performance appraisals need to consider which methods best suits the overall mission and objectives of the organization. Each of the methods discussed below focuses on a specific set of criteria (traits, behaviors, or outcomes) that may or may not be suitable for the particular organization in question or particular jobs. In fact, many organizations might mix and match elements of one or more of the methods below to arrive at a customized performance appraisal instrument.

One consideration is whether to utilize a single performance appraisal instrument for all employees in the organization or to tailor parallel evaluations that suit the purposes of different groups of employees or units within the agency (McCurdy and Lovrich 2004, 62). Another factor is the relative costs and benefits of implementing each method. Methods that are more time-consuming and detailed (e.g., BARS or management by objectives) can be costly to implement and may necessitate contracting with external vendors. At the same time, however, they tend to provide a more complete and accurate assessment of employee performance.

The examples below are some of the more commonly used methods for evaluating employee performance in the public sector. The discussion here is not exhaustive, and additional resources for performance appraisal methods are provided at the end of the chapter.

Nonprofits in Focus	Poor Performers in NPOs

Dealing with poor performers can be a challenging issue for employers. Accurately assessing performance is the first step in identifying those who exceed expectations and those who do not. Like their counterparts in the for-profit and public sectors, nonprofit HR managers face the problem of addressing performance in the workplace. For full-time employees in nonprofits, the issue is straightforward. Just as a for-profit firm has performance expectations, nonprofits can demand that their paid staff accomplish defined goals. The key is to identify beforehand the nonprofit's expectations of the employee and his or her position and evaluate the employee accordingly. Those failing to meet the required standards of performance should be disciplined and, if they continue to fail to meet expectations, ultimately terminated.

Unfortunately, dealing with poor-performing volunteers is not so clear-cut. Volunteers are essential to the overall mission of many nonprofits. Indeed, Brudney (2010) stated, "One of the most distinctive features of the nonprofit sector is its ability to harness the productive labor of literally millions of citizens in service to organizational goals without benefit of remuneration" (753). Having to tell someone working without pay that his or her services are no longer needed is no easy task. Managers are often reluctant to discipline volunteers who are seen as "comrades-in-arms" (Drucker 1992). Further complicating the matter is the potential fallout among other volunteers if a dismissal is not handled diplomatically (*Inc.* 2013).

Yet, nonprofit HR managers are often tasked with the difficult task of disciplining poorly performing volunteers. Even though volunteers are not paid, they are still an important part of the organization; they are often the public face—knocking on doors, making phone calls—and the way they interface with the public can influence the organization's reputation and how much people are willing to donate to the cause. If a volunteer's work is proving detrimental to the NPO's mission, then HR managers should hold that individual accountable just as would be done in the private sector. Failure to do so can result in continued poor performance and ultimately lead to the NPO's downfall (Kennedy 1991).

For many NPOs, dealing with those who volunteer to allay feelings of loneliness can be particularly problematic (Drucker 1992). While the relationships forged from a sense of belongingness and community can be profoundly rewarding, these volunteers can come across as abrasive if they attempt to force the development of a friendship with a fellow volunteer where a natural personal connection does not exist. Drucker urged NPO executives to dismiss troublesome volunteers if they begin to damage the morale of other volunteers. According to Drucker, NPO managers should stick by the adage "If they try, they deserve another chance. If they don't try, make sure they leave. An effective nonprofit executive owes it to the organization to have a competent staff wherever performance is needed. To allow nonperformers to stay on means letting down both the organization and the cause."

Traditional Methods

Traditionally, supervisors have utilized narrative assessments—such as the example in Figure 7.1—to evaluate employee performance. Supervisors are instructed to write an essay that reviews the employee's performance over a designated period of time (e.g., annual or semiannual evaluation period). Specific criteria are usually listed and described briefly to provide structure for the supervisor in writing the essay and the employee in understanding it. Such criteria might include productivity, accuracy, and/or coordination. Employees should understand each of the criteria they are being assessed on. In addition, supervisors might be asked to provide an overall assessment of the individual's performance for the period. Often such overall assessments are based on a **Likert scale**, an ordinal scale of four or five responses.

While such narrative assessments might be easy to administer and provide a great deal of flexibility to supervisors in explaining their ratings, essays have many drawbacks. Narrative assessments can be time-consuming, training intensive, and biased toward the particular supervisor's writing style and focus (optimistic versus

Figure 7.1	**Example of Narrative/Essay Appraisal Method**

Instructions: Write an essay that describes how the employee performed for each of the rating criteria. Be sure to include examples of the employee's contributions to each of the criteria in your essay. Finally, select the overall performance rating that best describes the employee's productivity for the period.

Rating Criteria	Narrative Description
Productivity. Volume of work and major accomplishments for the period.	
Accuracy. Meeting quality standards and applicable regulations for the period.	
Coordination. Planning, organizing, and delegating of work for the period.	

Overall Rating of Employee (circle the most appropriate):

Outstanding exceeds Expectations meets Expectations needs Improvement not Acceptable

Sources: Adapted from Buford and Lindner 2002; McCurdy and Lovrich 2004.

pessimistic) (McCurdy and Lovrich 2004). Two equally performing employees may receive different evaluations, for example, if one's supervisor tends to give harsher assessments than the other's. Or, one supervisor may like to elaborate while another writes very terse evaluations. Over time, narrative assessments have a tendency to become inflated (overly complimentary) and are difficult to compare historically, especially if supervisors change over time (64).

Trait-Based Methods

Trait-based assessments often include a list of desirable (or undesirable) personality traits in a column with a Likert scale (e.g., *very satisfactory* to *very unsatisfactory*) indicating the employee's achievement with respect to each criterion. Figure 7.2 illustrates a trait-based appraisal method that requires supervisors to assess an employee's competency on a number of desirable traits such as communication, dependability, initiative, enthusiasm, persistence, team orientation, and decisiveness. Trait-based methods are often used in the private sector to assess employee performance and to communicate desirable behaviors (Schermerhorn, Hunt, and Osborn 2004). Traits such as the "**Big Five**"—extraversion, agreeableness, conscientiousness, emotional stability, and openness to experience—are frequently utilized by private firms looking to identify and develop qualities in employees that are conducive to performance (Barrick and Mount 1991; 1993). The **Myers-Briggs Type Indicator (MBTI)** is another trait-based instrument that assesses an individual's tendency to feel or act a certain way under different circumstances (Kunimerow and McAllister 1988; Rice and Lindencamp 1989; Roach 1988). Such instruments might prove useful to managers in the public sector eager to select and promote the individuals most qualified to move the agency forward. The MBTI may be applied to the development phase of the employee's performance appraisal.

Trait-based methods are used by firms evaluating salespeople on how outgoing they are and by law enforcement agencies evaluating officers on honesty and integrity. However, public agencies need to be careful when considering trait-based evaluations. When trait-based performance appraisals are not connected to specified job-related tasks, they seldom meet the standards of validity and scrutiny set by the courts (McCurdy and Lovrich 2004). In other words, if "enthusiasm" is not deemed related to the ability of a public employee to carry out his or her duties (e.g., filling out forms to authorize purchases), then it should not be utilized in evaluation of that employee's performance.

Figure 7.2	**Example of Trait-Based Appraisal Method**

Instructions: Check the rating that best describes the employee's competency in each trait.

Trait	Outstanding	Very Satisfactory	Satisfactory	Unsatisfactory	Very Unsatisfactory
Communication	☐	☐	☐	☐	☐
Dependability	☐	☐	☐	☐	☐
Initiative	☐	☐	☐	☐	☐
Enthusiasm	☐	☐	☐	☐	☐
Persistence	☐	☐	☐	☐	☐
Team Orientation	☐	☐	☐	☐	☐
Decisiveness	☐	☐	☐	☐	☐

Source: Adapted from McCurdy and Lovrich 2004.

Behavior-Based Methods

Generally, the traditional and trait-based methods reviewed thus far include Likert-like rating scales that instruct supervisors to indicate the degree to which employees' exhibit desirable criteria. This approach to assessing levels of performance can be problematic given the leeway afforded raters in determining what is meant by "outstanding." Without a substantive description of what actually constitutes "outstanding" work, performance evaluations can vary greatly depending on the judgments of supervisors. In other words, what one supervisor considers "outstanding" performance may be different than what another supervisor considers "outstanding," subjecting employee appraisals to the raters' varying attitudes and perceptions of performance (Shafritz et al. 2001).

Behavior-based methods, on the other hand, are based on clear and precise definitions of the desired behaviors accompanying each level of performance (or Likert scale rating); such unambiguous descriptions reduce the incidence of rater bias. As such, behavior-based criteria have been increasingly used in the public sector. Behaviorally anchored rating scales—such as the example in Figure 7.3—require agencies to develop a list of observable behaviors from a detailed job description (Schermerhorn, Hunt, and Osborn 2004). Careful attention to identifying desirable and undesirable behaviors is essential for HR managers and other specialists striving to raise the level of performance. Listing specific behaviors compels evaluators to consider carefully the type of behavior integral to organizational performance, rather than the individual biases of the rater. This approach also leaves less open to interpretation by the rater—what qualifies as good performance is clearly spelled out. More importantly, behaviorally anchored methods provide the detail and job-relatedness necessary to stand up to legal review (McCurdy and Lovrich 2004).

Behavior-based methods can be costly and time-consuming due to the work involved in identifying and describing examples of the employee behaviors (Schermerhorn, Hunt, and Osborn 2004). HR managers must also undergo training to develop the expertise necessary in implementation of behavior-based methods (McCurdy and Lovrich 2004). However, behavior-based methods provide useful feedback to employees regarding job-related positive and undesirable behaviors; other methods often fail to provide such information. This feedback can then be useful in the development of a plan for improvement.

Outcome-Based Methods

The desire to measure performance outcomes in the public sector has necessitated aligning performance appraisals to managing for results. Outcome-based methods integrate quantifiable metrics into the employee appraisal process. Appraisal methods such as **management by objectives (MBO)** are frequently touted as ways to link

Figure 7.3	**Example of Behaviorally Anchored Rating Scale (BARS) Criterion**

Planning & Organizing—Establishes priorities and work sequences to coordinate efforts, maintain work flow, and meet deadlines; ensures sufficient functioning through smooth interface with related processes.

Instructions: Select the statement that best reflects the work behavior of the employee.

Rating	*Score*	*Example*
Extremely Outstanding Performance	7	Could be expected to meet deadlines, no matter how unusual the circumstances, by increasing effort until the work is done.
Good Performance	6	Could be expected to meet deadlines comfortably by delegating the less important duties to others.
Fairly Good Performance	5	Could be expected to meet deadlines on time by delegating most of the work to others.
Acceptable Performance	4	Could be expected to meet deadlines within a reasonable length of time.
Fairly Poor Performance	3	Could be expected to be behind schedule all the time, but appear to work hard to catch up.
Poor Performance	2	Could be expected to be behind schedule and display little effort to catch up.
Extremely Poor Performance	1	Could be expected to ignore deadlines and get work in on time only infrequently.

Sources: Adapted from Buford and Lindner 2002; McCurdy and Lovrich 2004; State of Indiana n.d.a.

means and ends (Schermerhorn, Hunt, and Osborn 2004). In the context of a drive to become more strategic in HR planning, methods like MBO are advantageous because they chart both employee performance and long-term agency goals. Figure 7.4 provides an example of an MBO approach to performance appraisal for a public HR manager position. In the example, the HR manager is tasked with specific objectives and expectations that were negotiated between the supervisor and subordinate at an earlier date. The objectives and expectations are specific to the duties and responsibilities of the job, making the performance appraisal job related. For the HR manager in this example, the objective to "enhance workforce retention and recruitment" clearly specifies that the individual decrease the resignation rate and increase

Figure 7.4	**Example of Management by Objectives (MBO) Appraisal Method**

In the coming six months, the following objectives will be pursued, and success will be determined by these associated results.

Position	Objective	Expectation
Human Resource Manager	Increase workplace safety	Creation of a new position within the legal department responsible for ensuring compliance with federal and state laws regarding workplace safety. Increase workplace safety training opportunities throughout the organization. Increase awareness of potential safety hazards throughout the organization.
	Increase employee motivation and satisfaction	Survey employees regularly to assess motivation and satisfaction rates. Increase employee motivation and satisfaction rates over designated period. Decrease employee dissatisfaction rate over designated period.
	Enhance workforce retention and recruitment	Decrease resignation rate by 5 percent over the designated period. Increase two-year retention rate by 5 percent over the designated period. Renew focus on improving diversity in the workforce.
	Increase employee knowledge, skills, and abilities	Increase training and development opportunities over the designated period. Facilitate training opportunities outside the organization. Increase assistance for tuition reimbursement.
	Increase technology-related competencies	Increase technology-related training and development opportunities over the designated period. Provide assistance for technology-related training opportunities outside the organization. Increase assistance for tuition reimbursement related to technology studies.

Agreed to on:

Agreed to by:

Sources: Adapted from Buford and Lindner 2002; McCurdy and Lovrich 2004.

the two-year retention rate by a certain percentage during the evaluation period. Calculating the resignation and retention rates for the six-month period would be straightforward, as would making the comparison to the previous period to determine whether the HR manager achieved the stated objective or not.

Mutually agreed-upon objectives and expectations allow a supervisor to evaluate subordinates according to clear measures and motivate employees to strive for desired performance (Buford and Linder 2002, 268). However, basing performance evaluations strictly on objective results can be problematic, especially when outcomes are not easily quantifiable. Many public sector job outcomes are difficult to measure. For example, basing evaluations of social workers on the number of cases processed in a given period may not be useful; the work often varies from case to case, with some cases proving more complicated than others. In addition, a social worker's objective may not just be to process a case but also to ensure that a broader objective is accomplished (e.g., place a child in a safe home). A focus on a means-ends connection can lead to individualistic behavior (i.e., focusing only on what is necessary to meet one's own quota or objective instead of providing excellent service overall) that is detrimental to teamwork and morale. Moreover, agencies often have many different outputs and means for quantifying measures of efficiency and effectiveness (Shafritz, Russell, and Borick 2007, 325). Indeed, variation may occur within government agencies. Within the Department of Homeland Security, the desired outcomes of interest to the Federal Emergency Management Agency may differ markedly from those of Immigration and Customs Enforcement.

Each of the four appraisal methods has advantages and disadvantages, so public HR managers need to weigh the costs and benefits of each. Such an assessment must also consider the jurisdiction's mission and objectives. Public HR managers should consider a performance appraisal process that incorporates a mix of the four types of criteria—traditional, trait based, behavior based, and outcome based. The appendix at the end of this chapter provides an example of a comprehensive performance appraisal report from the State of Indiana (State of Indiana n.d.b). The example in the appendix uses many of the elements discussed in this chapter in a holistic and strategic manner. The strategic orientation of the performance appraisal is exemplified by the matching of employee goals and objectives with those of the overall agency. Moreover, the performance appraisal includes a work improvement plan (WIP) for employees who fail to meet expectations with regard to core competencies and agency-specific competencies. A WIP is meant to reinforce a coordinated commitment to employee, agency, and overall jurisdictional goals and objectives. Comprehensive performance appraisals like the example in the chapter appendix complement the pursuit of a strategic approach to HR—the subject of Chapter 12. As public agencies choose to be more strategic in their approach to managing services, a more comprehensive performance appraisal that incorporates employee development planning is a necessity.

Alternative Appraisal Methods

In addition to the four commonly used methods already discussed, there are a number of alternative appraisal methods that can enhance the evaluation of employee performance. These alternative approaches are often utilized as supplemental instruments to the appraisal process. Ratings of supervisors combined with those of an employee's subordinates (in the case of supervisor evaluations), peers, or clients/customers can be quite useful. Multirater approaches complement the supervisor's ratings with those of others who may be able to provide more firsthand details of the employee's work. However, multirater approaches can be costly and time-consuming, so agencies should carefully weigh the costs and benefits of augmenting the performance appraisal system in this way.

Multisource Appraisal Methods

Multisource appraisal processes (also referred to as **360-degree performance appraisals**) incorporate feedback from a variety of sources, not just the employee's direct supervisor. Ratings from the employee, supervisor, peers, and customers/clients are combined in the performance appraisal process. Multisource appraisal has the potential to be more objective and comprehensive than a single-source appraisal. If for some reason a supervisor is biased in favor of or against the employee, the presence of other evaluations will ensure a more balanced perspective. Moreover, the inclusion of multiple raters lends greater reliability and validity to the appraisal instrument (US Office of Personnel Management [OPM] 1997). In addition, by encouraging teamwork and cooperation, multisource appraisals can encourage the development of such traits in the agency subordinates. In conducting multisource appraisals, agencies and HR managers should take great care in handling paperwork in order to ensure the anonymity of those who provide evaluations.

Assessment Centers

Assessment centers are a constructive, hands-on alternative to the methods previously covered. Assessment centers are generally external to the agency and incorporate a variety of techniques in the appraisal process. The goal of assessment centers is to place the employee in a variety of work-like simulations so that performance can be observed. Such exercises are useful for selecting job external and internal job candidates. Assessment centers are particularly useful for identifying individuals capable of handling stressful situations, a skill useful in management positions. Through job analysis, assessment centers are able to identify job-related evaluation instruments. Simulations often include group discussions, in-basket exercises, interviews, interactions with subordinates, communication exercises, and written exercises. For example, employees who speak directly with citizens on a day-to-day basis (e.g., handling complaint calls) may be judged by raters on their ability to handle customer complaints over the phone. For many public safety agencies, hazard simulations for both selection and performance evaluation have become commonplace. Persons involved in the assessment activities may be an employee's supervisors or HR consultants who serve as participant-observers. Once the exercise is completed, the employee is given both oral and written feedback on the tasks completed.

Avoiding Rater Error and Bias

As alluded to earlier in the chapter, one of the primary concerns of performance appraisal is the error and bias of raters. Given that all performance appraisals are subject to human involvement, error and bias are constant threats to effective evaluation. Below are common errors and biases that tend to mitigate the effectiveness of performance appraisals. Knowing the types of errors and biases helps public HR managers identify potential pitfalls in the appraisal process and provide raters with appropriate training. With careful training, error and bias in the performance appraisal process can be minimized.

Personal Bias Errors or Stereotyping

Occasionally, raters bring certain biases (intentionally or unintentionally) to the evaluation process. Some raters may have a bias toward or against a specific ethnic group or other demographic category (e.g., gender, age, disability, sexual orientation) that is reflected in performance evaluations (Buford and Lindner 2002; Schermerhorn, Hunt, and Osborn 2004). Others may have a previous or current personal relationship with a co-worker that may influence the evaluation. Such errors and biases have been the subject of lawsuits that have resulted in compensatory and/or punitive damages for plaintiffs filing suit (e.g., the Jefferson County, Alabama, case study in Chapter 4). Thus, raters must carefully guard against personal biases and stereotypes when appraising employee performance. As discussed in Chapter 4, EEO and diversity training are important to ensuring that employees and managers know what kinds of bias are illegal.

Recency Errors

Recency errors occur when a rater allows current or recent events to influence the evaluation of employees (Buford and Lindner 2002; Schermerhorn, Hunt, and Osborn 2004). A rater may weight recent events heavily and fail to consider the employee's performance over the entirety of the designated period. For example, an employee may have a demonstrated record of workplace safety over the course of his five-year tenure but failed to wear a hardhat during a recent site visit by the safety manager. The safety manager may be inclined to use the recent incident as a reason for a poor rating, failing to account for the individual's five-year record of safety.

Halo Errors

Halo error occurs when a rater allows a rating on one criterion (e.g., arriving late to work) to influence ratings on subsequent criteria (e.g., processing paperwork, communicating with customers). The employee may be highly effective in the job overall, but a tendency to get to work late may cause the supervisor to write the entire evaluation in a negative light—an example of negative halo error. Both negative and positive halo errors are possible. With halo errors, the individual is viewed as being either incapable of success or unable to do wrong, neither of which is an accurate assessment. Raters should take great care in assessing an individual independently on the merits of each rating criteria; they should avoid generalizing the rating of one item to other criteria on the performance appraisal.

First-Impression Error

Making an initial judgment about an employee and then ignoring subsequent behaviors that disprove such a judgment is a first-impression error. Allowing an initial impression of an employee (flattering or unflattering) to influence subsequent performance appraisals discounts the individual's contribution to the agency over the course of the review period. Such errors generally occur during the hiring process or probation period, which can be stressful times for an employee; the supervisor may only remember the mistake made during the first week on the job while forgetting the improvements made in later weeks.

Leniency/Strictness Errors or Rater Patterns

Supervisors may be inclined to give everyone positive performance ratings (leniency error) or to be a tough evaluator (strictness error). Some supervisors may want everyone to like them and are hesitant to mar work relationships by evaluating a subordinate poorly. Conversely, some supervisors may be unwilling to see the positive in any subordinates, perhaps demanding too much of their employees. In such instances, supervisors are either unable or unwilling to differentiate between superior and poor performers (Schermerhorn, Hunt, and Osborn 2004). This can be especially problematic in multirater performance evaluations when peers are hesitant to provide negative feedback to one another.

The Similar-to-Me Effect

The similar-to-me effect occurs when raters favor employees they perceive as exhibiting the same qualities as themselves. This effect may occur when raters view employees who display the same attitudes, background, and experience as themselves more favorably. For example, a supervisor may gives employees who attended his or her alma mater higher performance ratings than other employees.

Comparison or Contrast Effects

Comparing and contrasting employees during the performance appraisal process, rather than evaluating each employee on his or her own merits alone, fails to account for individual job-related accomplishments. Raters often assume that there is a normal distribution of performance that supports a certain number of excellent, good, fair, and poor ratings. In other words, a supervisor may believe that not all employees in the department can be excellent, so someone has to be just fair or poor. A good employee may be compared to a group of exceptional performers and rated just fair, or a fair employee may be compared to a group of poor performers and rated excellent. Comparison effects can be detrimental to motivating individuals. Failure to see the potential in individuals due to comparisons with their peers may negatively affect employee development. Realizing that they might never match up to the potential of their peers, individuals (and their supervisors) may not be willing to invest in training and other development tools that could positively affect their growth as employees.

Central Tendency Error

A central tendency error occurs when a rater evaluates all employees as average. Fearing alienating employees by judging a few individuals as overachievers, the rater opts to assess everyone as exhibiting satisfactory performance. Central tendency errors mute the effectiveness of performance appraisal as every level of performance nets the same rating. Differentiating good performers from poor performers requires diligence in the documentation of noteworthy events in each employee's periodic reviews. It is the supervisor's responsibility to give fair evaluations so that employees who excel are rewarded and those who need improvement are given the help they need. Taking a middle ground is just taking an easy way out of making the hard decisions that come with performance appraisal.

Obviously, no process is immune to human error. Because the appraisal process is a personal interaction between rater and subordinate, it is prone to human biases. No appraisal process can approach the objectivity of the analysis carried out in the hard sciences (e.g., biology, physics, chemistry). For HR managers, recognizing that the process is prone to human error is fundamental. HR managers can select an appraisal instrument that suits the needs of employees, supervisors, and the organization and then train all its users so as to minimize bias and error.

Performance Appraisal in an Era of PHRM Reform

As has been discussed in the preceding chapters, the contemporary reform environment has focused on creating a more productive and performance-oriented public sector. The trend toward decentralization in PHRM has enhanced the decision-making authority of managers for many jurisdictions, and this has included giving them wide discretion over performance appraisal. Forgoing traditional seniority-based decisions, many jurisdictions have adopted deregulation, performance-based pay, and declassification efforts in an attempt to link job duties to organizational performance. Performance-based pay policies have proven to be a one of the more enduring developments toward creating more efficient PHRM practices (Kellough and Nigro 2002, 2006; Perry, Engbers, and Jun 2009). Likewise, the trend toward employment at will (EAW) in the public sector just shows the increasing importance of performance in the public service. Declassification efforts further the trend toward greater flexibility by providing agency-level managers the ability to modify job descriptions to better correspond to agency performance goals. Naturally, for reformers, modernizing the performance appraisal process so that it reflects outcome-driven criteria is viewed as essential.

Exemplifying the trend toward performance-oriented PHRM is the state of Georgia. Georgia's reform efforts have received considerable attention in recent years, especially the state's performance-based pay and appraisal systems (Kellough and Nigro 2002, 2006). The goal of GeorgiaGain was to establish a modern PHRM system that would base pay increases on performance ratings. The system-wide effort included a new performance appraisal system that linked individual job-related performance standards to agency and, ultimately, state government productivity. GeorgiaGain, like other performance-based personnel strategies, includes explicit performance goals, expectations, and annual performance plans that serve as the criteria by which employees are evaluated. These modifications have necessitated the creation of new job descriptions and HR information systems to continually monitor and update descriptions through routine job analysis.

GeorgiaGain, like many reform efforts, was established to replace traditional tenure-based performance appraisal systems with outcome-based evaluations (Kellough and Nigro 2002). Similar to private sector appraisal methods, GeorgiaGain sought to implement a standardized appraisal process in which supervisors clearly defined job-related expectations for their subordinates through one-on-one communication. Encouraging dialogue between managers and employees was considered a prerequisite to establishing a credible performance appraisal process. Moreover, clearly specifying job-related performance expectations would give supervisors a straightforward way to distinguish top performers from others in order to allocate rewards. Fundamental to performance-based initiatives was creating a climate of trust so that employees felt empowered and motivated to achieving the stated goals (Battaglio 2010; Battaglio and Condrey 2009; Kellough and Nigro 2002, 2006). And, like the reform efforts covered previously in the text, GeorgiaGain emphasized managerial flexibility in order to achieve measurable performance improvement and increased responsiveness to state citizens (153).

However, performance-based pay and deregulation efforts such as EAW have failed to meet expectations (Battaglio and Condrey 2009; Kellough and Nigro 2002; 2006; Perry, Engbers, and Jun 2009). While a lack of political support and financial backing factored into the reforms' inability to achieve their purpose, a lack of support among Georgia's state employees also proved problematic. Most importantly, contextual factors such as a climate of trust, adequate rewards for performance, and effective performance appraisal affect the viability of any HR reform (Perry, Engbers, and Jun 2009). In particular, for performance appraisal to drive performance, trust is critical (Kellough and Nigro 2002; Reinke 2003). Unfortunately, management reforms over the last few decades have tended to evoke widespread distrust of performance-based evaluation systems (Battaglio and Condrey 2009; Kellough and Nigro 2002). Employees often perceive reforms as having replaced civil service notions of fairness and security with a revival of patronage, resulting in unfair performance and promotion decisions. Thus, PHRM reforms may erode employee confidence in the evaluation system. Governments considering linking performance-based pay and EAW to appraisal systems should make every effort to foster employee confidence in the system. Otherwise, employees are less likely to improve their productivity (Kellough and Nigro 2002).

Conclusion

Effectively managing performance appraisal in the public sector is increasingly important given the drive toward greater accountability for results. The trend toward performance-based pay means that it is critical, more than ever, for the performance appraisal process to accurately capture whether an employee is meeting job expectations. For public HR managers, however, accurately assessing employee productivity is no easy task. Multiple values, roles, and desired outcomes among public agencies make objective measurement of employee performance challenging. At the same time, a great deal of skepticism exists among employees regarding the ability of management to effectively link performance appraisal with rewards. Performance appraisal systems that do not inspire confidence among employees are subject to failure.

Further complicating the matter for public HR management is the need to pursue efficiency while upholding constitutional values. Maintaining due process standards is an important legal objective that is not easily quantified and often conflicts with notions of efficiency. For example, it might be more efficient to expedite the termination of a poorly performing employee, but doing so without granting a hearing may be unconstitutional. Private companies and even nonprofit organizations have less of an obligation to consider constitutional values given their status as at-will employers. Generally speaking, the risks an organization faces in these two sectors for terminating an employee are limited to civil suits based on "wrongful termination" or "breach of contract." On the other hand, the government standard, articulated in Chapter 3, guarantees employees a grievance process before formal termination. Finally, setting expectations is only one part of the appraisal process. If employees fail to meet expectations, managers should be able to articulate a plan for developing knowledge, skills, and abilities to assist subordinates with future goal accomplishment.

Using outcome-based measures in the performance appraisal process for the sake of efficiency alone is not as advantageous as reformers would suggest. Recall from our discussion throughout the text that many reforms (e.g., employment at will, performance-based pay) are fraught with difficulties that erode trust and motivation—features vital to productivity. HR managers considering outcome-based measures must determine carefully which outcomes best reflect the mission and objectives of the jurisdiction, as well as the agency and divisions within. Additionally, the inclusion of multiple criteria in the appraisal process ensures greater objectivity. Over time, trial and error will inform the appraisal process, which should be updated as needed. Training and development are crucial to minimizing errors and bias. Most importantly, a work improvement plan should be incorporated into the appraisal so that employees know what skills and behaviors to improve to better contribute to organizational outcomes.

Job analysis is critical to effective performance appraisal. Selecting the right criteria for evaluating employees can come only from systematic, up-to-date job analysis. Moreover, identifying job-related criteria is important so that the performance evaluation process will withstand legal challenges. Incorporating job-related criteria into the performance appraisal process provides greater clarity for employees eager to develop mission-critical skills.

References

Barrick, Murray R., and Michael K. Mount. 1991. "The Big Five Personality Dimensions and Job Performance: A Meta Analysis." *Personnel Psychology* 44:1–26.

Barrick, Murray R., and Michael K. Mount. 1993. "Autonomy as a Moderator of the Relationship Between the Big Five Personality Dimensions and Job Performance." *Journal of Applied Psychology* 78:111–18.

Battaglio, R. Paul, Jr. 2010. "Public Service Reform and Motivation: Evidence from an Employment At-Will Environment." *Review of Public Personnel Administration* 30:341–63.

Battaglio, R. Paul, Jr., and Stephen E. Condrey. 2009. "Reforming Public Management: Analyzing the Impact of Public Service Reform on Organizational and Managerial Trust." *Journal of Public Administration Research & Theory* 19:689–707.

Battaglio, R. Paul, Jr., and Jerome S. Legge Jr. 2009. "Self-Interest, Ideological/Symbolic Politics, and Citizen Characteristics: A Cross-National Analysis of Support for Privatization." *Public Administration Review* 69:697–709.

Berman, Evan M., James S. Bowman, Jonathan P. West, and Montgomery Van Mart. 2006. *Human Resource Management in Public Service: Paradoxes, Processes, and Problems*. 2nd ed. Thousand Oaks, CA: SAGE.

Brown, Andrew. 2005. "Implementing Performance Management in England's Primary Schools." *International Journal of Productivity and Performance Management* 54:468–81.

Brudney, Jeffrey L. 2010. "Designing and Managing Volunteer Programs." In *The Jossey-Bass Handbook of Nonprofit Leadership and Management,* 3rd ed., edited by David O. Renz, 753–93. San Francisco, CA: Jossey-Bass.

Buford, James A., Jr., and James R. Lindner. 2002. *Human Resource Management in Local Government: Concepts and Applications for HRM Students and Practitioners*. Cincinnati, OH: South-Western.

Carroll, Stephen J., and Craig E. Schneider. 1982. *Performance Appraisal and Review Systems: The Identification, Measurement, and Development of Performance in Organizations*. Glenview, IL: Scott, Foresman.

Clifford, James P. 1999. "The Collective Wisdom of the Workforce: Conversations with Employees Regarding Performance Evaluation." *Public Personnel Management* 28:119–56.

Drucker, Peter F. 1992. *Managing the Non-Profit Organization: Principles and Practices*. Reprint ed. New York: HarperBusiness.

Facer, Rex L., II. 1998. "Reinventing Public Administration: Reform in the Georgia Civil Service." *Public Administration Quarterly* 22:58–73.

French, P. Edward, and Doug Goodman. 2012. "An Assessment of the Current and Future State of Human Resource Management at the Local Government Level." *Review of Public Personnel Administration* 32:62–74.

Friedman, D. 2006. "Exes Lash Out at Pay for Performance." *Federal Times,* September 25.

Inc. n.d. "Nonprofit Organizations, and Human Resource Management." Accessed June 19, 2013. http://www.inc.com/encyclopedia/nonprofit-organizations-and-human-resources-management.html.

Kellough, J. Edward. 2006. "Employee Performance Appraisal in the Public Sector." In *Public Personnel Management: Current Concerns, Future Challenges,* 4th ed., edited by Norma M. Riccucci, 177–89. New York: Addison Wesley Longman.

Kellough, J. Edward, and Lloyd G. Nigro. 2002. "Pay for Performance in Georgia State Government: Employee Perspectives on GeorgiaGain after 5 Years." *Review of Public Personnel Administration* 22:146–66.

Kellough, J. Edward, and Lloyd G. Nigro. 2006. "Dramatic Reform in the Public Service: At-Will Employment and the Creation of a New Public Workforce." *Journal of Public Administration Research and Theory* 16:447–66.

Kennedy, Larry W. 1991. *Quality Management in the Nonprofit World: Combining Compassion and Performance to Meet Client Needs and Improve Finances*. San Francisco, CA: Jossey-Bass.

Kunimerow, J. M., and L. W. McAllister. 1988. "Team Building with the Myers-Briggs Type Indicator: Case Studies." *Journal of Psychology Type* 15:26–32.

McCurdy, Arthur H., and Nicholas P. Lovrich. 2004. "Maintaining a High-Performance Workforce." In *Human Resource Management in Local Government: An Essential Guide,* edited by Siegrun Fox Freyss, 59–91. Washington, DC: International City/Council Management Association.

Perry, James L., Trent A. Engbers, and So Yun Jun. 2009. "Back to the Future? Performance-Related Pay, Empirical Research, and the Perils of Persistence." *Public Administration Review* 69:39–51.

Reineke, Saundra J. 2003. "Does the Form Really Matter? Leadership, Trust, and Acceptance of the Performance Appraisal Process." *Review of Public Personnel Administration* 23:23–37.

Rice, George H., Jr., and David P. Lindencamp. 1989. "Personality Types and Business Success of Small Retailers." *Journal of Occupational Psychology* 62:177–82.

Roach, Ben. 1988. *Strategy Styles and Management Types: A Resource Book for Organizational Management Consultants.* Stanford, CA: Balestrand Press.

Schermerhorn, John R., Jr., James G. Hunt, and Richard N. Osborn. 2004. *Core Concepts of Organizational Behavior.* Hoboken, NJ: John Wiley & Sons.

Shafritz, Jay M., David H. Rosenbloom, Norma A. Riccucci, Katherine C. Naff, and Al C. Hyde. 2001. *Personnel Management in Government: Politics and Process.* 5th ed. New York: Marcel Dekker.

Shafritz, Jay M., E. W. Russell, and Christopher P. Borick. 2007. *Introducing Public Administration.* 5th ed. New York: Pearson Longman.

State of Indiana. n.d.a. "Behaviorally Anchored Rating Scale (BARS) Guide." Accessed April 21, 2014. http://www.in.gov/spd/files/bars.doc.

State of Indiana. n.d.b. "Employee Work Profile and Performance Appraisal Report." Accessed April 21, 2014. http://www.in.gov/dcs/files/12WorkProfilePracticeDirectorBlank.pdf.

Tompkins, Jonathan. 1995. *Human Resource Management in Government: Hitting the Ground Running.* New York: HarperCollins.

US Office of Personnel Management (OPM). 1997. "360-Degree Assessment: An Overview." http://www.opm.gov/perform/wppdf/360assess.pdf.

Additional Resources

American Educational Research Association (AERA), American Psychological Association (APA), and National Council on Measurement in Education. 1999. *Standards for Educational and Psychological Testing.* Rev. ed. Washington, DC: American Educational Research Association. https://law.resource.org/pub/us/cfr/ibr/001/aera.standards.1999.pdf. (See also http://www.apa.org/science/programs/testing/standards.aspx.)

Indiana State Personnel Department, "Performance Management," http://www.in.gov/spd/2394.htm.

US Department of Labor (DOL), Employment and Training Administration. 2006. *Testing and Assessment: A Guide to Good Practices for Workforce Investment Professionals.* http://www.onetcenter.org/dl_files/proTestAsse.pdf.

US Office of Personnel Management (OPM). "Assessment & Evaluation: Leadership Assessments." http://www.opm.gov/services-for-agencies/assessment-evaluation/leadership-assessments/.

US Office of Personnel Management (OPM). "Personnel Assessment and Selection Resource Center." http://apps.opm.gov/ADT/Content.aspx.

Appendix
Performance Appraisal Report Example

Performance Appraisal Report Example	
Name of Employee:	Employee ID Number:
Agency/Division:	Unit:
Class Title/Class Code:	Review Period:

Type of Evaluation:

☐ Annual Appraisal

☐ Employee is moving to a new supervisor or a new job classification

☐ Employee is going on leave of absence anticipated to last more than thirty (30) calendar days

☐ Other:

Purpose of Organization and Position

Organizational Vision, Mission and/or Objectives:

Purpose of Position (How does this position fit into the Organization/Division/Facility? What does this position contribute to the Organization/Division/Facility objectives):

Section A: Competencies

Instructions: Employees must be evaluated on the three (3) required/core Competencies and the additional agency-determined discretionary Competencies.

1. Job Knowledge—Possesses adequate knowledge, skills, and experience to perform the duties of the job; understands the purpose of the work unit and how position contributes to the overall mission of the agency; maintains competency in essential areas.

Rating	Behaviors during the review period which support the rating
☐ Meets	
☐ Exceeds	
☐ Does Not Meet	

2. Teamwork—Encourages and facilitates cooperation, pride, trust and group identity; fosters commitment and team spirit; works cooperatively with others to achieve goals.

(Continued)

(Continued)

Rating	Behaviors during the review period which support the rating
☐ Meets	
☐ Exceeds	
☐ Does Not Meet	

3. Customer Service—Demonstrates knowledge of internal and external customers; is sensitive to customer needs and expectations; anticipates needs and responds promptly and willingly to provide information, services and/or products as needed.

Rating	Behaviors during the review period which support the rating
☐ Meets	
☐ Exceeds	
☐ Does Not Meet	

4. Agency-Determined Discretionary Competencies

Rating	Behaviors during the review period which support the rating
☐ Meets	
☐ Exceeds	
☐ Does Not Meet	

NOTE: Failure to meet expectations for any Competency may result in employee being placed on Work Improvement Plan or separation, and may result in employee receiving an Overall Performance Rating of "Does Not Meet Expectations" or "Needs Improvement."

B. Performance Expectations/Goals	
Expectation/Results (Rank in Order of Importance)	Rating
Performance Expectation #1:	☐ Meets
Results:	☐ Exceeds
	☐ Does Not Meet
Performance Expectation #2:	☐ Meets
Results:	☐ Exceeds
	☐ Does Not Meet
Performance Expectation #3:	☐ Meets
Results:	☐ Exceeds
	☐ Does Not Meet
Performance Expectation #4:	☐ Meets
Results:	☐ Exceeds
	☐ Does Not Meet
NOTE: Failure to meet expectations for any goal or objective may result in employee being placed on Work Improvement Plan or separation, and may result in employee receiving an Overall Performance Rating of "Does Not Meet Expectations" or "Needs Improvement."	

Overall Performance Rating		
☐	Outstanding	Consistently exceeds expectations on all evaluation factors
☐	Exceeds Expectations	Overall high performance; frequently exceeds expectations on many factors
☐	Meets Expectations	Consistently meets the requirements of the job in all aspects
☐	Needs Improvement	Sometimes acceptable, but not consistent; needs improvement to meet expectations
☐	Does Not Meet Expectations	Does not meet the minimum standards of performance

Is a Work Improvement Plan (WIP) generated as a result of this appraisal? ☐ Yes ☐ No

Is so, please attach the WIP and ensure that the WIP pertains to the specific competency(s) and/or expectation(s) for which a Does Not Meet rating was given.

Is an Employee Development Plan generated as a result of this appraisal? ☐ Yes ☐ No

---

C. Employee Development Plan

Education, Expertise, Licensure, Certification suggested for career development:

Personal Learning Goals:

Development Objectives	**Developmental Training/Assignments**
(*Knowledge/Skills/Abilities Needed to Reach Goals*)	(*On-the-job Training/Details*)

If this form is being used as communication of the Work Profile, not a Performance Appraisal, please sign on the appropriate line below.

Signature of Employee   Date (*month, day, year*)

Signature of Supervisor   Date (*month, day, year*)

If this form is being used as a Performance Appraisal, please sign on the appropriate line below.

I hereby certify that this report constitutes an accurate evaluation using my best judgment of the service performed by this employee for the review period covered.

                                                        Signature of
Signature of Evaluator   Signature of Reviewer   Appointing Authority   Date (*month, day, year*)

I hereby certify that I have had an opportunity to review this report and understand that I am to receive a copy. I am aware that my signature does not necessarily mean I agree with the rating.

Signature of Employee   Date (*month, day, year*)

Source: State of Indiana n.d.b

Case 7.1   The Mouse That Roared

After examining the material presented in this chapter, consider the situation described below and the questions that follow:

Larry Fine recently accepted a new position as human resource manager for the Department of Health and Wellness in a western state. Several years ago, the governor of the state signed into law a bill enacting employment-at-will status for all employees, effective immediately. The intent was to give HR managers the authority to terminate poorly performing employees and to put everyone on notice that all employees would be held accountable for poor performance (i.e., that job security was no longer a given). The legislation also created a new performance appraisal system that was intended to reward superior performance with merit raises.

One of the issues Larry has been tasked with is the failure of previous supervisors and HR managers to hold employees accountable for lapses in performance. Larry has been reviewing the past performance of employees and finds that one employee in particular, Pat Smith, has consistently underperformed in her job. Unfortunately, previous supervisors and HR managers never held Pat accountable. They simply gave her a pass each time her evaluation came up. According to Larry's discussion with supervisors who have worked with Pat, a number of personal issues have affected her work at the office. Pat is a single mother raising two children and works two jobs in order to make ends meet.

Larry has been working with Pat over the last few evaluation periods, meeting with her to convey the message that her work has consistently been lacking. In these discussions, Larry set forth a work plan that would provide a road map for Pat to improve her productivity. Initially, the plan seemed to work; colleagues and managers noted a change in Pat's behavior and performance. Indeed, her first evaluation after the implementation of the road map noted a remarkable improvement in her job performance. Unfortunately, subsequent evaluations have noted a decline in Pat's performance. For the last few months, Pat has consistently shown up late for work and failed to coordinate work with her peers when she was out of the office for personal matters. Recently, an on-the-job incident has brought the issue to a head. When confronted by a supervisor about her consistently late arrivals, Pat lashed out, causing a major disruption to the work environment. This incident brought Larry back into the matter again. Larry has met with the supervisor, who now feels he can no longer work with Pat and has recommended terminating her. Larry's superiors are less inclined to terminate Pat and have suggested demoting her as an alternative. Larry is scheduled to meet with Pat in an hour to resolve the issue. Larry is faced with either continuing to give Pat a pass, demoting her, or terminating her.

1. What are the essential talking points for Larry to prepare before he meets with Pat? How might her performance appraisals over the last few periods be used in such a discussion?

2. Given her status as an at-will employee, should Larry simply terminate Pat for consistently underperforming? Legally speaking, Larry may have the right to recommend Pat's termination, but is this the right thing to do?

3. How might you advise Larry in this matter? Would you recommend sending Pat to continued training and development, demoting her, or terminating her? Are there any other alternatives for Larry to consider?

4. What biases or errors may have occurred in the performance evaluations?

5. What would have been a better course of action for Larry over the course of the entire period described?

Exercises

1. The chapter appendix illustrates the methods and criteria used by the state of Indiana to evaluate state employees. Using the material presented in this chapter, assess the appropriateness of the criteria used in the state's performance appraisal. Do you think the state emphasizes the right criteria in each section for appraising employee performance? What improvements (if any) would you recommend for each of the sections?

2. You've recently been hired as an assistant HR manager in a department of economic development for a local government. The agency HR director has tasked you with redesigning the performance appraisal process. The agency has incorporated a new mission

(Continued)

(Continued)

statement that emphasizes attracting innovative industry to the region. The goals of the new mission are to

- increase new industry startups;
- identify key industries for economic growth;
- enhance workforce competencies;
- identify and cultivate small businesses; and
- develop regional capacity for promoting new industry and economic growth.

3. Using the chapter appendix as a model, design a performance appraisal that fits this jurisdiction's and agency's needs for assessing employee performance. Given the goals of the new mission statement, how might you identify agency-determined competencies? In addition, the local government's vision statement emphasizes the values of customer service, fiduciary duty, open government, and free enterprise. How might these values influence the core competencies you identify?

Managing Motivation in the Public Service

Public human resource management (PHRM) reform efforts over the past few decades have aimed to improve the efficiency of the public service. In particular, these efforts have taken aim at the perception of an inefficient bureaucracy composed of public employees who are unmotivated and unproductive. In an effort to increase workplace productivity, many of the PHRM reforms discussed thus far have sought to motivate public employees to be more performance oriented. Motivation is seen as a crucial element of productivity in both the public and private sectors. Jurisdictions, such as the state of Georgia, have implemented performance-based pay and employment at will (EAW) as tools for improving motivation in the public service.

However, the incentives offered via reforms like performance-based pay can be at odds with the factors that have traditionally motivated people working in public service. We now know that public employees are not motivated just by pay and prestige but often respond to a call to serve a higher purpose or common good. Because many PHRM reforms have emphasized monetary rewards, they have failed to boost employee productivity. This lapse is important given that many public sector agencies are still considering using such reforms to motivate their employees. Unless policy makers take stock of the results achieved to date, improving productivity will continue to be problematic. HR managers should consider how the objectives of the public sector contrast with those of the private sector and appreciate what motivates public employees to pursue a common good.

This chapter will review the literature on **public service motivation (PSM)** and reflect on the impact recent PHRM reforms have had on motivation in the public service. The chapter will also offer approaches that public managers can employ to effectively leverage PSM to achieve productivity and work objectives.

Defining Public Service Motivation

Research into what motivates public sector employees has seen greater activity in recent decades in light of reform activity and its emphasis on private sector know-how. Traditionally, organizational theorists took for granted that people are motivated by similar incentives regardless of the sector they work in—public, private, or nonprofit. More recently, however, the topic has captured the attention of practitioners and scholars alike as uniquely suited to PHRM literature (Crewson 1997; Horton 2008; Houston 2000; Naff and Crum 1999; Oh and Lewis 2009; Perry 1996, 1997; Perry and Porter 1982; Perry and Wise 1990; Rainey 1982). The essential question is, What motivates people to pursue the public good? For researchers, this is a different question from what motivates people to choose work in the public sector over work in other sectors. Rather, this question concerns what drives the public sector employee to recognize and respond to causes uniquely oriented toward the public sector (e.g., the elimination of poverty) (Perry and Wise 1990).

Recent research suggests that the service ethic, a desire to pursue the public interest, or **public service motivation (PSM)** might be behind the decision to pursue public institution causes (Rainey 2009, 266). Findings from this vein of research suggest that motivating factors differ between public and private sector workers. Rainey (1983), in his comparative assessment of managers in state government and the business community, found that people employed in state agencies regarded meaningful public service as more important than did their private sector counterparts. Similarly, federal employees indicated that serving social causes and making a difference in public affairs—much more so than pay and job security—were their primary motivators for entering government employment (Crewson 1995). Rainey (2009) suggested that these findings identify a typology of public servants that includes valuing work that assists others and benefits society, involves self-sacrifice, and promotes responsibility and integrity (267).

These recent findings contradict traditional political behavior literature, which suggests that humans—and, more specifically, public employees—are rational actors who are motivated by self-interest. In the context of bureaucracy, the classical economic explanation is that the public sector worker operates in his or her own self-interest to enhance power and position within the organization, regardless of whether the policies produced are efficient or in the public interest (Downs 1965; Tullock 1971). PSM challenges the economic rationale that people are self-maximizing individuals motivated only by securing their position within the organization. Rather, individual motivators are complex and include not only prestige and power but also social aspirations.

Perry (2000) further distinguished PSM from general motivation theories by emphasizing the "publicness" of motivation. This quality is shaped by four premises: sociohistorical context, including education, socialization, and other life events; motivational context, including institutional values, beliefs, ideology, job characteristics, organizational incentives, and work environment; individual characteristics, including abilities, competencies, self-concept, and self-regulatory processes; and behavior, including rational choice, rule-governed behavior, and obligation. Working for the federal, state, or local government, one might be shaped by life events (e.g., saying the pledge of allegiance at the beginning of school), values (e.g., constitutional values of equality, liberty, and justice), and/or individual characteristics and behaviors (e.g., a strong work ethic instilled by family members). Over time, individuals come to strongly identify with these life events, values, self-concepts, and behaviors, and their influence on work is unavoidable.

It is clear, then, that PSM theory offers an alternative explanation for why people enter government employment. They do not do so strictly out of self-interest, although that is certainly a consideration in any employment decision, but often also out of a desire to serve the wider public good.

Public Service versus Public Sector Motivation

To be clear, *public service motivation* should be distinguished from *public sector motivation*. People are motivated by many different considerations to work for and in the public sector as opposed to the for-profit and nonprofit sectors. The public sector includes all levels of government (federal, state, local) as well as quasi-public entities (e.g., public corporations or state-owned enterprises). Public sector employment is often attractive because it offers job security, career growth potential, and retirement/health benefits. The conventional perception is that the public sector offers better quality of life, balance of work and family, and opportunity for advancement through training and learning than can be found in the private sector. According to Perry and Hondeghem (2008, 3), these "specific motives for working for and in the public sector lie outside PSM, which refers generally to motives associated with serving the public good." So, it is important to recognize that some who are motivated to work for the public sector may not necessarily have a strong public service orientation, instead being more influenced by practical matters such as job security or generous health benefits. **Public sector motivation** is the desire to work in a certain type of organization (i.e., government), whereas **public service motivation** is the desire to do a certain type of work (i.e., serve the public good).

The Motives Underlying Public Service Motivation

Perry and Wise (1990) found three purposes underlying the public service motive: norm-based, affective, and rational. Norm-based and affective reasons for public employment convey more altruistic purposes. **Norm-based motives** include a desire to serve the public interest, a sense of loyalty or duty to government, and a belief in social equity. Valuing social equity might move a person to seek a position in an office responsible for ensuring equal employment opportunity (e.g., a diversity office in a university).

Affective motives constitute a commitment to a specific program out of a personal conviction. For example, citizens may be drawn to serve in veterans affairs agencies out of a sense of loyalty to the men and women in the armed services. According to Frederickson and Hart (1985), one type of affective motive, **patriotism of benevolence**, involves "an extensive love of all people within our political boundaries and the imperative that they must be protected in all of the basic rights granted to them by the enabling documents (i.e., the United States Constitution)" (549).

Finally, persons seeking public sector employment may not be influenced only by altruistic reasons. Indeed, **rational motives**, such as a desire to participate in the policy process, commitment to public programs based on personal identification, and/or advocacy for a special interest may also be motivating factors (Perry and Wise 1990, 370). For example, policy makers are often involved in crafting enabling legislation and then are motivated to see their ideas come to fruition in the form of operationalized programs. Some research suggests that rational motives, while often driven by self-interest, should not be perceived as overtly detrimental to the public good. Self-interest drivers (e.g., promotion, power, prestige, success in politics) may tip the balance in favor of policy pursuits over another career. Policy makers often have an advantage in public sector employment in that they possess the intimate knowledge and expertise requisite to launching a particular initiative. Their expertise is just as important to the policy process as is elected officials' knowledge of the legislative process required to pass enabling legislation. Ultimately, the fact that policy makers may seek to work on government initiatives benefits citizen end users (Downs 1965; Tullock 1971). The classic example is Niccolò Machiavelli's Italian prince whose "ends justify the means."

Given the many factors that motivate individuals to work in the public service, to expect that individuals adopt a purely rational approach to job selection, divorced from their belief systems, is implausible. Thus, PSM is a valuable theoretical construct; rather than seeking to eliminate values and beliefs, PSM embraces their worth as motivational tools.

Identifying Public Service Motivation

For public HR managers, identifying prospective candidates (or current employees) who exhibit PSM-like qualities can be useful in the recruitment and promotion process. How does one go about identifying these qualities in someone? Table 8.1 presents the findings from Perry's research, from which he built a model of PSM, broken into four constructs (or categories). This model could be used as a rough predictor of who might be inclined to exhibit PSM, based on how they respond to various survey questions (Perry 1996). Perry's model frames the questions along both rational and altruistic motivations. The first construct—*Attraction to Policy Making*—is a rational one and gauges individual perceptions of politics and the policy-making process. Persons exhibiting PSM qualities would be inclined to agree with statements in the table, while disagreeing with the statements marked with an asterisk (*). So, as an example, those with PSM would typically not think that *politics* is a dirty word, and they would tend to appreciate the give and take of public policy making.

The remaining constructs assess more altruistic perceptions of public service. *Commitment to the Public Interest* gauges an individual's sense of civic duty, especially as applied to public employees as integral stakeholders in the policy process. Tapping the norm-based motive of social equity, the *Compassion* construct assesses individual commitment to social programs. The questions about compassion also test moral imperatives through emotional responses to humanness (Frederickson and Hart 1985). *Self-Sacrifice* is another aspect of PSM. Self-sacrifice gauges the individual's willingness to put others' interests before his or her own. This sacrifice is demonstrated by the willingness of public servants to forgo financial rewards for the intangible rewards they receive from serving the public (Perry 1996, 7). For example, a public servant who has expertise in finance may have eschewed a lucrative career in the private sector as an investment banker in order to become a regulator for the Federal Reserve; this person is sacrificing a high income in favor of pursuing goals beneficial to the broader public.

While others have experimented with alternative versions of Perry's original constructs, the questions included in Table 8.1 have proven useful. Indeed, Perry's PSM questionnaire has been established as a reliable means for validating public service motives not only among public employees but also among workers in other sectors. International applications of PSM have validated its importance as a universal characteristic in public service employees, with some variation according to national context (e.g., country-specific culture and values) (Vandenabeele and Van de Walle 2008). For example, recent research has suggested that the rational constructs of this model of PSM may not adequately explain the motives of Korean public servants (Kim 2009)

Table 8.1	**Identifying Public Service Motivation**

*Answering in the negative. Persons exhibiting PSM qualities should disagree with these statements.

Construct	Statement
Attraction to Policy Making	• *Politics* is a dirty word.* • The give and take of public policy making doesn't appeal to me.* • I don't care much for politicians.*
Commitment to the Public Interest	• It is hard to get me genuinely interested in what is going on in my community.* • I unselfishly contribute to my community. • Meaningful public service is very important to me. • I would prefer seeing public officials do what is best for the community, even if it harms my interests. • I consider public service a civic duty.
Compassion	• I am rarely moved by the plight of the underprivileged.* • Most social programs are too vital to do without. • It is difficult for me to contain my feelings when I see people in distress. • To me, patriotism includes seeing to the welfare of others. • I seldom think about the welfare of people whom I don't know personally.* • I am often reminded by daily events about how dependent we are on one another. • I have little compassion for people in need who are unwilling to take the first step to help themselves.* • There are few public programs I wholeheartedly support.*
Self-Sacrifice	• Making a difference in society means more to me than personal achievements. • I believe in putting duty before self. • Doing well financially is definitely more important to me than doing good deeds.* • Much of what I do is for a cause bigger than myself. • Serving citizens would give me a good feeling even if no one paid me for it. • I feel people should give back to society more than they get from it. • I am one of those rare people who would risk personal loss to help someone else. • I am prepared to make enormous sacrifices for the good of society.

Why would it be useful for public HR managers to recruit prospective candidates who exhibit PSM? The following sections explore the influence of PSM in public sector and how it can be leveraged in the organization.

Nonprofits in Focus	**Do Public Employees Volunteer?**

Now that we've discussed the subject of motivation in the public sector, we turn to consider whether or not such a motive transcends to volunteering. Public service motivation (PSM) suggests that many people in the public sector have answered "a call" to public service. This call stems from a commitment to serving the public interest, serving others, and self-sacrifice. But does this commitment to the public interest and serving others carry over to volunteering for causes outside the scope of paid employment.

David Houston (2006) recently took up this question by analyzing respondents to the 2002 General Social Survey who were employed in the public, nonprofit, and private sectors. His primary research question was whether public service employees are more likely than others to engage in volunteer work. To shed light on this query, he studied self-reported levels of giving of time, blood, and money to charitable organizations among the respondents. Houston's research demonstrates that public employees are indeed more likely to volunteer than are their counterparts in the private sector, lending credence to the idea that a strong PSM commitment exists among persons in the public service. His research indicates that nonprofit employees are also more likely to volunteer than their counterparts in the private sector. Nonprofit employees, like their peers in the public sector, exhibit a strong PSM streak in their work.

Why is this discovery important? The predictive power of PSM has important implications for recruiting, retaining, and rewarding employees in both the public and nonprofit sectors. Houston (2006) suggested that recruitment efforts should begin by seeking out individuals in public affairs and nonprofit management programs at universities who exhibit PSM-like qualities. Focusing recruitment efforts on finding such people is crucial to building an applicant pool of qualified and motivated employees. Perhaps most important, Houston argued that the satisfaction that individuals with high PSM find in public and nonprofit employment should be a strong rebuttal to the negative press often given to working in "the faceless bureaucracy." Shedding a light on the positive work these sectors accomplish may be a powerful recruitment tool for persons showing a proclivity for self-sacrifice.

PHRM reforms that seek to utilize private sector know-how might be tapping a set of motivational triggers that are not as effective for persons employed in the public and nonprofit sectors. Reformers would be wise to consider triggers that tap PSM rather than monetary rewards as an inducement for productivity.

Finally, nonprofits are increasingly involved in the formation of public policy. The role of nonprofits in championing social causes has made them key stakeholders in the policy process. This has been especially true of faith-based initiatives supported by the White House meant to buttress the social causes of the public sector. In this context, PSM may be a valuable tool for building overall social capital among the broader public (Brewer 2003). Civically active persons, such as those in the public and nonprofit sectors, may be able to improve communication among various political communities by building trust and legitimizing the work of both sectors (Behn 1998). Given the frequently combative climate of politics, trust and legitimacy may be significant assets.

PSM and Public Human Resource Management

PSM research has gained ground in recent decades, expanding upon the earlier work of Perry and others. PSM has intrigued many scholars and practitioners because it can be an effective means for tapping employee potential. For example, people demonstrating high levels of PSM may be ideal candidates for leadership positions. While directly relating PSM to productivity has proven problematic (see Alonso & Lewis 2001; Bright 2007, 2013), more indirect measures have demonstrated that PSM is an important construct in the development of productivity and trust in the public workforce (Crewson 1997; Houston 2000; Jurkiewicz, Massey, and Brown 1998; Naff & Crum 1999). In fact, a strong association exists between PSM and job performance, commitment, and retention (Crewson 1997; Jurkiewicz, Massey, and Brown 1998; Perry & Wise 1990). PSM has also proven to be a valuable construct in evaluating the effectiveness of PHRM functions such as recruitment, compensation, performance appraisal, and strategic management.

Job Performance and Satisfaction with the Work Environment

The most direct influence of PSM is its positive association with job performance and satisfaction. Surveys of federal employees have found that PSM is strongly correlated with better performance ratings and more positive work-related attitudes (Alonso and Lewis 2001; Naff and Crum 1999). Those who exhibit high levels of PSM also perceive their organization more positively and feel a more powerful connection with its goals and values. In particular, research on federal employees has shown that PSM is positively associated with commitment to the organization, work satisfaction, perceived performance, lower turnover intention, better relationships with other employees, and more philanthropic attitudes (Houston 2006; Pandey and Stazyk 2008; Pandey, Wright, and Moynihan 2008; Park and Rainey 2008).

Interestingly, PSM is also correlated with personal integrity. Assessing perceptions of federal employees regarding whistle-blowing, Brewer and Selden (1998) found that PSM-related qualities were greatest among employees who exposed wrongdoing in the workplace.

When it comes to the future leadership in public service, succession planning might use PSM as a tool for identifying employees with the potential to lead. Qualities identified with PSM—integrity, trust, benevolence—are the same qualities we associate with good leadership. Emphasizing PSM competencies in performance appraisal might help managers identify those employees best suited for promotion (see Chapter 7).

Compensation and Incentives

Research incorporating motivational concepts in the development of compensation and other incentives is particularly relevant/useful to PHRM (Perry 2009). A richer appreciation for the impact of intrinsic motivation has the potential not only to improve our understanding of PHRM but also to link PHRM with broader theoretical themes in organizational behavior, social psychology, and public management (Perry 2009).

Workplace incentives may be based on remuneration and reward (e.g., performance-based pay) or tap into the altruistic behavior embodied in PSM theory. When practitioners understand PSM, they can leverage the intrinsic motivators that may be just as powerful as traditional extrinsic motivators, like financial gain or promotion, to improve organizational performance. PSM is uniquely suited for this purpose because it provides a deeper understanding of the intrinsic factors that motivate employees to be effective in their jobs and fulfill their potential. It should be noted that the traditional merit system values (e.g., job security, procedural fairness, and neutral competence) that have been the foundation of our civil service system are intrinsic in nature.

While much of the PSM research suggests that a calling to public service is a primary motivator for public employment, however, the importance of wages and benefits should not be downplayed. Public employees, like employees in other sectors, are drawn to government employment in no small way by the total compensation package. They may be willing to sacrifice for the greater good, but they are also pragmatic and need to pay the bills. Therefore, developing an incentive system with the right mix of intrinsic and extrinsic rewards is an important goal of HR managers. For example, performance appraisals often focus on the technical aspects of a job in order to measure productivity (e.g., job knowledge, teamwork, customer service). A PSM focus in performance appraisal would supplement such measures with a concern for competencies like the motivation of oneself and others, service orientation, trustworthiness, emotional maturity, relationship building, and the development of self and others.

Job Design

With regard to job analysis, paying more attention to motivation in the design of jobs and work is crucial. While many acknowledge the critical connection between motivation and effective job design, the research on this topic is lacking (Perry, Mesch, and Paarlberg 2006; Perry 2009; Perry & Porter 1982). Recent research on emotional labor (covered in Chapter 4) suggests that motivational factors can be incorporated into job design and performance appraisal to emphasize skills related to PSM (e.g., self-sacrifice, service to others) that are often important in the performance of demanding public safety and law enforcement jobs (see Guy, Newman, and Mastracci 2008). However, motivation has also been important to reformers looking to galvanize public sector employees. Unfortunately, reforms have in some cases replaced robust intrinsic motivators (like self-sacrifice and service to others) with a set of less predictable extrinsic rewards (like compensation) (Moynihan 2008; Perry 2009).

Recruitment and Retention

Attracting the right people to the public service is important (see the Nonprofits in Focus box). Hiring decisions have a critical impact on organizational performance.

As previously mentioned, PSM is correlated with commitment to the organization, work satisfaction, perceived performance, lower turnover intention, better relationships with other employees, and more philanthropic attitudes (Houston 2006; Pandey and Stazyk 2008; Pandey, Wright, and Moynihan 2008; Park and Rainey 2008). Ensuring you hire the right people may mean selecting employees dedicated to serving others versus serving themselves. Retaining, appraising, rewarding, and motivating employees are crucial HR functions that might benefit from tapping the public service work ethic. What's more, the public sector faces a number of distinctive challenges in recruiting qualified persons with the right knowledge, skills, and abilities. Public HR managers are tasked with recruiting in an increasingly competitive environment in which public service is often not the first choice of new entrants to the labor market (Light 1997; Partnership for Public Service and Grant Thornton LLP 2010; Ritz & Waldner 2011). Recent college graduates are often drawn to the financial rewards of private sector employment. Further complicating hiring for the public sector is the erosion of job security and other traditional recruitment offerings in the wake of PHRM reforms (Battaglio and Condrey 2009). Therefore, recruiting and selecting people who exhibit PSM-like qualities, who are less concerned about financial compensation, may improve the prospects of finding enough qualified and motivated personnel.

Unfortunately, according to Clerkin and Coggburn (2012), many public agencies lack the HRM capacity to identify people with PSM qualities and recruit them to the public service. Research supports Clerkin and Coggburn's assertion that recruitment to the public sector is a key challenge for 21st-century HRM (MSPB 2010; Partnership for Public Service 2010). Indeed, the economic downturn of the last decade has exacerbated the problem, as many of the unemployed from the private sector have sought work in the public sector. This flood of new applicants has the potential to exhaust PRHM capacities to select the best candidates at all levels of government. For Clerkin and Coggburn, this challenge provides an opportunity for PHRM to refine recruitment practices by using PSM as an additional selection criterion, thereby narrowing the pool of applicants to the strongest group (see also Mann 2006). According to Perry and Wise (1990), employees joining the public service often exhibit PSM-like values before entering the workplace. Therefore, HR managers can use PSM as a recruitment criterion to tap this preexisting sentiment toward the public service. PSM can be a powerful tool for attracting and retaining a motivated workforce in the public sector.

Clerkin and Coggburn (2012) suggested that an awareness of PSM also has the potential to improve HRM practices and reinforce performance outcomes. The need is critical for public HR managers who use pragmatic means to improve recruitment and retention since, as discussed earlier, employees who exhibit PSM tend to be more motivated at work, be more productive, and experience more job satisfaction. Using tools to evaluate PSM (such as a questionnaire, as shown in Table 8.1) in the hiring process is perhaps the best way to recruit people exhibiting qualities conducive to the public service. PSM may also be incorporated into structured interviews and behavioral interviews during the selection process (Paarlberg and Lavigna 2010; Paarlberg, Perry, and Hondeghem 2008). For example, a hiring manager might query applicants about their interest in serving others and volunteering or their interest in self-development and the development of others through training.

Furthermore, Clerkin and Coggburn (2012) proposed the use of PSM as a part of the overall marketing and recruitment strategy of PHRM (see Jacobson 2011; Ritz & Waldner 2011). Advertising for public service positions should include mention of the positions' potential to make a difference in society, serve the citizenry, and provide for the public good (Doverspike et al. 2011; Liu et al. 2011). To recruit a workforce that embodies PSM-like qualities, public HR managers should make clear their desire for people who exhibit qualities of self-sacrifice, compassion, and commitment and who have an interest in public policy making. Clerkin and Coggburn (2012) asserted that putting this message first and foremost may increase the likelihood that persons who espouse PSM qualities will apply and deter those who are not truly interested in public service. Targeting such recruitment efforts in the appropriate trade publications (e.g., public sector employment websites)—especially when the traditional extrinsic public sector employment motivators such as job security, retirement, benefits, and quality of life are also included—may prove most fruitful (Clerkin and Coggburn 2012, 227). Presenting the practical benefits of public employment alongside the public service motive may be a very persuasive recruiting tactic. In fact, there is also the potential for persons in the private sector who embrace PSM to move to the public sector (Steijn 2008; Wright and Christensen 2010). In this way, public HR managers can be positioned to select from the strongest possible group of job candidates.

Organizational Climate

HR managers with a deep appreciation for PSM have the potential to champion the public service ethic associated with agency mission. For example, PSM may strengthen human capital frameworks that align employee and organizational values, facilitate communication, and, ultimately, enhance buy-in. For human service-related organizations—like the Department of Health and Human Services—service to others and self-sacrifice is mission critical. PSM may be useful in aligning agency goals (e.g., overcoming poverty) with those of staff (e.g., helping individuals one case at a time). Incorporating PSM throughout all PHRM processes can ensure that assessments of applicants during the hiring phase are confirmed and reinforced throughout the employment relationship (Clerkin and Coggburn 2012, 227).

Motivation and PHRM Reform

A central tenet of public management reform is that the public service is seen as inefficient, lacking the motivation and organization necessary to improve productivity and performance; hence, there is a need for reform (Battaglio 2009; Battaglio and Condrey 2009; Kellough and Nigro 2002; 2006). Affording public HR managers greater flexibility in the administration of HR activities and functions (e.g., pay, performance appraisal, hiring, termination) has been viewed as important to improving performance.

Since the 1980s, performance-based pay and deregulation through the use of employment-at-will (EAW) policies have been seen as the primary mechanisms for motivating poor-performing employees to produce better results (Kellough and Nigro 2002; 2006). Reforms have attempted to tap employees' self-interest and incentivize productivity through extrinsic rewards. The assumption underlying performance-based pay is that monetary remuneration is the most important means for motivating employees. Likewise, EAW is seen as a means to strip away the "red tape" associated with the traditional civil service system; EAW is intended to dismantle long and involved hiring and termination processes. The expectation is that market-oriented reforms like EAW and performance-based pay will increase employee (and organizational) productivity (Kellough and Nigro 2002; 2006).

However, scholars have questioned the purported benefits and efficacy of these public management reforms (Battaglio 2009; Houston 2000; Naff & Crum 1999). In reform environments, policies tend to be based on market principles of efficiency, managerial flexibility, and results. These principles differ from the traditional merit system motivators of job security and procedural fairness, to name a few. Any assumption that public employees respond to traditional merit system motives is often minimized or abandoned (Battaglio and Condrey 2006; 2009; Condrey 2002; Condrey and Battaglio 2007). So, gauging the impact that reforms have had on traditional motives for working under a merit system warrants investigation. To this end, recent efforts (see Battaglio and Condrey 2009; Condrey and Battaglio 2007; Kellough and Nigro 2002; 2006) have concluded that these reforms, specifically performance-based pay and EAW, have failed to act as effective motivators for performance.

Performance-Based Pay and Employment at Will

The state of Georgia presents an opportunity to assess the ability of public management reforms to motivate the public workforce. The intent of the Georgia reforms was to develop a more productive and responsive public service by implementing performance-based pay and EAW policies (Condrey and Battaglio 2007; Kellough and Nigro 2002). Unfortunately, Georgia State employees have tended to voice pessimism about the reforms' ability to achieve the intended purpose (Battaglio and Condrey 2009; Condrey and Battaglio 2007; Kellough and Nigro 2002; 2006). Using more traditional kinds of motivation (e.g., job security, benefits) may be a better means for promoting workforce efficiency (Kellough and Nigro 2006).

The evidence seems to show that the implementation of EAW systems has by and large had a negative effect on motivation levels of those employed in the public service. In Battaglio and Condrey's analysis of a survey of Georgia HR professionals, many indicated a great deal of pessimism about the ability of EAW—the removal of job security in an effort to create a more responsive and motivated workforce—to improve productivity. Any motivating influence of EAW appears to have been muted by the potential for procedural abuse stemming from a lack of due process and the loss of job security. The authors' research has shown that EAW has not worked.

The loss of job security, in particular, has had a significant impact on HR professionals' perceptions of the potential for EAW to motivate employee performance. Why would a public employee be willing to go the extra mile for the employer when the employer is not taking care of the employee and does not have his or her interests at heart? The findings of Battaglio (2009) and others (see Coggburn et al. 2010) suggest that deregulation has not produced a more productive public sector workforce. Indeed, the research suggests that deregulation has negatively impacted motivation and morale among public employees. Public employees expressed significant levels of mistrust regarding management and the use of EAW (Battaglio & Condrey 2009), a significant relationship between the loss of job security and reduced motivation (Battaglio 2010), and a fear that the use of spoils would reappear in a deregulated environment (Battaglio & Condrey 2009; Condrey & Battaglio 2007). Moreover, further research suggests that such misgivings tend to intensify over time (Coggburn et al. 2010). Coggburn and colleagues (2010) found that HR directors in Georgia and Texas, states where EAW has been in place longer, had greater levels of dissatisfaction with EAW than directors in Florida and Mississippi, which have only recently enacted similar deregulation policies. These findings support Kellough and Nigro's (2006) suggestion that retooling management practices alone is not enough to improve productivity and motivation in the public service.

Motivation among Minorities

A troubling finding from this stream of research has been the impact HR reforms have had on motivation among minorities in the public service (Battaglio 2009; Battaglio and Condrey 2009). Civil service employment has a long history of pursuing practices that improve representation and diversity in the workforce. For many African Americans, recent reform efforts have made them rethink their perceptions of the public service as a great equalizer; they may even perceive these reforms as a move in the wrong direction regarding diversity (see Wilson 2006). By giving managers the upper hand in HR decisions, practices such as EAW may be viewed by African Americans as a tool for "discrimination-induced job dismissals" (Wilson 2006, 178). When a manager does not need to have cause to dismiss a public employee, some worry that a prejudiced public manager would dismiss employees he did not like because of their race. All of the considerations in the Civil Service Reform Act and Civil Rights Act seemed to level the playing field and ensure equal opportunity for all, but the potential for EAW and other reforms to erode years of progress in the promotion of diversity in the public sector must not be ignored. HR managers should take care to remain impartial themselves and to be aware of the potential for EAW to allow discrimination to sneak back into the public workplace.

Public Service Motivation and Compensation

Public service motivation theory offers a promising link between compensation and motivation for those considering performance-based pay. PSM theory posits that public servants are motivated by commitment, compassion, and self-sacrifice with regard to public policy and the public interest (Perry 1996; Perry and Hondeghem 2008). Grounded in the assumption that people who choose public sector work do so based on both rational and altruistic considerations, the theory has garnered considerable empirical support from a variety of social science disciplines (Perry and Hondeghem 2008).

Proponents of performance-based pay assume that managers will apply such pay schemes evenhandedly, rewarding strong performers. Unfortunately, performance-based pay might actually be detrimental to motivation. More nuanced research suggests that pessimism toward performance-based pay may result from a negative view of external control rather than opposition to change in general (Brehm and Gates 1997). In other words, employees are not necessarily dismissive of change; their negativity has more to do with whether they feel those who implement performance-based pay are doing so fairly. Such negative perceptions may be exacerbated in a heightened reform environment. Evidence suggests that performance-based pay may sour employee perceptions of their leadership and the work environment (Kellough and Nigro 2002) and that other reforms, such as EAW, may also negatively impact employee motivation (Battaglio 2009; Battaglio and Condrey 2009). Employees may begin to feel as if a monetary value is being bestowed simply on how much work they can produce and not as though they are valued holistically for the contributions they can make and their worth as individuals.

Perry, Engbers, and Jun (2009) considered the potential for PSM in the performance-based pay arena, suggesting that it may be a valuable factor to include in the equation for assessing job performance and rewarding employees. Because PSM accounts for the differences in what motivates employees in the public sector versus private sector, it can help managers accurately reward performance in the public sector. Instead of focusing on bottom-line goals or job objectives, PSM can broaden the scope of performance evaluations to include "more applicable levers for improving performance in public agencies" (Perry, Engbers, and Jun 2009, 45–46).

Recently, research has suggested that public management reform efforts over the last decade have eroded PSM (Leisink and Steijn 2008; Moynihan 2008). The market-driven atmosphere that emphasizes monetary incentives has proven harmful to intrinsic motivators like those embodied in PSM theory. In fact, the pursuit of extrinsic reward systems, such as performance-based pay, may be futile. The PHRM reforms certainly have value, but some practices may not be the best fit for the public sector. People who choose to work in the public sector are often motivated by intangibles, so attempting to incentivize them with tangible rewards is not likely to be as effective in the public sector as in the private sector.

Looking Ahead: Leveraging PSM

PHRM reforms favor a management-centered, private sector approach that is opposed to the traditional bureaucratic model. Eschewing the perceived problems of bureaucratic systems and civil service protections, reformers have advocated that greater flexibility be afforded to managers. Over time, however, public management reforms may breed a contempt that runs counter to the public interest, thus undermining the very public management systems they were intended to strengthen (Battaglio and Condrey 2009). PSM may prove productive in countering the challenge to public service that PHRM reforms have posed by reinvigorating the public service commitment to self-sacrifice and service to others and the public good. HR managers can leverage PSM by including PSM constructs (see Table 8.1) in the evaluation of public employees.

Moynihan (2008) suggested that public sector managers reconsider how they motivate performance by including intrinsic values—like those personified by the call to public service—in the selection process (260). In fact, these values are really the original principles on which the merit system is based. Unfortunately, establishing agreement on which values are the right ones and linking those values to performance is problematic. However, studies suggest that "pro-social" behavior and motives can be tapped in a way that improves work performance (Rainey 2009 271; see also Grant 2008).

For HR managers, a greater emphasis on PSM constructs—attraction to policy making, commitment to the public interest, compassion, self-sacrifice—is a must given the recent decades of PHRM reform. PHRM reform efforts have targeted public service as outmoded, inefficient, ineffective, and overly bureaucratic. However, bureaucracy bashing may not be the best path to positive reinforcement of high performance among public servants. HR managers should instead emphasize the positives of public service. A focus on PSM in recruitment, retention, and performance evaluations can be a good start to reinvigorating the public service. HR managers can look for PSM-like qualities in potential public employees during job interviews. Moreover, finding such qualities in persons already employed may be important as well for overall morale. Performance appraisals can be retooled to focus not only on how well the individual is meeting individual and agency objectives but also on the employee's exhibition of PSM-like qualities. Querying stakeholders (e.g., peers, managers, customers) regarding an employee's PSM qualities may be a useful way to assess such constructs (see Chapter 7 for a more detailed discussion of 360-degree appraisal methods).

Clearly, a more thorough assessment of the public sector motivation is necessary. What we do know is that many recent reforms have been less than enthusiastically embraced by those who work in the public sector. This is especially true when EAW has been perceived as facilitating racial discrimination or at least showing less emphasis on diversity and proportional representation. Both public service motivation and diversity raise interesting questions for researchers interested in exploring workforce dynamics in employment-at-will systems. Moreover, many HR professionals appear to be conflicted over the potential of PHRM reform efforts to serve as a motivational tool and advance the discussion of HR policy (Battaglio 2009). Although dubious of EAW's ability to encourage policy innovation, managers may also be keenly aware that their jobs are on the line if productivity does not improve. If employees in EAW systems are interested only in meeting minimum requirements—as research findings suggest—then an EAW environment may be problematic. The focus on extrinsic motivators may prove corrosive to underlying intrinsic motives (Moynihan 2008). Policy innovation may take a back seat to keeping one's job.

Recent scholarship on the emotional capacity of individuals within the public service may also serve as an important addition to the literature on PSM and job performance (Guy and Newman 2004; Guy, Newman, and Mastracci 2008). Emotional labor—caring, negotiating, empathizing, relationship building—can be an important aspect of public servant interactions with others in the public service as well as with citizens. For many public servants, the prospect of performing such emotional labor provides a strong call for public service. Much as with PSM, the range of skills that play out in such dynamic situations are often neglected. Therefore, public HR managers have an opportunity to incorporate in job analysis a more robust description of the capacities needed for particular jobs. A more determined focus on emotive job requirements, rather than market determinants, provides public HR managers with an advantage in tapping PSM aptitudes. The research on emotional labor may prove useful to public HR managers looking to revise job descriptions and performance appraisals to incorporate a broader skill set. Like PSM, emotional labor can contribute to feelings of pride in one's work and a belief that the work one does is meaningful (Guy, Newman, and Mastracci 2008, 186).

Incorporating PSM into PHRM functions must be done with great care. Measuring PSM has proven problematic, resulting in concerns about the reliability and validity of assessments that include it (Clerkin and Coggburn 2012). The need for a more reliable and valid tool for measuring PSM continues to be a concern among scholars and practitioners alike (Kim et al. 2011). Also, PSM is only one measure of public service aspirations, and it does not necessarily consider performance on the job. Furthermore, the inclusion of PSM does not necessarily mean a diminished emphasis on performance-based evaluation and compensation. Public HR managers should include PSM along with the measures of knowledge, skills, and ability that are traditionally included in job analysis and descriptions.

References

Alonso, Pablo, and Gregory B. Lewis. 2001. "Public Service Motivation and Job Performance: Evidence from the Federal Sector." *American Review of Public Administration* 31:363–80.

Battaglio, R. Paul, Jr. 2009. "Privatization and Citizen Preferences: A Cross-National Analysis of Demand for Private versus Public Provision of Services in Three Industries." *Administration & Society* 41:38–66.

Battaglio, R. Paul, Jr. 2010. "Public Service Reform and Motivation: Evidence from an Employment At-Will Environment." *Review of Public Personnel Administration* 30: 341-63.

Battaglio, R. Paul, Jr., and Stephen E. Condrey. 2006. "Civil Service Reform: Examining State and Local Cases." *Review of Public Personnel Administration* 26:118–38.

Battaglio, R. Paul, Jr., and Stephen E. Condrey. 2009. "Reforming Public Management: Analyzing the Impact of Public Service Reform on Organizational and Managerial Trust." *Journal of Public Administration Research & Theory* 19:689–707.

Behn, Robert D. 1998. "What Right Do Public Managers Have to Lead?" *Public Administration Review* 58:209–24.

Brehm, John, and Scott Gates. 1997. *Working, Shirking, and Sabotage: Bureaucratic Responses to Sabotage.* Ann Arbor: University of Michigan Press.

Brewer, Gene A. 2003. "Building Social Capital: Civic Attitudes and Behavior of Public Servants." *Journal of Public Administration Research and Theory* 13:5–26.

Brewer, Gene A., and Sally Coleman Selden. 1998. "Whistle Blowers in the Federal Civil Service: New Evidence of the Public Service Ethic." *Journal of Public Administration Research and Theory* 8:413–40.

Bright, Leonard. 2007. "Does Person-Organization Fit Mediate the Relationship Between Public Service Motivation and the Job Performance of Public Employees?" *Review of Public Personnel Administration* 27:361–79.

Bright, Leonard. 2013. "Where Does Public Service Motivation Count the Most in Government Work Environments? A Preliminary Empirical Investigation and Hypotheses." *Public Personnel Management* 42:5–26.

Clerkin, Richard M., and Jerrell D. Coggburn. 2012. "The Dimensions of Public Service Motivation and Sector Work Preferences." *Review of Public Personnel Administration* 32:209–35.

Coggburn, Jerrell D., R. Paul Battaglio Jr., James S. Bowman, Stephen E. Condrey, Doug Goodman, and Jonathan P. West. 2010. "State Government Human Resource Professionals' Commitment to Employment At Will." *American Review of Public Administration* 40:189–208.

Condrey, Stephen E. 2002. "Reinventing State Civil Service Systems: The Georgia Experience." *Review of Public Personnel Administration* 22:114–24.

Condrey, Stephen E., and R. Paul Battaglio Jr. 2007. "A Return to Spoils? Revisiting Radical Civil Service Reform in the United States." *Public Administration Review* 67:425–36.

Crewson, Philip E. 1995. *The Public Service Ethic.* Washington, DC: American University Press.

Crewson, Philip E. 1997. "Public-Service Motivation: Building Empirical Evidence of Incidence and Effect." *Journal of Public Administration Research and Theory* 7:499–518.

Downs, Anthony. 1965. "A Theory of Bureaucracy." *American Economic Review* 55:439–46.

Doverspike, Dennis, Lei Qin, Marc Porter Magee, Andrea F. Snell, and L. Pamela Vaiana. 2011. "The Public Sector as a Career Choice: Antecedents of an Expressed Interest in Working for the Federal Government." *Public Personnel Management* 40:119–32.

Frederickson, George H., and David K. Hart. 1985. "The Public Service and the Patriotism of Benevolence." *Public Administration Review* 45:547–53.

Grant, Adam M. 2008. "Employees Without a Cause: The Motivational Effects of Prosocial Impact in Public Service." *International Public Management Journal* 11:48–66.

Guy, Mary Ellen, and Meredith A. Newman. 2004. "Women's Jobs, Men's Jobs: Sex Segregation and Emotional Labor." *Public Administration Review* 64:289–98.

Guy, Mary Ellen, Meredith A. Newman, and Sharon H. Mastracci. 2008. *Emotional Labor: Putting the Service in Public Service.* Armonk, NY: M. E. Sharpe.

Horton, Sylvia. 2008. "History and Persistence of an Idea and an Ideal." In *Motivation in Public Management: The Call of Public Service,* edited by James L. Perry and Annie Hondeghem, 17–32. Oxford, England: Oxford University Press.

Houston, David J. 2000. "Public Service Motivation: A Multivariate Test." *Journal of Public Administration Research and Theory* 10:713–28.

Houston, David J. 2006. "'Walking the Walk' of Public Service Motivation: Public Employees and Charitable Gifts of Time, Blood, and Money." *Journal of Public Administration Research and Theory* 16:67–86.

Jacobson, Willow S. 2011. "Creating a Motivated Workforce: How Organizations Can Enhance and Develop Public Service Motivation." *Public Personnel Management* 40:215–38.

Jurkiewicz, Carole L., Tom K. Massey Jr., and Roger G. Brown. 1998. "Motivation in Public and Private Organizations: A Comparative Study." *Public Productivity & Management Review* 21:230–50.

Kellough, J. Edward, and Lloyd G. Nigro. 2002. "Pay for Performance in Georgia State Government: Employee Perspectives on GeorgiaGain after 5 Years." *Review of Public Personnel Administration* 22:146–66.

Kellough, J. Edward, and Lloyd G. Nigro. 2006. "Dramatic Reform in the Public Service: At-Will Employment and the Creation of a New Public Workforce." *Journal of Public Administration Research & Theory* 16:447–66.

Kim, Sangmook. 2009. "Testing the Structure of Public Service Motivation in Korea: A Research Note." *Journal of Public Administration Research & Theory* 19:839–51.

Kim, Soonhee, Wouter Vandenabeele, Lotte B. Andersen, Francesco Paolo Cerase, Robert K. Christensen, Céline Desmarais, Maria Koumenta, et al. 2011. "The Development of an International Instrument to Measure Public Service Motivation: A Research Note." Paper presented at the 11th National Public Management Research Conference, Syracuse, NY.

Lasseter, Reuben W. 2002. "Georgia's Merit System Reform 1996 -2001: An Operating Agency's Perspective." *Review of Public Personnel Administration* 22:125-132.

Leisink, Peter, and Bram Steijn. 2008. "Recruitment, Attraction, and Selection." In *Motivation in Public Management: The Call of Public Service,* edited by James L. Perry and Annie Hondeghem, 118–35. Oxford, England: Oxford University Press.

Light, Paul. 1997. *The Tides of Reform: Making Government Work, 1945–1995.* New Haven, CT: Yale University Press.

Liu, Bangcheng, C. Hui, J. Hu, W. Yang, and X. Yu. 2011. "How Well Can Public Service Motivation Connect with Occupational Intention?" *International Review of Administrative Sciences* 77:191–211.

Mann, Gregory A. 2006. "A Motive to Serve: Public Service Motivation in Human Resource Management and the Role of PSM in the Nonprofit Sector." *Public Personnel Management* 35:33–48.

Merit Systems Protection Board (MSPB). 2010. "The New Importance of Job Announcements." *Issues of Merit* 15:1–7.

Moynihan, Donald P. 2008. "The Normative Model in Decline? Public Service Motivation in the Age of Governance." In *Motivation in Public Management: The Call of Public Service,* edited by James L. Perry and Annie Hondeghem, 247–67. Oxford, England: Oxford University Press.

Moynihan, Donald P., and Noel Landuyt. 2008. "Explaining Turnover Intention in State Government: Explaining the Roles of Gender, Life Cycle, and Loyalty." *Review of Public Personnel Administration* 28:120–43.

Naff, Katherine C., and John Crum. 1999. "Working for America: Does Public Service Motivation Make a Difference?" *Review of Public Personnel Administration* 19:5–16.

Oh, Seong Soo, and Gregory B. Lewis. 2009. "Can Performance Appraisal Systems Inspire Intrinsically Motivated Employees?" *Review of Public Personnel Administration* 29:158–67.

Paarlberg, Laurie E., and Bob Lavigna. 2010. "Transformational Leadership and Public Service Motivation: Driving Individual and Organizational Performance." *Public Administration Review* 70:710–18.

Paarlberg, Laurie E., James L. Perry, and Annie Hondeghem. 2008. "From Theory to Practice: Strategies for Applying Public Service Motivation." In *Motivation in Public Management: The Call of Public Service,* edited by James L. Perry and Annie Hondeghem, 268–93. Oxford, England: Oxford University Press.

Pandey, Sanjay K., and Edmond C. Stazyk. 2008. "Antecedents and Correlates of Public Service Motivation." In *Motivation in Public Management: The Call of Public Service,* edited by James L. Perry and Annie Hondeghem, 101–17. Oxford, England: Oxford University Press.

Pandey, Sanjay K., Bradley E. Wright, and Donald P. Moynihan. 2008. "Public Service Motivation and Interpersonal Citizenship Behavior in Public Organizations: Testing a Preliminary Model." *International Public Management Journal* 11:89–108.

Park, Sung Min, and Hal G. Rainey. 2008. "Leadership and Public Service Motivation in US Federal Agencies." *International Public Management Journal* 11:109–42.

Partnership for Public Service and Grant Thorton LLP. 2010. "Closing the Gap: Seven Obstacles to a First-Class Federal Workforce." http://ourpublicservice.org/OPS/publications/viewcontentdetails.php?id=147.

Perry, James L. 1996. "Measuring Public Service Motivation: An Assessment of Construct Reliability and Validity." *Journal of Public Administration Research & Theory* 6:5–22.

Perry, James L. 1997. "Antecedents of Public Service Motivation." *Journal of Public Administration Research & Theory* 7:181–97.

Perry, James L. 2000. "Bringing Society In: Toward a Theory of PSM." *Journal of Public Administration Research & Theory* 10:471–88.

Perry, James L. 2008. "The Civil Service Reform Act of 1978: A 30-Year Retrospective and a Look Ahead." *Review of Public Personnel Administration* 28:200–4.

Perry, James L. 2009. "A Strategic Agenda for Public Human Resource Management Research." *Review of Public Personnel Administration* 30:20–43

Perry, James L., and Annie Hondeghem, eds. 2008. *Motivation in Public Management: The Call of Public Service.* Oxford, England: Oxford University Press.

Perry, James L. Trent A. Engbers, and So Yun Jun. 2009. "Back to the Future? Performance-Related Pay, Empirical Research, and the Perils of Persistence." *Public Administration Review* 69:39–51.

Perry, James L., Debra Mesch, and Laurie Paarlberg. 2006. "Motivating Employees in a New Governance Era: The Performance Paradigm Revisited." *Public Administration Review* 66:505–14.

Perry, James L., and Lyman W. Porter. 1982. "Factors Affecting the Context for Motivation in Public Organizations." *Academy of Management Review* 7:89–98.

Perry, James L., and Lois Recascino Wise. 1990. "The Motivational Bases of Public Service." *Public Administration Review* 50:367–73.

Rainey, Hal G. 1982. "Reward Preferences among Public and Private Managers: In Search of the Service Ethic." *American Review of Public Administration* 16:288–302.

Rainey, Hal G. 1983. "Public Agencies and Private Firms: Incentive Structures, Goals, and Individual Roles." *Administration & Society* 15:207–42.

Rainey, Hal G. 2009. *Understanding and Managing Public Organizations.* 4th ed. San Francisco, CA: Jossey-Bass.

Ritz, Adrian, and Christian Waldner. 2011. "Competing for Future Leaders: A Study of Attractiveness of Public Sector Organizations to Potential Job Applicants." *Review of Public Personnel Administration* 31:291–316.

Steijn, Bram. 2008. "Person-Environment Fit and Public Service Motivation." *International Public Management Journal* 11:13–27.

Tullock, Gordon. 1971. "Public Decisions as Public Goods." *Journal of Political Economy* 79:913–18.

Vandenabeele, Wouter, and Steven Van de Walle. 2008. "International Differences in Public Service Motivation: Comparing Regions across the World." In *Motivation in Public Management: The Call of Public Service,* edited by James L. Perry and Annie Hondeghem, 223–44. Oxford, England: Oxford University Press.

Walters, Jonathan. 2002, October. "Life After Civil Service Reform: The Texas, Georgia, and Florida Experiences." *Armonk, NY: IBM Endowment for the Business of Government.*

Wilson, George. 2006. "The Rise of At-Will Employment and Race Inequality in the Public Sector." *Review of Public Personnel Administration* 26:178–87.

Wright, Bradley E., and Robert K. Christensen. 2010. "Public Service Motivation: A Test of the Job Attraction-Selection-Attrition Model." *International Public Management Journal* 13:155–76.

Additional Resource

International Research Society for Public Management—http://www.irspm.net

Case 8.1   "Radical" Civil Service Reform in Georgia

In 1996, the state of Georgia embarked upon an unprecedented experiment in decentralizing personnel authority. Georgia Act 816 removed civil service protections for employees hired after July 1, decentralizing personnel policy and administration to the agency level. The act was part of a larger reform initiative in the state to establish a new performance management system buttressed by performance-based pay (Kellough and Nigro 2002). The establishment of an EAW system for state personnel in Georgia was the result of a convergence of factors: a very powerful governor (Zell Miller, later a US senator) with experience in HR management and a distaste for the state's numerous and archaic personnel rules and regulations; an imbedded central personnel management hierarchy unwilling or unable to reform itself; well-placed, powerful bureaucratic actors that wanted more direct control over their agencies' personnel management system; and very weak employee unions (Battaglio and Condrey 2006, 121).

The EAW system was put in place piecemeal by filling vacant positions with "unclassified" titles effective July 2, severely limiting State Personnel Board jurisdiction. The establishment of EAW abrogated property interest or tenure rights normally afforded employees after they had served the traditional one-year probationary period. The state of Georgia's efforts mirror a desire among the public and politicians alike for more private sector–oriented management practices in recruitment, hiring, compensation, promotion, downsizing, and discipline (Walters 2002). This is especially true for agency line managers, who now expect to be able to hire immediately and with greater flexibility than under traditional civil service systems. No longer obligated to confer with the central HR department on matters of recruitment and selection, state agencies now have the authority to hire employees at any step within a given pay grade. The intent is to provide agencies with greater flexibility as they compete for a qualified workforce. Managers are also tasked with ensuring consistent and fair salary management practices for agency personnel (Lasseter 2002).

The intent of EAW is to streamline the downsizing and disciplinary functions in the public sector in order to improve productivity. Moreover, Georgia's EAW system removes seniority as a measure of performance, allowing agencies to reassign and relocate at-will employees as needed. Streamlining discipline and grievance practices places unclassified, at-will employees at the mercy of managers, because these employees do not have the right to appeal disciplinary decisions. In contrast, traditional classified employees are disciplined according to a standard progressive method that begins with an oral or written reprimand, then moves to suspension without pay or salary reduction, and leaves dismissal as a last resort. Concerns about cronyism, favoritism, and unequal pay for equal work—features of spoils systems of the past—have proven to be problematic (Battaglio 2010, Battaglio and Condrey 2009; Condrey and Battaglio 2007). Accountability continues to be a concern for future EAW efforts.

Discussion Questions

Clearly, there are concerns about accountability in the Georgia reform model. The lack of uniformity across the various personnel systems in the operating agencies exacerbates this problem. Without a strong state office of personnel management to ensure uniformity in practice, how does one ensure fairness in such a reform model? How might a lack of uniformity of HR policy and practice effect personnel loyalty and commitment? Trust? Motivation?

Exercise

Below are job descriptions for several types of positions within a government agency. The HR manager has tasked you with updating these job descriptions before upcoming job openings are advertised. The HR manager would like you to include language that would attract candidates exhibiting PSM-like qualities. What language might you include or change in the job descriptions below? How might you assess PSM-like qualities in potential candidates for these positions?

Table 8.2	Job Descriptions
Grade	**Description**
Clerical	**Administrative Assistant.** Responds to requests for information; may require interpretation of department rules and regulations. Independently composes and types correspondence for signature of supervisor regarding administrative matters, office policies, or programs. Compiles and types special reports by selecting relevant information from a variety of sources such as reports, documents, correspondence, electronic files, etc. Organizes and maintains files and reference manuals/materials; ensures confidentiality of information, as necessary. Prepares materials needed for meetings, such as agendas, handouts, binders, etc. May perform administrative functions such as payroll preparation, travel reports, supply requisitions, etc. Sets up and types a wide variety of correspondence, reports, tables, records, case histories, hearings, etc. from rough draft, dictation, dictating machine, or instructions. Types materials that involve knowledge of special terminology. Attends meetings and transcribes minutes; may serve as

(Continued)

(Continued)

Grade	Description
	hearings reporter by recording verbatim testimony and transcribing into prescribed format. Proofs typing results for typographical errors, spelling, punctuation, and format accuracy. Establishes and maintains electronic files for identifying, recording, and classifying stored data; extracts, assembles, and merges stored information to create new documents.
Professional	**Park Ranger.** Explains rules and regulations to park visitors for the purpose of protecting and preserving natural, historic, and cultural features; sites; and structures. Prepares and maintains various records and reports pertaining to park activities. Performs general painting, carpentry, masonry, plumbing, electrical, and related trades work as required. Cleans and supplies restrooms, removes refuse from trash receptacles and grounds, and performs other general cleanup functions. Operates numerous power tools, trucks, and other equipment. Collects and accounts for fees.
Professional	**Human Resource Management Director.** Participates in the development and implementation of personnel management programs for the state classified service, including position classification, pay, recruitment, testing and selection, tenure, employee relations, equal employment opportunity, performance appraisal, and career development and training. Provides administrative and technical direction to the various division administrators. Reviews, formulates, or directs the revision of rules, regulations, policies, and procedures for the state classified service. Reviews current and long-range programs, plans, and policies for DSCS and identifies areas of conflict, prepares revisions to enhance operations, and prepares reports of recommendations. Directs all program activities for the department in the absence of the Civil Service Director with line authority over all programs and serves as principal assistant to the director. Meets with the governor, legislators, federal and state officials, classified and unclassified state employees, members of professional organizations, and other special interest groups on matters relating to civil service programs. Prepares or directs the preparation of regular and special reports as required or desired relating to the department's programs. Prepares and reviews correspondence on complex and sensitive matters affecting the department of clerical work and minor administrative and business detail. Knowledge of word-processing, decision-making, and business software required.

Grade	Description
Executive	**Agency Undersecretary.** Directs the work activities of all programs in the absence of the assistant secretary, serves as principal assistant to the assistant secretary, and has administrative line authority over all programs. Advises the assistant secretary regarding program, office, or departmental problems. Reviews current and long-range programs, plans, and policies for the office, identifying and resolving areas of conflict. Reviews, formulates, or directs the revision of rules, regulations, and procedures for the office. Reviews and evaluates work of subordinates and gives technical guidance when needed. Coordinates budget recommendations. Conducts staff meetings and conferences with subordinates to resolve problems and conflicts. Meets with officials of federal, state, and local agencies, legislators, professional organizations, and interested groups on matters relating to the office. Directs the preparation of special reports relating to office programs. Prepares correspondence on complex and sensitive matters affecting the department or office.

Source: Louisiana Department of State Civil Service, http://agency.governmentjobs.com/louisiana/

9

Labor Relations in the Public Sector

LEARNING OBJECTIVES

Upon completion of the chapter, you will be able to do the following:

- Discuss the history of labor relations in the United States.
- Explain the process of collective bargaining between labor and management.
- Describe alternative dispute resolutions that can be applied to resolving labor-management impasses.
- Explain the right to strike of public sector employees in the United States.
- Discuss the prospect of federal regulations concerning labor-management relations in the public sector.
- Discuss labor-management relations in an era of PHRM reform.

Unions are legally recognized organizing units for labor in the United States. Many people may be familiar with private sector unions like the United Auto Workers, which represents employees who work for private companies like GM or Ford. Likewise, public sector employees can also have union representation through public sector unions. The 1981 standoff between the Professional Air Traffic Controllers Organization (PATCO) and President Ronald Reagan is one of the more well-known labor disputes between management and a public sector labor union. PATCO represented the interests of air traffic controllers, who at the time were demanding better working conditions. They ultimately decided to strike—a move that violated federal law prohibiting **strikes** (work stoppages) by public labor unions. President Reagan ordered the air traffic controllers back to work, resulting in a standoff. Reagan then dismissed 11,345 air traffic controllers for violating his back-to-work order in a move that is considered "the biggest, most dramatic act of union-busting in 20th-century America" (Early 2006).

Labor-management relations in the public sector encompass the sum total of interactions among public employees, public managers, government entities, and public employee labor unions (Selden 2009, 5). These interactions and activities may include, for example, discussions over pay and benefits, working conditions, reorganizations, transfers, and discipline procedures. In 2012, the US union membership rate—the percentage of workers who were members of a union—was 11.3 percent. In contrast, public sector workers had a union membership rate of 35.9 percent (BLS 2014b). Thus, understanding the central issues of labor relations is important for public HR managers.

Private and public labor unions are similar because both serve the same purpose—they advocate on behalf of workers. However, they are not the same in other respects; most importantly, different laws govern public and private labor relations. Private sector labor unions are governed by national legislation—the National Labor Relations Act of 1935 (the Wagner Act)—and regulated by a central federal authority—the National Labor Relations Board (NLRB). On the other hand, laws governing public sector labor relations differ according to the level of government (federal, state, and local) and even the type of agency (e.g., postal workers are governed by a different set of laws). Such a varied legal landscape can make the work of public HR managers challenging.

Jurisdictions across the country have implemented their own guidelines and legislation regarding labor-management relations, resulting in variation from state to state. Public HR managers therefore must be familiar with the labor laws governing their jurisdictions. Organized labor in the public sector has also undergone significant challenges to its influence and power over the past decade due to reform legislation at the state level and homeland security legislation at the federal level.

The focus of this chapter is the contemporary environment of labor-management relations in the public sector. The chapter begins with a concise historical review of labor-management relations in the United States, and it ends with a review of labor-management relations in an era of public human resource management (PHRM) reform and an assessment of how reforms have impacted public unions.

Unions and Labor-Management Relations

In discussing labor relations, we often hear the words *labor* and *management* used as though they describe two opposing factions. *Labor* refers to labor unions and union members, while *management* refers to the interest of the organization—in the context of this chapter, the government—and its managers.

Labor unions are typically most concerned with the rights of the workers represented by the union; they seek to ensure that workers are not mistreated or subject to unfair or illegal labor practices. Unions tend to support the view that all union members deserve equal fair and equal treatment. They also emphasize solidarity—that members will support each other as they work collectively to achieve a fair workplace. Employees may choose to join a union to get the benefits of organized representation, which can include higher wages and greater job security (Aldt and Tzannatos 2002). Unions typically collect dues from each union member in exchange for the services they provide. Not all employees may join a union; employees who are managers are not permitted to join a union, because in the adversarial legal framework of US labor relationships, they are on the "management side."

Management is usually most concerned with ensuring that all employees are working as they should and meeting their productivity or performance objectives. Because management tends to prioritize overall performance, it is more open to implementing strategies that "get the job done" like rewarding individual performance, even if doing so may result in unequal treatment of employees. Management may view what unions consider to be necessary for the fair treatment of workers as costing time and money and negatively impacting efficiency. At the same time, unions may feel that management is more worried about performance targets than about the individuals who work to achieve those targets. As such, labor and management are traditionally at odds with each other, and labor-management relations can be highly contentious. Disputes may arise if the union feels that management has put in place an unfair labor practice (e.g., a change in working conditions) or if management feels the union has refused to work in good faith toward reaching an agreement.

When a union forms, and is legally recognized, such an organized unit can be a powerful voice for workers. One of the key activities that unions engage in is **collective bargaining**, which is the process of developing legally binding terms of employment. Unions also lodge complaints against **unfair labor practices** perpetuated in the workplace by management. The details of these activities will be discussed throughout the chapter.

While most unions have the same general objectives, they are indeed different entities, as we will see. As mentioned, private sector unions are different from public sector unions, and public unions at the federal level operate within a different legal framework than do unions at the state and local levels. Understanding the history of unions and how their relationship with management has developed over time provides the HR manager with a useful perspective.

The next section discusses the development of unions in both the private and public sector, and it examines the similarities and differences between the two.

Setting the Stage: Rise of Private Sector Labor Unions

Public sector unions emerged from private sector labor movements. Therefore, to understand how public sector labor unions function, it is important to understand the history of private sector labor unions.

The modern union has its origins in the workers' guilds that began to form before the peak of the Industrial Revolution in the mid- to late 19th century. Guilds were typically made up of individuals who worked in the same craft or trade. Focused on enforcing safe work conditions and fair wage standards in the face of the harsh working conditions of early industrialization, these early labor associations were the main voice of labor during this period; they were also limited mostly to regional or local organizing efforts. Moreover, labor associations were viewed suspiciously by government and the general public, being seen as an obstacle to free-market enterprise and even as having subversive communist/socialist tendencies. Efforts such as strikes or work stoppages were often illegal. Private employers claimed that worker unionizing efforts were illegal conspiracies, citing the conspiracy doctrine, a legal tenet that maintained labor unions were criminal organizations whose aim was to pressure management for higher wages and thus restrict competition. Unions were also held to violate antitrust laws. The courts tended to side with employers, repeatedly issuing injunctions that prohibited strikes (Chaison 2006).

Not until the 1842 decision in *Commonwealth v. Hunt* did the Massachusetts Supreme Court refute the notion that labor union activities were criminal in nature, thus dismissing the validity of the conspiracy doctrine in the state of Massachusetts (Chaison 2006, 2). Before *Hunt*, the future of labor unions was uncertain in the United States. The *Hunt* case affirmed that unions—in this case a guild of boot makers—could legally organize and strike on behalf of workers and their wages. This landmark decision contributed to a more constructive environment for labor union efforts elsewhere in the United States.

By the time of the Great Depression in the 1930s, the legal framework for labor-management relations had progressed to the point where employees were granted the right to unionize nationally (Chaison 2006). This change in policy was linked to passage of the **National Labor Relations Act (the Wagner Act)** in 1935. The Wagner Act recognized private sector workers' rights to unionize and collectively bargain with employers. Section 7, the key section regarding labor relations, states, "Employees shall have the right to self-organization, to form, join, or assist labor organizations, to bargain collectively through representatives of their own choosing, and to engage in other concerted activities for the purpose of collective bargaining or other mutual aid and protection." The act also permitted employees to engage in activities such as strikes, picketing, and boycotts—a right previously only granted at the state level in *Hunt* (Chaison 2006; Mosher 1982). In addition to giving unions significantly greater legitimacy, the Wagner Act created the **National Labor Relations Board (NLRB)** to oversee representation elections for labor unions and preside over instances of unfair labor practices perpetrated by management.

The 1935 act was subsequently amended by the **Taft-Hartley Act of 1947**, which forbade specific instances of unfair labor practices on the part of unions. The **Labor Management Reporting and Disclosure Act of 1959** (also "LMRDA" or the "Landrum-Griffin Act") further defined the rights of union members, extending the Bill of Rights to union members; establishing reporting requirements for labor organizations, union officers and employees, employers, labor-relations consultants, and surety companies; creating standards for the regular election of union officers; and setting up safeguards for protecting labor organization funds and assets (DOL 2010). The federal legislation that was enacted to regulate union activity for the private sector would serve as the model for public sector labor policies in the mid-20th century.

Private sector unionization reached its zenith in the mid-1950s with over one-third of nonagricultural workers in the United States having union representation (Chaison 2006, 56; Kearney 2010, 94). However, beginning in the 1960s, private sector union representation began a gradual decline, with membership reaching just 8.5 percent of private sector workers as of 2008 (Kearney 2010, 94). Private sector union density—the percentage of workers who pay dues to unions—is even lower, at 7.7 percent of the private nonagricultural labor force (Chaison 2006; Kearney 2010, 94). The reasons for the precipitous decline of unions over the last decade are debatable, but Chaison (2006) cited several, including structural shifts in the labor force (i.e., an aging workforce), greater employer opposition, an increasing inability and unwillingness among unions to organize in a more hostile climate, and changes to labor law that have placed more restrictions on labor union activities (Chaison 2006, 60–63). Growth in public sector employment before and after World War II has also been cited as contributing to the decline in private sector unionization, as more employees left the private sector to take government jobs (Chaison 2006; Kearney 2010). The proportionally larger numbers of public employees grew public employee union membership, making it another focal point of power in the labor-management environment.

Unionism in the Public Sector

Unlike private sectors unions, which have experienced a gradual decline in membership and influence over the last several decades, public sector unions have enjoyed a period of relative growth since the 1960s. This is not surprising given that the government has continuously expanded, beginning with exponential growth in government employment during the New Deal Era of the 1930s and continuing after World War II during the Cold War and again during the Great Society initiatives of the 1960s. Unionization in the federal government was paralleled by an extension of union and bargaining rights at the state level as well.

History of Labor-Management Relations in the Public Sector

Initial efforts to secure public sector labor rights began in the late 1800s with employees in public safety agencies. Aware of similar activities of private unions, police officers and firefighters sought expanded rights for bargaining over wages and working conditions through their respective fraternal orders (Chaison 2006). These public employees joined associations, which were more like fraternal organizations than labor unions. During this period, union representation of public employees was controversial and deemed a violation of the sovereignty of government (Kearney 2010). Unionization was viewed as a means for public servants to coerce public officials into granting favorable employment terms given the workers' control over the function of government. Such power was seen as incompatible with democratic principles of plurality in the political system. In fact, President Theodore Roosevelt imposed a 1902 "gag rule" that forbade federal employees from engaging in all lobbying activities (Mosher 1982; 189; Van Riper 1958, 216). Thus, the legal environment during this period was not favorable to the rights of public employees to unionize and bargain.

In the early part of the 20th century, US postal workers were the first public employees to garner support for the rights of public service workers to unionize at the federal level. The postal workers petitioned for better wages and working conditions as well as the removal of President Theodore Roosevelt's gag order. Their campaign ultimately attracted congressional attention, resulting in passage of the **Lloyd-Lafollette Act** in 1912, which guaranteed federal employees the right to join unions and lobby Congress (Van Riper 1958, 216–18). But, while the 1912 act afforded public employees the right to either individually or through their organization petition Congress, public service unions still had no statutory basis for collective bargaining; that is, they were not allowed to negotiate labor contracts with management. Political support for legislation guaranteeing collective bargaining rights was also marginal, leaving public management the upper hand until the 1960s.

In the 1960s and 1970s, the climate of opposition to public employee unionization ebbed. Fraternal associations already in place for public servants found organization easier than in the past. Public employers and political officials were also less likely to overtly challenge labor for fear of disenchanting the large block of the voting public that supported unions (Chaison 2006). Recognizing changing attitudes toward public sector unionization, President John F. Kennedy issued **Executive Order 10988** in 1962, which for the first time recognized the rights of federal employees to organize and collectively bargain—although strikes were still strictly forbidden (Kearney 2010). While only applicable to federal employees, President Kennedy's executive order nonetheless set a significant positive standard in public sector labor relations and ushered in a new era of unionization.

In 1969, President Richard Nixon's **Executive Order 11491** superseded the precedent established by Executive Order 10988, expanding organized labor rights for federal employees even further. Executive Order 11491 afforded a more standardized framework of collective bargaining rights for federal employees, creating the **Federal Labor Relations Council (FLRC)** as an oversight body that reviewed appeals and made policy decisions (Mosher 1982, 198). The 1969 executive order also clarified union election procedures, alternative dispute resolution mechanisms, and ultimately placed authority to resolve disputes and alleged unfair practices in the Department of Labor. In 1970, postal workers were afforded collective bargaining rights under the **Postal Reorganization Act**, which established the quasi-corporate and independent nature of the US Postal Service. The act guaranteed the right of postal workers to bargain over wages and working conditions, a right other federal employees still do not have.

Finally, the passage of the **Civil Service Reform Act of 1978** set out the legal parameters of federal labor-management relations for all federal employees. Under the 1978 act, the authority of the FLRC was made permanent, and the agency was transformed into the **Federal Labor Relations Authority (FLRA)**. The FLRA was responsible for overseeing labor-management relations and administering alternative dispute resolution mechanisms to resolve grievances (Mosher 1982, 199). This body is the public sector counterpart of the NLRB, which oversees labor relations in the private sector. Federal employees are still strictly forbidden from striking, however. The Civil Service Reform Act of 1978 and the FLRA continue to govern federal labor-management relations. Today, federal labor unions represent over 1 million workers or 31.2 percent of the federal workforce (BLS 2014a). Examples of federal labor unions are the American Federation of Government Employees (AFGE), the National Federation of Federal Employees (NFFE), and the National Treasury Employees Union (NTEU); Table 9.1 describes each in more detail.

Since the PATCO strike of 1981, public sector labor-management relations have continued to be strained. As we will discuss below, reforms over the last few decades have tended to give management greater leverage in collective bargaining. During the Clinton administration, there was an attempt at reconciliation with the signing of Executive Order 12871. This executive order created the Labor-Management Partnership Council to foster greater communication between the two sides. The goal was to facilitate the implementation of the Clinton administration's National Performance Review (NPR) objectives. However, President George W. Bush revoked 12871 with Executive Order 13203, effectively dissolving the partnership.

Public Sector versus Private Sector Unions

Clearly, there are several significant differences between private and public sector unions. Particularly salient is the difference in how the different types of unions are

| Table 9.1 | Examples of Federal Labor Unions | | | |

Union	Persons Represented	Number of Workers Represented	Agencies Where Workers Are Represented	Year Founded
American Federation of Government Employees	Represents both supervisory and nonsupervisory employees.	650,000 federal employees; 5,000 Washington, D.C., employees; a few hundred private sector employees	Numerous federal agencies and Washington, D.C., government employees	1932
National Federation of Federal Employees	Represents both supervisory and nonsupervisory employees.	110,000	8 federal agencies	1917
National Treasury Employees Union	Represents nonsupervisory employees only.	150,000	31 federal agencies	1938

Sources: Compiled from http://www.afge.org, http://www.nffe.org, and http://www.nteu.org.

regulated. The laws governing public sector unions are complex and differ according to the level of government and the type of agency. While there is some degree of standardization at the federal level (i.e., the Civil Service Reform Act of 1978), there are also some deviations. For example, the US Postal Service is governed by its own specific labor legislation, and more recently the Departments of Homeland Security and Defense have had exceptions that provide management with greater bargaining authority. Each state has its own set of laws governing the formation and activities of unions. As noted above, federal workers may not strike. However, public workers represented by unions are permitted to strike in some states.

Whether public sector workers have the right to strike or not touches upon consequences for national sovereignty. Public sector employees are often tasked with vital services (e.g., public safety), and any disruption to those services via labor activities (e.g., work stoppage, strike) may have a dramatic impact on the functioning of society. While strikes in the private sector might affect the availability of consumer products, such work stoppages do not pose a threat to the safety of citizens. Weighing the rights accorded organized labor in the public sector should be done with careful consideration of the impact that such rights could have on the vital services government provides its citizens.

Unionization at the State and Local Levels

In the early 20th century, state, and local governments experienced a surge in growth similar to that of the federal government. Early on, it was argued that unionization at the regional level was a threat to states' sovereignty, but the gradual expansion of labor rights at the federal level without major difficulties eventually allayed these concerns. The favorable climate for federal unionization unmistakably trickled down to the state and local levels. The presidential executive orders of the 1960s set a precedent and paved the way for unionization and collective bargaining legislation regionally. Like their federal counterparts, state and local public employees were also spurred to organize and petition for statutory expansions to worker rights (Shaw and Clark 1972, 901–4; Kearney 2010). Yet, the expansion of such rights to public sector (and private sector) unions varied regionally, with the North having a more receptive environment and the South a more hostile one. Early urbanization in the North meant a much larger industrial workforce and a better educated one as opposed to the mostly agrarian workforce of southern states. Many southern states also enacted right-to-work laws (see "State and Local Legal Frameworks" below) that limited the activities of labor. The legal environment also improved for labor as state legislatures witnessed dramatic changes in their membership. Before 1970, many state legislatures consisted mostly of rural, antiunion politicians; however, in the 1970s, many of these politicians were replaced with more progressive freshman legislators voted in by an expanded electorate that now included minorities and 18- to 20-year-olds, thanks to civil rights legislation of the 1960s. These representatives tended to be less trustful of elites in government and more inclined to side with labor rights.

Initial organizing efforts at the state and local levels were driven mostly by professionals (e.g., teachers, firefighters, and police), and state and local public employee unionization tends to be structured along specific professions (i.e., the American Federation of Teachers). Professional labor unions are generally national in scope with local chapters representing regional or local interests. Because of varying state laws, public employees who work in similar jobs in different states may enjoy different levels of rights to negotiate or organize. Two national unions, the American Federation of State, County, and Municipal Employees (AFSCME)—founded in Wisconsin in 1932—and the American Federation of Teachers, have capitalized on strong national operations centers supported by a vibrant network at the state and local levels. These unions' national operations tend to be well funded and capable of pressuring politicians at all levels of government to enact or obstruct legislation that would affect union members.

Frameworks for Labor-Management Relations

The legal frameworks governing labor-management relations are important in any labor dispute or negotiation because they set out what activities are permitted and/or required as well as the procedures that must be followed by both labor and management. Public labor relations at the federal level are based on the Civil Service Reform Act of 1978 and the Postal Reorganization Act of 1970, but no overarching act or legislation applies to all states.

Federal Legal Frameworks

As discussed earlier, several executive orders and congressional legislation have over time established various frameworks for labor relations in the federal government. The Civil Service Reform Act of 1978 currently provides the statutory basis for all federal labor relations. Specifically, the act covers all federal employees except for supervisory personnel; members of the armed services; and employees in the postal service, Foreign Service, Federal Bureau of Investigation (FBI), Central Intelligence Agency (CIA), General Accounting Office (GAO), National Security Agency (NSA), Federal Labor Relations Authority, Federal Service Impasses Panel (FSIP), Tennessee Valley Authority (TVA), and US Secret Service. As previously mentioned, the statutory right to bargain for postal employees is mandated in separate legislation, the Postal Reorganization Act of 1970.

Title VII of the 1978 Civil Service Reform Act, also known as the **Federal Service Labor-Management Relations (FSLMR) statute**, synthesized earlier provisions of various executive orders to provide detailed guidelines for the labor rights of federal employees (Thompson 2007). The statute also created the FLRA as an independent administrative agency to oversee labor relations in the federal government. The FLRA is tasked with resolving complaints of unfair labor practices, determining the eligibility of employees to be represented by labor unions, adjudicating exceptions to arbitrators' awards, adjudicating legal issues relating to the duty to bargain in good faith, and resolving impasses during negotiations. The FLRA is comprised of three main bodies—the Authority, the Office of the General Counsel, and the Federal Services Impasses Panel. The Authority adjudicates unfair labor practices allegations, issues raised by petitions to be represented by a union, and exceptions to grievance arbitration awards. It also resolves disputes raised by the parties during collective bargaining and provides specific guidance upon request. The Office of the General Counsel investigates alleged unfair labor practices, files and prosecutes unfair labor practice complaints, processes and determines matters concerning whom can be represented by a union, and provides training and alternative dispute resolution services. The FSIP serves as a medium for resolutions of bargaining impasses by offering assistance with negotiations (FLRA n.d.).

The FSLMR tends to be more favorable to management than to labor. Moreover, the statutory language prohibits the right to strike and the right to arbitration when bargaining impasses occur (Masters and Albright 2003, 176). If an impasse occurs at the federal level, both parties to the negotiation can use as a mediator either a neutral third party or use the **Federal Mediation and Conciliation Service (FMCS)**, an independent agency that mediates public labor disputes. If the parties fail to reach a voluntary settlement, the assistance of the FSIP may be sought.

State and Local Legal Frameworks

There is no single piece of legislation or comprehensive framework that all states or localities follow, although Congress has attempted to regulate state and local government labor relations in the past. The most recent attempt was the Public Safety Employer-Employee Cooperation Act introduced in 2007 and 2009 with the intent of setting minimum standards for collective bargaining among state public safety officers. However, the bill—like previous legislation—remains stalled in Congress. Barring any new initiatives to establish comprehensive labor relations at the state level, local jurisdictions are subject to the labor laws of each state as well as applicable federal case law.

State Labor Laws

Variation in state laws revolves around the extent to which labor has a right to collectively bargain. Six states—Arkansas, Louisiana, Mississippi, North Carolina, South Carolina, and Virginia—have outlawed collective bargaining rights altogether for public employees. In fourteen states—Alabama, Arizona, Colorado, Georgia, Idaho, Indiana, Kentucky, Maryland, Nevada, Oklahoma, Utah, Texas, West Virginia, and Wyoming—collective bargaining is permissible but not mandated by state legislation. The majority of states (30) follow some form of collective bargaining approach to labor-management relations, though the laws, policies, and frameworks in these states vary. States may choose to follow NLRB protocol (which governs private unions) or opt for a meet-and-confer approach (see "Contract Negotiation" below). Figure 9.1 depicts the extent of collective bargaining rights across the country (Kearney 2010).

Many states that do not have comprehensive labor laws are right-to-work states. **Right-to-work laws** give states the authority to determine whether workers can be required to join a labor union to get or keep a job (National Conference of State Legislatures [NCSL] n.d.). In contrast, states that have not adopted right-to-work laws may require employees to join the labor union that represents workers in the organization. Even if an employee refuses membership, he or she may still be required to pay for costs associated with joining a union (e.g., advertising, negotiating), since the

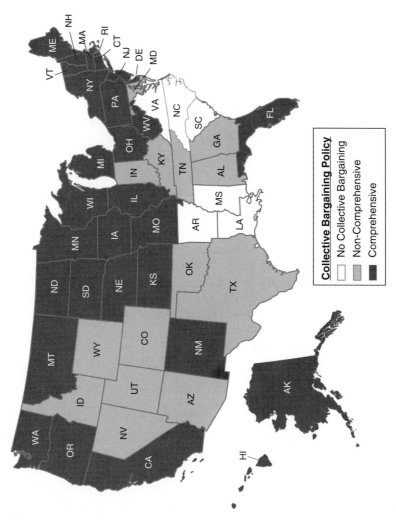

Figure 9.1 Collective Bargaining Rights by State for Public Sector Employees

Collective Bargaining Policy
- No Collective Bargaining
- Non-Comprehensive
- Comprehensive

Source: Kearney 2010

worker will ultimately benefit from such activities. Costs are generally equivalent to membership dues (NCSL 2014).

Right-to-work laws emerged in the states in the 1940s and 1950s, after passage of the Taft Hartley Act in 1947, which outlawed closed union shops. Right-to-work laws are predominantly in southern and western states (see Table 9.2) (Kearney and Carnevale

Table 9.2	States with Right-to-Work Laws	
State	**Year Constitutional Amendment Adopted**	**Year Statute Enacted**
Alabama		1953
Arizona	1946	1947
Arkansas	1944	1947
Florida	1968	1943
Georgia		1947
Idaho		1985
Indiana		2012
Iowa		1947
Kansas	1958	
Louisiana		1976
Mississippi	1960	1954
Michigan		2012
Nebraska	1946	1947
Nevada	1952	1951
North Carolina		1947
North Dakota	1948	1947
Oklahoma	2001	2001
South Carolina		1954
South Dakota	1946	1947
Tennessee		1947
Texas		1993
Utah		1955
Virginia		1947
Wyoming		1963

Source: US Department of Labor (DOL) 2009

2001, 9–10). Since the initial wave of interest in the 1940s, a handful of additional states adopted right-to-work laws. Over the last decade, a handful of states in the Midwest have adopted or are considering adopting right-to-work laws as a part of PHRM reform—a measure that has proven contentious in a region traditionally favorable to unions.

In addition to individual state's labor laws, federal court case decisions can also serve as guidance for state labor relations. The Supreme Court's decision in ***Garcia v. San Antonio Metropolitan Transit Authority* (1985)** leaves open the possibility of comprehensive labor relations legislation. Prior to *Garcia*, the Supreme Court ruled had ruled that Congress did not have the power to regulate wages and hours of governmental employees performing "traditional governmental functions" (see *National League of Cities v. Usery* 1976). In the late 1970s, the San Antonio Metropolitan Transit Authority (SAMTA, now known as VIA Metropolitan Transit) declared that it would no longer observe federal labor requirements that obligated it to pay overtime wages to its employees. In 1979, the Wage and Hour Division of the US Department of Labor contested SAMTA's decision, declaring that the local transit workers were indeed covered by federal wage laws and therefore eligible for overtime pay. SAMTA countered by arguing their transit operations were not regulated by Congress. SAMTA employee Joe G. Garcia and his peers filed suit in federal court, seeking their overtime pay. In *Garcia,* the Court overruled previous decisions, finding that the commerce clause of the Tenth Amendment, typically used to argue for state sovereignty or states' rights, does not preclude application of the Fair Labor Standards Act (FLSA) to state and local government (Kearney and Carnevale 2001, 58). In other words, federal labor law governing overtime pay for employees working forty or more hours a week, applies to state and local employees as well (Buford and Lindner 2002, 377).

Despite the *Garcia* ruling, however, state and local governments still abide by their own established labor relations laws. Unless national legislation is passed to standardize labor relations, states will continue to vary in their treatment of unions. Given the lack of bipartisan efforts in Congress over the last decade, such legislation is not likely anytime soon.

Developing a Framework for Collective Bargaining

In states without right-to-work laws, collective bargaining is often the way that work conditions are determined in unionized workplaces. Collective bargaining is a structured process by which labor and management negotiate to reach agreement. When contracts between labor and management need to be formalized or have expired, collective bargaining provides the structure for ironing out differences between the two parties. Collective bargaining may also be utilized to manage disputes between the two parties. Unlike meet-and-confer approaches, which give management the upper hand, collective bargaining puts the parties on equal terms and provides a formal framework for bargaining in good faith.

The Civil Service Reform Act of 1978 guarantees a collective bargaining process for most federal employees. The act strictly regulates activities that are nonnegotiable (e.g., pay and benefits), permissible (e.g., classification grades), and mandatory (e.g., grievance process) for federal employees. (These terms are defined and discussed below under "Contract Negotiation.")

In states with a legal framework for collective bargaining, the law generally considers factors such as the extent of union activity in the jurisdiction, permissible bargaining issues and activities, who has contract-bargaining authority, the extent of alternative dispute resolutions, and the regional/local history of labor-management relations (Selden 2009, 5). In the absence of their own legislation, many state and local jurisdictions that permit collective bargaining for public employees emulate NLRB rules governing private and nonprofit organizations.

Specific procedures must be followed before collective bargaining can begin. First, each party must determine its respective bargaining unit. Next is the negotiation of the contract. Then if contract negotiations fail, certain grievance procedures must be followed.

Representation, Election, and Certification

The first step in the collective bargaining process is to determine the bargaining unit, that is, the group of employees eligible to be represented by the union in the negotiation. These groups may be determined by professional category; for example, a bargaining unit might be made up of law enforcement personnel or of clerical workers. Alternatively, bargaining units might represent a variety of public sector employees; for example, federal labor unions represent federal employees from a variety of agencies. The FLRA governs federal employee unit determinations, while state and local laws vary (Buford and Lindner 2002, 379).

Once a bargaining unit is determined, the legal right of the unit to representation must be ascertained. Just because a group of employees agree on a set of grievances and wish to petition management for changes does not mean that management will negotiate with them. Complying with legislation gives the bargaining unit the legal status to negotiate on behalf of the employees it represents. Otherwise, employee associations might be viewed as hostile or subversive. Attaining the legal right to representation as a bargaining unit entails a number of steps set forth by the appropriate labor relations board (e.g., FLRA or a state regulatory body), which makes the final decision about who is included in the bargaining unit. Allowing for variation among governments, the criteria used to determine representation typically include the following:

- *Community of interest*—commonly held job characteristics among employees (e.g., similar professions or working conditions)

- *Bargaining history*—pattern of labor-management relationship within jurisdiction (e.g., whether the government jurisdiction has bargained with similar labor unions)
- *Union organizing history*—pattern of labor-organizing efforts (e.g., whether employees have sought legal status, conducted elections for representation, and established a leadership structure)
- *Efficiency of agency operations*—the extent that labor-organizing efforts constrain personnel practices in the jurisdiction
- *Unit size and occupational characteristics*—the size of the organizing unit, which can affect the ability of government to negotiate effectively and equitably with labor (e.g., large unions might have difficulties administering provisions fairly across various occupations)
- *Exclusion of supervisory employees*—restriction of supervisors, who are part of management, from bargaining in league with their subordinates (Kearney and Carnevale 2001, 86–92)

The relevant labor relations board will approve the bargaining unit for representation as long as it meets the appropriate criteria. A bargaining unit should typically have a shared community of interest and a formalized structure. Similarly, the jurisdiction should have a history of bargaining with similar employee units. A labor relations regulatory body may deny a bargaining unit status if the regulatory body determines that the unit has no leadership structure or if the unit is so large that negotiating would be too unwieldy. Once a bargaining unit has been determined and a decision has been made about representation, elections of representatives and certification of the unit take place. While the FLRA oversees certification of federal labor union elections, state and local procedures vary. Typically, recognition is afforded to the unit either by voluntary recognition (e.g., all union members agree to the unit) or an election indicating that a significant proportion of employees seek representation. Such evidence is generally provided when at least 30 percent of the bargaining unit has expressed a "showing of interest" (i.e., that they want to be represented by the union) (Kearney and Carnevale 2001, 92).

Once an election has confirmed the desire for union representation, the FLRA or the appropriate state or local regulatory agency approves certification of the bargaining unit, providing the union with the legal status to collectively bargain with management. Certification of the bargaining unit normally stands for at least one year. If after one year the unit has not finalized its status through the regulatory body, a decertification election may take place based on the same parameters as used for certification.

Contract Negotiation

Once representation has been established, labor and management must attempt to negotiate a contract. Contract negotiation is the crux of collective bargaining, during which labor and management seek to come to an agreement on any and all issues that fall within the established scope of bargaining.

Federal Scope of Bargaining

As previously mentioned, the FSLMR regulates labor relations at the federal level. The FSLMR specifically lays out the scope of bargaining issues between labor and management (i.e., what matters are up for negotiation). Every issue is classified as nonnegotiable, permissive, or mandatory in nature. The specific matters that fall into each classification include the following:

- *Nonnegotiable*—(1) matters established by law (i.e., position classification, Hatch Act enforcement, and pay); (2) government-wide rules and regulations; (3) rules and regulations of an agency or primary national subdivision, unless the FLRA has determined that there is no compelling need to prohibit negotiations or that a union represents a majority of the affected employees (who make up a single bargaining unit); (4) management rights, including interpretation of the agency's mission, determination of its budget, organization, number of employees, and internal security, and the right to take personnel actions involving the assignment of work, contracting out, promotions, and emergency actions
- *Permissive*—(1) the numbers, types, and grades of employees or positions assigned to an organizational subdivision, work project, or tour of duty; and (2) technology—the means or the methods of performing work
- *Mandatory*—(1) conditions of employment that do not fall into either of the above categories; (2) procedures for implementing actions within management's preserved rights; (3) appropriate arrangements for employees adversely affected by management's exercise of its reserved rights; and (4) a grievance procedure, which must allow for conclusion by binding arbitration (Shafritz et al. 2001, 483–84)

Matters that are nonnegotiable are simply that—they are never up for negotiation. An example of a nonnegotiable federal matter would be pay and benefits. The US Constitution affords only Congress the right to handle the appropriation of funds. Thus, permitting federal employees the right to negotiate over pay would be unconstitutional. Matters that are permissive may be negotiated, but negotiation is not required. If an agency is considering reforming the classification structure, employees may request for the changes to be part of negotiations, but management does not have to agree to negotiate this issue. Matters that are mandatory are required to be negotiated. Mandatory matters typically involve the grievance process for employees, a right guaranteed by due process of the law.

As noted earlier, the FSLMR gives the upper hand to management in contract negotiations. The above classifications notwithstanding, it should be noted that the language of the FSLMR limits the scope of bargaining to matters not related to pay and benefits. At the federal level, then, pay and benefits may *never* be negotiated.

State/Local Scope of Bargaining

In states that allow collective bargaining, a similar tripartite framework holds for state and local contract negotiations. Scope of bargaining is usually determined by the individual state labor laws or regulations of state labor regulatory boards. According to Buford and Linder (2002, 380), bargaining issues at the state and local levels generally fall into the following three categories:

- *Mandatory*—typically wages, hours, and other terms and conditions of employment (Note that while at the state level, negotiation of wages may be mandatory, federal employees are prohibited from bargaining over wages and hours.)
- *Prohibited*—generally issues covered by civil service regulations, matters of organizational "mission," and items set forth in state legislation as management rights (For example, states considering changing the state civil service code to implement employment at will do not have to consult with employees; because this is a matter of writing law, the issue is left up to elected representatives.)
- *Permissive*—items not covered under mandatory and not excluded by prohibited categories (e.g., other terms and conditions of employment)

At the state level, all matters regarding wages, hours, and other conditions of employment may require a contract to be executed (Buford and Lindner 2002, 380). Contracts between labor and management may also include benefits, control over work scheduling and work rules, overtime and holiday pay, dismissal and disciplinary procedures, and pay equity or comparable worth.

At both federal and state levels, the scope of bargaining classification sets out very clearly what types of issues may and may not be negotiated.

State Collective Bargaining: Adopting the NLRB Framework

The influence of private sector labor on state and local government labor-management relations is apparent, as states that want to adopt more comprehensive labor relations for public employees typically view the framework established by the NLRB as a standard for collective bargaining (Buford and Lindner 2002). The NLRB approach includes the following:

- Employee rights to union formation and collective bargaining
- Establishment of an administrative agency for oversight and unit certification
- Exclusive recognition of any union that wins majority support
- Obligation of the employer to bargain with the union
- Explicit language recognizing management rights
- The exclusion of certain matters from negotiations (management prerogatives)
- Impasse resolution procedures/alternative dispute resolutions
- Union security provisions
- Codes of unfair labor practices for both management and labor (377)

State Collective Bargaining: Meet-and-Confer Approach

Some jurisdictions that lack comprehensive collective bargaining agreements may choose to take a less structured approach to labor relations. One such mechanism is the **meet-and-confer approach**, which establishes a minimum set of principles allowing unions to bring concerns to management. This approach greatly favors the employer in labor relations because it does not require management to recognize the issues raised by employees. According to Buford and Lindner (2002), meet-and-confer approaches to labor relations often include the following:

- Management and labor are on unequal terms.
- The employer has no obligation to bargain.
- The employer sets the agenda for discussion.
- Management has final say on the outcomes of any discussion.
- Management retains most rights.
- Final authority rests with management.
- No administrative oversight is in place, leaving labor law enforcement up to state courts (376).

According to Buford and Lindner (2002), such an approach represents a "middle ground," allowing for some minimal parameters rather than interacting in an environment with no labor relations structure at all. Many governments seek a less structured approach to collective bargaining to improve efficiency or attract industry to the jurisdiction. Although the meet-and-confer approach is management centered, labor is not entirely deterred from seeking redress. The effectiveness of the meet-and-confer approach may depend upon the relationships established over time between management and labor. If appointed officials in a particular agency and union leaders have a good working relationship with open channels of communication, management may be more receptive to issues raised by labor representatives. If the relationship is more hostile, then management is less likely to consult with labor leaders.

Reaching an Agreement

The crux of any labor-management relationship is the commitment and responsibility of each party—management and labor—to **bargain in good faith**. Bargaining in good faith means that each party actively contributes to deliberations, thus signifying an intention to reach an agreement (NLRB n.d.a). Such a good-faith effort demonstrates not only a willingness to reach agreement but a commitment to find common ground. The criteria by which a good-faith effort is evaluated include a willingness of both parties to meet at reasonable times and regular intervals and to deal with persons of authority from the other party. Good-faith efforts may also include conduct away from the bargaining table. Kearney and Feldman (2004) suggested that the following principles be considered when determining whether a party is bargaining in good faith:

- Time restrictions on contract modifications, terminations, and negotiations
- Duty to disclose relevant bargaining information
- Presence of people with the authority to bargain during negotiations
- Preclusion of employer making unilateral changes to existing compensation and working conditions during negotiations
- Prohibition of work stoppages during negotiations
- Inclusion of alternative dispute resolution mechanisms to resolve impasses
- Obligation to execute a written agreement
- Outlining terms of bad-faith bargaining to prevent such practices (98)

The contract is an extension of this good-faith effort, as it puts into writing the terms agreed upon by both labor and management. As such, representatives of both labor and management are tasked with bringing to the negotiating table an open mind and a sincere effort to reach agreement. As long as both management and labor continue to bargain in good faith, the parties to the negotiation are under no obligation to agree to either side's proposals or concessions. The hope is that the two parties will eventually be able to negotiate a contract that is mutually acceptable.

However, in some cases, the parties may not be able or willing to compromise. Failure to agree on a contract results in an impasse. Most jurisdictions have an independent body responsible for overseeing a resolution to impasses (e.g., the FSIP for federal labor impasses or a corresponding state body). Typically, such governing bodies resort to **alternative dispute resolutions (ADR)** such as mediation, fact-finding, and arbitration, to resolve the impasse. Table 9.3 presents the basic elements of each of the ADRs commonly used to resolve impasses.

The benefit of using ADR to overcome an impasse is that it avoids the courts. Litigation can be time-consuming and expensive. The informal nature of ADR allows for more open dialogue between the two parties and greater flexibility in determining the parameters of the process. Ultimately, it is a timely, cost-effective, and less adversarial approach to dispute resolution for labor and management (O'Leary and Raines 2001, 682).

Strikes in the Public Sector

Despite the best efforts of both parties to reach an agreement on a contract, including attempts via ADRs, sometimes an impasse is still unavoidable. In some cases, the union will choose to take the extreme measure of going on strike, meaning that the

Table 9.3	**Alternative Dispute Resolution**

Mediation—A neutral third party (mediator) facilitates a voluntary settlement to the impasse. The mediator uses communication and persuasion to assist labor and management in reaching an agreement. Mediators cannot enforce a solution, but they may offer potential resolutions.

Fact-finding—This more structured, quasi-judicial approach may be used as an initial step or when mediation fails. Both parties present evidence and arguments in a hearing before the fact-finder(s). The fact-finder(s) then presents a report of the most objective facts and recommends a nonbinding settlement, which either or both parties may reject.

Arbitration—Like fact-finding, arbitration is a judicial type of proceeding in which the parties submit evidence and arguments to the arbitrator. However, arbitration is final and binding upon both parties. Arbitration, seen as a means for expediting a resolution to the impasse to minimize disruption of work, is often mandated by state law. Arbitration may come in two forms:

- *Conventional*—The arbitrator is given the discretion to choose one or the other party's evidence or a combination.
- *Final-offer*—Each party presents its "last best offer" for the arbitrator to choose from, binding the parties to one or the other's "offer." The entire package of issues under negotiation may be submitted for determination, or each issue may be submitted separately.

Source: Kearney and Feldman 2004

employees walk out or refuse to report for work. Employees who strike do so to pressure politicians and public sector managers to accede to their demands. When all else fails, strikes are seen as a means to cultivate public support for workers' plights and to make it difficult for management to meet productivity goals.

The right to strike is problematic in the public sector. The democratic process affords citizens a voice through congressional representatives. When labor unions are permitted to strike, government is yielding power to a group not elected by citizens, thus violating the concept of sovereignty. Furthermore, critics contend that public employees and their unions have an unfair advantage because their position within government gives them insider information that they can leverage to influence policy. Finally, strikes have the potential to disrupt public services that may be essential to life, liberty, and property, thereby threatening the public welfare. For example, a Baltimore police strike in 1974 resulted in strife and unrest, including fires and looting. The Baltimore incident provoked labor unrest among law enforcement officers in other jurisdictions as well (Prout 2010).

Only 11 states afford public employees the right to strike (Kerrigan 2012). In jurisdictions where strikes are illegal, dissatisfied employees may take part in a work slowdown, deliberately slowing their work and reducing productivity. Another, more common, tactic is the "blue flu," where public employees collectively call in "sick." Jurisdictions that permit strikes generally do not allow public employees in vital services such as public safety or law enforcement to strike. Public managers in jurisdictions that permit strikes should prepare a contingency plan that focuses on maintaining services during the strike, considers public support for labor rights, and provides for legal remedies to end the strike when necessary (Shafritz et al. 2001).

Grievance Procedures

Once bargaining is completed and the contract is signed, the written agreement between the two parties must be enforced in the workplace. Unfortunately, not all contracts between labor and management operate smoothly. Often bad-faith efforts on the part of one or both parties result in complaints that must be resolved. Tables 9.4 and 9.5 list instances of unfair labor practices at both the federal and state/local levels that might produce complaints.

The grievance procedure establishes a structured process for assessing when the terms of the contract have been violated or misapplied and how the situation might be resolved (Chaison 2006). According to Kearney and Feldman (2004), a grievance procedure typically includes three stages. Initially, an informal attempt is made to resolve the complaint through a conversation or informal meeting with one's immediate supervisor. If the issue is not resolved, the second stage requires union involvement; labor representatives speak on behalf of the aggrieved party, and a written

Table 9.4	Typical Examples of Unfair Labor Practices in Federal Government

By Management	By Union
• Making threatening statements to employees to discourage the filing of a representation petition • Conveying the impression that employees' conduct will be closely monitored as a result of filing an unfair labor practice charge • Making implied threats against union representatives for aiding employees in the filing and prosecution of grievances under the parties' negotiated grievance procedure • Issuing a written reprimand to a unit employee in retaliation for activity on behalf of the union • Failing to promote an employee because of that employee's union activities or inactivities	• Informing an employee that membership in the labor organization is required to obtain union assistance processing a grievance • Attempting to get management to discipline an employee who did not join the labor organization • Attempting to get management to discharge an employee because he or she was organizing on behalf of a different labor organization • Imposing fines on unit employees who exceed a certain predetermined standard of efficiency • Restricting an employee from serving as an officer of the labor organization if the employee has received an outstanding performance award

Source: FLRA 2001

Table 9.5	Typical Examples of Unfair Labor Practices in State and Local Government

By Management	By Union
• Interfering, restraining, or coercing public employees in the exercise of statutory rights • Interfering or assisting in the formation or operation of an employee organization • Refusing to follow statutory impasse procedures • Instituting a lockout • Dealing directly with employees rather than with their bargaining representatives on bargaining issues	• Interfering, restraining, or coercing public employees in regard to protecting the exercise of statutory rights • Refusing to meet and bargain in good faith • Refusing to follow statutory impasse procedures • Engaging in or instigating a strike • Interfering with an employee's work performance or productivity

Source: Kearney and Carnevale 2001

record of the grievance is forwarded to a department head or upper management. At the third stage, if the complaint is still unresolved, human resources professionals and union committee members will step in to assess the grievance and provide a possible solution. If a compromise fails, both parties move to ADR or, as a last resort, litigation.

Labor-Management Relations in a PHRM Reform Environment

Public labor unions have faced tremendous challenges to their power and authority in the reform era. They have felt the impact of all five reform themes to varying extents. Homeland security legislation at the federal level and reforms at the state and local level over the last decade have sought to restrict the bargaining rights of labor (Brook and King 2008; Riccucci 2011b). While proponents of labor unions argue that they are an integral part of the effective delivery of government services, PHRM reforms contend that labor unions are recalcitrant impediments to productivity that cost taxpayers millions of dollars in work stoppages (McCartin 2011). As a result, public sector labor unions have frequently been a prime target of PHRM reform. Recent reforms in the states of Michigan and Wisconsin—resulting in work stoppages, litigation, and political strife—highlight the contentious climate of contemporary labor-management relations.

Federal Reform Era: Changing Economic and Political Environment

As detailed earlier in the chapter, public sector labor unions flourished during the mid- to late 20th century, unlike their counterparts in the private sector. However, by the 1970s, serious efforts to reform labor-management relations were under way in both the United States and abroad in response to fiscal austerity brought on by energy shortages and inflation. In the United States, labor unions were viewed as an obstruction to the efficient running of government. Negotiations for improved working conditions, and work stoppages when negotiations fail, can be costly and time-consuming. As a result, proponents of reform have targeted labor-management frameworks that include collective bargaining (traditionally viewed as antithetical to free enterprise) in favor of more management-centered policies.

Unlike the National Partnership Council established by the Clinton administration in the 1990s in order to foster labor-management cooperation, President Bush's Management Agenda proposed a variety of government reform efforts that collectively sought to minimize the power of labor unions. These reforms were characterized as a drive toward a more "citizen-centered, market-based, and results-oriented" public service (Bradbury, Battaglio, and Crum 2010, 448). In 2001, President Bush's Executive Order 13203 abolished the NPC and directed all heads of agencies to "promptly move to quash any orders, rules, regulations, guidelines or policies implementing or enforcing Executive Order 12871" (Office of Personnel Management [OPM] 2001). The new order effectively reversed the arrangements put in place by the Clinton administration to foster labor-management partnerships.

In addition, in the wake of the tragedy of September 11, 2001, the Bush administration oversaw a number of initiatives to overhaul the personnel systems of federal agencies, including the National Security Personnel System at the Department of Defense (Brook and King 2008; Bradbury, Battaglio, and Crum 2010). The personnel changes provided the secretaries of the agencies with the power to act on personnel matters without consulting with labor and installed a performance-based pay system. Along with the largest reorganization of the federal executive branch in the modern era by way of the creation of the Department of Homeland Security (DHS), the Bush administration oversaw significant changes to labor-management relations in the federal workforce. The Aviation and Transportation Act of 2002 gave DHS management the right to bar some 50,000 employees of the newly created Transportation Security Administration (TSA) from union representation (Kearney 2010, 103). Moreover, the Homeland Security Act (2002) and the National Defense Authorization Act (2002) provide the secretaries of the Departments of Homeland Security (DHS) and Defense (DOD) the right to oversee and restrict the scope of bargaining, going so far as to provide the head of DHS the authority to declare any part of an existing collective bargaining agreement "null and void" (Kearney 2010, 103). This legislation also further restricted—in some cases "exempted"—collective bargaining and unionization guidelines under Title VII in both DHS and DOD (Ferris and Hyde 2004; Kearney 2010). The National Defense Authorization Act of 2002 mandated further civil service reform, giving the DOD exemption from Title V civil service protections for public employees as well as the right to fashion its own pay, classification, performance evaluation, labor relations, and employee appeals systems (Bradbury, Battaglio, and Crum 2010; Kearney 2010, 104).

In 2008, however, federal courts struck down several of these provisions as violating civil servants' rights; these decisions prompted the Bush administration to restore labor-management relations under previous civil service guidelines (Ballenstedt 2008; Riccucci and Thompson 2008, 883). Additionally, the performance-based pay system proved controversial. Divisive elements of the plan included the awarding of higher performance ratings to white employees than to nonwhite employees and civilians employed in defense agencies. Moreover, raises and bonuses were largely inconsistent with performance ratings (Losey 2008). The administration of President Barack Obama repealed the pay system on October 29, 2009, restoring all DOD employees to the General Schedule by January 1, 2012.

State Pressures on Unions

At the state level, recent high-profile reforms of labor-management legislation have spurred interest in collective bargaining rights of public employees (Kearney 2010; Riccucci 2011a; 2011b). Most prominent among reform efforts have been those of the states of Michigan and Wisconsin, which sought to curtail public sector employees' rights concerning collective bargaining.

Passed in 2011, Wisconsin Act 10—also known as the Budget Repair Bill—outlined a number of austerity measures aimed at controlling state spending (State of Wisconsin 2011). The measures were implemented to cut expenses and increase state revenues in order to balance the budget, and they negatively impacted union rights in the process. One of the key provisions that directly affected labor-management relations was a requirement that state employees increase their contributions to their health care and pension plans, thereby reducing the state's financial contributions. The act also placed restrictions on government employees' collective bargaining rights, stipulating that they could only negotiate over wages; they no longer had a say in other issues such as restructuring efforts at the state level. In addition, the act capped base wage increases at changes in the Consumer Price Index (CPI).

The Budget Repair Bill also restricted contracts to one year with no extensions; contracts would have to be renegotiated each year rather than every few years. It prohibited automatic deductions of union dues from paychecks, allowed any employee to opt out of paying union dues, and required that unions hold annual certification votes via secret ballot. If a majority of total union members failed to vote for certification, the union would be decertified and barred from representating those workers for one year.

The legislation has prompted a great deal of opposition from public employee unions. Some labor unions have requested that the courts strike down the bill as a violation of the state's open meeting laws. While a recent federal court decision struck down elements of the bill as unconstitutional, the measure is still unresolved in terms of state law as this book goes to press (Vielmetti and Marley 2012).

Similar efforts in the state of Michigan have curtailed public sector union rights. Specifically, right-to-work laws were enacted in that state in 2012 as part of Public Act 349, making it illegal to require employees to contribute financially to a union as a condition of employment. Public sector unions in Michigan fought the act on the grounds that right-to-work laws cannot apply to the public sector. The Michigan Court of Appeals disagreed, arguing that the right-to-work laws do indeed apply to civil servants represented by unions (Gray 2013).

Several other states—including Arizona, Colorado, Indiana, and Tennessee—are also considering reform legislation that would restrict collective bargaining rights in the public sector (Maynard 2012). For reformers, unions are seen as stumbling blocks to overcome because unions tend to oppose the negative impact of such reforms on wages and job security. Not surprisingly, these states are also considering decentralization, deregulation, performance-based pay, declassification, and privatization as part of a larger overhaul of government. There is a very apparent push to roll back public union influence, a trend that is of great concern for public union leaders.

Impact of PHRM Reforms

In addition to the specific legislation discussed above, public labor has been impacted by all five of the reforms. Decentralization efforts tend to place greater authority in the hands of management, thus insulating labor unions from involvement in the policy-making process. Likewise, deregulation efforts like employment at will tend to weaken the influence of labor unions in civil service systems. Reformers argue that the job security afforded public employees within civil service systems strengthens the bargaining power of labor unions, so EAW policies naturally have the opposite effect. Fearing reprisals, employees will hesitate to speak out against reform-related issues in an EAW environment. It is not coincidental that most deregulation reform efforts have taken place in right-to-work states, which tend to be less hospitable to unions and do not guarantee labor involvement in the reform process.

Public employee unions may temper the extent of EAW but really cannot preclude its adoption in jurisdictions across the country (Condrey and Battaglio 2007). The result of this decentralized, at-will environment is the replacement of traditional rule-bound, centralized personnel practices with more agency-specific, manager-centered systems. This occurs more often in states with weak employee unions. Evidence from Service First reforms in Florida in 2001 suggests that at-will employment schemes might be mitigated to an extent by public sector unions (Bowman and West 2006). Since its inception in 2001, Florida's Service First program has placed approximately 16,000 senior state government managers—out of a total of approximately 124,000 state employees—in at-will status. However, notable exceptions are law enforcement and nursing employees, who have strong union representation in the state.

Decentralization and deregulation efforts at the federal level have also diminished labor rights in favor of greater managerial flexibility (Brook and King 2008). Reforms in the DHS and DOD have increased the use of performance-based pay systems, given management greater flexibility vis-à-vis labor relations, and afforded agencies authorization to design and operate their own personnel systems (Brook and King 2008, 215). Ultimately, dissatisfaction among federal employees and discrepancies in the management of the National Defense Personnel System (NDPS) led to its abolishment in 2012.

Labor unions have been at odds with performance-based pay and declassification efforts. The view of labor is that both of these reforms create inequalities in terms of individual performance evaluation and pay. It can be difficult to quantify productivity in public sector jobs because they often entail improving the quality of life of others and the general public interest. Declassification is problematic because it may result in higher pay grades and salaries for newly hired employees, an outcome that runs counter to the traditional classification system that rewards seniority.

Clearly, labor unions are opposed to the privatization of work carried out by the public servants they represent. Hiring private sector employees to carry out public sector services means that public employees will either be terminated or displaced. This is an attractive option to proponents of reform because private sector workers, who do not enjoy the costly benefits associated with public employment, are less expensive. Consequently, reformers have sought to curtail or outright eliminate labor union participation in negotiations over HR activities, especially any discussion of farming out work to private contractors.

Interestingly, despite the pervasiveness of public employee unions and collective bargaining, many of these reform efforts continue unchallenged. Kearney (2010) suggested that public sector unions face a number of challenges. To survive, they need to do the following:

- Validate union relevance to current and prospective dues-paying members.
- Petition state and local governments for new enabling legislation for uncovered categories of workers.
- Resist privatization and outsourcing of traditional public service functions.
- Recognize changing demographics and technologies in the workplace.
- Foster positive public opinion of public unions (105).

With the fiscal constraints placed on governments as a result of the economic downturn that began in 2008, public sector unions have been faced with the prospect of continued reductions in force, modest wage increases, reductions in the level and scope of benefits, and increased employee costs for those benefits. Furthermore, the future of labor-management cooperation appears to be very tenuous—a situation that may only further constrain government performance. For public HR managers, maintaining an open and friendly dialogue with unions is essential to ensuring cooperation. Open channels of communication can prevent resentment and protests, which can negatively affect productivity.

Nonprofits in Focus	Labor Relations, Collective Bargaining, and NPOs

Since the 1970s, labor relations in the nonprofit sector have been governed by the same regulations as those in the private sector. The National Labor Relations Board (NLRB) enforces labor laws affecting nonprofits, including the National Labor Relations Act of 1935, the Labor-Management Relations Act of 1947, and the Labor-Management Reporting and Disclosure Act of 1959 (Pynes 2006, 237–38). The NLRB's authority over nonprofits is triggered by gross annual volume (i.e., the total annual revenue of the nonprofit organization). Health care and child care institutions (e.g., hospitals, medical and dental offices, social services organizations, child care centers, and residential care centers) with a gross annual volume of at least $250,000 are under NLRB jurisdiction; for nursing homes and visiting nurses associations, the threshold is $100,000. For cultural and educational centers (such as private and nonprofit colleges, universities, and other schools; art museums; and symphony orchestras), the minimum annual revenue is $1 million. The NLRB's authority over religious organizations depends on the activity of the nonprofit. According to the NLRB, "the Board will not assert jurisdiction over employees of a religious organization who are involved in effectuating the religious purpose of the organization, such as teachers in church-operated schools" (NLRB n.d.b). However, the NLRB has become involved in labor-management disputes when the religious organization's activities are not of a "religious character" (e.g., providing health care). For example, disputes arising at a Catholic hospital involving religious orders, management, and employees carrying out secular activities can involve state regulatory bodies and national labor unions. Unions have sued Catholic hospitals for using public funds for antiunion activities. Such disputes have resulted in the US Conference of Catholic Bishops (USCCB), with leaders of Catholic health care providers and labor unions, releasing guidelines for a "fair process" by which health care workers can decide whether or not to form a new union. NPOs that fall below the relevant revenue thresholds are not subject to the national labor relations acts.

NPOs tend to have charitable objectives, but they are not immune from labor-management disputes. This was recently demonstrated by the firing of five nonprofit employees of Hispanics United of Buffalo for posting criticism of workplace conditions on the social media site Facebook. While Hispanics United argued that the individuals involved were terminated because they had committed workplace harassment of another employee, the NLRB sided with the fired employees. The NLRB cited Section 7 of the National Labor Relations Act, which defines protected activity. Section 7 states, "Employees shall have the right to self-organization, to form, join, or assist labor organizations, to bargain collectively through representatives of their own choosing, and to engage in other concerted activities for the purpose of collective bargaining or other mutual aid and protection." Additionally, Section 7 protects employees engaged in grievances, on-the-job protests, picketing, and strikes (Lester 2011).

Now that social media websites have become the proverbial watercooler, many HR managers question the extent of protections afforded employees to speak their minds. Are such websites an appropriate place for nonprofit employees to air grievances? The NLRB seems to think so, ruling in favor of employees in a number of cases. Unfortunately, until the issue comes to the courts' attention, nonprofit HR managers may be left with little guidance. While the courts have recognized the right of employees to exercise labor-related freedoms outside the workplace, the line separating work from leisure has become complicated in the age of social media. For example, would it be permissible for a nonprofit employee to post a message about work on a personal social media site while on the job? Thus, nonprofit organizations would be wise to establish a social media policy that oulines appropriate and inappropriate workplace-related conduct.

Given the policy statement issued by the USCCB, nonprofits are treating the issue of labor-management relations seriously. Clear guidelines established through a formal policy can streamline labor-management relations and avoid costly litigation.

Conclusion

Continuing with our five themes of reform, several lessons can be drawn. We see that PHRM reforms have seriously threatened the influence of labor unions and the right of public employees to organize. In particular, the trend toward decentralization and deregulation has had a profound impact on public sector labor unions, giving management more power and labor correspondingly less. Thus, practitioners advocating reforms should expect to encounter the greatest resistance in states with strong public employee unions. However, research suggests that even in states with a strong labor presence, the move to greater managerial discretion may still erode due process protections (Hays and Sowa 2006, 111). As the public sector has more experience with decentralization and deregulation and abuses are chronicled, we can expect a backlash in some states. In other states, however, the story may be more subtle. Particularly in those states without union protection and a vigilant press, excellent civil servants may be replaced by well-connected cronies (Condrey and Battaglio 2007). The result may well be reduced trust in public management and organizations on the part of employees and the public alike.

Public HR managers need more guidelines for interacting with labor. Informal activities—such as meeting regularly and establishing lines of communication with union representatives—can streamline labor-management relations. Even in a PHRM reform environment, regular informal contact can be an important way to avoid disputes that can spill over into political protests and costly legal action. Communication may be key to resolving labor-management conflicts in the reform environment.

References

Aldt, Toke, and Zafiris Tzannatos. 2002. *Unions and Collective Bargaining: Economic Effects in a Global Environment.* Washington, DC: The World Bank.

Ballenstedt, Brittany R. 2008. "Pentagon Drops Plans to Convert Union Employees NSPS." *Government Executive,* September 30. http://www.govexec.com/defense/2008/09/pentagon-drops-plans-to-convert-union-employees-to-nsps/27783/.

Battaglio, R. Paul, Jr. 2010. "Public Service Reform and Motivation: Evidence from an Employment At-Will Environment." *Review of Public Personnel Administration* 30:341–63.

Battaglio, R. Paul, Jr., and Stephen E. Condrey. 2006. "Civil Service Reform: Examining State and Local Government Cases." *Review of Public Personnel Administration* 26:118–38.

Battaglio, R. Paul, Jr., and Stephen E. Condrey. 2009. "Reforming Public Management: Analyzing the Impact of Public Service Reform on Organizational and Managerial Trust." *Journal of Public Administration Research & Theory* 19:689–707.

Bowman, James S., Mark C. Gertz, Sally G. Gertz, and Russell L. Williams. 2003. "Civil Service Reform in Florida State Government: Employee Attitudes 1 Year Later." *Review of Public Personnel Administration* 23:286–304.

Bowman, James S., and Jonathan P. West. 2006. "Ending Civil Service Protections in Florida Government: Experiences in State Agencies," *Review of Public Personnel Administration* 26:139–57.

Bradbury, Mark D., R. Paul Battaglio Jr., and John L. Crum. 2010. "Continuity Amid Discontinuity? George W. Bush, Federal Employment Discrimination, and 'Big Government Conservatism.'" *Review of Public Personnel Administration* 30:445–66.

Brook, Douglas A., and Cynthia L. King. 2008. "Federal Personnel Management Reform: From Civil Service Reform Act to National Security Reforms." *Review of Public Personnel Administration* 28:205–21.

Buford, James A., Jr., and James R. Lindner. 2002. *Human Resource Management in Local Government: Concepts and Applications for HRM Students and Practitioners.* Cincinnati, OH: South-Western.

Bureau of Labor Statistics (BLS). 2014a. "Union Members News Release 2013." Press release, January 24. http://www.bls.gov/news.release/pdf/union2.pdf.

Bureau of Labor Statistics (BLS). 2014b. "Union Members Summary." Press release, January 6. http://www.bls.gov/news.release/union2.nr0.htm.

Chaison, Gary N. 2006. *Unions in America.* Thousand Oaks, CA: SAGE.

Commonwealth v. Hunt, 45 Mass. 111 (1842).

Condrey, Stephen E., and R. Paul Battaglio Jr. 2007. "A Return to Spoils? Revisiting Radical Civil Service Reform in the United States." *Public Administration Review* 67:424–36.

Early, Steve. 2006. "An Old Lesson Still Holds for Unions." *The Boston Globe,* July 31, http://www.boston.com/news/globe/editorial_opinion/oped/articles/2006/07/31/an_old_lesson_still_holds_for_unions/.

Federal Labor Relations Authority (FLRA). 2001. *A Guide to the Federal Service Labor-Management Relations Program.* https://www.flra.gov/webfm_send/441.

Federal Labor Relations Authority (FLRA). n.d. "Introduction to the FLRA." Accessed January 7, 2014. http://www.flra.gov/introduction-flra/.

Federal Service Labor-Management Relations Statute (FSLMR), 5 U.S.C. §71 et seq.

Ferris, Frank, and Albert C. Hyde. 2004. "Federal Labor-Management Relations for the Next Century—or the Last? The Case of the Department of Homeland Security." *Review of Public Personnel Administration* 24:216–33.

Gray, Kathleen. 2013. "Court: Michigan Right-to-Work Law Must Cover Unionized State Employees." *Detroit Free Press,* August 15, http://www.freep.com/article/20130815/NEWS06/308150140/michigan-right-to-work-civil-service-employees/.

Guy, Mary E. 2004, April. *Civil Service Reform: A Comparative Perspective.* Paper presented at the University of Georgia, Athens.

Hays, Steven W., and Jessica E. Sowa. 2006. "A Broader Look at the 'Accountability' Movement: Some Grim Realities in State Civil Service Systems." *Review of Public Personnel Administration* 26:102–17.

Kearney, Richard C. 2010. "Public Sector Labor–Management Relations: Change or Status Quo?" *Review of Public Personnel Administration* 30:89–111.

Kearney, Richard C., and David Carnevale. 2001. *Labor Relations in the Public Sector*. 3rd ed. New York: Marcel Dekker.

Kearney, Richard C., and Barry M. Feldman. 2004. "Labor-Management Relations and Collective Bargaining." In *Human Resource Management in Local Government: An Essential Guide*, edited by Siegrun Fox Freyss, 93–108. Washington, DC: International City/Council Management Association.

Kerrigan, Heather. 2012. "Why Public-Sector Strikes Are So Rare." *Governing*, October 10, http://www.governing.com/topics/public-workforce/col-why-public-sector-strikes-are-rare.html.

Lester, Aaron. 2011. "Facebook Firings and the Labor Relations Board: What Nonprofits Need to Know." *Nonprofit Quarterly*, June 16, https://nonprofitquarterly.org/index.php?option=com_content&view=article&id=13201.

Losey, Stephen. 2008. "Is DoD's New Pay System Fair?" *Federal Times*, April 11, http://www.federaltimes.com/article/20080811/DEPARTMENTS01/111122001/1023/DEPARTMENTS01/.

Masters, Marick F., and Robert R. Albright. 2003. "Federal Labor-Management Partnerships: Perspectives, Performance, and Possibilities." In *Going Public: The Role of Labor-Management Relations in Delivering Quality Government Services*, edited by Jonathan Brock and David B. Lipsky, 171–210. Champaign, IL: Industrial Relations Research Association.

Maynard, Melissa. 2012. "States Push to Shake Up Personnel Practices." *Stateline*, February 16, http://www.stateline.org/live/details/story?contentId=632584.

McCartin, Joseph A. 2011. "What's Really Going on in Wisconsin?" *The New Republic*, February 19, http://www.tnr.com/article/politics/83829/wisconsin-public-employees-walker-negotiate/.

Mosher, Frederick C. 1982. *Democracy and the Public Service*. 2nd ed. Oxford, England: Oxford University Press.

National Conference of State Legislatures (NCSL). n.d. "Right-to-Work Resources." Accessed January 7, 2014. http://www.ncsl.org/research/labor-and-employment/right-to-work-laws-and-bills.aspx.

National Labor Relations Board (NLRB). n.d.a. "How is 'Good Faith' Bargaining Determined?" Accessed April 30, 2014. http://www.nlrb.gov/rights-we-protect/employerunion-rights-and-obligations#main-content.

National Labor Relations Board (NLRB). n.d.b. "Jurisdictional Standards." Accessed April 30, 2014. http://www.nlrb.gov/rights-we-protect/jurisdictional-standards#main-content.

National League of Cities v. Usery, 426 U.S. 833 (1976).

Office of Personnel Management (OPM). 2001. "Memorandum for Heads of Departments and Agencies." Memorandum, March 1. http://main.opm.gov/LMR/guide413203.asp.

O'Leary, Rosemary, and Susan Summers Raines. 2001. "Lessons Learned from Two Decades of Alternative Dispute Resolution Programs and Processes at the US Environmental Protection Agency." *Public Administration Review* 61:682–92.

Prout, Bob. 2010. "The Most Important Profession." *FBI Law Enforcement Bulletin,* April. http://www.fbi.gov/stats-services/publications/law-enforcement-bulletin/april-2010/notable-speech/.

Pynes, Joan E. 2006. "Human Resource Management Challenges for Nonprofit Organizations." In *Public Personnel Management: Current Concerns, Future Challenges,* 4th ed., edited by Norma M. Riccucci, 225–42. New York: Longman.

Riccucci, Norma M. 2011a. "Human Resource Management: Current and Future Challenges." In *The State of Public Administration: Issues, Challenges, and Opportunities,* edited by Donald C. Menzel and Harvey L. White, 127–41. Armonk, NY: M. E. Sharpe.

Riccucci, Norma M. 2011b. "Public Sector Labor Relations Scholarship: Is There a 'There,'" There?" *Public Administration Review* 71:203–9.

Riccucci, Norma M., and Frank J. Thompson. 2008. "The New Public Management, Homeland Security, and the Politics of Civil Service Reform." *Public Administration Review* 68:877–90.

Selden, Sally Coleman. 2009. *Human Capital: Tools and Strategies for the Public Sector.* Washington, DC: CQ Press.

Shafritz, Jay M., David H. Rosenbloom, Norma A. Riccucci, Katherine C. Naff, and Al C. Hyde. 2001. *Personnel Management in Government: Politics and Process.* 5th ed. New York: Marcel Dekker.

Shaw, Lee C., and R. Theodore Clark Jr. 1972. "Collective Bargaining and Politics in Public Employment." *UCLA Law Review* 19:887.

State of Wisconsin. 2011. Wisconsin Legislative Documents, Wisconsin Act 10. http://docs.legis.wisconsin.gov/2011/related/acts/10.pdf.

Thompson, James R. 2007. "Federal Labor-Management Relations Reforms under Bush: Enlightened Management or Quest for Control?" *Review of Public Personnel Administration* 27:105–24.

US Department of Labor (DOL), Office of Labor Management Standards. 2010. "Labor Management Reporting and Disclosure Act." http://www.dol.gov/olms/regs/compliance/lmrda-factsheet.htm.

US Department of Labor (DOL), Wage and Hour Division. 2009. "State Right-to-Work Laws and Constitutional Amendments in Effect January 1, 2009 with Year of Passage." http://www.dol.gov/whd/state/righttowork.htm.

Van Riper, Paul P. 1958. *History of the United States Civil Service.* Evanston, IL: Row, Peterson.

Vielmetti, Bruce, and Patrick Marley. 2012. "Federal Court Strikes Down Parts of Union Law." *Journal Sentinel,* March 30. http://www.jsonline.com/news/wisconsin/federal-court-strikes-down-parts-of-act-10-4k4qdap-145208985.html.

Walters, Jonathan. 2002. *Life after Civil Service Reform: The Texas, Georgia, and Florida Experiences.* Arlington, VA: IBM Endowment for the Business of Government.

Walters, Jonathan. 2003. "Civil Service Tsunami: Florida's Radical Overhaul of Its Personnel System Is Making Big Political Waves." *Governing,* May. http://www.governing.com/topics/politics/Civil-Service-Tsunami.html.

West, Jonathan P. 2002. "Georgia on the Mind of Radical Civil Service Reformers." *Review of Public Personnel Administration* 22:79–93.

Additional Resources

American Federation of Government Employees—http://www.afge.org

American Federation of Labor and Congress of Industrial Organizations (AFL-CIO)—http://www.aflcio.org

American Federation of State, County, and Municipal Employees (AFSCME)—http://www.afscme.org

Federal Labor Relations Authority (FLRA)—http://www.flra.gov

National Federation of Federal Employees—http://www.nffe.org

National Labor Relations Board (NLRB)—http://www.nlrb.gov

National Treasury Employees Union—http://www.nteu.org

Case 9.1 Labor Unions and Civil Service Reform: Florida and Service First

In 2001, the state of Florida reformed its civil service system with the assistance of private sector ingenuity. Then-governor Jeb Bush aligned himself with the Florida Council of 100, an influential body of top businesspeople within the state who supported civil service reform. The governor's office and the Florida Council of 100 produced a report documenting alleged incidents of mismanagement and abuse in state government and detailing the inefficiencies of the traditional civil service. The result of the report was the Service First initiative, civil service reforms that became law on May 14, 2001. This sweeping reform package incorporated most of the reform trends discussed in this text, and did so in an abrupt fashion.

In contrast to the Georgia reforms, which incorporated conversion to EAW in stages, Florida's reforms were more drastic, eliminating seniority immediately for all state employees affected by the Service First initiative. The measure immediately gave managers the ability to target people or positions for downsizing as they saw fit, for any "reasonable cause." This is a much looser standard than "just cause," which requires a statement of a specific, justified rationale for dismissal (West 2002). Additionally, Service First eliminates state employees' rights to appeal suspensions and dismissals so that an affected employee has little or no recourse. Grievance guidelines under Service First no longer permit the Public Employee Relations Commission (PERC)—the independent state governing body that considers appeals for adverse actions (e.g., wrongful termination)—the authority to hear appeals relevant to layoffs or transfers. Moreover, civil service employees requesting disciplinary appeals are now subject to curtailed timelines and reduced remedies. While capricious or prohibited personnel actions can still be appealed to PERC, PERC is no longer authorized to alter penalties imposed by state agencies, and it is incapable of considering the alleged unfair treatment of employees (West 2002).

To simplify and expedite recruitment, Service First emphasizes minimum qualifications for a job rather than adequate job analysis and validated criteria in hiring (West 2002). Accordingly, the Florida governor's office circulated a memo mandating that at least two of three candidates for a new position be recruited from outside the public sector before internal candidates could be considered. This is a clear move toward privatization as embodied under the People First initiative (Guy 2004). Furthermore, pay raises are no longer based on formal pay tiers organized to reward seniority. Service First dramatically simplified job titles and pay structures along the lines of broadbanding, giving managers greater flexibility in rewarding employees. Promotions are based on management's perceptions of an employee's knowledge, skill, and abilities rather than formal tests.

In addition, state employees in supervisory positions were placed in EAW status. While the initial goal was to consign all state employees to EAW status, political pressure—particularly from public safety and nursing unions opposed to eliminating classified positions—forced the state to reduce the number of positions affected. This compromise amounted to 16,000 positions being placed in the newly dubbed Selected Exempt Service, subject to EAW. About 120,000 employees in the Florida personnel system remained classified, still enjoying the full protections afforded by grievance procedures and appeals for adverse job actions. Those 120,000 classified employees are not completely unaffected though because of the shift from "just cause" as the standard for adverse action to "reasonable cause" (Walters 2002).

Two factors distinguish Florida from the other case studies discussed in the text. First, People First is aimed at outsourcing many HR management functions. While other states have considered outsourcing agency-specific HR functions, no state besides Florida has encompassed the entire state's HR function. In an effort to make HR a more market-like enterprise, the initiative has contracted out many transactional functions to a private entity, Convergys (Condrey and Battaglio 2007; Guy 2004). Under the terms of the contract between the state and the "service provider," Convergys is to support the state's workforce in the areas of HR administration, benefits administration, payroll administration, and staffing administration functions (see also the discussion in Chapter 10, "Privatizing Human Resource Functions in the Public Sector").

The second issue that distinguishes Florida is the role that collective bargaining has played in the process. Unlike many other southern states (e.g., Georgia) that have utilized right-to-work legislation to implement civil service reforms, Florida has a sizable union presence that was vocal in its opposition to the Service First reforms. Therefore, unions were able to limit the extent of EAW among state government employees. AFSCME Council 79 filed a three-count lawsuit against the state of Florida and the administration of Governor Jeb Bush, alleging that Service First initiatives have "unconstitutionally waived and impaired collective bargaining rights protected by the Florida Constitution" (Walters 2002; 2003). While succeeding in limiting the extent of EAW by applying political pressure, the union lost the lawsuit before the Florida Supreme Court. Even so, as a result of efforts by AFSCME, greater attention to civil service reform actually led to an increase in union membership in the state.

The Florida case highlights the dilemma of balancing the greater administrative flexibility gained by pursuing PHRM reforms with the cost of lost political accountability. Previous research was unable to gather critical comments on the record from state employees, since they feared political retribution (Battaglio and Condrey 2006). Service First reforms have led to an atmosphere of apprehension (Bowman et al. 2003). Polling state employees, Bowman and colleagues found serious reservations concerning Service First, especially about its ability to enhance productivity in the civil service. State employees expect EAW to be extended to more employees, reject the idea that pay will be enhanced, see reform as a distraction from real issues (e.g., fiscal reform), and claim that citizen suspicion of government derives largely from activities in the political arena, not from citizen displeasure with services. These findings mirror research elsewhere that has challenged the idea that EAW leads to improved productivity (Battaglio 2010; Battaglio and Condrey 2009; Condrey and Battaglio 2007). Changes in traditional civil service hiring, suspension, and dismissal procedures are a particularly alarming threat to political neutrality in Florida's civil service. These changes, like those in Georgia, represent a dramatic shift in HR management in the public sector. Furthermore, the trend toward privatization in the delivery of government services, underscored by the contract with Convergys, has placed traditional merit systems in conflict with the private sector.

Discussion Questions

1. Assess the Service First initiatives from both a labor and a management perspective. To what extent do you agree with the governor's office and the Florida Council of 100? To what extent do you agree with the claims presented by AFSCME regarding the constitutionality of Service First?

2. You are a manager in a Florida state agency and receive the memorandum sent by the governor's office regarding the hiring of private sector candidates. How would you respond to the memo? Would you respond differently if you were a union leader or representative?

3. The state of Florida is considering expanding EAW to all state employees and has hired you as a consultant to evaluate this proposal. What conclusions might you draw from the state's experience thus far with EAW that might assist policy makers in moving forward? Would you include representatives from labor unions in your discussions? Why or why not?

Exercise

Role-Play a Labor-Management Dispute

As part of a broader push to improve government productivity and save taxpayer dollars, the State of Texiana recently passed sweeping legislation that, among other things, reduced the bargaining power of public sector labor unions and authorized privatization initiatives. The governor of Texiana is targeting a number of agencies and their operations for privatization opportunities. The HR division of the Department of Environmental Resources (DER) has been chosen for a trial effort at privatization. This effort would eliminate in-house administration of certain HR functions (e.g., payroll, benefits, workers' compensation) in favor of having a private vendor supply these services.

At a recent agency-wide meeting of employees within DER, the chief of staff for the governor's office announced that the privatization initiative was a priority and would be taking place over the next six to eight months. At the meeting, many employees expressed strident reservations about the initiative. The result has been an all-out war in the press between the two rival camps—the governor's office on one side and the employees and

(Continued)

(Continued)

their union representatives on the other. The employees and their union representatives are raising the following questions:

What will be the fate of workers displaced by the privatization initiative? Will these workers be displaced? Transferred? Or given right of first refusal to jobs offered by the vendor?

What, if any, is the potential windfall from an outsourcing initiative? Is it actually a less expensive alternative to in-house HR administration?

Will the workers being displaced be allowed to bid on the privatized work just as actual vendors will?

If the privatization initiative proves unsuccessful, what will be the fate of the workers displaced and the overall initiative?

Role-Play

Given the political quagmire that has developed in the wake of the privatization initiative in DER, the governor has appointed you as a mediator between labor and management. You have a reputation as having been a fair dealer in previous labor-management disputes within the state. The class will divide into groups representing the various sides: one or more students might participate as mediators, and the other students might represent labor, management, and the media.

The Future

10

Privatizing Human Resource Functions in the Public Sector

LEARNING OBJECTIVES

Upon completion of the chapter, you will be able to do the following:

- Discuss the opportunities and challenges of privatization in public human resource management (PHRM).
- List the benefits and pitfalls of privatization.
- Discuss the types of laws affecting privatization in the public sector, including constitutional law, regulatory law, statutory law, and general contract law.
- Explain transparency considerations for privatization and democratic governance.

Privatization is an often controversial topic that has garnered a great deal of attention over the last few decades. The idea of turning over government functions to a private company may seem radical, but it has become an increasingly common strategy. Facing pressure from politicians and managers for cost savings, many governments have endeavored to improve traditional public sector practices by tapping private sector know-how. In some cases, a public agency may not be well equipped to handle production or delivery of traditional government services in-house and insufficient knowledge, resources, infrastructure, so the outsourcing and contracting out of these services becomes an attractive alternative.

The terms *privatization*, *outsourcing*, and *contracting* are often used interchangeably. *Privatization* is a more general term describing the process of transferring ownership from the public sector to the private or nonprofit sector. *Outsourcing* refers more specifically to the contracting out of a business function or process to a third party (also called a contractor or vendor). In the public sector, *contracting* has often entailed the outsourcing of services to a private or nonprofit contractor.

Private companies may also outsource certain activities to other private companies or even public or nonprofit organizations.

The benefits of privatization can include increased efficiency, reduced costs, higher-quality service, and the ability of the agency to focus on more strategic concerns since day-to-day functions are being handled externally. However, outsourcing public services redefines the nature of public service provision and the nature of governance itself. There can also be political fallout if the project causes public employees to lose their jobs, is mismanaged, or goes over budget. There is considerable debate over whether privatization is wise; suffice it to say, it is usually a case-by-case decision.

The George W. Bush administration made outsourcing a priority with such programs as the Competitive Sourcing Initiative (CSI). The federal government has also outsourced its entire workforce recruitment system, USAJOBS (Llorens and Kellough 2007; Shafritz, Russell, and Borick 2007). At the state and local level, outsourced PHRM activities include specific functions, agency HRM services, and even the entire HR function. For example, the state of Nevada outsourced its workers' compensation system to a private firm, eliminating approximately $2 billion in unfunded liabilities and over 800 positions in government (Chi, Arnold, and Perkins 2003).

So, of all the PHRM reform themes, why does privatization deserve its own chapter? Quite simply, privatization entails more than simply retooling how we perform specific HR processes such as compensation or job classification. Privatization involves transferring HR functions or even the entire HR operation to a third party: a for-profit company, a nonprofit organization, or even another government. Such actions represent a fundamental shift in the purpose of providing government products and services—companies have a profit motive, while governments do not. In addition, governments must operate in a way that is accountable to the public, while companies do not have this obligation. It is important to consider the implications of these conflicting motives. Turning over certain government functions (e.g., defense, space exploration, health care) to a third party may disturb politicians and citizens who hold that the most basic premise of government is that it serves its people. For example, privatization of education or prisons often proves controversial: Are students or prisoners better off with a private entity running the system?

With an increased reliance on private and nonprofit firms to provide HR functions, scholars and practitioners have considered the wisdom of such initiatives. To be sure, outsourcing has proven to be productive in many instances. However, there have also been a number of instances in which public/private arrangements have not proven fruitful, resulting in both waste and legal issues. At times, swept up in enthusiasm for possible cost savings and efficiency gains, reformers overlook the potential downside of contractors' profit motives. Accordingly, the material presented in this chapter will assess the successes and failures associated with privatizing PHRM functions and provide public HR managers with practical advice for managing outsourcing contracts. The reader will find historical antecedents, case studies, and direct advice. Most importantly, the chapter provides guidance on how to use the best of what government and business have to offer the public service.

Privatization of Public HR Management

Beginning in the 1980s, popular political dogma has championed private sector efficiency. Government has been viewed as bureaucratic, bloated, and inefficient, making privatization an attractive option. It is seen as a fresh start, a new approach that will help government to run more efficiently, and many jurisdictions have opted for third-party alternatives to deliver services. Consequently, interest groups and private interests have lobbied to win lucrative government contracts (Condrey and Battaglio 2007; Thompson and Elling 2000). The increasingly political nature of the privatization process has led some to charge: "Who gets what from government is no longer determined by the simple formula of votes for jobs; rather, it is a complex calculus involving contracts and large private interests" (Condrey and Battaglio 2007, 430).

As discussed in Chapters 1 and 2, reformers at all levels of government have taken a keen interest in the performance deficiencies attributed to traditional PHRM and in improving it. By their nature, governments need to be large organizations in order to carry out all of their duties and responsibilities; of course, this may mean that they are not the leanest or most efficient of operations. For example, the red tape associated with carrying out recruitment, selection, compensation, and other traditional PHRM functions has proven cumbersome and inefficient. Therefore, public HR departments have increased their use of contractors who can hire new personnel quickly and dismiss poor performers (Maranto 2001). For many governments, HR functions such as payroll and benefits administration, consulting, wage and salary surveys, job analysis, and job evaluation are seen as being easily contracted out (Battaglio and Condrey 2006; Coggburn 2007; Fernandez, Rainey, and Lowman 2006; Shafritz, Russell, and Borick 2007). More recently, governments have insisted that they have no other option but to pursue privatization initiatives to cut costs.

Reasons to Privatize or Outsource

Why would a public agency choose to privatize PHRM instead of provide services in house? The rationale for many governments is twofold: economies of scale and access to higher-quality products and services (Fernandez, Rainey, and Lowman 2006). The many large for-profit firms that specialize in the delivery of HR services (e.g., Deloitte, PricewaterhouseCoopers, The Segal Company) have already invested the time and capital to obtain the equipment and know-how necessary to carry out these functions. The incremental cost for the private company to take on an additional client (the public agency) is usually much smaller than the cost to the public agency of handling these functions itself. Privatization allows public agencies to take advantage of larger firms' economies of scale or quality advantage, saving government much needed money (Fernandez, Rainey, and Lowman 2006). For example, the private consulting firm Deloitte often contracts with governments throughout the world on a number of HR activities, including workforce development, labor market analysis, and training. Governments might opt to work with Deloitte in order to tap the consulting firm's human capital knowledge. In addition, by unburdening current HR employees from more mundane tasks like filling out paperwork for payroll and benefits, privatization gives HR managers greater flexibility to pursue mission-critical functions that require greater thought and strategic consideration, such as workforce planning (Fernandez, Rainey, and Lowman 2006; Rainey 2009).

Additionally, for-profit firms specializing in HR have advantages in human capital; they are the experts, and in order to be successful they need to hire the "best and the brightest" in HR-related fields. In turn, they accumulate specialized knowledge that gives them a quality advantage in service delivery. A public agency may have an antiquated payroll system that needs to be upgraded but not know how best to implement a more efficient system, since the personnel working there have not been trained in the latest software. For example, Maricopa County in Arizona sought the expertise of Automatic Data Processing (ADP)—a for-profit HR consulting firm—in the automation and integration of HR services such payroll, time and attendance, and benefits administration by moving to SaaS (Software as a Solution) (see Chapter 11 for a full discussion of HR software).

Whether privatization makes sense and why it makes sense may depend on the degree of difficulty associated with the tasks being considered for outsourcing (Coggburn 2007; Rainey 2009). HR services associated with more mundane tasks, such as payroll, are often outsourced as a way of saving public expenditures and freeing up personnel to focus on more strategic functions (Coggburn 2007; Kellough and Nigro 2006; Rainey 2009). Using the private sector to provide functions such as workforce planning and performance management may be more oriented toward tapping expertise not readily available in the public sector (Coggburn 2007; Rainey 2009).

Deciding to Privatize or Outsource

The decision to privatize or outsource public functions is often referred to as the "make-or-buy decision," meaning that organizations have a choice between "making" (relying on internal or in-house resources) or "buying" (using an external vendor or contractor). Privatizing is a significant undertaking and should not be approached lightly. The decision makers should be sure to evaluate the different options and conduct a cost-benefit analysis to determine whether privatizing is worthwhile. Moreover, managers should be acquainted with the potential providers of the service under discussion, including who the potential vendors are and their reputations. For HR functions, the uniqueness and type of service as well as the availability of vendors are important considerations for determining privatization effectiveness (Coggburn 2007). Generic transactional HR activities (e.g., payroll and benefits) are more likely to be successfully privatized when responsibilities are clearly specified and vendors are abundant. A familiarity with the political forces that may facilitate or hinder privatization is also essential. Stakeholders in the political environment—politicians, the media, the courts, and the public—influence the make-or-buy decision in the public sector (Battaglio and Khankarli 2008).

It should also be said that any outsourcing arrangement includes not only the public agency and the private contractor but also the individuals who work for these organizations. The federal government relies on thousands of people who work for private contractors but whose ultimate client may be the Department of Education or Defense, for example.

Nonprofits in Focus	Outsourcing Volunteer Management

Like their counterparts in the public and private sectors, nonprofits may also opt to contract out certain functions. Nonprofits may do so for similar reasons as do organizations in the other sectors: to concentrate on core activities central to the organization's mission, reduce costs and time, capitalize on market economies of scale, and/or improve efficiency. NPOs face the same challenges as for-profits and government agencies of managing their people, even when those people are volunteers. During the recent economic downturn, many volunteer organizations experienced a windfall of volunteers eager to assist those in need. Unfortunately, many of these volunteers were turned away, not because their services were not needed but because the NPOs lacked the human capital capacity to take on and manage large numbers of volunteers. In New York City, 54 percent of city nonprofits surveyed did not have the capacity to handle increased volunteerism and were forced to turn away volunteers (Bloomberg 2009). As a result, one out of every three potential volunteers could not be utilized (Bagley 2009).

As a result of such human capital capacity constraints, a number of organizations have begun to outsource volunteer management to experts. For example, the nonprofit New York Cares specializes in providing tailored volunteer programs for partner organizations, identifying critical needs; creating projects to bridge gaps; and recruiting, training, and deploying teams of volunteers (New York Cares 2013). New York Cares's partners include nonprofits, local governments, and public schools who need to focus on their core missions and lack the manpower to manage and coordinate volunteers. Services include afterschool and recreational programs for children living in homeless shelters, free SAT preparation classes for low-income high school students, and job-readiness training for unemployed adults (Bagley 2009). The New York Cares volunteer management model has been emulated by more than 370 volunteer organizations across the country, united under the umbrella of HandsOn Network/Points of Light Institute. This nonprofit organization connects other nonprofits to boost community awareness and attract volunteerism among younger volunteers and corporate America.

The Legal Environment of PHRM Outsourcing

As we have discovered throughout this text, those making changes to public sector HR practices must consider the legal environment (see Battaglio and Ledvinka 2009). Public and private organizations operate under different laws, so joining the two in an outsourcing contract entails navigating a host of legal questions. Choosing to outsource PHRM functions is a major project; it comes with potential liabilities and requires consideration of and adherence to many constitutional, statutory, and regulatory laws. As a result, HR managers are increasingly being tasked with not only managing contracts (discussed below) but attaining a basic understanding of contract law as well. After all, when the public sector outsources to a private entity, the contract is the foundation of that business relationship: it outlines who is responsible for doing what, the financial terms of the agreement, how quality will be ensured, and the type and frequency of monitoring activities. Familiarity with constitutional, statutory, and regulatory constraints is critical to successful PHRM privatization (Fernandez, Rainey, and Lowman 2006). Table 10.1 summarizes the four types of laws affecting the outsourcing of the HR function in the public sector: constitutional law, statutory law, regulatory law, and contract law. The sections below review each of these categories and the specific laws in greater detail. These laws ensure that both

Table 10.1	Laws Affecting Privatization of Human Resource Functions*
Constitutional Law	*Board of Regents of State Colleges v. Roth* (1972)
	State action doctrine
Statutory Law	The Freedom of Information Act (FOIA, 1966)
	Public function approach
Regulatory Law	Reduction in Force (RIF, 1986)
	Voluntary Early Retirement Authority (VERA, 1998)
	Voluntary Separation Incentive Pay (VSIP, 2003)
	Federal Acquisition Regulation (2005)
Contract Law	State and local laws governing the execution of contracts and the terms of outsourcing agreements

Source: Battaglio and Ledvinka 2009

*In addition to the laws covered here, states and municipalities have myriad laws and regulations that might also impact the outsourcing of HR functions.

public employers and private contractors are accountable for their decisions, have legitimacy, and operate transparently.

Constitutional Law

The US Constitution and federal statutes prohibit government entities from violating citizens' civil rights, mandating that government cannot deprive a citizen of property without due process of law (Battaglio and Ledvinka 2009). As discussed in Chapters 3 and 4, public employees have property rights attached to their jobs, rights guaranteed by the Supreme Court (Riccucci and Naff 2008). Public employees also have the right to a hearing after adverse employment actions brought by their employer (*Board of Regents v. Roth* 1972). Furthermore, federal statutory law provides individuals whose rights may have been violated by contractors and government entities "acting under color of state law" (e.g., a private entity carrying out a public sector function in fulfilling an outsourcing contract) the right to initiate civil proceedings against the alleged wrongdoers (Civil Rights Act of 1871).

While these constitutional protections generally do not apply to interactions between private citizens and private sector firms, they sometimes do apply when a contractual relationship exists between a government and a private vendor (Rosenbloom and Piotrowski 2005). "Coordinated joint public-private participation in an activity," such as the contracting out of PHRM to a private company, may trigger constitutional protections normally not granted to private employees (Rosenbloom and Piotrowski 2005, 104). In instances of coordinated activity, the courts have considered private firms as "state actors," meaning that they are acting as a proxy government and thus are liable for any violation of citizen/employee constitutional rights. For example, in *Board of County Commissioners v. Umbehr* (1996), an independent trash collector named Umbehr contracted with Wabaunsee County, Kansas, and was a frequent critic of the elected commissioners of that county. When Umbehr was terminated, the contractor took issue with his termination, claiming that he was targeted for his criticism of the county commissioners. In *Umbehr*, the Supreme Court sided with the contractor and ruled that independent contractors, while not technically employed by the government, still enjoy the same First Amendment protection from termination or prevention of contract renewal as a public employee has when they exercise freedom of speech. The Court said that "independent government contractors are similar in most relevant respects to government employees" (Board of County Commissioners 1996).

Likewise, in *O'Hare Truck Service v. City of Northlake* (1996), the Court ruled in favor of the First Amendment rights of a contractor who had refused to contribute to a mayoral candidate's campaign for reelection. O'Hare Truck Service's contract with the city was subsequently terminated. The Court ruled that "we decline to draw a line excluding independent contractors from the First Amendment safeguards of political association afforded to employees" (*O'Hare* 1996). The Supreme Court has been quite adamant in maintaining that privatization does not mean that government employers can forgo their constitutional responsibilities to contractors, clients, or customers (see also *Lebron v. National Railroad Passenger Corp.* 1995; *West v. Atkins* 1988).

For public managers supervising PHRM contracts, an appreciation for the law is essential for them as well as for the contractor to avoid liability for civil rights and due process violations (Battaglio and Ledvinka 2009). To avoid liability, public managers and contractors must be vigilant in protecting citizens' individual rights and ensuring that the contracting authority (e.g., a government agency) does not abdicate its constitutional responsibilities (Rosenbloom and Piotrowski 2005, 112). Transferring management and performance to a private vendor does not give public agencies immunity from prosecution or civil lawsuits alleging violations of their constitutional duties as an employer. In addition, private firms in a contractual relationship with a public entity are potentially liable for any violation of their employees' individual constitutional rights.

Statutory Law: Open Records Laws and Open Meetings Laws

Along with accountability and legitimacy, transparency is an important consideration for PHRM outsourcing (Battaglio and Ledvinka 2009). Governments must operate transparently; the public has a right to know how its government functions. Laws that open public records to inspection, such as the **Freedom of Information Act (FOIA)** (5 U.S.C. § 552), guarantee government transparency by granting citizens access to records of how decisions were made. Open public meeting laws in the United States generally require that meetings be open to the general public and the public be given advance notice of meetings. Exceptions to the statutory requirements are limited, so most information related to PHRM may be subject to transparency laws. Complicating the issue is the treatment of private sector autonomy, especially in instances where trade secrets have legal protection. FOIA does not necessarily require a private contractor to reveal trade secrets or other proprietary information. While federal courts have generally been unwilling to apply FOIA directly to private firms that contract to provide government services, the information produced by a private firm while in a contractual relationship with a government agency and is in that agency's custody can be subject to FOIA (Rosenbloom and Piotrowski 2005).

At the state level, there is no general consensus regarding transparency regulations. State courts have attempted to balance the rights of both private vendors and the public in their decisions. For some states, the **public function approach** governs the disclosure of documents in certain situations (Rosenbloom and Piotrowski 2005). How much a private firm may be required to disclose depends on the extent to which a private firm is engaged in a public function—including human resources. The more involved it is, the more likely the open records law will be triggered. State courts in California, Delaware, Georgia, Kentucky, Louisiana, Missouri, New Hampshire, New York, Ohio, and Utah use the public function approach when assessing whether to release documents (Battaglio and Ledvinka 2009, 13).

Regulatory Law

Certain regulations, primarily federal, apply to private vendors taking over PHRM functions. These regulations apply specifically to the job security of public employees, especially if job loss may result from the transfer of work to the private firm (see 5 C.F.R. part 351). If, upon contracting work out to a private firm, the public agency needs or chooses to reduce its workforce, it must first obtain congressional approval for a **reduction in force (RIF)**. After approval for an RIF is obtained, affected employees must be notified of the impending action. In some instances, federal employees may be granted the **right of first refusal** with respect to jobs generated by private vendors from the contracting out of the government activity (Fernandez, Rainey, and Lowman 2006, 216; Office of Management and Budget [OMB] 2003). In this case, the affected public employees have the right to refuse, or accept, a new job opportunity with the contractor before the vendor advertises the position to the general labor market. In the case study at the end of the chapter, employees of Louisiana's Department of Economic Development were initially offered the right of first refusal or transfer to another department within state government when the governor's office introduced privatization.

Reduction-in-force requirements are also impacted by the **Voluntary Early Retirement Authority (VERA)** and **Voluntary Separation Incentive Pay (VSIP)** regulations. These two pieces of legislation authorize federal employers to offer financial incentives to employees who voluntary resign to facilitate privatization of HR functions (5 CFR § 831.114, 5 CFR § 842.213, and 5 CFR § 576). Federal agencies considering RIFs may ask the Office of Personnel Management for authorization to implement VERA and VSIP provisions. VERA authorizes federal employers to temporarily reduce retirement age and service eligibility requirements for early retirement, giving employees the option to retire earlier than usual (5 CFR § 831.114). In addition, federal employers may implement VSIP, giving employees in targeted positions a lump sum separation incentive payment of up to $25,000 (5 CFR 576). These regulations ensure that outsourcing in the public sector considers the rights of public employees during the transition to a private vendor (Elam 1997; Fernandez, Rainey, and Lowman 2006). Even so, some employees may still be disadvantaged by privatization.

Federal contracting is also guided by the **Federal Acquisition Regulation (FAR)**. With respect to HR functions, FAR is meant to protect public employees hired under civil service system rules from layoffs (Fernandez, Rainey, and Lowman 2006) (48 CFR § 1). FAR also prohibits public managers from directly or indirectly supervising employees of a private sector firm (Fernandez, Rainey, and Lowman 2006). Limiting federal supervision may pose a threat to the authority of public managers, whom the general public often sees as the agents of accountability. Mismanagement and lack of oversight with regard to contractors in the wars in Iraq and Afghanistan illustrate the potential problems associated with diminishing federal authority over the supervision of privatization.

Contract Law

The expansion of privatization efforts at all levels of government has required public managers to acquire greater technical knowledge of contract law (Battaglio and Ledvinka 2009). This knowledge must encompass procurement, or a government's procedures for securing goods and services. Obviously, contract law varies from state to state, but most states (excluding Louisiana) are signatories to the Uniform Commercial Code (UCC), which provides a standardized set of rules for transactions. Knowledge of the contracting-out process is one of the most important components of successful outsourcing efforts (Fernandez, Rainey, and Lowman 2006). This is especially true for public HR managers, who are often tasked with effectively drafting, interpreting, and enforcing contracts to ensure accurate performance by a private contractor. The legislation reviewed above places a legal duty on public managers to ensure the protection of employee and citizen constitutional rights when private vendors are responsible for HR functions such as recruitment and selection. Unfortunately, most public HR managers are not trained in contract law.

Thus, it is prudent that public managers get the requisite training in contract law and consult with government attorneys when a legal concern arises during privatization. Failure to monitor contractual performance, especially when HR functions are involved, may result in liability on the part of government. If the contract fails to mention the government's duty to enforce and monitor the vendor's actions, the government may be liable for any damages resulting from the contractor's actions. Monitoring contract performance as the service is provided and then auditing performance once the contract is completed are key elements of HR outsourcing (Coggburn 2007). According to Coggburn (2007), taxpayer financing of privatization efforts places a special responsibility on public managers to ensure fair and equitable treatment of employees and remain accountable to the public interest.

Managing Privatization

Once the decision to outsource has been made, the next concern is how the contract will be managed and who will administer it. This section reviews specific managerial skills that public HR and other managers might find useful for the administering of contracts. Ideally, a jurisdiction should have a contracting-out team that includes lawyers, accountants, and an expert in the service being contracted (e.g., an HR manager for HR services). However, this is not always the case, especially in smaller jurisdictions or cities that lack the resources and personnel to manage contracts. The additional resources listed at the end of the chapter provide a more thorough review of contract management practices. Table 10.2 gives a concise overview of skills and practices essential to the contract management process (see LeRoux and Harney 2007, 29).

Public managers should be knowledgeable about the basics of *contract and project management*. Privatization is a significant undertaking, so HR managers need to know how to oversee long-term, complicated projects.

From the discussion above, it should be clear that public managers have a responsibility to be apprised of the legalities involved in privatizing public services. It is essential for all stakeholders to ensure that the privatization process is conducted fairly, legally, and ethically (Battaglio and Ledvinka 2009; Cohen and Eimicke 2008). Therefore, conflicts of interest with potential vendors should be avoided. This is particularly important for HR functions, given the obligation to protect the constitutional rights granted to public personnel. Knowledge of *contract and procurement*

Table 10.2	**Essential Skills and Considerations for Managing Contracts in the Public Sector**

- General understanding of contract and project management
- Contract and procurement law for public sector privatization, including relevant constitutional, statutory, and regulatory law
- Public ethics of contracting, including ethical standards, accountability to the public interest, and avoiding conflicts of interest
- Clear delineation of individual duties and responsibilities for those involved in contract management
- Effective techniques for team building and communication
- Negotiation skills
- Developing contract specifications, including scope of work, evaluation, and the criteria for awarding the contract
- Methods for monitoring and providing effective feedback
- Evaluating contractor performance
- Record keeping and documentation

Source: Adapted from LeRoux and Harney 2007

law, including relevant constitutional, statutory, and regulatory law, is essential to ensure accountability. According to Cohen and Eimicke (2008), contracting in the public sector poses a potential challenge to ethics, accountability, and democratic representation. The responsibilities imposed by government regulations can sometimes be at odds with optimizing contractor performance. It can be difficult to balance the two objectives, but doing so is necessary for ensuring contract performance.

Public ethics compels managers to establish standards that enforce accountability to the public interest. Cohen and Eimicke (2008) suggest:

> The potential for conflict of interest issues and corruption are a clear danger given the complexity, size, and duration of the contracting process. Staff members may be hired from time to time, but contracts are renewed all the time. The financial stakes are high, and the pressure on often poorly paid government staff members can be intense. . . . We frequently see a clash of cultures as the values of the private sector and those of the public intersect. (210)

Once a jurisdiction decides to embark on a privatization initiative, managers, politicians, and the public should have a clear understanding of who is *responsible* for government contracting. Furthermore, their *duties* must be clearly specified. The first step in delineating responsibility is to determine who in government will manage the contract. Depending on the size of the jurisdiction, responsibility for privatization may rest in the executive office (e.g., mayor or city-manager) or in a separate procurement office (see LeRoux and Harney 2007, 20–26). Increasingly, the responsibility for contracting out has been complicated by the trend toward networked government, such that multiple vendors or entities from various sectors (public, private, nonprofit) are tasked with contract performance. For example, transportation and infrastructure projects often include federal and state departments of transportation, private contractors, regional and local governments (e.g., county and city), and in some cases quasi-governmental authorities (e.g., toll-road authorities) in the performance of operations—and these parties may disagree. Achieving objectives efficiently can be complicated in such a structure; therefore, it is important for each stakeholder's responsibilities to be clearly defined.

In such dynamic environments, *effective techniques for team building and communication* are essential to contract performance. This is especially true for HR managers because coordinating personnel decisions and actions across sectors can be challenging. HR managers must agree on who is responsible for which HR functions and how to deal with problem employees. Some public employees may not welcome "outsiders" who come in to take over. Contract managers and vendors should have predetermined communication channels; these become especially important when problems arise with the privatization process. Establishing regular meetings and points of contact is important to effective team building and communication between public and private stakeholders. Moreover, people who are designated points of contact should be trained in *negotiation skills* so they can effectively resolve contract disputes without needing to procede to costly litigation. Public contract managers also need to be familiar with alternative means of dispute resolution—fact-finding, mediation, and arbitration (see Chapter 9 for a full discussion).

Public managers should be familiar with drafting, interpreting, and enforcing *contract specifications,* including the scope of the work to be done and the criteria for evaluation of prospective vendors. Initially, public managers must decide on the type of bidding process (i.e., whether the process is open and competitive). Bidding and evaluation techniques come in a variety of forms, but what is most essential is that the process be open and competitive to ensure accountability (Cohen and Eimicke 2008; Savas 2000; 2005). However, whether or not the process is open and competitive is determined by the law and elected officials of a given jurisdiction. A carefully constructed scope of work for the service being privatized is crucial for ensuring what will be expected of both parties. A scope of work will detail what the vendor will do, outlining the type and extent of operations that the vendor has agreed to perform. The scope of work should clearly specify the conditions, requirements, and responsibilities of the contractor's provision of services (LeRoux and Harney 2007). For example, it should specify the schedule for delivery of services and payments, as well as performance standards, technical requirements, and the consequences for performance failure. The scope of work should also be sure to incorporate correct terminology and legal language. If public managers are unsure about the proper terminology, they should consult with jurisdiction attorney's or use boilerplates provided by relevant associations as a model (e.g., the American Bar Association's Model Procurement Code for State and Local Government). As public HR managers have taken on some of these legal responsibilities, it is becoming increasingly useful and possibly necessary for them to have legal training. Care should be taken in drafting the contract; if there is a dispute, the contract is the final word in resolving the issue.

Once the public good or service has been contracted out, the public manager is not relieved of his or her responsibilities, especially to the public interest. *Monitoring and providing effective feedback* are essential during the period of the contract and after the relationship has ended. Monitoring the contractual relationship minimizes the potential for principal-agent problems (Globerman and Vining 1996; Johnston and Romzek 1999). A principal-agent problem may arise if the agent (contractor) does not have the best interest of the principal (government/public) in mind. Contractors are first and foremost interested in making a profit, while government's primary responsibility is to the citizens. Careful monitoring is typically touted as a necessity to deter contractors from cutting corners and pursuing deleterious behavior (Brown and Potoski 2003; Fernandez 2007; Rehfuss 1989). A recent Pennsylvania case illustrated how privatization can go wrong: A judge was sentenced for accepting over $1 million in a kickback scheme in payments to send juveniles to a for-profit detention facility (Warner 2011). Public HR managers have a responsibility to ensure that taxpayer funds are being used efficiently to obtain high-quality services or products. The data collected should focus on work inputs, work processes, work outputs, timeliness, cost-effectiveness, accuracy of invoicing, legal compliance, and number of customer complaints (Fernandez 2007, 1124; LeRoux and Harney 2007). Any feedback should be reported back to the contractor through established communication channels so that the contractor can improve performance.

Furthermore, public managers should be prepared to *evaluate contractor performance,* including by inspecting work in progress and work completed, monitoring service complaints, examining contractor data and records, and administering citizen satisfaction surveys (Fernandez 2007, 1124; LeRoux and Harney 2007). *Record keeping and documentation* of the government's monitoring activities and contractor performance are indispensable to successful privatization.

All of these steps and skills are necessary for successful privatization. The ultimate objective in outsourcing is to tap the efficiencies of the market in a way that is transparent and accountable to public scrutiny; a privatization initiative can be considered successful if it has saved taxpayers money and improved service quality while preserving public value.

Pitfalls of PHRM Privatization

While outsourcing PHRM functions offers many advantages, it also presents considerable risks that can jeopardize the legitimacy of such endeavors. Even in the private sector, privatizing HR services carries risks (Greer, Youngblood, and Gray 1999; Lawler et al. 2004). HR privatization efforts have the potential to disrupt service if doing so detracts from core competencies such as employee relations and performance appraisal (Greer, Youngblood, and Gray 1999). There is also the potential for loss of in-house expertise when an HR department increasingly relies on vendors (Lawler et al. 2004). Privatization may also damage the culture within an organization, as attitudes toward management sour when poor vendor services reflect badly on the firm.

Public agencies must consider some specific risks when faced with the make-or-buy decision. Initially, there is the potential for abuse and corruption during the bidding process (Condrey and Battaglio 2007; Shafritz, Russell, and Borick 2007). Interest group politics can galvanize electoral politics around the privatization process. For example, the Ohio-based firm Convergys was awarded lucrative contracts to provide HR functions in the states of Florida and Texas that have been the subject of debate (see Battaglio and Condrey 2006; Coggburn 2007; Condrey and Battaglio 2007). In the case of Florida, Convergys was awarded a $350 million, nine-year contract to provide benefits, payroll, and staffing services (Battaglio and Condrey 2006, 31–32). In Texas, Convergys was awarded an $85 million, five-year contract with the state Health and Human Service Commission to provide, among other services, performance management, recruitment and selection, benefits and payroll administration, and compensation and classification administration (Coggburn 2007, 319). In both instances, delays and mismanagement led to cost overruns. In Florida, a former Convergys employee was indicted for stealing state employees' identities; five state employees filed suit against Convergys for identity theft; a subcontractor of Convergys was accused of selling information concerning 100,000 state employees to an outfit in India; and an internal audit by the Florida Department of Management Services found Convergys's security software to be subpar, allowing unauthorized access to confidential information on state leaders (Kromm 2006). From this example we learn that the project management can be compromised by a political push to outsource to the private sector. Such machinations have the potential to diminish cost savings and disregard employees' well-being at the expense of satisfying private organizational interests.

The worst outcome is that the contractor performs at a level below that of the public agency. For example, a recent report by the nonprofit Project on Government Oversight found that the federal government was consistently overpaying contractors for services that could have been performed in-house (Project on Government Oversight [POGO] 2011). The report compared federal government and private sector employee compensation across a number of outsourced services, including human resources. The federal government paid contractors on average an annual rate of $228,488, more than twice the $111,711 to have the same services done in-house (Nixon 2011)

Additionally, garnering support from public sector employees has proven important for achieving outsourcing efforts (Battaglio and Legge 2009; Durant and Legge 2002; Fernandez and Smith 2006). Public employees may view privatization as a threat to their job security and benefits (Becker, Silverstein, and Chaykin 1995; Dudek & Company 1988; Kuttner 1997). Job security and benefits serve as powerful incentives to work in the public service (see Rainey 2009), so such a threat may prove detrimental to morale. In jurisdictions where public employees enjoy the right to collectively bargain, opposition to privatization can take the form of media campaigns and legal action to halt outsourcing efforts. Such actions can prove costly to government—both politically and financially—and potentially sour public service morale and job satisfaction (Fernandez and Smith 2006).

While there is ample evidence of the efficiency gains from outsourcing (see Savas 2005; Siegel 1999), there is also substantial evidence that suggests privatization is not a panacea for all government ills (see Greene 2002; Hodge 2000). Efficiency gains are often the result of reductions in the cost of labor (Greene 2002; Rehfuss 1989; Savas 2005; Sclar 2000; see also Fernandez and Smith 2006). However, cost savings calculations often ignore the costs of coordinating activities and exchanging information in a complex operating environment (Lawler et al. 2004; Meier and Krause 2005; see also Globerman and Vining 1996). The cost-benefit analysis of privatization tends to focus on costs such as labor, capital, and land (Meier and Krause 2005). However, it often excludes the **transaction costs** associated with contractual arrangements—both before and after the contract is finalized—such as the difficult-to-measure costs of negotiating, bargaining, monitoring performance, and correcting inefficiencies (Globerman and Vining 1996; Williamson 1985). Thus, the benefits of privatization may be overstated.

PHRM contractual relationships also need to consider accountability to the greater public and the legitimacy to be gained from transparency and accountability. Fundamental differences may arise out of an uneasy friction among issues associated with legal, political, and market accountability (Cooper 2003). Relinquishing legal accountability for private sector performance may not be simple in a PHRM contractual relationship. Oftentimes, managers overlook individual legal rights and legislation that gives public managers and their agencies legally enforceable obligations (Cooper 2003). This oversight may erode public employee support and result in legal challenges seeking monetary damages and/or back pay for displaced employees (Coggburn 2007; Fernandez and Smith 2006).

Conclusion: Incorporating Public Value into Privatization

Privatization is a trend that is here to stay, at least for the near future. The increasing reliance on private delivery of public HR services raises a number of important issues and challenges for all stakeholders involved. Public and private actors must comply with a broad array of laws and regulations. Public agencies have an obligation to uphold the values that our government holds dear—like equal employment opportunity and the right to due process. When entering into an outsourcing contract, private companies are held to the same obligation, and public values should be specifically incorporated into the language of the contract (Fernandez, Rainey, and Lowman 2006; Moe 1987; Moe and Gilmour 1995). Requirements set forth by constitutional, regulatory, statutory, and case law also reinforce accountability among private vendors.

At the same time, the government is motivated by efficiency and budget constraints. Privatizing HR activities in the public sector is a balancing act. The key challenge is how to draft contracts that explicitly heed public values while also allowing for flexible HR management that can be more cost-efficient (see the case study on Louisiana in this chapter for an example). Writing contracts to express specific public values, such as equal employment opportunity and due process, is the right thing to do, but it may also decrease cost-effectiveness and limit managers' decision-making ability (Battaglio and Ledvinka 2009). The costs and benefits of outsourcing need to be evaluated case by case.

As discussed in previous chapters, the recent shift away from civil service systems to employment at will (EAW) means that concern over the erosion of public values has a credible basis (Battaglio and Condrey 2009; Condrey and Battaglio 2007). Privatization, likewise, has the potential to displace public values, particularly when contracted-out services involve how employees are managed (Woodard 2005). Contractors tend to be guided by managerial directives rather than legal requirements in HR practices (Woodard 2005, 111). Additionally, when public HR managers do not have a direct role in managing contract personnel, they are less likely to have the opportunity to promote equity and due process (Fernandez, Rainey, and Lowman 2006). With the proper legal training, public managers have the potential both to reduce liability and to reinforce the merit system and equity in contractual language (Battaglio and Ledvinka 2009).

Of primary importance during outsourcing PHRM functions is responsiveness to citizens' considerations throughout the process. Monitoring contract compliance, conducting cost-benefit analyses, and assessing legal liabilities are essential to managing outsourced HR activities in the public sector. Concerns about fraud persist, and actual instances of wrongdoing occur. The politics of privatization has at times reared its ugly head, as with missteps regarding civilian contracts in Iraq (Adams, Balfour, and Reed 2006). Many of these contracts were awarded with little or no public and congressional input. They were given to civilian contractors with few qualifications for the job, and government exercised minimal oversight of the contractors. The result was a number of investigations uncovering gross mismanagement, the torture of prisoners at Abu Ghraib being the most flagrant example (Schooner 2005). Proper monitoring of contracts then becomes a crucial component of ensuring the legitimacy of the make-or-buy decision (Coggburn 2007).

The debate regarding how much cost savings can be attributed to privatization continues. As noted earlier, the research here is decidedly mixed. While many public agencies have enjoyed success with outsourcing, there are also many instances of unsuccessful contracting. In addition to often complex constitutional issues and legal obligations, public managers must attempt to figure transaction costs into the decision process. A robust cost-benefit analysis of the make-or-buy decision includes these costs. To fulfill constitutional and contractual obligations, public managers at times must engage in negotiations, which can take a toll on the contractual relationship and add to the costs of contract compliance. These obligations are particularly germane to the public personnel arena, where constitutional values are salient (Coggburn 2007; Siegel 2000). In light of the need for stringent monitoring of contract performance, transaction costs must be given careful consideration.

Finally, outsourcing public personnel-related services to the private sector involves a number of liability and fairness issues. Public managers need to anticipate the public and private sector HR values that will come into conflict (Coggburn 2007). Reformers cite the efficiencies and productivities that privatization promises to achieve as reasons to pursue such initiatives (Kettl 2002; Savas 2000). Public managers must, however, temper such considerations by raising the myriad constitutional and contractual obligations regarding PHRM to ensure that public values of fairness and equity, especially in reference to equal employment opportunity and due process rights, are not eroded. Public managers are accountable to the public for not only delivering services efficiently but also for producing high-quality services that reflect constitutional values and comply with the law (Coggburn 2007; see also Chi, Arnold, and Perkins 2003; Siegel 2000).

Given the drive for improved performance in the public sector, governments will continue to pursue reforms like privatization in order to get as much value as possible from taxpayer dollars. This will be especially true for jurisdictions experiencing financial setbacks and those seeing a large number of retirements as the baby boom generation leaves the workforce. Privatization promises a quick fix to governments tasked with finding novel solutions to human capital crises. Contracting out to the private sector is also a popular alternative for many politicians looking to capitalize on perceived government ineffectiveness. In addition, many citizens view private sector know-how as the best resource government can draw on. However, privatization is not always the most efficient option and, in fact, can prove more costly than in-house production. Governments that pursue privatization should do so prudently and ensure that the process remains as transparent as possible.

References

Adams, Guy B., Danny L. Balfour, and George E. Reed. 2006. "Abu Ghraib, Administrative Evil, and Moral Inversion: The Value of "Putting Cruelty First." *Public Administration Review* 66:680–93.

Bagley, Gary. 2009. "Don't Let Goodwill Slip through the Cracks." *The Huffington Post*, October 12. http://www.huffingtonpost.com/gary-bagley/dont-let-goodwill-slip-th_b_318077.html.

Battaglio, R. Paul, Jr., and Stephen E. Condrey. 2006. "Civil Service Reform: Examining State and Local Government Cases." *Review of Public Personnel Administration* 26:118–38.

Battaglio, R. Paul, Jr., and Ghassan A. Khankarli. 2008. "Toll Roads, Politics, and Public-Public Partnerships: The Case of Texas State Highway 121." *Public Works Management & Policy* 13:138–48.

Battaglio, R. Paul, Jr., and Christine Ledvinka. 2009. "Privatizing Human Resources in the Public Sector: Legal Challenges to Outsourcing the Human Resource Function." *Review of Public Personnel Administration* 29:293–307.

Battaglio, R. Paul, Jr., and Jerome S. Legge Jr. 2009. "Self-Interest, Ideological/Symbolic Politics, and Citizen Characteristics: A Cross-National Analysis of Support for Privatization." *Public Administration Review* 69:697–709.

Becker, Fred W., Gail Silverstein, and Lee Chaykin. 1995. "Public Employee Job Security and Benefits: A Barrier to Privatization of Mental Health Services." *Public Productivity and Management Review* 19:25–33.

Bloomberg, Michael R. 2009. "NYC Service: A Blueprint to Increase Civic Engagement." http://www.nycservice.org/liberty/download/file/944/.

Board of County Commissioners v. Umbehr, 518 U.S. 668 (1996).

Board of Regents of State Colleges v. Roth, 408 U.S. 564 (1972).

Brown, Trevor L., and Matthew Potoski. 2003. "Transaction Costs and Institutional Explanations for Government Service Production Decisions." *Journal of Public Administration Research & Theory* 13:441–68.

Chi, Keon S., Kelley A. Arnold, and Heather M. Perkins. 2003. "Privatization in State Government: Trends and Issues." *Spectrum: The Journal of State Government* 76:12–21.

Civil Rights Act of 1871 (as amended), 42 U.S.C. § 1983.

Coggburn, Jerrell D. 2007. "Outsourcing Human Resources: The Case of Texas Health and Human Services Commission." *Review of Public Personnel Administration* 27:315–35.

Cohen, Steven, and William B. Eimicke. 2008. *The Responsible Contract Manager: Protecting the Public Interest in an Outsourced World.* Washington, DC: Georgetown University Press.

Condrey, Stephen E., and R. Paul Battaglio Jr. 2007. "A Return to Spoils? Revisiting Radical Civil Service Reform in the United States." *Public Administration Review* 67:425–36.

Cooper, Phillip J. 2003. *Governing by Contract: Challenges and Opportunities for Public Managers.* Washington, DC: CQ Press.

Dudek & Company. 1988. *Privatization and Public Employees: The Impact of City and County Contracting Out on Government Workers.* Washington, DC: National Commission for Employment Policy.

Durant, Robert F., and Jerome S. Legge Jr. 2002. "Politics, Public Opinion, and Privatization in France: Assessing the Calculus of Consent for Market Reforms." *Public Administration Review* 62: 307–23.

Elam, L. B. 1997. "Reinventing the Government Privatization-Style—Avoiding the Legal Pitfalls of Replacing Civil Servants with Contract Providers." *Public Personnel Management* 26:15–33.

Federal Acquisition Regulations, 48 C.F.R. § 1.

Fernandez, Sergio. 2007. "What Works Best When Contracting Services? An Analysis of Contracting Performance at the Local Level in the US." *Public Administration* 85:1119–41.

Fernandez, Sergio, Hal G. Rainey, and Carol E. Lowman. 2006. "Privatization and Its Implications for Human Resources Management." In *Public Personnel Management: Current Concerns, Future Challenges,* 4th ed., edited by Norma M. Riccucci, 204–24. New York: Longman.

Fernandez, Sergio, and Craig R. Smith. 2006. "Looking for Evidence of Public Employee Opposition to Privatization: An Empirical Study with Implications for Practice." *Review of Public Personnel Administration* 26:356–81.

Freedom of Information Act, 5 U.S.C § 552.

Globerman, Steven, and Aidan R. Vining. 1996. "A Framework for Evaluating the Government Contracting-Out Decision with an Application to Information Technology." *Public Administration Review* 56:577–86.

Greene, Jeffrey D. 2002. *Cities and Privatization: Prospects for the New Century.* Upper Saddle River, NJ: Prentice Hall.

Greer, Charles R., Stuart A. Youngblood, and David A. Gray. 1999. "Human Resource Management Outsourcing: The Make or Buy Decision." *Academy of Management Perspectives* 13:85–96.

Hodge, Graeme A. 2000. *Privatization: An International Review of Performance.* Boulder, CO: Westview.

Johnston, Jocelyn M., and Barbara S. Romzek. 1999. "Contracting and Accountability in State Medicaid Reform: Rhetoric, Theories, and Reality." *Public Administration Review* 59:383–99.

Kellough, J. Edward, and Lloyd G. Nigro, eds. 2006. *Civil Service Reform in the States: Personnel Policy and Politics at the Subnational Level.* Albany: SUNY Press.

Kettl, Donald F. 2002. *The Transformation of Governance: Public Administration for Twenty-First Century America.* Baltimore: Johns Hopkins University Press.

Kromm, Chris. 2006. "Florida's Privatization Nightmare." *Facing South,* April 12. http://www.southernstudies.org/2006/04/floridas-privatization-nightmare.html.

Kuttner, Robert. 1997. *Everything for Sale: The Virtues and Limits of Markets.* New York: Alfred A. Knopf.

Lawler, Edward E., III, Dave Ulrich, Jac Fitz-enz, and James C. Madden V. 2004. *Human Resources Business Process Outsourcing: Transforming How HR Gets Its Work Done.* With Regina Maruca. San Francisco, CA: Jossey-Bass.

Lebron v. National Railroad Passenger Corp., 513 U.S. 374 (1995).

LeRoux, Kelly, and Donald F. Harney, eds. 2007. *Service Contracting: A Local Government Guide.* 2nd ed. Washington, DC: ICMA Press.

Llorens, Jared J., and J. Edward Kellough. 2007. "A Revolution in Public Personnel Administration: The Growth of Web-Based Recruitment and Selection Processes in the Federal Service." *Public Personnel Management* 36:207–22.

Maranto, Robert. 2001. "Thinking the Unthinkable in Public Administration: A Case for Spoils in the Federal Bureaucracy." In *Radical Reform of the Civil Service,* edited by Stephen E. Condrey and Robert Maranto, 69–86. Lanham, MD: Lexington Books.

Meier, Kenneth J., and George A. Krause. 2005. "The Scientific Study of Bureaucracy: An Overview." In *Politics, Policy, and Organizations: Frontiers in the Scientific Study of Bureaucracy,* edited by George A. Krause and Kenneth J. Meier, 1–19. Ann Arbor: University of Michigan Press.

Moe, Ronald C. 1987. "Exploring the Limits of Privatization." *Public Administration Review* 47:453–60.

Moe, Ronald C., and Robert S. Gilmour. 1995. "Rediscovering Principles of Public Administration: The Neglected Foundation of Public Law." *Public Administration Review* 55:135–46.

New York Cares. 2013. Accessed June 17, 2013. http://www.newyorkcares.org.

Nixon, Ron. 2011. "Government Pays More in Contracts, Study Finds." *New York Times,* September 12. http://www.nytimes.com/2011/09/13/us/13contractor.html.

O'Hare Truck Service v. City of Northlake, 518 U.S. 712 (1996).

Office of Management and Budget. 2003. "Circular No. A-76, Revised." http://www.whitehouse.gov/omb/Circulars_a076_a76_incl_tech_correction/.

Project on Government Oversight (POGO). 2011. "Bad Business: Billions of Taxpayer Dollars Wasted on Hiring Contractors." http://pogoarchives.org/m/co/igf/bad-business-report-only-2011.pdf.

Rainey, Hal G. 2009. *Understanding and Managing Public Organizations,* 4th ed. San Francisco, CA: Jossey-Bass.

Reduction in Force, 5 C.F.R § 351. http://www.gpo.gov/fdsys/pkg/CFR-2011-title5-vol1/pdf/CFR-2011-title5-vol1-part351.pdf.

Rehfuss, John A. 1989. *Contracting Out in Government.* San Francisco, CA: Jossey-Bass.

Riccucci, Norma M., and Katherine C. Naff. 2008. *Personnel Management in Government.* 6th ed. Boca Raton, FL: CRC Press.

Rosenbloom, David H., and Suzanne J. Piotrowski. 2005. "Outsourcing the Constitution and Administrative Law Norms." *American Review of Public Administration* 35:103–21.

Savas, Emanuel S. 2000. *Privatization and Public-Private Partnerships.* New York: Chatham House.

Savas, Emanuel S. 2005. *Privatization in the City: Successes, Failures, Lessons.* Washington, DC: CQ Press.

Schooner, Steven L. 2005. "Contractor Atrocities at Abu Ghraib: Compromised Accountability in a Streamlined, Outsourced Government." *Stanford Law & Policy Review* 16:549–72.

Sclar, Elliott D. 2000. *You Don't Always Get What You Pay For: The Economics of Privatization.* Ithaca, NY: Cornell University Press.

Selden, Sally Coleman. 2006. "The Impact of Discipline on the Use and Rapidity of Dismissal in State Governments." *Review of Public Personnel Administration* 26:335–55.

Shafritz, Jay M., E. W. Russell, and Christopher P. Borick. 2007. *Introducing Public Administration,* 5th ed. New York: Pearson Longman.

Siegel, Gilbert B. 1999. "Where Are We on Local Government Contracting?" *Public Productivity & Management Review* 22:365–88.

Siegel, Gilbert B. 2000. "Outsourcing Personnel Functions." *Public Personnel Management* 29:225–36.

Thompson, Lyke, and Richard C. Elling. 2000. "Mapping Patterns of Support for Privatization in the Mass Public: The Case of Michigan." *Public Administration Review* 60:338–48.

Voluntary Early Retirement Authority, 5 C.F.R. § 831.114. http://www.gpo.gov/fdsys/pkg/CFR-2010-title5-vol2/pdf/CFR-2010-title5-vol2-sec831-114.pdf.

Voluntary Separation Incentive Pay, 5 C.F.R. § 842.213. http://www.gpo.gov/fdsys/pkg/CFR-2012-title5-vol2/pdf/CFR-2012-title5-vol2-sec842-213.pdf.

Warner, Dave. 2011. "Former Judge Sentenced to Prison for 'Kids for Cash' Scheme." Reuters, August 11, http://www.reuters.com/article/2011/08/11/us-crime-kidsforcash-idUS TRE77A6KG20110811/.

West v. Atkins, 487 U.S. 42 (1988).

Williamson, Oliver E. 1985. *The Economic Institutions of Capitalism: Firms, Markets, Rational Contracting.* New York: Free Press.

Woodard, Colleen A. 2005. "Merit by Any Other Name—Refraining the Civil Service First Principle." *Public Administration Review* 65:109–16.

Additional Resources

A. M. Best Company—http://www.ambest.com

American Bar Association (ABA). 2013. "State and Local Model Procurement Code." Revised November 11. http://apps.americanbar.org/dch/committee.cfm?com=PC500500.

National Institute for Public Procurement, "NIGP Code of Ethics"—http://www.nigp.org/eweb/StartPage.aspx?Site=NIGP&webcode=abt-codeofethics

US Bureau of Labor Statistics, Consumer Price Index (CPI)—http://www.bls.gov/cpi/

Case 10.1   Privatizing State Services in Louisiana

In the fall of 2000, Louisiana citizens voted on whether to privatize the Louisiana Department of Economic Development (LDED). The proposal, dubbed "Louisiana, Inc.," was part of then governor M. J. "Mike" Foster Jr.'s Vision 2020 initiative to bolster economic development in the state. The legislation proposed replacing the LDED with Louisiana, Inc., "a private sector corporation with a *new economy* strategy and responsiveness." The privatization initiative targeted human resources for reform as a means of removing red tape that typically slowed down the personnel process. According to the state constitution, a reorganization of agency personnel that affected civil service laws required legislative approval and a voter referendum. A positive outcome at the polls would have meant that supervisory appointments in the department, which had been protected by civil service laws, would be made by the governor's office, thus becoming subject to employment at will. While operating outside government personnel regulations, Louisiana, Inc. would have been subject to the state's open-meeting laws, public records laws, and ethics code.

Political abuses of the past weighed heavily on the minds of Louisiana voters as they ultimately rejected the privatization measure.[1] Moreover, department employees and key governor's office appointments—including the secretary of the department, Kevin Reilly—vocally opposed the measure. This opposition garnered considerable media attention, culminating in Governor Foster terminating the secretary because of his opposition to the measure. The ultimate failure of the proposal was anticipated by many in the governor's office. While the governor was traveling across the state to drum up support for the privatization effort, policy analysts were hard at work on contingency plans to implement some other type of reform.

The contingency plan put into place in the spring of 2001 via executive order called for the creation of a departmental reorganization task force, run by private sector consultants. The task force agreed on a "streamlining" process, compacting seven departmental offices into three: the Office of the Secretary, the Office of Management and Finance, and the Office of Business Development. The new Office of Business Development would include a "cluster-based" economic development function, which would focus on key "cluster" industries in the state (e.g., oil and gas, chemicals, agriculture). This department was composed of nine professionals with experience working in their respective clusters and staff, as well as five service groups. The directors of these cluster and service groups were unclassified positions whose incumbents would be appointed by the governor's office and serve at the governor's pleasure.

Along with privatization efforts at LDED, the Foster administration aimed to decentralize and reorganize Louisiana government under ASCEND 2020

---

[1]Former governor Edwin W. Edwards was sentenced to 10 years in prison on federal racketeering charges in October 2001. Edwards was released from prison in January 2011. Two other state officials, the commissioners of insurance and elections, were released from prison in 2005 after serving time for similar charges.

(Advancing Service, Creating Excellence, Nurturing Distinction). Like PHRM reforms elsewhere, ASCEND 2020 delegated personnel authority and discretion to agency HR directors. Under the decentralization plan, the Louisiana Department of State Civil Service, the central merit system authority, was tasked with refocusing its mission from enforcing rules to consulting. In this capacity, the Department of Civil Service assists state agencies with general policy development, skill development, communication, and assessment.

Decentralization of state human resources was accomplished by the creation of two divisions: the Human Resource Program Assistance Division and the Human Resource Accountability Division. The Assistance Division provides state agencies with a one-stop point of contact for general knowledge of merit principles, and it advocates for state agencies as they try to expedite solutions to HR problems. The Accountability Division addresses performance and accountability concerns for over 50 state agencies each year. Agencies in violation of merit system principles are cited and/or sanctioned, and agencies that practice excellence in HRM are duly recognized. Additionally, the Assistance and Accountability Divisions deliver training in line with the new practices to agency managers, supervisors, and HR directors.

Reform efforts also sought to modernize PHRM practices in the state. To meet recruiting and selection needs, agencies are now equipped with a modern human resource information system (HRIS) that provides them with better information about state employees. The state also created a vacancy-posting website and required job applicants to respond directly to the agency with the vacancy of interest. The website has reduced the time needed to fill a vacancy since vacancies can be posted immediately.

Commenting on the state of HRM reforms in Louisiana, Governor Foster explained how members of the administration were able to coordinate their efforts in an often dynamic political climate:

> I spent a lot of time being involved and knowing who was being appointed and knowing who was subject to appointment and trying to get those people and ended up with a very good board (Civil Service) and a very good executive director. You can take an interest and get a board that's a good board. We've got some ex-bankers who are very conscientious people. It's very easy. Again, it all goes back to who sits in this chair. If you get somebody who accepts that everything is political, everything is a political payoff; it's going to fail. If you can get somebody in this job that tries to do things not on a political basis, it will work well, and it has. (personal communication, August 6, 2003)

While the Foster administration was able to enforce its reorganization of LDED through the state civil service department, only supervisory/managerial positions became exempt from the state's civil service rules. Although PHRM reforms were implemented, change was not without costs in terms of resources and personnel. Secretary Kevin Reilly was forced to resign, along with other longtime supervisors within LDED. Employee morale also dropped, making the transition to the new system time-consuming. Whether or not the new organization has proven beneficial to attracting businesses to the state and retaining them remains uncertain.

Discussion Questions

1. Assume the role of a policy analyst in the Louisiana governor's office. What advice might you give the governor on the decision to privatize? What are the pros and cons to consider when outsourcing government services? Now assume the role of a public employee in the Department of Economic Development: Would you give the governor different advice?

2. In your opinion, what ultimately doomed the privatization effort in Louisiana? Use insight from this chapter in your explanation.

3. What might the governor's office have done differently to achieve a successful outcome in the privatization initiative?

4. After the failure of the privatization initiative, the governor's office was still able to implement change in the LDED and the state personnel system. What is your evaluation of these initiatives? Do you agree with the expansion of executive and administrative power in these efforts? Why or why not?

Exercise

Working in groups, investigate local efforts to contract out the HR function. Your group should write a research paper of at least 15 pages and give the class a 15–20 minute briefing on your findings. Your presentation should lead to class commentary/discussion about issues of accountability, measurement, the jurisdiction's political climate, and the culture of government agencies. The purpose of this assignment is to give you practice in developing a coherent and succinct presentation that describes your case study results. Using visual aids

(Continued)

(Continued)

and distributing handouts to the class are encouraged to aid understanding of your presentation and further discussion.

The following are some questions to think about when constructing your presentation. It may be that the answers to these questions are elusive. Keep in mind (1) the many difficulties in trying to improve the efficiency of a government agency's performance through contracting out work to the private sector alone and (2) the competing priorities, distinct work cultures, and institutional constraints that separate a government agency from a provider agency. Interviewing key employees involved in the contracted service is strongly suggested for unraveling the details.

- *General purpose*—What do you perceive as the objectives of the contract (e.g., increasing government efficiency, reducing costs)?
- *Scope of work/services*—What are some of the specific/key services identified in the contract for outsourcing (e.g., refuse collection, wastewater treatment)?
- *Financial terms*—Does the contract provide for incentives for meeting performance benchmarks, fiscal stability, cost savings, or other benefits?
- *Quality assurance*—What measures of accountability are included in the contract (e.g., Is there regular monitoring, and who is the monitoring authority)?
- *Overall evaluation*—In your opinion, has contracting out the service improved government performance? To what extent are the desired outcomes of privatization being realized? What, if any, recommendations would you make (e.g., Should the program be sustained, changed, or expanded)?

Human Resource Information Systems

Upon completion of the chapter, you will be able to do the following:

- Discuss the history of human resource information systems (HRIS).
- Define and explain the functions of HRIS.
- Describe the eight types of HRIS systems.
- Broadly describe the types of HRIS software available and their applications in the public sector.
- Discuss the legal considerations surrounding HRIS in the public sector.

Human resource departments, whether public or private, deal with vast amounts of information. For example, a public HR department houses all the personnel files on its employees—including employees' vital information like Social Security numbers and addresses, pay and benefits information, insurance forms, bank account numbers for direct deposit, and tax forms for every employee who's worked at the agency. It also houses employment information like performance evaluations, years of service, employment manuals, and company policies and procedures. Also included are documents like organizational charts, pay schedules, relevant federal or state employment policies and regulations—and the list goes on. A tremendous amount of information and knowledge is contained within any public organization.

Public managers must be able to manage and leverage this information efficiently to contribute to the overall performance of the organization. As such, **knowledge management** has become a key component of successfully navigating the information age. Knowledge management is the strategic process of creating, acquiring, capturing, aggregating, sharing, and using knowledge from a variety of sources to enhance organizational learning and performance (Bate and Robert 2002, 647; Scarborough, Swan, and Preston 1999). Public sector HR managers tasked with more complex tasks like human capital management or workforce planning also have a particular need for efficient knowledge management. Social, organizational, and demographic changes are forcing public HR managers to take stock of their capabilities (Hendrickson 2003). Employees, customers, and clients are increasingly demanding expanded services of higher quality and faster, and they want HR services to be seamlessly linked with other corporate functions (Hendrickson 2003, 381; Pfeffer 1997). Organizations are frequently operating in more fluid structures, relying less on hierarchy and more on the ability of managers to coordinate activities across agencies and sectors. Moreover, the impending retirements of an aging workforce necessitate a greater emphasis on recruiting talented people who can assume management positions or grow into them. The ever-changing landscape of the information age has made technology an integral part of the HR function. As a result, our reliance on human resource information systems (HRIS) is more apparent than ever.

HRIS is used to "acquire, manipulate, analyze, retrieve, and distribute information about an organization's human resources" (Kavanagh, Thite, and Johnson 2012, 29; see also Tannenbaum 1990). In the past, the "HRIS" used in many government offices involved paper and filing cabinets. Today, however, is a completely different story. The combination of technological advances and an increased need for strategic planning has had a profound impact on HR processes (Kavanagh, Thite, and Johnson 2012). Advances in computer hardware and software allow organizations to integrate copious amounts of HR data and monitor HR needs and activities through a variety of metrics (Hendrickson 2003, 381). Yet HRIS does not consist solely of computer applications; it also "includes the people, policies, procedures and data required to manage the HR function" (Hendrickson 2003, 381).

Unfortunately, very little literature exists on the application and usefulness of HRIS in the public sector (Durant, Girth, and Johnston 2009; McGregor and Daly 1989). This chapter will introduce the topic of HRIS and discuss its potential applications for building a knowledge-based organization (Ingraham, Selden, and Moynihan 2000).

History of HRIS

The evolution of HRIS began before World War II. At that time, HR was considered a noncore function of organizations and was limited to employee record keeping (Hendrickson 2003). The HR department was an isolated unit with little or no interaction with other core administrative functions such as budgeting and finance. The main function of record keeping was to compile employee data (e.g., name, address, phone number, employment history, etc.), typically in index card files.

Technological advances during World War II brought greater awareness to the field of human resources and knowledge management (Goerl 1975; Hendrickson

2003). Norbert Weiner's contributions to **cybernetics**—the discipline of regulating systems and structures—provided a way to use technology to effectively achieve organizational goals (Goerl 1975, 584). At the same time, new ideas in organization theory demonstrated that employee morale was an integral part of organizational success, leading to a greater appreciation of the individual in the organization (Hendrickson 2003; Rainey 2009). While the HR function was still relegated to being an informal part of the organization, these advances led to the development of more formal recruitment and selection processes.

By the 1960s, social and economic movements began to revolutionize thinking about the personnel function, especially about how organizations should be staffed. The personnel function achieved greater status within both private and public organizations, becoming viewed as a necessary function for accomplishing organizational goals (Hendrickson 2003). During this era, the term *personnel* was superseded by *human resource management*, leading to the acronym HR that is commonly used today. The landmark Civil Service Reform Act of 1978 reinvigorated the status of personnel in the public sector by creating the Office of Personnel Management to coordinate the staffing of the federal bureaucracy. More importantly, civil rights legislation and regulations governing diversity forced organizations to do a better job of recording demographic information about employees. To this end, large organizations used mainframe computers to maintain employee records, and computer-based HRIS was born (382). In the 1970s and 1980s, computer hardware and software became necessary tools for the HR function.

The human capital movement (see Chapter 12) over the last few decades has made HRIS an even more vital component of public and private organizations of all sizes. An organization's ability to track current and future workforce needs cannot be accomplished effectively without HRIS. The contemporary HRIS landscape has seen the function of HR departments evolve from basic record keeping to contributing significantly to the operation of the organization, for example, by sophisticated applications of labor analytics. As a result, HR professionals are equipped with technology that can assist in key strategic processes like workforce decision making.

HRIS Applications

The uses of HRIS in the private and public sectors are similarly broad in scope. For example, HRIS allows public HR managers to keep track of EEOC metrics to report workplace demographics. Moreover, HRIS gives HR managers the ability to track instances of discrimination in personnel actions. Thus, HRIS allows the organization to reduce or avoid potential legal liability. HRIS may also be useful for tracking metrics for specific programs or policies, enabling managers to assess the usefulness and efficiency of such practices. For example, HRIS lets managers assess the effectiveness of training and development programs over time, evaluating such programs' impact on productivity. Managers can also use HRIS to keep track of employee absences, paid and unpaid time off, and other day-to-day operational metrics (Kavanagh, Thite, and Johnson 2012). Most importantly, HRISs provide automated and integrated data solutions needed for strategic HR planning.

According to the Society for Human Resource Management (SHRM), HRIS serves six vital organizational functions: strategic management, workforce planning and employment, human resource development, total rewards, employee and labor relations, and risk management (SHRM 2008). Table 11.1 provides examples that illustrate these six functions. In terms of strategic management, HRIS assists with scanning the external environment and tracking improvements in quality and productivity. HRIS can provide workforce-planning metrics by tracking promotions, transfers, new hires, and termination rates. HRIS can also help in the maintenance of regulatory records and forms (i.e., EEOC, OSHA, and affirmative action reports). HRIS is useful to employees too. It can help them manage their career development by tracking training and development opportunities, for example. Other functions include tracking an employee's performance evaluations and compensation over time, as well as health and retirement benefits enrollment and interfacing pay and deductions to payroll. HRIS allows HR managers to use salary survey data efficiently, and HRIS can store disciplinary and grievance records, union membership and dues information, and attitude survey data. Finally, HRIS can assist the organization with **risk management** by identifying trends in on-the-job reportable incidents for workers' compensation and workers' compensation claims.

HRIS offers organizations a number of advantages (Beckers and Bsat 2002). An integrated HRIS collects information in a single database, offering better information processing and knowledge management (Kavanagh, Thite, and Johnson 2012; Lengnick-Hall and Lengnick-Hall 2006). It provides managers with timely, comprehensive assessments of information across the organization. In addition, real-time reporting of important HR metrics expedites and better informs the decision-making process. Timely and accurate information processing also improves the organization's HR operations and management and streamlines administrative functions associated with HR; for example, automation of payroll reduces labor costs (Roberts 1999). The advanced use of HRIS changes the overall function of HR from a top-down process to a more strategic approach. Such a transformation entails a move away from rule-bound hierarchies to a more fluid structure, in which HR takes into account the stakeholders in the internal and external environment. For public agencies moving toward strategic human resource management (SHRM), HRIS enables them to improve connectivity and collaboration and make better-informed decisions

Table 11.1	HRIS Application

HRM Application	Examples
Strategic Management	• Environmental scanning • Tracks quality and productivity improvements
Workforce Planning and Employment	• Tracks promotion, transfer, hiring, and termination rates • Maintains and reports EEOC data in the required format • Produces applicant flow and utilization reports for affirmative action programs
Human Resource Development	• Outlines career path development • Tracks education, skills, and training programs completed • Registers employees in courses • Tracks employee performance
Total Rewards	• Tracks salary survey information • Tracks retirement planning, tuition reimbursement, COBRA and HIPAA information • Facilitates benefits administration and salary analysis across job classifications
Employee and Labor Relations	• Stores employee disciplinary records • Records union data and labor distribution data for budgeting payroll expenses associated with labor. • Tracks attitude survey results
Risk Management	• Identifies accident and illness trends • Tracks safety records, insurance, and workers' compensation claims • Monitors departments and jobs with higher risks

Source: SHRM 2008

about future needs. Moreover, HRIS provides accurate delivery of HR services and benefits to employees—a boon to overall employee satisfaction. For example, employees' paychecks are deposited electronically in their bank accounts. Also, intranets (proprietary websites that contain information specific to individual agencies) are repositories of information on any number of topics—such as open job postings or expense report forms—that employees can access at any time and from remote locations or even from home.

Particularly insightful is the application of HRIS to **enterprise resource planning (ERP)**. According to Kavanagh and colleagues (2012), ERP is

> a set of integrated database applications or modules that carry out the most common business functions, including HR, general ledger, accounts payable, accounts receivable, order management, inventory control, and customer relationship management. (20)

ERP houses the essential functions of management (i.e., human resources and finance) in a readily accessible software system. The potential efficiencies from integrated delivery of a variety of management and HR functions include enhanced knowledge management, human capital stewardship, and improved collaboration among organizational units (Kavanagh, Thite, and Johnson 2012; Lengnick-Hall and Lengnick-Hall 2006). For agencies embarking on more strategic HR efforts like workforce planning or human capital management, which involve substantial intra-organizational coordination, ERP is essential (see also Dery and Wailes 2005).

Implementation of HRIS

The potential for organizations to implement and manage HRIS effectively varies according to their characteristics. Ngai and Wat (2004; see also Kavanagh, Thite, and Johnson 2012) suggested that factors such as organizational size, management support and commitment, resources available, HR philosophy, managerial competence, and aptitude for change are important. Larger organizations tend to enjoy more marginal benefits from HRIS applications than do smaller organizations; the larger the organization, the more information it needs to manage, and the more it will benefit from HRIS efficiencies. The success of HRIS also depends on the commitment of top management to driving and implementing the development of new hardware and software. Finally, the installation and maintenance of computerized systems require a significant investment of money, time, and personnel with key skills, so the amount of resources the organization can dedicate to HRIS determines what can be done.

A supportive HR environment is also crucial to the success of HRIS. An HR philosophy that embraces the use of technology in the application of the organization's vision, culture, and structure is important. Finally, the technological capacity of employees determines whether they will buy in to the technological changes brought about by HRIS. A necessary step in the adoption of HRIS is to motivate employees to adopt the new technologies that automate the HR function.

Types of HRIS

Several types of computer-based HRIS applications are available; Table 11.2 provides an overview (Kavanagh, Thite, and Johnson 2012, 20–22). HRIS can be described

Table 11.2	**Information Systems Providing Support for HRM**		
Organizational Level	**Type of System**	**Major Goals and Focus**	**HRM Examples**
Operational	Transaction processing system	Improved transaction speed and accuracy More efficient processing of daily business transactions Automation of routine transactions Reduced transaction costs	Payroll processing Time and attendance entry Online creation and dissemination of application forms
Managerial	Management information system	Provision of key data to managers Improved decision making Scheduled and ad hoc reports	Producing EEO reports Calculating recruiting and selection yield ratios Calculating per capita merit increases
Executive	Executive information system	Provision of aggregate, high-level data Assistance with with long-range planning Support of strategic direction and decisions	Succession planning Aggregate data on balanced scorecard (see Chapter 12)
Boundary spanning	Decision support system	Interactive and iterative managerial decision making Support of forecasting and "what-if" analysis Running of business simulations	Staffing needs assessment Labor market analysis Employee skills assessment
	Expert system	Embedding of human knowledge in information systems Automation of decisions with technology	Résumé keyword searches

(Continued)

(Continued)

Organizational Level	Type of System	Major Goals and Focus	HRM Examples
	Office automation systems	Designing documents Scheduling shared resources Communication	Online training-room scheduling
	Collaboration technologies	Electronic communication and collaboration between employees Support of virtual teams	E-learning Online meetings and shared documents HR department wikis
	Enterprise resources planning system	Integration and centralization of corporate data Sharing of data across functional boundaries Single data source and common technology architecture	Systems such as OrangeHRM, Oracle/PeopleSoft, Lawson HRM, and SAP

Source: Kavanagh, Thite, and Johnson 2012

based on the organizational function it serves (i.e., operational, managerial, executive, or boundary spanning). Organizational functions include daily operating tasks (operational), managerial functions (managerial), strategic functions (executive), and integrated operations (boundary spanning).

Operational functions are transaction-based processes such as calculating payroll, tracking time and attendance, and processing forms. HRIS can improve the speed and accuracy of daily operations by automating routine transactions. Adopting such systems has the potential to reduce transaction costs associated with routine data entry and cut down on human error. Such efficiencies can be realized through online applications that can disseminate forms and information and collect data.

Management information systems help mangers deliver vital data that support decision making in the organization. Management-based systems may also provide predefined reports as well as ad hoc analyses. Such automated reporting is particularly useful to HR managers interested in producing EEO reports and calculating metrics for recruitment and compensation (e.g., yield ratios for recruitment and per capita merit increases).

Executive-level information systems provide aggregate data to inform long-term decision-making. Executive-based HRIS supports strategic planning on key objectives (e.g., balanced scorecard reporting on financials, customers, internal processes, and future objectives, discussed in depth in Chapter 12) (Kaplan and Norton 1996). For HR managers, such systems might be particularly useful for succession planning, that is, identifying and developing future leaders for the organization.

HRIS also facilitates boundary-spanning activities, or activities that integrate services across different organizational units. Such boundary-spanning applications are designed to support decision making, knowledge management, office automation, collaboration, and ERP. Decision support systems allow real-time information gathering that assists with interactive and iterative managerial decision making. Iterative applications, which examine multiple decision scenarios and their potential consequences, are valuable in forecasting analysis. For HR managers, decision support systems can aid in workforce planning by forecasting staffing and other resource needs. Expert systems support knowledge management; HR managers can apply expert systems to managing résumés and keeping track of the knowledge, skills, and abilities deemed vital to future productivity. Likewise, HRIS can automate routine office functions such as document design, scheduling, and communication through shared applications. HRIS also utilizes Web 2.0 technologies to support electronic communication and collaboration across the organization, for example, virtual teams and online meetings (e.g., video calls over the Internet via Skype), e-learning (e.g., online classrooms using services like Adobe Connect), and HR department wikis (web applications that host information that anyone can update). Finally, as discussed above, ERP is a necessary step toward the integrated management of HR functions across the organization. ERP systems centralize important data, enabling employees to share information across functional boundaries. ERP software (e.g., OrangeHRM, Oracle/PeopleSoft, Lawson HRM, and SAP) houses data in a single database, fostering increased data integrity and minimizing data entry, and use common technology architecture, enabling more efficient hardware and software maintenance.

Clearly, the types of systems available to organizations are impressive. However, as noted earlier, organizations are limited by a number of contextual factors such as organizational size, management commitment, and resources available. Organizations considering implementing or upgrading their HRIS must do so based on a careful analysis of its costs and benefits.

HRIS Software

Many software packages exist for HRIS applications. OrangeHRM, Oracle/PeopleSoft, Lawson HRM, and SAP are but a few of the more widely implemented HRIS software packages, used in both the public and private sectors. Most HRIS applications specialize in open-source and advanced host applications (i.e., cloud computing). Open-source software is free and allows any user to develop and publish modifications of its source code (OrangeHRM 2012). According to the OrangeHRM website, "Open Source has evolved as a flexible low cost alternative to proprietary software owned by corporations, typically created as a collaborative effort in which programmers improve upon the code and share the changes within the community." In cloud-based computing, the software and data are centrally hosted on the vendor's website or server and then delivered as a service over the Internet or private network to the end-user organization (NIST 2011). Open-source and cloud-based computing is a departure from the traditional configuration of proprietary software, once the norm in large organizations, which was installed on servers or machines physically located at the organization. Instead, organizations are increasingly using open-source software solutions that are not installed on their own servers but delivered to them virtually, via the "cloud." The next sections discuss the offerings of some of the leading HRIS providers.

HRIS Software Providers

OrangeHRM, based in New Jersey, specializes in open-source and advanced hosted applications in the form of software as a service (SaaS) for automated HR management. Founded in 2005, OrangeHRM has over 1 million users globally across both public and private sectors (OrangeHRM 2012). It offers applications customizable for small and medium organizations. The software includes human capital management and HRM applications for functions such as employee information, employee time-off, recruitment, and employee performance evaluation management. The company also offers a variety of support and training services for clients, including online and on-site instruction.

Oracle/PeopleSoft offers a variety of HRIS applications to large corporations, governments, universities, and other organizations. Its applications include human capital management, workforce management, workforce service delivery, talent management (i.e., recruitment, retention, and motivation), and HR analytics (i.e., analysis of staffing and productivity) (Oracle 2012). While initially focused on providing a single-client server software approach, as does OrangeHRM, Oracle/PeopleSoft has moved toward integrating cloud computing into its offerings.

Like Oracle/PeopleSoft software, the Lawson Human Resource Management suite (Lawson HRM) is utilized by a variety of public sector organizations, including school districts, local governments, and public utilities (Lawson HRM 2012). Lawson HRM is designed to support routine and strategic planning processes. Applications include benefits, payroll, tracking and managing employee information, time-off management, and general performance management. Like the two software packages discussed above, Lawson HRM also offers applications for human capital management, workforce management, and talent management.

The German multinational software company SAP is the largest business software provider in the world, specializing in software for managing operations and customer relations (SAP 2012). SAP's ERP system (SAP ERP) integrates data into a single-source application for sharing and analysis. SAP's public sector applications are designed to better link government at all levels to citizens (SAP 2012). Public sector applications include planning, budgeting, and shared services.

In addition to the more comprehensive HR software, a number of specialized products are on the market. Specialized software tends to focus on automating HR solutions to reduce workload and costs (Anderson 2004). For example, the software company Kronos offers workforce management solutions through a variety of cloud-based HRIS products (Kronos 2012). Workforce HR, Workforce Payroll, Workforce Scheduler, Workforce Timekeeper, Timekeeper Center, and ShopTrac Pro are Kronos software packages that help organizations with time and attendance, scheduling, absence management, payroll, hiring, and labor analytics. Ultimate Software provides cloud-based human capital management solutions for for-profit and nonprofit organizations. The company's UltiPro software provides an integrated, single-source solution for benefits, payroll, workforce analytics, talent management, mobile applications (apps), global human capital management, time and attendance, scheduling, payment services, salary planning and budgeting, and position management (Ultimate Software 2012). Epicor Human Capital Management (Epicor HCM; formally Spectrum) offers automated HR capabilities organizations can use to track, manage, and analyze employee data (Epicor HCM 2012). Specific HR applications include recruitment management, benefits, and absence tracking. Epicor HCM also develops and provides tools for performance management, HR reporting, and workforce analytics.

Nonprofits in Focus	**Volunteer Management Software**

Like any other type of organization, nonprofits look to HRIS to keep track of vast amounts of personnel data. For nonprofits, HRIS software needs to be able to track data on volunteers and donors as well as employees. Having access to such information is vital to improving the lifeblood of nonprofits: people and money. Nonprofits depend on growing their donor bases and maintaining close ties with those stakeholders. TechSoup Global and IdealWare—two nonprofit-centered IT-savvy firms—compiled a list of volunteer and donor management software programs and assessed their capabilities.

(Continued)

(Continued)

Software can be divided into stand-alone volunteer management software, which just tracks volunteers, and consolidated software, which allows for cross-listing of volunteers with donors. Cross-listing allows managers to identify volunteers who might be willing financial donors, and vice versa. TechSoup Global and IdealWare's assessment was based on a software's capacity to compile volunteer profiles, track volunteer activities, schedule volunteers, communicate with volunteers, manage online volunteer profiles, be customized and easy to use, and manage additional constituent information. Among the stand-alone software packages profiled were eRecruiter/eCoordinator by Samaritan, Volgistics by the company of the same name, and Volunteer Reporter by Volunteer Software. Consolidated software reviewed included DonorPerfect by SofterWare, The Raiser's Edge(i) by Blackbaud, and Volunteers for GiftWorks by Mission Research. For more detailed information on each software package, you can view the report at http://www.techsoup.org/SiteCollectionDocuments/article-consumers-guide-to-software-volunteer-management-document.pdf.

Source: Quinn, L., Bernard, C., Leslie, J., & Andrei, K. (2011). *A Consumer's Guide to Software for Volunteer Management.* TechSoup Global/IdealWare. http://www.techsoup.org/SiteCollectionDocuments/article-consumers-guide-to-software-volunteer-management-document.pdf.

HRIS Applications in the Public Sector

The private sector has been the trendsetter in innovative computer-based solutions to HR challenges of the 21st century (see Ulrich, Younger, and Brockbank 2008). As this text has highlighted throughout, public sector organizations are increasingly looking to the private sector for inventive solutions to HR challenges. In the past, HR departments often used myriad applications, which could be difficult to manage. The more recent trend has been to adopt more integrated HRIS solutions.

Increasingly, public sector organizations are adopting shared delivery of HR services that taps into the potential for efficiencies from combining centralized and decentralized operations (Cooke 2006; Selden and Wooters 2011). **Shared services** involves a collaborative approach to combining business functions (e.g., all of the HR departments within an organization) into an integrated, semiautonomous unit (an HRM shared services agency) tasked with managing and promoting efficiency, quality, cost savings, and internal customer service (Bergeron 2003, 3). Integrating HR services into one unit allows the organization to take advantage of economies of scale, eliminate duplication, and promote efficiency (Selden and Wooters 2011, 352; see also Bergeron 2003; Corporate Leadership Council 2006).

Table 11.3 presents a comparison of the three HR service models (centralized, shared, and decentralized) adapted by Selden and Wooters (2011) from Ulrich, Younger, and Brockbank (2008). The public sector has traditionally used the centralized HR service model. Typically, administration of centralized HR services tasks specialists with the design of and responsibility for HRM policies and procedures. Central HRM specialists and staff are also responsible for handling any issues or problems with HR

Table 11.3	Comparison of Centralized, Shared, and Decentralized HRM		
Dimension	**Centralized**	**Shared services**	**Decentralized**
Design responsibility for HRM policies and procedures	Central HRM specialists	Specialists in shared services unit	Departmental HRM professionals with variation across units
Implementation of HRM practices	Governed by central HRM specialists	Governed by agency HRM professionals who select from a menu of services; menu designed by shared services agency	Governed by departmental HRM professionals
Accountability	Central HRM	Split between agency HRM/managers and HRM shared services agency	Agency HRM
Services Orientation	Standardized HRM policies and services across government	Tailored to agency; agencies are allowed to choose from a standardized set of service options	Agency needs and priorities
Flexibility	Mandated use of central resources	Flexibility allowed as governed by shared services unit and permitted by law	Up to agencies
Skill requirements for HRM	Technical expertise in functional design and delivery (specialists)	Design expertise but also consulting and support expertise	"General" HRM knowledge (generalists)
Role	Provide HRM services that are consistent with the mission/mandates of central HRM; enforce mandated rules	Agencies helped to determine which available HRM services best fit their needs	Provides HRM services specific to needs of agency

Sources: Selden and Wooters (2011, 353); Ulrich, Younger, and Brockbank (2008)

practices and for policing compliance with HR policies and procedures. Implementing HRM practices under a centralized model uses a top-down approach and standardized policies and procedures across the government agency or jurisdiction.

In contrast, the trend toward decentralized delivery of HRM has focused on localized development of HR policies and procedures by agency-level HR managers (Condrey 2010; Selden and Wooters 2011). HRM professionals within agencies are tasked with the implementation of HR functions. Employees are directed to HR managers at the department level for grievances and other issues. The focus of HRM is to prioritize agency needs and goals. Without a standardized process, there is the potential for a great deal of variation among units within the organization (Selden and Wooters 2011; Ulrich, Younger, and Brockbank 2008), which can be problematic.

The increasingly popular hybrid approach to HRM services attempts to blend the benefits of centralization with decentralization (Condrey 2010; Selden and Wooters 2011). Establishing a shared services unit allows the organization to enjoy the advantages of centralization: economies of scale, greater expertise, and integrated technology. At the same time, tasking shared services personnel to adopt an internal customer focus and meet the needs of the respective agencies taps the benefits of decentralization (Selden and Wooters 2011, 352). Specialists within the shared services unit are responsible for the design of HRM policies and procedures. Collaborating with agency HR managers, shared services specialists are able to offer a menu of uniform HRM services that, at the same time, can also be tailored to the specific needs of the internal customer. Issues may be handled by both agency HR managers and specialists in shared services, depending on the nature of problem. The role of the shared services unit is to assist agencies in determining the level of HR service that suits their needs.

According to Selden and Wooters (2011) 16 states have embarked upon shared services models, with another 11 indicating they are leaning in that direction as well (356). The extent of the implementation of shared HR services among these states varied. For example, some states (Arizona, Louisiana, Michigan, New Mexico, Oklahoma, Oregon, and Wisconsin) focus on shared delivery of a specific set of activities, while others (Connecticut, Indiana, Tennessee, and Virginia) offer shared services for select agencies (357). Four states (Georgia, Maryland, Massachusetts, and Utah) offer shared HR services for all agencies, and two states (Iowa and Kansas) offer shared services options for other functions (e.g., information technology or security). For public organizations considering the shared HR services model, integration of technology is crucial to accurate and timely service delivery.

Having the right technology in place enables improved communication and distribution of relevant information in the shared services model (Selden and Wooters 2011; Ulrich, Younger, and Brockbank 2008). Advances in information technology have made HRIS an integral and distinct function of the HR function (Hendrickson 2003). For public HR managers, a greater appreciation of technology is necessary for the effective delivery of services. Moreover, a greater awareness of the benefits of IT has raised the expectations of public employees, managers, customers, regulators, and clients (Hendrickson 2003, 381).

Managing institutional knowledge is an exceedingly important task of public HR managers (Selden 2009). HR managers, as the arbiters of organizational information, face increased demand from stakeholders (Hendrickson 2003, 392–93) and thus play a vital role in the implementation and integration of HRIS (see also Ulrich 1997). While the private sector came to this realization decades ago, the public sector has only recently adopted the human capital mantra (Brook and King 2008; Selden 2009). Public HR managers now are challenged to integrate vital information for the maintenance of organizational knowledge in a rapidly changing environment.

Legal Considerations Related to HRIS

Since HR departments handle so much personal employee information, the maintenance of and dissemination of this information requires great care. Because many of the records being stored contain sensitive information, knowledge of the relevant laws is essential. While advances in technology have allowed HR managers to effectively manage organizational knowledge, HRIS is also vulnerable to security breaches and other cyberthreats. As a result, HR and IT managers must determine what employee information is appropriate to gather and establish the necessary cybersecurity for keeping it private. Access to information should be limited to only those whose jobs require it.

The lack of a comprehensive federal law regulating the protection of employee information has led to a variety of responses at the state level (SHRM 2008). As a result, HR managers must be familiar with the relevant laws guiding employee privacy. Table 11.4 reviews several important laws that bear on electronic record keeping (*HR Focus* 2006; Sotto and McCarthy 2007).

The **Fair Credit Reporting Act (FCRA)** regulates background checks conducted during the recruitment and selection process. The FCRA mandates the privacy of employee background information and requires that the organization get written authorization from the prospective employee for permission to obtain consumer reports. If the information leads to an adverse action on the part of the employer, the employee must be notified. Several states have enacted similar laws safeguarding the information procured by background checks. The **Electronic Communications Privacy Act** regulates the protection of federal employee communications, in particular those stored in computers. Employers must obtain prior authorization from the employee or secure a search warrant before accessing such data. The **Health Insurance Portability and Accountability Act (HIPAA)** regulates employee privacy with regard to health records and information. The **Privacy**

Table 11.4	**Laws Regulating Employee Privacy**

Fair Credit Reporting Act (FCRA)—Regulates the administration of background checks conducted by the employer during recruitment and selection. The FCRA mandates the privacy of employee background information and requires the organization to get written authorization from the prospective employee for permission to obtain consumer reports. If the information obtained leads to an adverse action on the part of the employer, the employee must be notified. Several states have similar laws.

Electronic Communications Privacy Act—Regulates the protection of federal employees' communications, in particular those stored in computers (e.g., emails). Employer must have prior authorization or secure a warrant.

Health Insurance Portability and Accountability Act (HIPAA)—Regulates employee privacy with regard to the transmission of health records and information. The Privacy Rule requires covered entities to adopt written policies and procedures regarding the use and disclosure of protected health information.

Sarbanes-Oxley Act of 2002—Regulates employee privacy and prohibits retaliation against whistle-blowers.

Fair and Accurate Credit Transactions Act of 2003 (FACTA)—Requires people who maintain or otherwise possess consumer information, or any other pertinent information, derived from consumer reports for a business purpose to properly dispose of such information or a compilation of it. Several states have similar laws.

Social Security number laws—Thirty-eight states prohibit or restrict the dissemination of Social Security numbers.

Security breach notification laws—Several states require employers to notify employees of potential or real security breaches that involve computerized data.

Sources: *HR Focus* 2006; SHRM 2008; Sotto and McCarthy 2007

Rule of HIPAA requires covered entities to adopt written policies and procedures regarding the use and disclosure of protected health information. **The Sarbanes-Oxley Act of 2002** further regulates employee privacy and prohibits retaliation against whistle-blowers. The **Fair and Accurate Credit Transactions Act of 2003 (FACTA)** requires people in the possession of consumer information acquired for a business purpose to properly dispose of such information; several states have enacted similar laws.

In addition, a number of laws regulate the dissemination of Social Security numbers. Social Security number laws have been enacted by 38 states. In addition, software that collects personnel records is increasingly susceptible to hackers (see the case study below). Therefore, several jurisdictions have enacted security breach notification laws, which require employers to notify employees of a potential or actual security breach that has or could compromise employee information.

HRIS and PHRM Reforms

Decentralization has transferred the responsibility for HR functions to agency-level staff, which poses a number of challenges to the coordination of HR activities government-wide. In turn, this means that coordinating the implementation of the other reforms discussed in this text (performance-based pay, declassification, deregulation, privatization) can also be a daunting task. Ensuring fairness and consistency in the application of these reforms is problematic in a decentralized HR authority environment.

HRIS has the potential to ameliorate the coordination problems inherent in decentralization. While an increasing reliance on shared services models has improved coordination gaps, reorganizing the delivery of HR services may pose a political hurdle that is too difficult to overcome. Technology may offer an easier solution to coordinating information management within and across departments, and investing in improved HRIS applications may be a wise choice for governments.

Privatization has raised significant issues with regard to the dissemination of information under the Freedom of Information Act. The increasing use of private contractors to carry out public HR functions has meant that private companies have custody of public information. Contractors may be required to disclose sensitive information obtained in the course of fulfilling their duties because they are acting for the government. As such, they too have a responsibility to maintain personnel records securely.

As the case study below details, the threat to information security is real. Data lapses cause irreparable harm to efficiency, workplace culture, and overall accountability. Having the right HRIS software in place might not be enough. Governments increasingly need to maintain IT expertise in the safekeeping of personnel information. Providing HR managers with greater access to information comes with a cost— a greater likelihood that the information will be at risk. Balancing the needs of management with security obligations will be a responsibility of both public HR managers and their IT counterparts.

Conclusion

Advances in information technology have ushered in a new era of managing human resources information, and policies governing HRIS are more important than ever. Computer networks and cloud-based software have given HR managers tools that allow them to administer HR functions in a more productive manner. HRIS in particular allows HR managers to effectively navigate large amounts of employee information, while providing greater access to this information to employees, customers, and clients. HRIS gives HR managers in the 21st century an integrated, single-source data stream for managing strategic planning, performance management, workforce planning, human resource development, compensation and rewards, benefits, and risk management. With such information now readily available to HR managers, the HR function can play a critical role in strategic planning for the organization. Public HR managers possess the information agencies need to plan for goal achievement.

Managing vast amounts of employee information also comes with a special responsibility to safeguard vital data. The potential for security breaches has resulted in jurisdictions passing laws and regulations governing the handling of sensitive information. For public HR managers and IT staff, familiarity with the law is essential for protecting employee privacy rights.

Public HR managers seeking to capitalize on rapidly changing social and economic environments must be able to analyze vast amounts of data in a timely fashion. HRIS provides public HR managers with the tools critical to meeting the information age's challenge of managing knowledge. Familiarity with HRIS portends untold possibilities for the future of the public service.

References

Anderson, Martin W. 2004. "The Metrics of Workforce Planning." *Public Personnel Management* 33:363–79.

Bate, S. Paul, and Glenn Robert. 2002. "Knowledge Management and Communities of Practice in the Private Sector: Lessons for Modernizing the National Health Service in England and Wales." *Public Administration* 80:643–63.

Beckers, Astrid M., and Mohammad Z. Bsat. 2002. "A DSS Classification Model for Research in Human Resource Information Systems." *Information Systems Management* 19:1–10.

Bergeron, Bryan P. 2003. *Essentials of Shared Services.* Hoboken, NJ: John Wiley.

Brook, Douglas A., and Cynthia L. King. 2008. "Federal Personnel Management Reform: From Civil Service Reform Act to National Security Reforms." *Review of Public Personnel Administration* 28:205–21.

Condrey, Stephen E. 2010. *Handbook of Human Resource Management in Government.* 3rd ed. San Francisco, CA: Jossey-Bass.

Cooke, Fang Lee. 2006. "Modeling an HR Shared Services Center: Experience of an MNC in the United Kingdom." *Human Resource Management* 45:211–27.

Corporate Leadership Council. 2006. "HR Shared Services: Determining the Scope, Scale, and Structure." Washington, DC: Corporate Executive Board. http://www.spa.ga.gov/pdfs/CLCHRSharedServicesDeterminingtheScopeScaleandStructure.pdf.

Dery, Kristine, and Nick Wailes. 2005. "Necessary but Not Sufficient: ERPs and Strategic HRM." *Strategic Change* 14:265–72.

Durant, Robert F., Amanda M. Girth, and Jocelyn M. Johnston. 2009. "American Exceptionalism, Human Resource Management, and the Contract State." *Review of Public Personnel Administration* 29:207–29.

Epicor Human Capital Management (Epicor HCM). 2012. "Human Capital Management." Accessed September 4. http://www.epicor.com/Products/Pages/Epicor-HCM.aspx.

Goerl, George Frederick. 1975. "Cybernetics, Professionalization, and Knowledge Management: An Exercise in Assumptive Theory." *Public Administration Review* 35:581–88.

Hendrickson, Anthony R. 2003. "Human Resource Information Systems: Backbone Technology of Contemporary Human Resources." *Journal of Labor Research* 24:381–94.

HR Focus. 2006. "Balancing HR Systems with Employee Privacy." 83:11–13.

Ingraham, Patricia W., Selden, Sally C., and Donald P. Moynihan. 2000. "People and Performance: Challenges for the Future Public Service—The Report from the Wye River Conference." *Public Administration Review* 60:54–60.

Kaplan, Robert S., and David P. Norton. 1996. *The Balanced Scorecard: Translating Strategy into Action.* Boston: Harvard Business School Press.

Kavanagh, Michael J., Mohan Thite, and Richard David Johnson. 2012. *Human Resource Information Systems: Basics, Applications, and Future Directions.* 2nd ed. Thousand Oaks, CA: SAGE.

Kronos, Inc. 2012. Accessed September 4. http://www.kronos.com.

Lawson Human Resource Management Suite (Lawson HRM). 2012. Accessed September 3. http://www.lawson.com/Solutions/Software/Human-Capital-Management/Human-Resource-Management/.

Lengnick-Hall, Cynthia A., and Mark L. Lengnick-Hall. 2006. "HR, ERP, and Knowledge for Competitive Advantage." *Human Resource Management* 45:179–94.

McGregor, Eugene B., Jr., and John Daly. 1989. "The Strategic Implications of Automation in Public Sector Human Resource Management." *Review of Public Personnel Administration* 10:29–47.

National Institute of Standards and Technology (NIST). 2011. "The NIST Definition of Cloud Computing." http://csrc.nist.gov/publications/nistpubs/800-145/SP800-145.pdf.

Ngai, E. W. T., and F. K. T. Wat. 2004. "Human Resource Information Systems: A Review and Empirical Analysis." *Personnel Review* 35:297–314.

Oracle. 2012. "PeopleSoft Human Capital Management." Accessed September 3. http://www.oracle.com/us/products/applications/peoplesoft-enterprise/human-capital-management/overview/index.html.

OrangeHRM. 2012. Accessed September 3. http://www.orangehrm.com.

Pfeffer, Jeffery. 1997. "Does Human Resources Have a Future?" In *Tomorrow's HR Management: 48 Thought Leaders Call for Change,* edited by David Ulrich, Michael R. Losey, and Geraldine S. Lake, 190–96. New York: John Wiley.

Quinn, L., Bernard, C., Leslie, J., & Andrei, K. (2011). *A Consumer's Guide to Software for Volunteer Management.* TechSoup Global/IdealWare. http://www.techsoup.org/SiteCollectionDocuments/article-consumers-guide-to-software-volunteer-management-document.pdf.

Rainey, Hal G. 2009. *Understanding and Managing Public Organizations.* 4th ed. San Francisco, CA: Jossey-Bass.

Roberts, Bill. 1999. "Calculating Return on Investment for HRIS." *HR Magazine* 44:122–28.

SAP. 2012. Accessed September 3. http://www.sap.com/index.epx.

Scarborough, Harry, Jacky Swan, and John Preston. 1999. *Knowledge Management: A Literature Review.* London, England: Institute of Personnel Development.

Selden, Sally Coleman. 2009. *Human Capital: Tools and Strategies for the Public Sector.* Washington, DC: CQ Press.

Selden, Sally Coleman, and Robert Wooters. 2011. "Structures in Public Human Resource Management: Shared Services in State Governments." *Review of Public Personnel Administration* 31:349–68.

Society for Human Resource Management (SHRM). 2008. "SHRM Learning System: Module 1; Strategic Management," 1–41. Alexandria, VA: Society for Human Resource Management.

Sotto, Lisa J., and Elisabeth M. McCarthy. 2007. "An Employer's Guide to US Workplace Privacy Issues." *The Computer & Internet Lawyer* 24:1–13.

Tannenbaum, Scott I. 1990. "HRIS Information: User Group Implications." *Journal of Systems Management* 41:27–36.

Ulrich, David. 1997. *Human Resource Champions: The Next Agenda for Adding Value and Delivering Results.* Boston: Harvard Business School Press.

Ulrich, David, Jon Younger, and Wayne Brockbank. 2008. "The Twenty-First-Century HR Organization." *Human Resource Management* 47:829–50.

Ultimate Software. 2012. Accessed September 4. http://www.ultimatesoftware.com.

Case 11.1 Edward Snowden and the Safeguarding of Information

The recent leaking of classified information by data analyst Edward Snowden highlights the sensitive nature of securing classified information. Snowden was employed by Booz Allen Hamilton as a computer specialist and worked as a contractor for the National Security Agency (NSA). He was allegedly motivated to disclose perceived illegal counterintelligence information-gathering secrets of the United States and its allies. Recent headlines suggest that Snowden's disclosure represents the most significant breach of US security since the leaking of the Pentagon Papers by Daniel Ellsberg in 1971 (Mirkinson 2013). Snowden detailed his revelations to the UK-based periodical *The Guardian* in a June 2013 interview.

Prior to his revelations, Snowden was employed in various capacities as a computer specialist for the NSA, CIA, and Dell, before gaining employment with Booz Allen Hamilton. As recently as 2012, Snowden was the subject of a government inquiry because of his downloading of sensitive NSA material in April of that year while employed by Dell (Hosenball 2013b). At this time, Snowden enjoyed access to top-secret information because of his various clearances granted by the NSA and USIS, a private company specializing in background checks.

Upon joining Booz Allen Hamilton in 2013, Snowden was employed as a "system administrator" according to the firm. However, Snowden disputes this, suggesting his job was to look for innovative ways to conduct surveillance on Internet and telephone traffic around the world (Shane and Sanger 2013). Thus began his infamous efforts to collect information on classified US intelligence-gathering operations. Interestingly, a recent investigation of Snowden's background suggested a number of irregularities, including misleading his employers about educational accomplishments he never actually achieved (Hosenball 2013a).

Public agencies have a special responsibility to safeguard personal information of employees and clients. Relevant federal laws are the Consolidated Omnibus Budget Reconciliation Act of 1985 (COBRA) and the Health Insurance Portability and Accountability Act of 1996 (HIPPA), discussed in the present chapter (see Table 11.4) and in Chapter 6's discussion of pay and benefits. Our discussion of the privatization process in Chapter 10 also underscored the government's responsibilities with respect to information held by a contractor that might be subject to the Freedom of Information Act (FOIA). That being said, "Technology confers awesome power on those who can harness it for good or bad. Fashioning smart policies that protect security and liberty is the way forward. We live in a "post-Snowden" age. Although his deeds were despicable, this public debate could yield real dividends" (Harman 2013).

The case of Edward Snowden has important implications not only for the application of HRIS but also for the contracting out of functions that bring the worker into contact with sensitive information. According to a recent story on National Public Radio, two factors aided Snowden's exploitation of the IT infrastructure at the NSA: (1) the agency's delay in installing the most current antileak software in its systems at the Hawaii station and (2) the sense of inclusion and security that can lead people to drop their guard when they believe their co-workers have been vetted. It was recently reported that Snowden was able to gain access to sensitive information not only through technical means but also by convincing co-workers that he needed their login information to carry out his duties. This is a security lapse that has every IT employee cringing.

Discussion Questions

With the prospect of more leaked information to come as Snowden continues to evade arrest, many public managers are considering changes that can prevent such lapses. At this point in the text, we have discussed issues of privacy, privatization, and the management of information as part of the HR function in the public sector. Given the wealth of information controlled by the HR function, what trends do you predict for the future of contracting out for IT services in the public sector? What lessons might we draw from the respective chapters in the text that could help prevent another incident such as the Snowden case? Should the outsourcing of sensitive information be centralized, decentralized, or a shared responsibility? Why or why not?

Sources

Chappell, Bill. 2013. "Snowden Reportedly Used Others' Login Info to Get Secret Data." National Public Radio, November 8. http://www.npr.org/blogs/thetwo-way/2013/11/08/243942091/snowden-reportedly-used-others-login-info-to-get-secret-data.

Harman. Jane. 2013. "Security Policies for a Post-Snowden Age." *Washington Post*, November 7. http://www.washingtonpost.com/opinions/security-policies-for-a-post-snowden-age/2013/11/07/be307c90–464c-11e3-a196–3544a03c2351_story.html.

Hosenball, Mark. 2013a. "NSA Contractor Hired Snowden Despite Concerns about Resume Discrepancies." Reuters, June 20. http://www.reuters.com/article/2013/06/21/us-usa-security-snowden-idUSBRE95K01J20130621.

Hosenball, Mark. 2013b. "Snowden Downloaded NSA Secrets While Working for Dell, Sources Say." Reuters, August 15. http://www.reuters.com/article/2013/08/15/us-usa-security-snowden-dell-idUSBRE97E17P20130815.

Mirkinson, Jack. 2013. "Daniel Ellsberg Calls Edward Snowden a 'Hero,' Says NSA Leak Was Most Important in American History." *Huffington Post*, June 10. http://www.huffingtonpost.com/2013/06/10/edward-snowden-daniel-ellsberg-whistleblower-history_n_3413545.html.

Shane, Scott, and David E. Sanger. 2013. "Job Title Key to Inner Access Held by Snowden." *New York Times*, June 30. http://www.nytimes.com/2013/07/01/us/job-title-key-to-inner-access-held-by-snowden.html.

Exercise

You work in your state's Department of Labor. For the last decade, the agency has lagged behind corresponding agencies in other states in terms of IT capability. The agency needs a revitalized HRIS system that can handle the vast amounts of personnel data collected for the 200-plus employees who work there. As the assistant HR manager for the state's Department of Labor, you have spoken with the department secretary and the head of HR about the need to recruit IT personnel to build in-house the capacity for maintaining an HRIS. The secretary and HR director have asked you to put together a job advertisement for three key IT personnel: an IT director and two IT specialists. Write up job descriptions for the two positions. What types of knowledge, skills, and abilities would you include? What tasks and duties would each of the positions be responsible for carrying out? Where might you advertise the job? As a contingency plan, the secretary has also asked you to consider outsourcing the agency's IT requirements. What criteria might you include in a request for proposals to administer the IT function? What legal issues might you consider when outsourcing IT-related functions?

12

Strategic Public Human Resource Management

LEARNING OBJECTIVES

Upon completion of the chapter, you will be able to do the following:

- Discuss the concept of human capital in terms of the public sector.
- Explain the balanced scorecard as a framework for managing organizational goals and objectives.
- Discuss the development of the workforce-planning process.
- Understand how to develop a strategic human resource management (SHRM) plan, including forecasting, analyzing, implementing, and evaluating such a plan in the public sector.
- Discuss how to link individual productivity to overall organizational performance.

Strategic human resource management (SHRM) has been mentioned periodically in this text, but what what is it? The SHRM perspective is that the HR department not only manages recruitment, compensation, and other personnel matters but also takes a proactive, forward-looking approach to addressing the future needs of the organization and its employees. When taking a SHRM approach, the HR department plays a more significant role in the performance of the organization. It is not strictly focused on the day-to-day matters that many people think constitute the HR function. Instead it also very deliberately looks ahead at long-term goals and objectives for the entire organization, thinking strategically about its mission and anticipating future staffing needs. It views employees as "human capital" instead of as costs incurred or just people who work in jobs. As human capital, employees are viewed as assets that the organization invests in over the long term. Developing their skills, capabilities, and knowledge brings value, improves performance, and furthers the organization's mission. In addition, SHRM seeks to ensure that various elements of the organization are coordinated in pursuing the same mission. The SHRM approach originated in the private sector, but its tactics and principles can be applied in the public sector as well.

While the literature on SHRM is expansive, this chapter seeks to provide a concise overview of the potential a human capital management approach has to offer the public sector. It begins by discussing the dynamics of applying an SHRM approach to the public sector, with particular emphasis on how such an approach might complement efforts to operate within a more performance-oriented environment. The sections below discuss the key elements of SHRM—strategic planning, improving internal processes and employee capacity, workforce planning, and accountability—in the public sector context. These features are now considered to be essential to the future of public HR management.

Human Capital Management

The term *human capital* has roots in the economics literature concerning the valuation of the human element in firms' behavior. According to Becker (1962), a human capital perspective is "concerned with activities that influence future real income through the embedding of resources in people" (9). Thus, the human capital approach to management emphasizes investment in the knowledge, skills, abilities, and/or competencies of employees, with the expectation of a return in the form of improved organizational performance. Despite its private sector roots, human capital has proven appealing to managers in the public sector eager to invest in the capacity of public servants. Since 2000, the US Government Accountability Office (GAO) has emphasized a human capital approach to the federal workforce, viewing investments in individuals' capabilities as an important positive influence on organizational performance. The GAO (2000) concluded: "People are assets whose value can be enhanced through investment. . . . As the value of people increases, so does the performance capacity of the organization, and therefore its value to clients and other stakeholders" (1–2).

A topic that frequently arises in discussions of public HRM reform efforts is the need to increase the productivity of public sector employees. Performance-oriented HR management has gradually attracted interest among scholars and practitioners interested in applying a human capital management approach to assessing future public sector workforce demands (e.g., Battaglio and Llorens 2010; Selden and Wooters 2011).

Thinking Strategically about Human Resource Management in the Public Sector

Public HR practitioners operate under constant pressure to reevaluate the skills and competencies necessary for improving government effectiveness. Thinking critically about performance measurement means giving greater consideration to the human capital and management needs of the organization. All of the five elements of PHRM reform that we have addressed throughout the text have in some way sought to accomplish a more productive public sector. Reformers touting private sector efficiencies gained through practices such as employment at will (EAW) and performance-based pay have proposed using such strategies to improve public sector productivity. However, designing performance-based compensation systems has proven tricky and even damaging to employee performance when the systems are not managed properly (see Battaglio 2010; Battaglio and Condrey 2009; Kellough and Nigro 2002, 2006). For governments considering alternatives to these reform efforts, adopting a human capital perspective that focuses on specific public sector metrics (i.e., benchmarks or targets for measuring and analyzing performance) is appealing (Selden 2009). Such an approach to improving public service is less drastic and more prudent approach than some popular reform efforts.

PHRM traditionally focused on the maintenance of merit-based civil service systems and, when politically expedient, viewed public employees as "costs to be cut rather than assets to be valued" (GAO 2001, 1). The traditional approach did not include a significant strategic component in its mission. A 2000 GAO report highlighted the federal government's human capital shortcomings, noting that "many agencies have not sufficiently indicated how they will identify their human capital needs, nor how they will acquire, develop and deploy their human capital to improve the economy, efficiency, and effectiveness with which they serve the American people" (1). Demographic changes in the workforce, such as the wave of retirements among baby boomers, along with increasingly competitive hiring environments have prompted many governments to take human capital management seriously.

Public HR managers increasingly realize that to continue fulfilling their core functions in an environment of shrinking resources, a strategic plan for meeting organizational needs is critical. As a result, many public organizations have developed or started to develop long-term, strategic HR management plans, and many public HR professionals have a keen interest in strategic HR functions such as workforce planning, hiring, and employee retention.

Strategic Human Resource Management and Workforce Planning

Measuring current and anticipating future workforce capacities—**workforce planning**—has become increasingly important to public HR managers (Hays and Kearney 2001; Selden 2009). Human capital approaches to public sector HR incorporate exacting processes for planning workforce needs. Public employers adopting SHRM seek to anticipate the skills and abilities—the organizational knowledge— that will be needed in the future. Managing organizational knowledge becomes increasingly important as retirement rates rise. Knowledge management requires planning for the exodus of important skill sets and anticipating competencies that will contribute to organizational goals and objectives. SHRM requires public managers to use metrics that assess the efficient use of resources (Selden 2009).

Able public servants represent arguably the most important public sector resource (Ingraham et al. 2000). Therefore, it is imperative that public HR managers invest, cost-effectively, in a more knowledgeable public service. Such an effort requires a culture shift in the way that the public and politicians view the public service, as they must embrace the idea that training and development will improve productivity. This shift toward investment in human capital proved to be constructive in the private sector during the 1990s.

The **balanced scorecard approach** (see Kaplan and Norton 1996b), originally developed for and used in the private sector, maintains that investment in employee learning is crucial for achieving organizational objectives. In contrast to the traditional view, which focuses more narrowly on profits, the balanced scorecard is a more comprehensive approach to putting strategy into action that places value on diverse factors. In addition to profitability, it includes targets for customer satisfaction, internal process quality and efficiency, and employee learning (Kaplan and Norton 1996).

The focus of SHRM is to incorporate human capital into strategic planning (Selden 2009) and to align human capital objectives with overall agency goals. Accordingly, agency mission and vision statements contain language that emphasizes investment in employees as crucial to achieving agency objectives. The aim is to persuade management to lead strategic efforts and to get buy-in from line mangers and street-level service providers. Strategic planning requires agencies to assess current operations, forecast future operations, and develop a plan that will achieve future objectives. This process engages public managers in scanning the environment (internal and external); links objectives with those of other actors (federal, state, local); develops strategic goals; identifies core competencies; develops operational objectives and strategies; implements a plan; and monitors, evaluates, and adjusts the plan accordingly (Selden 2009, 16).

Commitment on the part of management, employees, and stakeholders is important for successful strategic planning (Bryson 2004; Selden 2009). Getting buy-in from all stakeholders requires that strategic planning incorporate elements of both top-down and bottom-up approaches to managing (Selden 2009, 19). That is, a successful strategic plan will include directives from management and feedback from employees on the feasibility of such directives in day-to-day operations. Coordinating strategic plans requires collaboration among all employees as they carry out directives to achieve agency goals.

Practical Steps toward Strategic Public Human Resource Management

Table 12.1 presents a practical framework for applying SHRM to the public sector. Building on previous research and practice (see Huselid et al. 2005; Kaplan and Norton 1996a; Niven 2003; Selden 2009), the framework includes five elements: strategic planning, internal processes, employee capacity, workforce planning, and accountability.

Table 12.1	**Elements, Objectives, and Measures for Strategic Human Resource Management in the Public Sector**	
Core Element	**Objective**	**Performance Measure**
Strategic planning	• Gain management/leader commitment • Secure employee buy-in • Establish clear mission, vision, and goals	• Idea champions and change agents • Priorities and timetables • Access to planning, information, opportunities, risks, and uncertainties • Focus on long-term value • Alignment of external and internal information reporting • Stakeholder input
Internal processes	• Increase employee access to information • Improve employee productivity • Reward employees	• Employee satisfaction with access to information • Technology audit • Pay philosophy and strategy • Pay differentials between top performers and others • Variable pay schemes • Labor market analysis
Employee capacity	• Increase employee motivation and commitment • Improve training and development • Enhance information technology capacity • Identify potential managers and leaders	• Routine surveys of employee motivation and commitment • Public service motivation metrics • Diversity initiatives • Routine satisfaction surveys for training and development • Succession planning

(Continued)

(Continued)		
Core Element	**Objective**	**Performance Measure**
Workforce planning	• Assess current workforce capacities • Forecast workforce needs • Analyze gaps between current and future workforce • Develop strategies for meeting gaps between current and future workforce • Monitor and evaluate workforce metrics	• Assessment of resignation and retention rates • Assessment of voluntary turnover rates • Absentism rates • Percentage of sick time and vacation used • Grievance rates (and resolutions) • Appeals rates (and resolutions) • Discrimination charge rates • Exit surveys • Turnover costs
Accountability	• Evaluate results • Comply with law • Enhance employee participation • Enhance civic participation • Identify areas for improvement	• Evaluation of investment and costs • Advisory committee of employees • Employee satisfaction with objectives and goals of plan • Advisory committee of citizens • Citizen satisfaction with access to government • Periodic revision of plan(s)

Sources: Choudhury 2007; Huselid et al. 2005; Kaplan and Norton 1996a, 1996b; Niven 2003; Selden 2009

The sections below review each of the elements in greater detail and provide actionable metrics that public HR managers can use to operationalize them.

Strategic Planning

Strategic planning entails garnering information to align organizational plans with potential opportunities, risks, and uncertainties in both the internal and external environment. Thus, greater attention is given to factors that build long-term value for the organization, including nonfinancial assets such as human capital; the lessons drawn from the balanced scorecard approach emphasize that there is more to organizational success than financial performance. The result is a precise plan that allows the organization to accurately assess whether it is managing to the plan.

This strategic orientation has intrigued HR managers in the public sector. For public human capital enthusiasts, strategic planning represents an opportunity for institution building in the public sector. Long-term planning gives management and employees alike a vision of where the agency is going and how it plans to get there. Strategic planning clarifies for public managers what the long-term goals and decisions of the agency should be. More specifically, strategic planning establishes a clear mission and vision to which organizational and job goals can be aligned. To this end, timetables are laid out for aligning activities such as budgeting and workforce planning. For example, a target for public HR managers might be to reduce employee turnover or improve retention. To develop a plan to achieve these goals, HR might survey current employees to investigate the factors affecting intent to quit. Ultimately, the establishment of objective measures will aid the organization and management in conducting periodic performance assessments and obtaining feedback from employees.

Communicating the mission and vision is critical to the success of strategic planning. A strategic plan serves as an instrument for communicating strategy to public managers throughout the organization in order to build consensus around the plan. Clearly, commitment from management is critical to gaining employee buy-in to strategic planning. Once key opinion leaders buy in to the strategic mission, management can use them as idea champions to facilitate change.

Implementation of strategic planning is somewhat different in the public sector since public sector organizations consider other factors besides the bottom line in their missions. Their goals and objectives will understandably be somewhat different from a private company's. While cost savings and efficiency are important, public (and nonprofit—see the Nonprofits in Focus box) organizations aspire toward purposes in line with public or stakeholder interests. Great care should be taken in the articulation of strategic goals for public interest pursuits (e.g., reducing poverty, improving public safety, preventing the spread of disease, etc.). It can be more difficult to define objective measures for such programs than to measure total revenues or profits. Management should consider the unique setting of each public agency in order to effectively respond to its specific challenges and opportunities. Organizations in need of a new direction can also use strategic planning to "recharge" the organization. Routine activities can become monotonous, but reinvigorating the organization with a new vision/mission and goals for achieving it can lift employee morale and, consequently, productivity.

Strategic planning should aid public HR managers in using evidence-based decision making to monitor, evaluate, and revise workforce needs (Selden 2009). Once a strategic plan is in place, the elements of the HR function—internal processes, employee capacity, workforce planning, and accountability—are used to translate and implement the plan throughout the organization.

Internal Processes

Integrating the internal processes of an organization is a key component not only of SHRM but of high-performance organizational cultures in general (Schermerhorn et al. 2004). The purpose of integration is to ensure that individual job goals are aligned with organizational goals. Coordinating the activities of individuals within an agency through effective communication is critical to mission success. Integrating work processes has the potential to turn challenges into opportunities (see Schein 1985).

Along with identifying the most effective ways to communicate within the organization, SHRM clarifies how employees are rewarded, sanctioned, and promoted (Schermerhorn et al. 2004). This is especially important for SHRM in the public sector given the dynamics set in motion by the implementation of performance-based pay (see Chapters 6 and 7). At the core of integrating internal processes is assessing to what extent the organization has succeeded. Success is ultimately a measure of productivity; for example, has the organization improved the time involved in processing paperwork, conducting grievance proceedings, or other internal processes? The hope is that successfully coordinating the activities of groups and individuals within the organization will lead to improved productivity.

Performance Appraisal

Measuring the extent of integration within the organization can be accomplished by aligning the goals of the agency with those of divisions and individuals within it. The instrument for ensuring alignment is performance appraisal (see Chapter 7). Job analysis should ensure that the tasks, behaviors, and goals of individuals are in sync with organizational directives. The feedback derived from the appraisal process should guide other internal processes such as hiring, training and development, succession planning, and compensation (Selden 2009, 135). Selden noted that employees should be involved in the process of building and implementing effective performance appraisal systems. Also, to effectively manage employee performance by distinguishing top performers from others, managers and supervisors need appropriate training in performance appraisal. Employees and subordinates need access to information about how their positions contribute to overall agency performance. Discrepancies between organizational and employee orientations can be remedied through training and development.

Compensation

Clearly, adequately rewarding top-performing employees is fundamental to achieving high performance. Human capital plans should create a compensation scheme according to a philosophy that values the organization's strategic objectives. Reward systems should evaluate whether compensation is driven mostly by experience, tenure, or performance (Selden 2009, 158). If it is not driven by performance, then changes need to be made. Additionally, labor market analysis will provide a comparison of pay rates for internal positions to those of similar positions in the public, nonprofit, and for-profit sectors (see Chapter 6). Performance-based pay has often been used to recognize top performers in the public sector, albeit with mixed results. Selden suggested that organizations should measure the degree of correlation between employees' pay increases and performance ratings (159). The organization should also compare pay rate increases for top performers with those of others. Finally, internal salary surveys provide valuable insight regarding the integration of internal processes. Figure 12.1 lists questions that might be used in a survey to evaluate an organization's pay and performance systems (Selden 2009). Survey questions should assess the extent of coordination between organizational goals and employee rewards as well as to what degree employees perceive compensation decisons are fair. An organization whose employees by and large feel its processes are fair and agree with its goals has a cohesive work environment amenable to implementing its strategic plan.

Figure 12.1	**Perceptions of Pay and Performance in the Organization**

Please indicate your level of agreement or disagreement with each of the following statements related to pay and performance and your performance appraisal. Please be assured that your responses are completely anonymous. (5-point Likert scale: *strongly agree, agree, neither agree/disagree, disagree, strongly disagree*).

- My performance appraisal accurately reflects the agency's goals and priorities.
- I am satisfied with my opportunities for advancement.
- I am held accountable for achieving results.
- My performance appraisal accurately identifies competencies and skills that need improvement.
- I have incentives for improving my competencies and skills.
- My performance appraisal takes into account the most important parts of my job.
- My supervisor and I agree on what "high performance" on my job means.
- My performance appraisal is a fair reflection of my performance.
- Feedback from my supervisor/team leader about my performance is constructive.
- Employees are expected to perform at a high level.
- Low performance is not acceptable in the organization.
- High performers tend to stay with this organization.
- Low performers tend to stay with this organization.
- For promotion opportunities, the best qualified applicant is chosen.
- In my organization, differences in performance are recognized in a meaningful way.
- Managers communicate the goals and priorities of the organization.
- Managers/supervisors are fair in recognizing individual contributions.
- Managers/supervisors are fair in recognizing team contributions.

Please indicate your level of agreement or disagreement with each of the following statements related to pay and performance in your agency. Please be assured that your responses are completely anonymous (5-point Likert scale: *strongly agree, agree, neither agree/disagree, disagree, strongly disagree*).

(Continued)

(Continued)

- Pay raises depend on how well employees perform their jobs.
- In this organization, my pay raises depend on my contribution to the organization's mission.
- I understand how pay raises are given.
- Performance-based pay makes me want to stay in my organization.
- Competency- or skill-based pay makes me want to stay in my organization.
- Seniority pay makes me want to stay in my organization.
- Step increases make me want to stay in my organization.
- Flexible pay upon promotion makes me want to stay in my organization.
- The organization's recognition programs make me want to stay in my organization.
- I see the rewards the organization offers as valuable.
- Peers or colleagues recognize and reward each other.
- The organization shows some form of appreciation to its employees.
- The organization recognizes small improvements as well as major ones.
- Employees in the organization see the rewards the organization offers as valuable.
- In this organization, teams compete for recognition and reward.

Source: Selden 2009, 160–61

Employee Capacity

Employee capacity is the degree to which employees have the technical and general know-how to perform current and future tasks the organization needs done. Incorporating strategic elements of the organization's mission in performance appraisals assists HR managers in assessing gaps between current skills and competencies and those needed to drive performance. Incorporating an understanding of these gaps in future efforts to achieve agency goals, objectives, programs, and services is a crucial element of SHRM (Thomas 1996, 6). Assessing employee capacity means monitoring and evaluating HR functions in order to meet the organization's needs with respect to recruiting, retaining, developing, and motivating personnel. Coordinating employee capacity-building measures with the agency's mission, structure, and operational activities is indispensable to achieving strategic HR management.

Public HR management often requires government agencies to develop, maintain, and evaluate human capital capacity (Bozeman and Feeney 2009, 146). Foremost among the responsibilities of HR professionals is to provide employees with adequate training and development. Agencies should have a training and development plan that incorporates methods for filling the gaps identified in strategic planning. Training and development plans should also seek employee input as to how to build future employee capacity. Once the plan is implemented, HR managers should evaluate its effectiveness. Training effectiveness can be measured by three metrics—investment, efficiency, and learning:

- *Investment*—the average training expenditures per employee and manager or training expenditures as a percentage of payroll
- *Efficiency*—training expenditures divided by the number of training hours for all employees
- *Learning*—average number of training hours per employee and manager; skill level after training versus skill level before training; performance appraisal rating after training versus rating before training (Selden 2009, 113–14)

Training evaluations can identify shortcomings in the current training plan and incorporate feedback to guide future employee development efforts. For example, routine reevaluation of training and development will identify changing needs for technology skills and lagging employee knowledge in this area, thereby ensuring that employees are trained in the latest technology. Employee surveys that ask about the quality and appropriateness of development opportunities provide important feedback to the planning process.

Training and developing future agency leaders is another element of building workforce capacity. **Succession planning** reflects a long-term organizational commitment to identifying and training future leaders. Part of developing an effective succession plan is recognizing core knowledge areas of the organization, especially those embodied in leaders nearing retirement. Typically, organizations identify candidates to replace current leaders and track their progress through leadership development programs (Selden 2009). To evaluate whether succession planning is identify the right candidates and developing them appropriately, the organization can track candidates' completion of development program stages, their length of service after they complete training, and their rates of promotion.

Improving employee motivation and commitment is an essential element of developing employee capacity. Indeed, recent public HR management reform efforts have utilized motivational tools, such as performance-based pay, to improve productivity in the public service (Houston 2000; Naff and Crum 1999). Yet motivation in the public service has unique characteristics (Crewson 1997; Horton 2008; Houston 2000; Naff and Crum 1999; Oh and Lewis 2009; Perry 1996, 1997; Perry and Porter 1982; Perry and Wise, 1990; Rainey 1982). Understanding the unique factors that motivate public service is important to the development of productivity and trust in the workforce (Crewson 1997; Houston 2000; Jurkiewicz et al. 1998; Naff and Crum 1999). In fact, there is a strong association between public service motivation and job performance, commitment, and retention (Crewson 1997; Perry and Wise 1990).

Nonprofits in Focus	Strategic Planning in the Nonprofit Sector

Like their counterparts in the for-profit and public sector, nonprofit organizations (NPOs) often face an uncertain future. The economy, social and natural crises, unrest in foreign countries, and other opportunities and threats often influence organizations in all sectors, forcing them to reinvigorate their employees to face the challenges at hand. As we have discussed, strategic planning is a tool for "recharging" the organization when a change is needed (Miller 2013). The organization needs to renew its employees' buy-in to the mission. An organization's mission, vision statement, and goals/objectives should not be seen as permanent. Rather, change can be a positive event if it is planned correctly. Miller (2013) suggested that in the case of nonprofits, strategic planning often disappoints key stakeholders (management, employees, volunteers, donors, boards of directors) when the plan lacks the following elements:

- An upfront, comprehensive assessment of the organization
- A clear vision with established measures of progress
- A comprehensive funding plan to secure the necessary resources
- A detailed plan for implementation and execution with buy-in from both board and staff

HR offices are often tasked to conduct comprehensive assessments of the organization. HR professionals are often ideally prepared to assess the organization, particularly the knowledge, skills, and abilities it needs in its workforce to face upcoming challenges. A comprehensive assessment of the organization's HR function entails reviewing job descriptions and compensation to ensure external as well as internal competitiveness. Further, interviewing key personnel within the NPO will provide a more comprehensive picture of the strengths, weaknesses, opportunities, and threats the organization faces.

Once the organization has a clearer picture of the current state of its employees' capacities and future workforce needs, aligning workforce planning with the new vision statement is critical. To achieve a successful transformation, HR professionals must write job descriptions to include objectives that align with those of the organization. For example, if an NPO provides hurricane relief, personnel on the ground should be equipped with the right skills (e.g., emergency care, first aid, disease prevention) to meet the situation at hand. Not all the people working for the NPO may be employees; some may be volunteers. However, using a volunteer workforce does not mean taking on any person willing to assist; recruiting volunteers with the right skill set is important.

Unlike many for-profit and public sector organizations, nonprofits are often required to maintain comprehensive development plans to secure funds. While for-profit firms rely on profits, and public agencies receive resources from taxpayers, NPO funding depends on grants and donors. Maintaining a healthy development division within the NPO is critical so that it can maintain solvency, especially in lean economic times. This means recruiting and hiring professionals who are skilled in fund-raising and public relations.

Finally, NPOs must have a detailed plan to implement the tasks outlined above. However, simply having a detailed plan is not enough. Once a plan is put together, it must be executed. The likelihood of its success is closely tied to the degree of buy-in from management and staff. Obviously, if management is not enthusiastic about the strategic plan, employees are less likely to follow through on its goals. Fostering enthusiasm for the strategic plan is the responsibility of management. Management's duty is to make sure employees "get" the importance of the strategic plan and understand how it will be implemented. Gaining support from individuals whom rank-and-file employees respect will help management to achieve buy-in. Such "champions" can serve as spokespersons, representing management's aspirations to employees and volunteers.

Workforce Planning

Traditional **workforce planning** involves analyzing current capacities within the agency, forecasting future needs, and assessing anticipated knowledge gaps. Workforce planning resided with the HR department and was mostly concerned with filling open positions. More recently, strategic planners have sought to link future workforce needs to overall agency and government objectives (Selden 2009). Thus, workforce planning now involves not only the expertise of HR staff but input from key managers as well (e.g., those tasked with budgeting and financial oversight). The result is a team effort toward using a variety of innovative workforce-planning approaches to reconcile government, agency, and individual goals.

Workforce-planning practices now combine traditional efforts (identifying future positions, skills, and competencies) with aligning with the goals established during strategic planning. The objective is to develop strategies that fill current gaps in competencies, as well as diversity, in a way that is consistent with the organization's overall strategic objectives. Identifying future knowledge, skill, and ability needs and developing strategies to meet them should contribute to the mission, vision, and goals of the agency as outlined in the strategic plan. Revisiting Table 12.1, elements of workforce planning include the following:

1. *Assess current workforce capacities*—Analyze current competency, diversity, and staffing levels; assessment should include impact of turnover, transfers, and promotions. Conduct labor market analysis.

2. *Forecast workforce needs*—Analyze future competency, diversity, and staffing needs. Needs assessment should take into account how competencies will contribute to the objectives of the agency outlined during strategic planning.

3. *Analyze gaps between current and future workforce*—Analyze gaps identified between current workforce and forecast needs. Objective is to focus agency workforce-planning efforts on strategically relevant short-term and long-term gaps.

4. *Develop strategies for meeting gaps between current and future workforce*—Integrate gap analysis with the strategic plan of the organization. HR professionals track key metrics and identify the resources necessary for recruiting and developing the workforce as needed. The ultimate product is an implementation of a workforce plan oriented toward accomplishing the agency's strategic objectives.

5. *Monitor and evaluate workforce metrics*—Monitor and evaluate progress toward strategic objectives of the workforce plan. Tracking metrics

and timetables allows HR professionals and agency management to evaluate the status of goal attainment. Feedback from monitoring and evaluation is used to update the workforce plan.

For example, the Office of Personnel Management (OPM) has a five-step model for addressing workforce planning (Figure 12.2). OPM's model, like the discussion above, addresses current and future workforce issues, identifies gaps, and offers solutions for filling the gaps. OPM also ensures progress toward meeting workforce goals by monitoring and evaluating the plan. The result is a comprehensive approach to accomplishing the strategic objectives of OPM by modeling its future workforce needs.

Assessing appropriate metrics is fundamental to tracking progress toward the plan's objectives. A key element of the plan is improving recruitment and retention. To monitor progress toward recruiting and retaining the right people in the right jobs at the right time, Selden (2009) suggested the following metrics are useful:

- Diversity of applicants and hires
- Job acceptance/fill rate
- Mission-critical acceptance/fill rate
- Career path rate
- Accession rate
- Vacancy rate
- Time to hire
- Voluntary turnover rates (age, tenure, group, new hires)
- Absentee rates
- Percentage of sick time and vacation used
- Grievance rates (and resolutions)
- Appeals rates (and resolutions)
- Discrimination charge rates
- Exit survey responses
- Costs associated with hiring and turnover (59–60, 81–82)

These and other metrics can be used depending on the goals of the workforce plan. For example, an organization may have a problem with high absenteeism and choose to target lower rates of absenteeism as one of its strategic objectives. The other chapters in the text outline measures for assessing many of the various goals of workforce planning in greater detail (e.g., diversity plans in Chapter 4).

Accountability

Clearly, evaluating the investment in SHRM and the payoff in results is important to overall accountability. The accountability element in Figure 12.1 gives agencies the

| Figure 12.2 | Office of Personnel Management's Workforce-Planning Model |

Step 1: Set Strategic Direction
- Link workfroce plan with agency strategic plan and annual performance
- Activities required to carry long term and short term goals and objectives

Step 2: Analyze Workforce, Identify Skill Gaps, and Conduct Workforce Analysis
- Determine current workforce resources
- Develop specification to accomplish agency strategic plan
- Determine gaps between current and forcasted workfroce needs

Step 3: Develop Plan of Action
- Identify strategies to close gaps
- Implement strategies and measures for assesing progress
- Include strategies for recruitment, training, retaining, restructuring, outsourcing, succession planning, technology

Step 4: Implement Action Plan
- Ensure human and fiscal resources are in place
- Assign roles and coordinate communication

Step 5: Monitor, Evaluate, and Revise
- Monitor progress against milestones
- Assess for continuous improvement
- Adjusting plans, make course corrections, and addresss new workforce issues.

Source: OPM 2014

opportunity to take stock of the coordinated efforts of the SHRM plan. By way of example, the strategic efforts of OPM focus on promoting a results-oriented performance culture that emphasizes high standards, accountability, and excellence (Crumpacker and Crumpacker 2004). Accountability is evidenced based. Metrics are used that evaluate OPM's ability to coordinate strategy, systems, policies, programs, and practices with performance appraisals, program evaluation, budgeting, and financial management (245). The metrics reviewed in this chapter measure how well organizational capacity is advanced so that accountability can be enforced. Ultimately, considering accountability in strategic efforts allows the organization to identify areas where improvement is possible or needed and revise the plan accordingly.

Incorporating accountability into SHRM also provides employers with motivation to solicit employee feedback. Giving employees the opportunity to participate in monitoring and evaluating strategic plans—in either a formal or informal capacity—can motivate them and garner their commitment to resolve future workforce issues. To this end, governments should consider establishing formal points of contact among HR professionals responsible for strategic planning (Crumpacker and Crumpacker 2004). For example, the position of chief human capital officer (CHCO) could be established to further coordination and communication needs of the organization (see Selden and Wooters 2011).

The public interest is also at stake in the assessment of strategic planning efforts. Successful SHRM has the potential to save taxpayers money. Many local governments incorporate citizen feedback in their strategic planning efforts to ensure that customer service goals are being met (Battaglio and Llorens 2010). Governments that embrace the balanced scorecard approach, discussed earlier, are committed to using citizen input to improve their experience with the agency. Such input may be particularly important if outsourcing human capital functions is under consideration. Finally, compliance with employment law and respect for constitutional values should always be a part of accountability in the public sector.

SHRM in an Era of PHRM Reform

Implementing SHRM efforts may prove difficult in a reform climate. The public service reforms discussed throughout the text—decentralization, performance-based pay, declassification, deregulation, and privatization—place HR systems under a great deal of stress. For example, decentralization transfers operational responsibilities from central personnel departments to agency-level HR professionals. Without the guidance of experienced central personnel staff, HR professionals will need extensive training to implement and administer reform efforts in their agencies. HR departments in smaller agencies may have insufficient resources and expertise to undertake the training needed to build SHRM capacity (Coggburn 2000; Hou et al. 2000). Another potential barrier is the need to conform to government-wide standards despite agency differences, as when HR professionals need to implement performance-based pay systems (Hays and Sowa 2006; Kellough and Nigro 2002; Perry et al. 2009). Additionally, deregulation efforts such as EAW may prove detrimental to long-term recruitment efforts, compromising agency performance (Battaglio 2010; Battaglio and Condrey 2009; Condrey and Battaglio 2007). Eliminating job security in favor of managerial flexibility may streamline the dismissal of poor-performing employees, but at the cost of employee motivation and trust—factors crucial to organizational productivity. In a reform climate, meeting the recruitment and retention goals stated in a strategic workforce plan may prove difficult.

Strategic HR efforts require coordination and collaboration, elements often missing or deemphasized in PHRM reform. As we have discussed throughout the text, consequences of PHRM reform often include derision and distrust. Such a workplace environment is hardly conducive to the teamwork that strategic efforts require. If employees are already skeptical of HR reforms that have been implemented, getting their buy-in to SHRM may be difficult.

Going forward, HR managers considering strategic planning may need to first "reenergize" the agency's employees before embarking on another organizational transformation. Given the work involved in strategic planning, winning over employees should be the first priority. This might mean meeting individually or in groups with employees to provide further clarification about strategic planning; the more open and transparent the process, the more likely employees will trust it and give it their best effort. Further, drawing on employees who believe in the necessity of strategic planning as "idea champions" will help win over more skeptical workers. Ultimately, the success of strategic efforts will depend upon support from everyone involved.

Conclusion

Strategic human resource management (SHRM) offers public managers an opportunity to invest in employees as part of the human capital initiative. Rather than eliminating incentives for training and development as part of cost-cutting measures, SHRM views employees as organizational assets (GAO 2001). As such, training and development are crucial to the coordinated effort of implementing a strategic plan. Assessing the human capital needs of the organization and adopting HR practices to meet these needs are necessary steps toward developing an organization prepared to meet future challenges.

As with public service reforms in general, there are no "one-size-fits-all" SHRM operating plans. Public agencies vary extensively according to history, geography, size, mission, and institutional level (federal, state, local). More importantly, differences in internal operations and accountability have the potential to exacerbate system-wide SHRM efforts. Classifying and analyzing agency differences to assess their needs and potential for change is critical to ensuring inter- and intra-agency coordination (Longo 2008, 7).

HR professionals need to understand the intricacies of public agencies so that they can develop plans that meet a particular agency's objectives. Developing plans that align employees' objectives with those of the agency is not easy task in the public sector. Coordinating SHRM efforts requires linking strategic goals and objectives with a performance appraisal system that accurately rewards the behaviors that contribute to success. To adopt a strategic approach, HR professionals must identify and observe the metrics that show whether results are being achieved.

References

Battaglio, R. Paul, Jr. 2010. "Public Service Reform and Motivation: Evidence from an Employment At-Will Environment." *Review of Public Personnel Administration* 30:341–63.

Battaglio, R. Paul, Jr., and Stephen E. Condrey. 2009. "Reforming Public Management: Analyzing the Impact of Public Service Reform on Organizational and Managerial Trust." *Journal of Public Administration Research & Theory* 19:689–707.

Battaglio, R. Paul, Jr., and Jared J. Llorens. 2010. "Human Resource Management in a Human Capital Environment." In *Handbook of Human Resource Management in Government*, 3rd ed., edited by Stephen E. Condrey, 27–43. San Francisco, CA: Jossey-Bass.

Becker, Gary S. 1962. "Investment in Human Capital: A Theoretical Analysis." *The Journal of Political Economy* 70:9–49.

Bozeman, Barry, and Mary K. Feeney. 2009. "Public Management Mentoring: A Three-Tier Model." *Review of Public Personnel Administration* 29:134–57

Bryson, John M. 2004. *Strategic Planning for Public and Nonprofit Organizations: A Guide to Strengthening and Sustaining Organizational Achievement.* 3rd ed. San Francisco, CA: Jossey-Bass.

Choudhury, Enamul H. 2007. "Workforce Planning in Small Local Governments." *Review of Public Personnel Administration* 27:264–80.

Coggburn, Jerrell D. 2000. "Is Deregulation the Answer for Public Personnel Management? Revisiting a Familiar Question: Introduction." *Review of Public Personnel Administration* 20:5–8.

Condrey, Stephen E., and R. Paul Battaglio Jr. 2007. "A Return to Spoils? Revisiting Radical Civil Service Reform in the United States." *Public Administration Review* 67:424–36.

Crewson, Philip E. 1997. "Public Service Motivation: Building Empirical Evidence of Incidence and Effect." *Journal of Public Administration Research and Theory* 7:499–518.

Crumpacker, Martha, and Jill M. Crumpacker. 2004. "Elevating, Integrating, and Institutionalizing Strategic Human Capital Management in Federal Agencies through the Chief Human Capital Officer." *Review of Public Personnel Administration* 24:234–55.

Hays, Stephen W., and Richard C. Kearney. 2001. "Anticipated Changes in Human Resource Management: Views from the Field." *Public Administration Review* 61:585–97.

Hays, Steven W., and Jessica E. Sowa. 2006. "A Broader Look at the 'Accountability' Movement: Some Grim Realities in State Civil Service Systems." *Review of Public Personnel Administration* 26:102–17.

Horton, Sylvia. 2008. "History and Persistence of an Ideal." In *Motivation in Public Management: The Call of Public Service,* edited by James L. Perry and Annie Hondeghem, 17–32. Oxford, England: Oxford University Press.

Hou, Yilin, Patricia Ingraham, Stuart Bretschneider, and Sally Coleman Selden. 2000. "Decentralization of Human Resource Management: Driving Forces and Implications." *Review of Public Personnel Administration* 20:9–22.

Houston, David J. 2000. "Public Service Motivation: A Multivariate Test." *Journal of Public Administration Research and Theory* 10:713–28.

Huselid, Mark A., Brian E. Becker, and Richard W. Beatty. 2005. *The Workforce Scorecard: Managing Human Capital to Execute Strategy.* Boston: Harvard Business School Press.

Ingraham, Patricia W., Sally Coleman Selden, and Donald P. Moynihan. 2000. "People and Performance: Challenges for the Future Public Service—the Report from the Wye River Conference." *Public Administration Review* 60:54–60.

Jurkiewicz, Carole L., Tom K. Massey Jr., and Roger G. Brown. 1998. "Motivation in Public and Private Organizations: A Comparative Study." *Public Productivity & Management Review* 21:230–50.

Kaplan, Robert S., and David P. Norton. 1996a. *The Balanced Scorecard: Translating Strategy into Action.* Boston: Harvard Business Review Press.

Kaplan, Robert S., and David P. Norton. 1996b. "Using the Balanced Scorecard as a Strategic Management System." *Harvard Business Review* 74:75–85.

Kellough, J. Edward, and Lloyd G. Nigro. 2006. "Dramatic Reform in the Public Service: At-will Employment and the Creation of a New Public Workforce." *Journal of Public Administration Research and Theory* 16: 447-66.

Kellough, J. Edward, and Lloyd G. Nigro. 2002. "Pay for Performance in Georgia State Government: Employee Perspectives on GeorgiaGain After 5 Years." *Review of Public Personnel Administration* 22:146–66.

Longo, Francesco. 2008. "Managing Public Reforms Effectively: A Strategic Change Management Approach." In *Strategic Change Management in the Public Sector: An EFMD European Case Book,* edited by Francesco Longo and Daniela Cristofoli, 1–20. Hoboken, NJ: Wiley.

Miller, Dennis. 2013. "Beyond Strategic Planning." *The Nonprofit Times,* March 18. http://www.thenonprofittimes.com/news-articles/beyond-strategic-planning/.

Naff, Katherine C., and John Crum. 1999. "Working for America: Does Public Service Motivation Make a Difference?" *Review of Public Personnel Administration* 19:5–16.

Niven, Paul R. 2003. *Balanced Scorecard Step-by-Step for Government and Nonprofit Agencies.* Hoboken, NJ: Wiley.

Office of Personnel Management (OPM). 2014. "OPM's Workforce Planning Model." Accessed April 30. http://www.opm.gov/policy-data-oversight/human-capital-management/reference-materials/strategic-alignment/workforceplanning.pdf.

Oh, Seong Soo, and Gregory B. Lewis. 2009. "Can Performance Appraisal Systems Inspire Intrinsically Motivated Employees?" *Review of Public Personnel Administration* 29:158–67.

Perry, James L. 1996. "Measuring Public Service Motivation: An Assessment of Construct Reliability and Validity." *Journal of Public Administration Research and Theory* 6:5–22.

Perry, James L. 1997. "Antecedents of Public Service Motivation." *Journal of Public Administration Research & Theory* 7:181–97.

Perry, James L., Trent A. Engbers, and So Yun Jun. 2009. "Back to the Future? Performance-Related Pay, Empirical Research, and the Perils of Persistence." *Public Administration Review* 69:39–51.

Perry, James L., and Lyman W. Porter. 1982. "Factors Affecting the Context for Motivation in Public Organizations." *Academy of Management Review* 7:89–98.

Perry, James L., and Lois Recascino Wise. 1990. "The Motivational Bases of Public Service." *Public Administration Review* 50:367–73.

Rainey, Hal G. 1982. "Reward Preferences among Public and Private Managers: In Search of the Service Ethic." *American Review of Public Administration* 16:288–302.

Rice, Mitchell F. 2001. "The Need for Teaching Diversity and Representativeness in University Public Administration Education and Professional Public Service Training Programmes in Sub-Saharan Africa." In *Managing Diversity in the Civil Service,* 99–110. Amsterdam, Netherlands: IOS Press.

Schein, Edgar. 1985. *Organizational Culture and Leadership.* San Francisco, CA: Jossey-Bass.

Schermerhorn, John R., Jr., James G. Hunt, and Richard N. Osborn. 2004. *Core Concepts of Organizational Behavior.* Hoboken, NJ: Wiley.

Selden, Sally Coleman. 2009. *Human Capital: Tools and Strategies for the Public Sector.* Washington, DC: CQ Press.

Selden, Sally Coleman, and Robert Wooters. 2011. "Structures in Public Human Resource Management: Shared Services in State Government." *Review of Public Personnel Administration* 31:349–68.

Shin, Roy W., and Debra J. Mesch. 1996. "The Changing Workforce: Issues and Challenges." *International Journal of Public Administration* 19:291–98.

Thomas, Mark A. 1996. "What is Human Resources Strategy?" *Health Manpower Management* 22:4–11.

Thomas, R. Roosevelt, Jr. 1991–92. "The Concept of Managing Diversity." *The Bureaucrat* 19–22.

US Government Accountability Office (GAO). 2000. "Human Capital: Key Principles from Nine Private Sector Organizations." GAO/GGD-00-28. http://gao.gov/assets/230/228623.pdf.

US Government Accountability Office (GAO). 2001. "Human Capital: Meeting the Governmentwide High-Risk Challenge." GAO-01-357T. http://www.gao.gov/assets/110/108710.pdf.

Additional Resources

City of Charlotte & Mecklenburg County Government, 2013. *Managing for Results (M4R)*. http://charmeck.org/mecklenburg/county/CountyManagersOffice/OMB/Budget/FY14%20Strategic%20Planning%20Conference%20Library/M4R%20Overview%20Final.pdf.

Driving Federal Performance—http://performance.gov

Federal Employment Reports—http://www.opm.gov/feddata/

FedScope—http://www.fedscope.opm.gov

Georgia Department of Administrative Services (DOAS), Human Resources Administration—http://doas.ga.gov/AboutUs/Pages/AboutHRA.aspx

Pew Charitable Trusts State and Consumer Initiatives. 2010. "Government Performance Project." http://www.pewstates.org/projects/government-performance-project-328600/.

US Government Accountability Office (GAO). 2000. *Human Capital: A Self-Assessment Checklist for Agency Leaders*. GAO/OCG-00–14G. http://www.gao.gov/special.pubs/cg00014g.pdf.

US Office of Personnel Management (OPM). Human Capital Management—https://www.opm.gov/policy-data-oversight/human-capital-management/

US Office of Personnel Management (OPM). 2008. *End-to-End Hiring Initiative*. http://www.opm.gov/publications/EndToEnd-HiringInitiative.pdf.

US Office of Personnel Management (OPM). 2014. "Required Outcome Metrics." http://www.opm.gov/policy-data-oversight/human-capital-management/reference-materials/results-oriented-performance-culture/requiredoutcomemetrics.pdf.

Case 12.1 Louisiana and Vision 2020

In 1999, then Louisiana governor Murphy J. "Mike" Foster Jr. embarked on an ambitious plan to change the direction of the state government. Governor Foster was elected in 1995 on a reform agenda aimed at not only turning around the ailing Louisiana economy but also changing the "anything goes" image of Louisiana politics. Governor Foster's predecessor, Governor Edwin W. Edwards, had been found guilty on seventeen of twenty-six counts—including racketeering, extortion, money laundering, mail fraud, and wire fraud—in 2001 and ordered to serve 10 years in federal prison. Edwards had received $845,000 in exchange for helping a contractor secure a bid to build a juvenile prison and had helped the then owner of the San Francisco 49ers, Edward J. DeBartolo Jr., "purchase" a casino license to the tune of $400,000. Louisiana's oil- and gas-based economy had been on a perilous slide since the oil boom had ended in the 1980s. Since then, the state had been struggling to diversify to new industries such as technology, while many firms relocated to neighboring states with better opportunities for growth. Needless to say, Governor Foster was facing a number of challenges during his first term in office.

Vision 2020, Governor Foster's strategic plan for recharging the state, was developed in conjunction with the Louisiana Economic Development Council (LEDC). The plan was officially tasked with creating a

> new and better Louisiana and a guide to economic renewal and diversification. It is a platform for innovative initiatives, and a process by which our progress toward long-term goals will be managed and monitored. In its first two years, the Council developed goals, objectives, and benchmarks designed to position the State to meet the challenge that has been articulated. By the year 2020, Louisiana will have a vibrant, balanced economy; a fully engaged, well-educated workforce; and a quality of life that places it among the top ten states in the nation in which to live, work, visit, and do business. (Vision 2020 2001)

The Action Plan 2001 set out the council's recommendations in the seven areas on which Vision 2020 would focus: agribusiness, culture and tourism, economic diversification, education and workforce training, environmental conservation, infrastructure development, science and technology, and tax and revenue policy. Below is the Action Plan recommendation, followed by a section from Vision 2020 that lays out two of the strategic plan's goals for improving the state's workforce and the objectives developed in order to meet those goals.

Action Plan 2001 Recommendation: Develop a strategic plan and implement available programs for universities, community and technical colleges, and secondary schools to provide training for jobs in the targeted technology areas in order to train a qualified workforce for technology-based companies requiring skilled employees.

> **Vision 2020 Goal**: 1: The Learning Enterprise
>
> **Vision 2020 Objective**: 1.6: To have a workforce with the education & skills necessary to work productively in a knowledge-based economy

Vision 2020 Goal: 2: The Culture of Innovation

Vision 2020 Objective: 2.14: To produce more flexible, adaptable, and innovative technicians for industry

Benchmark	Base	Update*	2003	2018
Number of certified, trained university graduates in targeted areas†		To be set		
Number of certified, trained community & technical college graduates in targeted areas		To be set		
Number of high school graduates with certifications in targeted areas		To be set		

†Targeted economic sectors include information technology, medical/biomedical, micromanufacturing, environmental technologies, food technologies, and advanced materials.
*Most recent data available

In the grid above, the actual figures for each benchmark would be entered into the "Base" column to show what the starting point was. Once the plan was put into action, the benchmarks would be assessed periodically, in 2003 and 2018. In this case, the objective is to have a continually increasing number of university, community and technical college, and high school graduates in the targeted fields.

Putting your knowledge of SHRM to work, consider the benchmarks proposed by Governor Foster's Economic Advisory Council to strengthen the workforce.

Discussion Questions

1. Develop a blueprint for a strategic plan that considers the following: How might you coordinate such efforts across agencies, industries, and sectors? What state agencies might be tasked with implementing the workforce-training benchmarks?
2. What roles might secondary and postsecondary education have in advancing toward the workforce-training benchmarks? How might community and technical colleges contribute to achieving these benchmarks?
3. What benefits might you champion as ensuing from the achievement of workforce-training goals for the state?

4. What, if any, other benchmarks might be affected by achieving a more educated and better trained workforce in the state?

For additional information on Vision 2020, you can access the full document, *Action Plan 2001*, through the Louisiana Digital Library at http://www.louisiana digitallibrary.org/cdm/ref/collection/p267101coll4/id/3790/.

Exercise

Developing a Strategic Vision for Public Human Resource Management

Answer the following questions regarding human resources in an agency or another organization that you work for. Using the questions in Figure 12.1 may prove useful. Then discuss your responses with the class or in groups. What advice might you offer to improve the strategic HR management environment where you work?

1. How would you change overall human resources management for your agency? How would the organization benefit if you were successful in achieving your strategic vision?

2. What are the most critical HR functions that should continue to be offered, be eliminated, be changed, or be initiated in the next three to five years?

3. What staffing, training, and development changes would need to be implemented to move your strategic vision forward?

4. What role do you see politicians and stakeholders as having in the achievement of your strategic vision?

5. What levels of resources do you see as necessary for achieving your strategic vision?

6. What facilities and technologies would be needed to achieve your strategic vision?

7. What considerations would need to be given to internal process, employee capacity building, and communication in order to implement your strategic vision?

8. If you could make only three changes that would significantly impact your ability to provide quality HR services to employees, what would these changes be? Why would you prioritize these changes?

9. What makes your agency and the HR function in your agency unique?

10. What do public employees in your agency consider to be the most important service provided by human resources? What do public employees need from human resources?

Source: Adapted from Niven 2003.

13

Public Human Resource Management Education

LEARNING OBJECTIVES

Upon completion of the chapter, you will able to do the following:

- Discuss the changes in public human resource education over the last few decades.
- Discuss the factors affecting changes in the vocation of human resources.
- Evaluate potential courses and materials for advancing the practice of human resources.
- Discuss the role of training and development for cultivating new knowledge within the organization.

After consideration of the material presented thus far in the text, a reevaluation of those subject areas and competencies that have long been considered the core of public sector human resources management (PHRM) education is needed. Exploring new HR management competencies is prudent given the contemporary reform environment. The sections below provide a preliminary assessment of the extent to which contemporary academic and practitioner-based educational programs reflect the current landscape of PHRM. The goal of the previous chapters has been to highlight critical PHRM changes in an era when the erosion of traditional civil service practices—such as civil service examinations, rigid classification and compensation schemes, and job security—has become commonplace. Given the changes in traditional civil service systems, a critical issue is the extent to which public administration programs have adapted PHRM courses to equip students with the skills necessary for today's HR positions. As discussed in previous chapters, performance-oriented reforms such as performance-based pay, employment at will, privatization, and broadbanding are increasingly being used at all levels of government. With no lessening of the appetite for reform-oriented PHRM on the horizon, public administration programs need to prepare students—future practitioners—for the contemporary public personnel environment.

The extent and impact of PHRM reforms have been well documented (e.g., Bowman and West 2007; Condrey and Battaglio 2007; Kellough and Nigro 2002; 2006a; 2006b). Unfortunately, this stream of research has not addressed the extent to which undergraduate and graduate programs in public administration have adapted their curricula in response to these changes (Llorens and Battaglio 2010). More specifically, an assessment of PHRM coursework is essential to provide future practitioners—especially HR managers—with a current tool kit for taking on private sector, market-oriented managerial changes (Lovrich, London, and Fredericksen 1994). As governments consider the merits of reform, HR managers and future practitioners should be equipped with an updated assessment in order to make themselves marketable.

This chapter begins with a review of traditional subject areas considered the core of PHRM education. Reflecting on the contemporary reform environment addressed in previous chapters, the chapter presents new competencies for comparison with the core PHRM curricula. The chapter concludes with an assessment of HR programs at the forefront of change management and draws conclusions about the state of HR management education in public administration/public affairs programs.

The Traditional Core of Public HRM

In 2010, Llorens and Battaglio reflected on the impact contemporary PHRM reforms have had on public administration programs. Their assessment examined the traditional core of PHRM, focusing on a number of textbooks that introduce the topic to public administration students.[1] Klingner and Nalbandian's (2003) PADS acronym—Planning, Acquisition, Development, and Sanction—represents the traditional activities of public personnel administration. Table 13.1 lists these functions and the specific HR activities associated with each.

Planning in traditional public sector HR focused on the foundations of traditional compensation and classification—job analysis and job description. Once these building blocks were in place, HR managers were tasked with accommodating future workforce needs through labor market analysis. The next stage—*acquisition*—charged HR managers with the selection of qualified applicants by means of an assessment tool that satisfied not only workforce needs but the legal mandates set

---

[1]Llorens and Battaglio (2010) reviewed Berman et al.'s *Human Resource Management in Public Service* (2006), Daley's *Strategic Human Resource Management* (2002), Klingner and Nalbandian's *Public Personnel Management: Contexts and Strategies* (2003), Nigro, Nigro, and Kellough's *The New Public Personnel Administration* (2007), Pynes's *Human Resources Management for Public and Nonprofit Organizations* (2004), and Shafritz et al.'s *Personnel Management in Government* (1992). The topics they identified as core subject matter are consistent with those identified by Fredericksen and London (1994), West (1994), and Witt (1994).

Table 13.1	**Traditional Core of Public HRM**
Planning	Job analysis
	Classification
	Compensation
	Workforce planning
Acquisition	Recruitment
	Assessment
	Selection
	Equal employment opportunity/affirmative action
Development	Training
	Performance management
	Safety and health
Sanction	Employee relations
	Labor relations/collective bargaining
Source: Klingner and Nalbandian 2003	

forth by equal employment opportunity (EEO), affirmative action, and diversity policies. *Development* activities are geared toward the appraisal of employees' performance in their position and training them so they can improve. Finally, *sanction* addresses the disciplining of employees under a civil service system.

HRM Reform: Factors Influencing Vocation

Throughout the text, we have discussed criticisms of traditional civil service systems by reformers (Kellough and Nigro 2006b; Selden 2006). In the pursuit of perceived private sector efficiencies, reforms have challenged the traditional core HR functions. The five reform themes addressed throughout the text—decentralization, performance-based pay, declassification, deregulation, and privatization—have generated novel approaches to current HR needs.

Llorens and Battaglio (2010) argued that the traditional PADS functions do not adequately address the issues emerging in the PHRM reform environment. Recall from earlier discussions that decentralization reforms in the public sector have set aside traditional centralized, rule-bound systems in favor of more flexible, private sector–oriented practices (Coggburn 2001; Kettl 2000; Thompson 2001). Specifically, decentralization and the accompanying elimination of top-down regulations shifts staffing and compensation decisions—traditionally the purview of a centralized personnel agency—to agency- and division-level managers. The result is that HR managers at the agency level and line managers are closely involved in staffing and compensation decisions.

Based on the logic of market mechanisms, performance-based pay systems attempt to reward individual, team, and/or organizational performance with financial incentives distributed as increases to base pay (i.e., merit pay), one-time bonuses, or a combination of the two (Kellough and Nigro 2002, 146). Instead of basing pay on longevity, performance-based pay systems are increasingly basing compensation on performance ratings. HR professionals entering the public sector need a solid understanding of effective job evaluation and job analysis methods to support this performance orientation. Knowledge of SHRM practices (see Chapter 12) is also essential in an environment that links merit increases to job performance and the employee's potential for career development. Additionally, performance-based pay can be used to improve the effectiveness of public sector recruitment and retention efforts.

Declassification efforts—such as broadbanding—aim to attract and retain a more qualified workforce. With broadbanding, the agency collapses groups of traditional grades into a single band, giving managers greater flexibility when determining pay during hiring and promotion decisions (Hays 2004; Whalen and Guy 2008). In contrast to traditional step-based compensation plans, broadbanding stresses the assessment of the knowledge, skills, and abilities an employee brings to the position, and it has the potential to reward employees who are likely to fill future workforce needs. Broadbanding is intended to promote egalitarianism by removing the distinctions accompanying traditional pay grades. It is also meant to complement other common elements of reform such as employee empowerment and customer service by deemphasizing titles and hierarchy. For students of public administration, a familiarity with nontraditional pay and benefits plans is essential. Public managers must be adept at negotiating total compensation packages with employees while operating within budgetary constraints.

Diminished job security due to deregulation policies such as employment at will (EAW) has also impacted traditional PHRM. Deregulation has limited or eliminated altogether the access of public sector employees to grievance and appeals procedures. Employees and managers in EAW jurisdictions operate in a system where employees have no guarantee of procedural due process before discipline or termination (Kuykendall and Facer 2002). Preparing students for public sector careers during which they may encounter EAW environments necessitates educating them thoroughly about the HR legal environment. PHRM systems under EAW may exhibit a mixture of classified and unclassified personnel, and HR professionals need to know how to design disciplinary systems in this more complex environment.

Privatizing PHRM functions has been an attractive alternative for reformers seeking to address recalcitrant public sector practices. Rigidity—especially in hiring, development, and discipline—has been targeted by reformers because of the ineffi- ciencies it is seen as perpetuating. Private contractors can hire new personnel quickly and just as briskly dismiss poor performers (Maranto 2001, 75). Also contracting out routine work frees public HR employees from more mundane tasks so they can focus on core mission-oriented tasks (Fernandez, Rainey, and Lowman 2006, 220; Rainey 2005). Furthermore, privatizing allows public agencies to tap private sector economies of scale and concentrated expertise. Public agencies have opted to outsource a wide range of HR activities, including workforce planning and performance management (Coggburn 2007, 220; Rainey 2005, 706). Consequently, future HR managers will need to be proficient in negotiation and cost-benefit analysis—skills essential for awarding contracts. HR personnel may also be tasked with managing and monitoring contracts and contract employees, necessitating an understanding of contract law.

Implications for Public HRM Education

Each of the reforms discussed in this book can dramatically alter traditional core functions of public sector HR practice (Thompson 2001), and such change suggests a need for significant reassessment of PHRM education. As governments decentral- ize, HR professionals at the agency level will have greater responsibilities, which may be particularly burdensome in smaller agencies. Lacking the expertise of central personnel staff, these HR professionals will need extensive training to handle the tasks expected of them (Coggburn 2001; Hou et al. 2000). For example, performance- based pay systems present difficulties in enforcing a government-wide standard across diverse agencies (Hays and Sowa 2006; Kellough and Nigro 2002). HR profes- sionals will need sufficient training in designing and implementing performance appraisal systems that support rewards for productive behaviors. Criticism of broad- banding often cites the potential of decentralized pay decisions to increase costs, legal liability, and internal and external pay inequities (Hays and Sowa 2006; Shafritz et al. 2001; see also Whalen and Guy 2008). Thus, HR professionals need adequate training in competitive compensation practices, salary negotiation, performance appraisal, budgeting, and labor market analysis.

As noted earlier, reduced public sector job security due to EAW has the potential to exacerbate recruitment and retention challenges. With job security no longer a viable incentive to work in the public sector, HR professionals need to be skilled at marketing public sector employment, as well as motivating and retaining employees. For example, federal agencies have begun to utilize student loan repayment incen- tives to recruit younger employees carrying ever-increasing levels of educational debt (US Office of Personnel Management [OPM] 2008). Guidelines for the student loan repayment program state that agencies are able to offer up to $10,000 in loan repayments per calendar year but are not to exceed $60,000 in total payments per employee. However, deciding the extent of payments to be offered and whether or not to pair payments with service requirements necessitates knowledge not commonly taught in PHRM coursework. Also, given more limited or outright nonexistent due process rights, HR professionals need to be aware of the legal environment of EAW systems (Kuykendall and Facer 2002; Lindquist and Condrey 2006). Last, privatization of HR functions requires extensive knowledge of cost-benefit analysis and contract management, and HR professionals charged with contract management will need the tools to ensure accountability through monitoring, legal restrictions, competition, cost accounting, and overall evaluation (Siegel 1999; 2000).

Evaluating Private Sector Models of HRM Education: Graduate Programs in HRM

At the core of many PHRM reforms is the emulation of private sector HR practices. The result is what is often termed a blurring of the distinctions between public sector and private sector practices. Thus, distinguishing between public sector and private sector HRM is increasingly difficult. In 2010, Llorens and Battaglio provided insight into the skills and competencies that are emerging as important for PHRM scholars and practitioners. Their research evaluated graduate-level HRM curricula for those seeking HR careers. They also reviewed alternative approaches to HRM education, assessing the curricula of a select sample of graduate programs offering degrees specifically in HR management.[2] Llorens and Battaglio selected the following schools from a listing of graduate education programs provided by the Society of Human Resources Management (SHRM) (2008):[3]

- *Cornell University*—Master of Industrial and Labor Relations
- *Pennsylvania State University*—Master of Human Resources and Employment Relations
- *Purdue University*—Master of Science in Human Resource Management
- *University of Minnesota*—Master of Arts in Human Resources and Industrial Relations
- *University of Illinois—Urbana-Champaign*—Master of Human Resources and Industrial Relations

---

[2]The listing is comprised of those programs that voluntarily chose to be included in SHRM's graduate directory.

[3]Rankings were based on the *U.S. News and World Report* ranking of top MPA/MPP/MPA programs.

Llorens and Battaglio (2010) noted two distinct advantages of these graduate programs: specialized training in HR rather than training in general management and a wide variety of course offerings within the HRM field. The specialized training in HR management offered at these graduate programs is unparalleled, especially when compared to that available in public affairs and administration programs. While it is not uncommon for Master of Public Administration (MPA) programs to include courses in HR management in their curriculum, concentrations in HRM are rare.

Furthermore, the variety of course offerings goes far beyond the traditional areas generally reviewed in the core PHRM course of a public administration program: recruitment, selection, classification, training, and labor relations. Indeed, many of the programs Llorens and Battaglio (2010) reviewed included a broad and interdisciplinary approach to HR education. Table 13.2 includes sample curricula from the HRM graduate programs Llorens and Battaglio reviewed.

We can look at Cornell University's Master of Industrial and Labor Relations (MILR) program as it existed more recently (Cornell 2014). The core requirements alone are impressive: staffing organizations, managing compensation, business strategy and HR, finance and HR management, and training and development in organizations. Additional HRM course offerings cover contemporary topics such as human resource information systems (HRIS), online research and reporting methods for executive decision making, strategic HR metrics, and competing in services—management, marketing, and HR strategies.

Table 13.2	**Sample Curricula in Graduate HRM Programs**
Cornell University (Master of Industrial and Labor Relations)	• Business Strategy and Human Resources • Finance and HR Management • Managing Compensation • Staffing Organizations • Training and Development in Organizations
Pennsylvania State University (Master of Human Resources and Employment Relations)	• Current Topics in Human Resources • Diversity in the Workplace • Employee Benefits • Employment Compensation • Employment Relations • Ethics

(Continued)

(Continued)

	• International and Comparative Employment Relations
	• Labor and Employment Law
	• Labor Market Analysis
	• Labor Relations in the Public Sector
	• Needs Assessment for Industrial Trainers
	• Organizations in the Workplace
	• Staffing and Training
	• Training in Industry and Business
Purdue University (Master of Science in Human Resources Management)	• Behavior in Organizations
	• Compensation and Reward Systems
	• Economics of Labor Markets
	• Employment Law
	• Financial Accounting
	• Financial Management I
	• Human Resources Information Systems I & II
	• Human Resources Systems
	• Industrial Relations I & II
	• Leadership and Ethics
	• Managerial Communication Skills
	• Marketing Management I
	• Operations Management
	• Quantitative Methods I & II
	• Staffing Systems
	• Staffing Tools
	• Strategic Management I & II
University of Illinois—Urbana-Champaign (Master of Human Resources and Industrial Relations)	• Employment Relations Systems
	• Human Resources Management and Organizational Behavior
	• International Human Resources Management
	• Labor Markets and Employment
	• Quantitative Methods
	• Research Methods
	• Unions, Management, and Labor Relations Policy

University of Minnesota (Master of Arts in Human Resources and Industrial Relations)	• Compensation and Benefits • Data Analysis • Labor Relations and Collective Bargaining • Managerial Economics and Labor Market Analysis • Organizational Behavior and Theory • Staffing, Training, and Development

Source: Llorens and Battaglio 2010

Based on the review of HRM curricula, Llorens and Battaglio (2010) revisited the traditional core competencies of PHRM (see Table 13.1). Table 13.3 offers the authors' insights into the competencies required in a rapidly changing PHRM environment.

Llorens and Battaglio's assessment is particularly salient in light of the elements of PHRM reform reviewed at the outset of this text (see Chapter 1, Table 1.1). Specialized courses on topics such as performance-based pay and broadbanding are essential for a 21st-century understanding of compensation, benefits, and reward systems. In a deregulated, decentralized, EAW environment, course offerings in labor market analysis, staffing systems, and HRIS are essential. Furthermore, an increased

Table 13.3	**Emerging Topics and Competencies in Public HRM**
Planning	• Conducting regional and national labor market analysis • Evaluating internal and external compensation equity within merit-pay or broadbanded pay systems • Ensuring workforce planning integration in decentralized operating environments
Acquisition	• Developing and marketing an agency or institutional brand • Assessing, selecting, and maintaining HR management information systems • Effectively utilizing automated recruitment and assessment technologies • Effectively negotiating salary and benefit packages in nonstructured pay systems
Development	• Staffing, developing, and managing contract employees • Developing enhanced performance appraisal techniques under merit-pay or at-will systems • Effectively utilizing advanced employee retention techniques
Sanction	• Navigating labor law in alternative or mixed personnel systems

Source: Llorens and Battaglio 2010

reliance on private contractors for PHRM functions necessitates a greater understanding of the costs and benefits of privatization and advanced coursework in employment law and strategic planning and management. While many public administration programs offer generalized coursework that may address some of these needs, few, if any, appear to do so specifically in an HR management context (Llorens and Battaglio 2010). Public affairs and administration programs would be wise to develop course offerings that incorporate the HR-related topics offered in Table 13.2.

Status and Future of PHRM Education

Given the critical issues facing PHRM, the future of PHRM education needs to be addressed. Though not all public administration/public affairs programs are accredited by the National Association for Schools of Public Affairs and Administration (NASPAA), the organization remains a powerful voice in determining which subject matter areas and competencies are deemed essential to an education in public administration. A recent review of NASPAA-accredited programs demonstrated that only 35.1 percent of the top 37 MPA programs require at least one course in HRM (Koven, Goetzke, and Brennan 2008).[4] Only 22.2 percent of top-ranked MPA programs not accredited by NASPAA have the same HRM requirement. None of the NASPAA accredited and nonaccredited Masters in Public Policy (MPP) programs require an HRM course (Koven, Goetzke, and Brennan 2008). Even more striking is the departure in the 2009 NASPAA standards from specifying coursework in PHRM (see Box 13.1). The 2008 standard stated:

> The common curriculum components shall enhance the student's values, knowledge, and skills to act ethically and effectively:
>> In the Management of Public Service Organizations, the components of which include:
>
> Human resources
>
> Budgeting and financial processes
>
> Information management, technology applications, and policy (§ 4.21).

While the 2008 standards included HRM, NASPAA does not prescribe courses under the standard; the courses mentioned were merely suggestions. In fact, the 2008 standard stated that

> these area requirements do not prescribe specific courses. Neither do they imply that equal time should be spent on each area or that courses must all

---

[4]Rankings were based on the *U.S. News and World Report* ranking of top MPA/MPP/MPA programs.

be offered by the public affairs, public policy or public administration programs. Nor should they be interpreted in a manner that might impede the
development of special strengths in each program. (§ 4.21)

The 2009 standards are even more lax, lacking any identifiable subject areas. The
new standards merely identify competencies that contribute to public service that
include five domains (see Box 13.1). At no point in the 2009 NASPAA standard is the
subject of HRM identified.

Box 13.1	**NASPAA Competency Standards for Peer Review and Accreditation, 2009**

Standard 5—Matching Operations with the Mission: Student Learning
   5.1 Universal Required Competencies: As the basis for its curriculum, the program will adopt a set of required competencies related to its mission and public service values.
   The required competencies will include five domains: the ability

- to lead and manage in public governance;
- to participate in and contribute to the policy process;
- to analyze, synthesize, think critically, solve problems and make decisions;
- to articulate and apply a public service perspective;
- to communicate and interact productively with a diverse and changing workforce and citizenry.

   5.2 Mission-specific Required Competencies: The program will identify core competencies in other domains that are necessary and appropriate to implement its mission.
   5.3 Mission-specific Elective Competencies: The program will define its objectives and competencies for optional concentrations and specializations.
   5.4 Professional Competencies: The program will ensure that students learn to apply their education, such as through experiential exercises and interactions with practitioners across the broad range of public affairs, administration, and policy professions and sectors.

Source: NASPAA 2009

In contrast to NASPAA's relatively broad, competency-based approach to the
subject matter and expertise required of public affairs programs, the American
Society for Public Administration (ASPA) task force Educating for Excellence in the
MPA Degree identified specific subject areas that it held to be critical to a quality
education in public administration. Critical coursework includes

> organizational concepts and institutions, policy evaluation, budgeting and
> finance, public administration, ethics and leadership, and politics and legal
> institutions. . . . Other courses that we think should be in an MPA program

worthy of the name are public human resources management, information resources and management, and intergovernmental/intersectoral relations, and leadership. (Henry et al. 2008, 21).

While recommending that "NASPAA, ASPA and other entities responsible for curricula in public administration and related masters programs take specific steps to foster a dialogue on the issues raised in our report," the task force report goes on to state that

> while NASPAA rather than ASPA conducts the accreditation for the MPA, if NASPAA feels that it cannot or will not participate in this discussion, or change its accreditation requirements, ASPA should consider a means of providing recognition for programs that meet its requirements in MPA structure, perhaps by publishing a list of approved programs. (21)

Clearly, the ASPA report should prompt a more targeted focus on HRM courses in MPA programs. Llorens and Battaglio (2010) argued that given recent PHRM reforms, now is an opportune time to initiate a more expansive and comprehensive evaluation of the presence and characteristics of public HR management education within the MPA curriculum.

Training and Development

To prepare HR professionals to practice in an increasingly strategically focused environment, training, career development, education, and learning must play a more vital role in PHRM education. Indeed, Perry (2009) suggested that training and development are important for three critical reasons: demographics, shifting institutional rules, and human capital (34). Demographic changes, especially an aging workforce that is approaching retirement, means that training and development are crucial to ensure that the organization's knowledge base is maintained with the next generation of leaders. PHRM reforms have shifted the values integral to public employment, suggesting that the traditional career that would sustain an employee throughout his or her working life may no longer be viable (Perry 1994; 2007); continual development will be essential to maintaining the relevance of one's skills and knowledge. Finally, Perry argued that the changing characteristics of the public workforce necessitate a better understanding of human capital, in other words, SHRM. Training and development of current and future public employees must reflect a more strategic approach to managing future knowledge and skills, especially to ensure that public agencies have necessary managerial and leadership capacities going forward. Perry suggested that a better understanding of "executive and leadership development should be among the training and development issues given high priority" (2009, 35). Adequate succession planning (discussed in Chapter 12) is key to meeting this critical need.

Training and development may also be important for maintaining an ethical climate in an era of PHRM reform. The potential for moral exemplars (Colby and Damon 1992) and even administrative evil (Adams and Balfour 2004) is well documented. While there are many examples of public officials fighting for social justice (e.g., civil rights attorney and US Supreme Court justice Thurgood Marshall), there is also the potential for immoral or even criminal action by those in government (e.g., torture in the Abu Ghraib prison in Iraq). It is the duty of professionals in HR "to inform members of their organizations about the specific forms of conduct that are either prohibited or especially welcomed" (Berman and West 2006, 191). Public HR managers would be wise to consider constituting regular training sessions that voice managerial priorities, as well as welcoming feedback on HR-related questions.

Conclusion: Proposals for Change

From the civil service reform efforts of the late 19th century to more recent market-oriented reforms, it is clear that the field of public HRM is anything but static. Scholars and educators operate under constant pressure to reevaluate the skills and competencies necessary for future generations of HRM professionals to meet the human capital and management needs of public organizations. Llorens and Battaglio (2010) suggested that recent reforms such as EAW and performance-based pay have called attention to the need for PHRM coursework to incorporate more market-oriented content, such as how to design performance-oriented compensation systems and labor market analysis. Llorens and Battaglio offered several proposals for improving instruction and curricula in HR coursework. For many practitioners, ongoing development may simply entail keeping up with the literature published in academic journals (e.g., *Review of Public Personnel Administration, Public Personnel Management, Public Administration Review,* and *Public Performance & Management Review*). Indeed, the literature assessed throughout this text should prove useful to faculty seeking to promote awareness of recent trends.

Clearly, the trends of decentralization, performance-based pay, declassification, deregulation, and privatization suggest that organizations may struggle to transition from traditional hierarchical structures (Risher 2005; Selden 2009). To counteract such difficulties, it may be useful to consider new metrics for analyzing performance. Chapter 12 on public SHRM provides a number of constructive measures for organizing and assessing agency progress in a reform climate. The chapter offers a number of practical examples of success at both the federal and state levels. Such examples may prove useful for classroom instruction, particularly for those practitioners hoping to benchmark successful practices.

Recruiting and retaining a qualified public workforce may prove difficult in an era of PHRM reform. HR professionals need to know how to assess employee attitudes, voluntary turnover, and absenteeism in a market-oriented environment (Selden 2009). Recent scholarship (Battaglio 2010; Battaglio and Condrey 2009) suggests that EAW may cause rifts in the employer/employee relationship, adversely affecting performance. Moreover, public managers will need to be well versed in the latest practical advice for managing outsourced HR functions. The lack of practical instruction in managing outsourced HR functions (Coggburn 2007) means that finding published information on HR privatization—like Chapter 10 of this text—is important. Faculty may also need to utilize more general texts (e.g., Cohen and Eimicke 2008; Cooper 2003) along with general PHRM textbooks.

Additional information may be found in many government reports and related materials. For example, the US Merit Systems Protection Board publishes a number of worthwhile reports on contemporary topics; examples include *Designing an Effective Pay for Performance Compensation System* (2006) and *Identifying Talent through Technology* (2004). Additionally, the Partnership for Public Service has published a number of valuable reports on key concerns like *Leaving Talent on the Table: The Need to Capitalize on High Performing Student Interns* (2009) and *Getting On Board: A Model for Integrating and Engaging New Employees* (2008). While the path toward successful HR management in the public sector may be varied, what is clear is that current and future reforms will dramatically alter the practice of HRM and, thus, the needs of current students in the field.

References

Adams, Guy B., and Danny L. Balfour. 2004. *Unmasking Administrative Evil.* Rev. ed. Armonk, NY: M. E. Sharpe.

Battaglio, R. Paul Jr. 2010. "Public Service Reform and Motivation: Evidence from an Employment At-Will Environment." *Review of Public Personnel Administration* 30:341–63.

Battaglio, R. Paul, Jr., and Stephen E. Condrey. 2009. "Reforming Public Management: Analyzing the Impact of Public Service Reform on Organizational and Managerial Trust." *Journal of Public Administration Research & Theory* 19:689–707.

Berman, Evan M., James S. Bowman, Jonathan P. West, and Montgomery R. Van Wart. 2006. *Human Resource Management in Public Service: Paradoxes, Processes, and Problems.* 2nd ed. Thousand Oaks, CA: SAGE.

Berman, Evan M., and Jonathan P. West. 2006. "Ethics Management and Training." In *Public Personnel Management: Current Concerns, Future Challenges,* 4th ed., edited by Norma M. Riccucci, 190–203. New York: Longman.

Bowman, James S., and Jonathan P. West. 2006. "Ending Civil Service Protections in Florida Government: Experiences in State Agencies." *Review of Public Personnel Administration* 26:139–57.

Bowman, James S., and Jonathan P. West, eds. 2007. *American Public Service: Radical Reform and the Merit System.* Boca Raton, FL: CRC Press.

Coggburn, Jerrell D. 2001. "Is Deregulation the Answer for Public Personnel Management? Revisiting a Familiar Question: Introduction." *Review of Public Personnel Administration* 20:5–8.

Coggburn, Jerrell D. 2007. "Outsourcing Human Resources: The Case of Texas Health and Human Services Commission." *Review of Public Personnel Administration* 27:315–35.

Cohen, Steven, and William B. Eimicke. 2008. *The Responsible Contract Manager: Protecting the Public Interest in an Outsourced World.* Washington, DC: Georgetown University Press.

Colby, Anne, and William Damon. 1992. *Some Do Care: Contemporary Lives of Moral Commitment.* New York: Free Press.

Condrey, Stephen E., and R. Paul Battaglio Jr. 2007. "A Return to Spoils? Revisiting Radical Civil Service Reform in the United States." *Public Administration Review* 67:425–36.

Cooper, Phillip J. 2003. *Governing by Contract: Challenges and Opportunities for Public Managers.* Washington, DC: CQ Press.

Cornell University. 2014. "MILR Concentration: Human Resources and Organizations." Accessed April 30. http://www.ilr.cornell.edu/graddegreeprograms/degrees/milr/hr.html.

Daley, Dennis M. 2002. *Strategic Human Resource Management: People and Performance Management in the Public Sector.* Upper Saddle River, NJ: Prentice Hall.

Fernandez, Sergio, Hal G. Rainey, and Carol E. Lowman. 2006. "Privatization and Its Implications for Human Resources Management." In *Public Personnel Management: Current Concerns, Future Challenges,* 4th ed., edited by Norma M. Riccucci, 204–24. New York: Longman.

Fredericksen, Patricia J., and Rosanne London. 1994. "A Comparison of Personnel Courses in Public and Business Administration." *Review of Public Personnel Administration* 14:101–26.

Hays, Steven W. 2004. "Trends and Best Practices in State and Local Human Resource Management: Lessons to Be Learned?" *Review of Public Personnel Administration* 24:256–75.

Hays, Steven W., and Jessica E. Sowa. 2006 "A Broader Look at the 'Accountability' Movement: Some Grim Realities in State Civil Service Systems." *Review of Public Personnel Administration* 26:102–17.

Henry, Nicholas, Charles T. Goodsell, Laurence E. Lynn Jr., Camilla Stivers, and Gary L. Wamsley. 2008. "Excellence in PA Report, Final Installment: Report of ASPA's Task Force on Educating for Excellence in the MPA Degree." *PA Times* (July): 21.

Hou, Yilin, Patricia Ingraham, Stuart Bretschneider, and Sally Coleman Selden. 2000. "Decentralization of Human Resource Management: Driving Forces and Implications." *Review of Public Personnel Administration* 20:9–22.

Kellough, J. Edward, and Lloyd G. Nigro. 2002. "Pay for Performance in Georgia State Government: Employee Perspectives on GeorgiaGain after 5 Years." *Review of Public Personnel Administration* 22:146–66.

Kellough, J. Edward, and Lloyd G. Nigro, eds. 2006a. *Civil Service Reform in the States: Personnel Policy and Politics at the Subnational Level.* Albany: SUNY Press.

Kellough, J. Edward, and Lloyd G. Nigro. 2006b. "Dramatic Reform in the Public Service: At-Will Employment and the Creation of a New Public Workforce." *Journal of Public Administration Research and Theory* 16:447–66.

Kettl, Donald F. 2000. *The Global Public Management Revolution: A Report on the Transformation of Governance.* Washington, DC: Brookings Institution Press.

Klingner, Donald E., and John Nalbandian. 2003. *Public Personnel Management: Contexts and Strategies.* 5th ed. Englewood Cliffs, NJ: Prentice Hall.

Koven, Steven G., Frank Goetzke, and Michael Brennan. 2008. "Profiling Public Affairs Programs: The View from the Top." *Administration & Society* 40:691–710.

Kuykendall, Christine L., and Rex L. Facer II. 2002. "Public Employment in Georgia State Agencies: The Elimination of the Merit System." *Review of Public Personnel Administration* 22:133–45.

Lindquist, Stefanie A., and Stephen E. Condrey. 2006. "Public Employment Reforms and Constitutional Due Process." In *Civil Service Reform in the States: Personnel Policy and Politics at the Subnational Level,* edited by J. Edward Kellough and Lloyd G. Nigro, 95–114. Albany: SUNY Press.

Llorens, Jared J., and R. Paul Battaglio Jr. 2010. "Human Resources Management in a Changing World: Reassessing Public Human Resources Management Education." *Review of Public Personnel Administration* 30:112–32.

Lovrich, Nicholas P., Rosanne London, and Patricia J. Fredericksen. 1994. "Overview: An Analytical Snapshot of the Contemporary Personnel Course." *Review of Public Personnel Administration* 14:5–7.

Maranto, Robert. 2001. "Thinking the Unthinkable in Public Administration: A Case for Spoils in the Federal Bureaucracy." In *Radical Reform of the Civil Service,* edited by Stephen E. Condrey and Robert Maranto, 69–86. Lanham, MD: Lexington Books.

National Association of Schools of Public Affairs and Administration (NASPAA). 2008. "General Information and Standards for Professional Master's Degree Programs." http://www.naspaa.org/accreditation/ns/pre2009standards.asp.

National Association of Schools of Public Affairs and Administration (NASPAA). 2009. "NASPAA Accreditation Standards." Adopted October 19. http://www.naspaa.org/accreditation/ns/naspaastandards.asp.

Nigro, Lloyd G., Felix A. Nigro, and J. Edward Kellough. 2007. *The New Public Personnel Administration.* 6th ed. Belmont, CA: Thomson/Wadsworth.

Partnership for Public Service. 2008. *Getting on Board: A Model for Integrating and Engaging New Employees.* http://ourpublicservice.org/OPS/publications/viewcontentdetails.php?id=128.

Partnership for Public Service. 2009. "Leaving Talent on the Table: The Need to Capitalize on High Performing Student Interns." http://ourpublicservice.org/OPS/publications/view contentdetails.php?id=133.

Perry, James L. 1994. "Revitalizing Employee Ties with Public Organizations." In *New Paradigms for Government: Issues for the Changing Public Service*, edited by Patricia Ingraham and Barbara Romzek, 191–214. San Francisco, CA: Jossey-Bass.

Perry, James L. 2007. "Democracy and the New Public Service." *American Review of Public Administration* 37:3–16.

Perry, James L. 2009. "A Strategic Agenda for Public Human Resource Management Research." *Review of Public Personnel Administration* 30:20–43.

Pynes, Joan E. 2004. *Human Resources Management for Public and Nonprofit Organizations.* 2nd ed. San Francisco, CA: Jossey-Bass.

Rainey, Glen W. 2005. "Human Resources Consultants and Outsourcing: Focusing on Local Government." In *Handbook of Human Resource Management in Government,* 2nd ed., edited by Stephen E. Condrey, 701–34. San Francisco, CA: Jossey-Bass.

Risher, Howard. 2005. "How Much Should Federal Employees Be Paid? The Problems with Using a Market Philosophy in a Broadband System." *Public Personnel Management* 34:121–40.

Selden, Sally Coleman. 2006. "The Impact of Discipline on the Use and Rapidity of Dismissal in State Governments." *Review of Public Personnel Administration* 26:335–55.

Selden, Sally Coleman. 2009. *Human Capital: Tools and Strategies for the Public Sector.* Washington, DC: CQ Press.

Shafritz, Jay M., Norma M. Riccucci, David H. Rosenbloom, and Albert C. Hyde. 1992. *Personnel Management in Government: Politics and Process.* 4th ed. New York: Marcel Dekker.

Shafritz, Jay M., David H. Rosenbloom, Norma A. Riccucci, Katherine C. Naff, and Al C. Hyde. 2001. *Personnel Management in Government: Politics and Process.* 5th ed. New York: Marcel Dekker.

Siegel, Gilbert B. 1999. "Where Are We on Local Government Contracting?" *Public Productivity & Management Review* 22:365–88.

Siegel, Gilbert B. 2000. "Outsourcing Personnel Functions." *Public Personnel Management* 29:225–36.

Society for Human Resources Management (SHRM). 2008. "Profiles: HR Graduate Programs." Accessed August 12. http://shrm.org (no longer available online; see http://www.shrm.org/ education/hreducation/pages/hrprogramdirectory.aspx).

Thompson, James R. 2001. "The Civil Service under Clinton: The Institutional Consequences of Disaggregation." *Review of Public Personnel Administration* 21:87–113.

Thompson, James R. 2007. "Federal Labor-Management Relations Reforms under Bush: Enlightened Management or Quest for Control?" *Review of Public Personnel Administration* 27:105–24.

US Merit Systems Protection Board (MSPB). 2004. *Identifying Talent through Technology: Automated Hiring Systems in Federal Agencies.* http://www.mspb.gov/netsearch/viewdocs .aspx?docnumber=253627&version=253914.

US Merit Systems Protection Board (MSPB). 2006. *Designing an Effective Pay for Performance Compensation System.* http://www.mspb.gov/netsearch/viewdocs.aspx?docnumber=224104& version=224323.

US Office of Personnel Management (OPM). 2008. "Pay & Leave: Student Loan Repayment." http://www.opm.gov/policy-data-oversight/pay-leave/student-loan-repayment/.

US News and World Report. 2008. "America's Best Graduate Schools 2009." Accessed August 12. http://grad-schools.usnews.rankingsandreviews.com (no longer available online; see http:// grad-schools.usnews.rankingsandreviews.com/best-graduate-schools).

West, Jonathan. 1994. "Teaching Public Personnel Management in Three Types of Higher Educational Institutions." *Review of Public Personnel Administration* 14:22–38.

Whalen, Cortney, and Mary E. Guy. 2008. "Broadbanding Trends in the States." *Review of Public Personnel Administration* 28:349–66.

Witt, Stephanie L. 1994. "Results of a National Survey of Instructors." *Review of Public Personnel Administration* 14:82–92.

Additional Resources

Cornell University, Industrial and Labor Relations (ILR) School—http://www.ilr.cornell.edu

Partnership for Public Service—http://www.ourpublicservice.org/OPS/

Pennsylvania State University, School of Labor & Employment Relations, Master of Science Degree in Human Resources and Employment Relations (HRER)—http://lser.la.psu.edu/ students/MSprogram.shtml

Purdue University, Krannert School of Management, Master of Science in Human Resources Management—http://www.krannert.purdue.edu/masters/programs/mshrm/

US Merit System Protection Board (in particular the MSPB's studies and reports on trends in HRM)—http://www.mspb.gov/studies/

University of Illinois at Urbana—Champaign, School of Labor and Employment Relations, Master's Program—http://www.ler.illinois.edu/prospectivestudents/mp_overview.html

University of Minnesota, Carlson School of Management, Master of Arts in Human Resources and Industrial Relations—http://www.csom.umn.edu/master-human-resources/

Case 13.1 — Assessing Future Knowledge and Skill Sets in a PHRM Reform Environment

Y ou are a newly hired employee in a local government's HR office. The juris-diction has recently instituted a number for HR-related reforms. The recently elected reform-minded mayor was instrumental in convincing the city council to hire a city manager who is receptive to the mayor's public management reforms. As a result, the city recently adopted a new performance-based pay policy for supervisory personnel. Supervisory personnel are also subject to employment at will due to a measure recently adopted by the city council and approved by the citizenry that removed civil service protections from some 500-plus managerial positions. In addition, the city is considering implementing broadbanding government-wide to recruit a more qualified workforce. Finally, the city manager and HR manager are considering outsourcing some of the more routine HR-related functions.

Discussion Questions

Your HR manager has asked you to gather feedback from government employees on the knowledge and skills they deem necessary for navigating the new landscape. You have also been tasked with identifying potential Master of Public Administration (MPA) programs to partner with for continuing education and training opportunities. Consider the following questions in your research:

1. What questions might you ask of employees (both supervisory and street level) regarding what knowledge and skills they need subsequent to the recent reforms?

2. Reviewing Table 13.2, what coursework/instruction might be useful to implement performance-based pay programs?

3. Reviewing Table 13.2, what coursework/instruction might you consider for improving the ability to recruit a qualified workforce?

Exercise

PHRM Literature Review Assignment

Now that you are familiar with the PHRM reform concepts, you are ready to dive into PHRM reform research. Prepare and present a paper reviewing an article from published PHRM research (see below for a list of human resource management and public administration journals). You should search academic websites (e.g., Google Scholar, JSTOR) for articles related to the five themes we have discussed: decentralization, performance-based pay, declassification, deregulation, and privatization. The search process may take some refinement. For example, you may want to search for specific reforms that are examples of the five themes in the public sector (e.g., employment at will, broadbanding, paybanding, outsourcing, and contracting out human resources).

The paper should be two to three pages. To promote discussion on the topic, provide copies of your paper to your instructor and classmates before your oral presentation. The written summary and the oral presentation will be evaluated in terms of their thoroughness and accuracy. When other students present their work, be prepared to engage in informed and spirited discussion of the issues debated.

Suggested sources for readings. The following are high-quality, readable publications usually oriented toward practicing public managers and human resource managers: *American Review of Public Administration, Governing, Government Executive, Human Resource Management Review, International Journal of Human Resource Management, The International Journal of Organization Theory and Behavior, Journal of Public Administration Research and Theory, Public Administration Review, Public Management Review, The Public Manager, Public Personnel Management, Review of Public Personnel Administration,* and *State and Local Government Review.*

14

Conclusion
Challenges and Opportunities

It should now be apparent that coordinating public human resource management (PHRM) activities in an era of public service reform is becoming increasingly complicated. The dynamic environment of PHRM in the 21st century necessitates that HR managers familiarize themselves with the trends in practice. For the past few decades, those trends have been dominated by the five PHRM reforms discussed through the text—decentralization, performance-based pay, declassification, deregulation, and privatization. These reforms, often termed "managerialist" reforms, adopt some of the guiding principles that govern the private sector, namely efficiency, high productivity, managerial flexibility, and an emphasis on results. When the popular perception of government is that it was highly inefficient, bureaucratic, and ineffective, some policy makers see these private sector–oriented reforms as an attractive alternative. Reformers who support implementation of these practices in public sector HR feel that they will be a "breath of fresh air," shaking up" the tired old practices of traditional PHRM. They further believe that implementing reform will ultimately lead to more efficient government.

These reforms have become pervasive at the federal, state, and local levels. In the wake of the 2008 financial crisis, financially strapped governments have faced even more pressure to increase efficiency, to improve productivity, and, most importantly, to cut costs. To be sure, implementation has at times been controversial. For example, allowing a private company to take over public services that our governments have traditionally performed is distasteful to some. Private sector firms are focused on profits, while governments have a duty to provide for the welfare of their citizens. Can the HR strategies developed to meet these differing objectives be reconciled? And what about the different legal environments of the public and private sectors? On the other hand, these reforms have indeed improved efficiency and streamlined the functioning of government in many respects. The key question now is, What has been the effect of these reforms in the public sector?

This aim of this textbook has been to provide a comprehensive introduction to the policies, practices, and regulations of public HR management while examining how these reforms have affected the practice of public HR. Part I of the book covered the foundations of PHRM, including the evolution and development of public service in the United States, the traditional merit-pay system, the laws and regulations governing public employment, equal employment opportunity, and, of course, the five reform themes. Part II discussed conventional HR functions and issues in the context of the public sector. These include recruitment and selection, pay and benefits, performance appraisal, labor unions, and the concept of public service motivation. Part III looked forward, addressing privatization, HR information systems, strategic public HR management, and PHRM education.

As mentioned at the beginning of this chapter, public HR managers need to be aware of current trends so they can respond to them or even implement them. However, before one decides to pursue reforms, it is important to consider first whether doing so is desirable. Each of the reforms discussed in this text presents a number of challenges to traditional PHRM, and as we have seen, the promise of improved HR functions has not always been fulfilled. In the context of the public sector, reforms rooted in private sector experience may not always be the best option.

This final chapter discusses both the challenges and opportunities for 21st-century PHRM, summarizing the lessons from previous chapters. We first assess the impact of PHRM reform to date and see that it does pose a number of challenges. However, the chapter goes on to suggest that with advances in information technology, strategic planning, and training and development, public HR managers will have many opportunities to make a positive difference (Battaglio and Jordan 2012).

Challenges of PHRM Reform

Challenge 1—The impact of public human resource management reform has been mixed at best, often failing to demonstrate promised benefits or producing unintended consequences. Supporters of reform have had a difficult time proving that changes to traditional PHRM have fulfilled their promise of creating a more effective and efficient government. A bevy of research indicate that different types of PHRM reform, individually or combined, have yet to yield the results promised (Battaglio and Condrey 2006; 2009; Hays and Sowa 2006; Kellough and Nigro 2005; Perry, Engbers, and Jun 2009; Selden, Ingraham, and Jacobson 2001; Shafritz et al. 2001; Whalen and Guy 2008). After several decades of experience with reform, we know very little about the impact it has had on productivity. This is troubling when one considers that many levels of government are weighing the merits of each of the public service reform elements as part of a potential reorganization of the civil service (Maynard 2012).

An unintended consequence of PHRM reforms is their potential to exacerbate recruitment and retention problems (Battaglio 2010; Battaglio and Condrey 2009; Coggburn et al. 2010; Condrey and Battaglio 2007). When employment at will (EAW) is implemented, for example, job security is no longer a viable recruitment incentive. Consequently, HR managers must be adept at selecting the appropriate recruitment and selection procedures that garner the largest possible pool of qualified applicants for the respective job. Public HR managers will be tasked with assessing the most optimal recruitment mechanisms available, including as Web 2.0 technologies and third-party e-recruitment.

Reforms have also had an impact on employee morale. Recent efforts (see Battaglio and Condrey 2009; Condrey and Battaglio 2007; Kellough and Nigro 2002, 2006; Leisink and Steijn 2008; Moynihan 2008) have highlighted the deleterious effects of reforms, specifically performance-based pay and EAW, on public employee motivation. Particularly interesting is the perceived failure of these reforms to act as motivators for performance. Public service motivation (PSM) theory offers a promising way for HR professionals to implement reforms while taking into account the drivers of government employees' morale and performance, which are not always the same as those of their private sector counterparts. PSM may be especially relevant to the implementation of performance-based pay. Repeatedly, performance-based pay has been unsuccessful at activating public employees' motivation. PSM and self-determination theory "may be more applicable levers for improving performance in public agencies than approaches applying expectancy and reinforcement theory" (Perry et al. 2009, 46). An emphasis on monetary incentives has proven harmful to intrinsic motivators like those embodied in PSM theory. Moynihan (2008) suggested that public managers consider intrinsic values—those held closely by those who feel the call to public service—in the selection process (260). Unfortunately, identifying the most salient values and linking them to job performance is problematic. However, studies suggest that pro-social behaviors can be tapped to improve work performance (Rainey 2009, 271; see also Grant 2008).

Finally, reforms affect how best to manage performance appraisal in the public sector. Performance evaluation is an increasingly important tool in the effort to drive greater accountability for results. However, accurately assessing employee productivity is no easy task. Multiple values, roles, and outcomes among public agencies make the objective measurement of employee performance challenging. Further complicating the difficulties of public sector performance appraisal is performance-based pay. Effective performance appraisal is critical to making performance-based pay work. Yet, a great deal of skepticism exists among employees regarding the ability of management to effectively link performance appraisal with rewards. Performance appraisal systems that do not elicit confidence among employees are subject to failure.

Challenge 2—Human resource systems are uniquely taxed by public human resource management reforms and do not receive adequate support to implement reforms. Each of the five PHRM reforms can dramatically alter PHRM's traditional focus on merit and equity (Thompson 2001). As governments dismantle central personnel offices, HR professionals at the agency level have more responsibilities and need HR systems that support their more demanding role (Coggburn 2001; Hou et al. 2000). Furthermore, many reforms attempt to create a single plan for the transformation of government operations, yet inter- and intra-organizational differences need to be accounted for.

> Public organizations differ extensively from each other: they differ in their "geography," size, mission, in the sector they belong to, and in their institutional level (supranational, national, regional, local, sublocal). They differ in their institutional history. They differ in their accountability systems and relations. They differ in their internal managerial and operational development rate. We have to learn to classify and analyze their contingent characteristics in order to assess their needs and possibilities of change. (Longo 2008, 7)

PHRM reform should be attuned to the intricacies of an organization. Public managers must align the processes and structures of the organization with the goals of the reform effort. PHRM reforms have value for politicians because they represent a desire to change a structure at the heart of how government is run. However, reforms, no matter how much flexibility is built into them, are blanket approaches that may not account for the nuances within and between organizations.

The trend toward adopting shared services models may be a viable alternative for dealing with differences across various organizational units. Shared services models create a centralized service function that treats employees and agency-based HRM professionals as internal customers (Selden and Wooters 2011). This approach is designed to better leverage existing resources, to reduce duplication of HRM activities across agencies, and to provide more consistent, higher-quality services by concentrating existing resources and streamlining processes.

Challenge 3—Public human resource management reforms have not demonstrated that they promote diversity in the workplace, and research indicates they may actually reverse the diversity gains made by merit systems. The last two decades of PHRM reform have generated considerable research regarding the impact that restructuring has had on public workplace diversity (Battaglio 2010; Battaglio and Condrey 2009; Bradbury, Battaglio, and Crum 2010; Condrey and Battaglio 2007; Daley, Vasu, and Weinstein 2002; Kellough and Nigro 2002; 2006; Kim 2009; Nigro and Kellough 2000; Schulz and Tanguay 2006). Given the historical precedents of discrimination against women and minorities, scholars have been eager to assess the impact of recent reforms on Title VII–protected classes in the public service (Battaglio 2010; Condrey and Battaglio 2007; Wilson 2006). Employment-at-will environments have proven controversial given the status of merit systems as tools to achieve equal opportunity (Mosher 1982, 224). In fact, merit system principles have been lauded for improving the status of women in the public workforce (Bernhardt and Dresser 2002; Moynihan and Landuyt 2008). Research findings suggest that minorities are pessimistic about the merits of PHRM reform efforts (Battaglio 2010; Battaglio and Condrey 2009; Bradbury, Battaglio, and Crum 2010; Condrey and Battaglio 2007). Many minorities believe that giving management and/or politicians greater discretion over PHRM functions, as in an EAW environment, may encourage "discrimination-induced job dismissals" (Wilson 2006, 178). Further, the impact these reforms have had on motivation among minorities in the public service is troubling (Battaglio 2010; Battaglio and Condrey 2009). Civil service employment practices have a long history of improving representation in the workforce, but HR reforms have made many African Americans skeptical that the public service is still the great equalizer (see Wilson 2006). The potential for EAW and other reforms to erode years of progress in the promotion of diversity must not be ignored.

Challenge 4—Public human resource management reforms raise a number of legal issues that must be carefully weighed before implementing changes. Effectively practicing PHRM requires understanding how employment law applies in the public sector. Employment law affects every aspect of day-to-day HR operations. For example, a public HR manager in an EAW environment should take great care to recognize this reform's potential risks to due process and procedural fairness. Moreover, legislation passed in the post–September 11 environment has reduced the privacy expectations of public employees.

HR policies should be communicated regularly to personnel. Advances in information technology allow HR managers to continuously impart the latest legal developments to managers and staff. Communicating what is expected of employees should not be relegated to orientation processes but be part of the ongoing training and development of the public service. Ignoring constitutional mandates for public employment practices could be costly.

Legal considerations are also important as government increasingly relies on private delivery of public HR functions. An understanding of the legal dynamics of privatization in the public sector can add "public value" to the contract (Battaglio and Ledvinka 2009). HR managers who are familiar with contract law can ensure that public values are incorporated in measures of contractor performance, thus mitigating the potential for diminished accountability for outsourced services (Fernandez, Rainey, and Lowman 2006; Moe 1987; Moe and Gilmour 1995). Awareness of the requirements imposed by constitutional, regulatory, statutory, and case law can reinforce accountability among private vendors.

The shift away from civil service systems to EAW has prompted a legitimate concern about the potential erosion of public values (Battaglio and Condrey 2009; Condrey and Battaglio 2007). Privatization, likewise, has the potential to displace public values during the contracting-out process, particularly in the way that personnel are managed (Woodard 2005). Because HR managers do not supervise contract personnel, they cannot directly control whether contracted-out HR activities comply with legal requirements or promote equity and due process values (Fernandez, Rainey, and Lowman 2006). With the proper legal training, however, public managers can draft and edit contracts so as to reduce legal liability and reinforce values of due process and equity (Battaglio and Ledvinka 2009).

Challenge 5—Politics often fuels the drive for public human resource management reforms. Governments should adopt PHRM reforms because such changes make sense for the organization and not simply because everyone else is doing it (Perry, Engbers, and Jun 2009). Given the lack of evidence documenting the benefits of many reforms, many change efforts are tied to external political demands based on a widespread perception of "good management" practices (DiMaggio and Powell 1983; Perry, Engbers, and Jun 2009). The result, Perry, Engbers, and Jun (2009) argued, is that public agencies adopt reforms either because they are coerced by those in power or because they seek to mimic private sector practices (47). Politicians often compel agencies to adopt perceived private sector efficiencies in order to play on antibureaucratic sentiment among the public (Condrey and Battaglio 2007; Kellough and Lu 1993; March and Olsen 1983; Perry 1988).

Indeed, contemporary labor-management relations in the public sector are often tied to politically driven reform efforts. Public sector labor unions have been challenged by state officials for their perceived inefficiencies (McCartin 2011). Appealing to ideological sentiment, reformers have sought to curtail or outright eliminate labor unions' ability to negotiate over HR activities. During a time of tight budgets, public sector unions face continued reductions in force, modest wage increases, and reductions in the quality of benefits with increased costs for those same benefits.

PHRM reforms have had a profound impact on public sector labor unions. Public employee unions may reduce the scope of EAW where it is implemented but not preclude its adoption (Condrey and Battaglio 2007). The result of a decentralized, at-will environment is the replacement of traditional HR practices with more agency-specific, manager-centered systems, especially in states where public employee unions are weak and public employees do not have the right to strike. Similarly, decentralization and deregulation efforts at the federal level have diminished labor rights, giving greater flexibility and authority to management (Brook and King 2008, 215).

Thus, practitioners advocating reforms should expect states with strong and effective employee unions to mount significant resistance. However, research suggests that even in states with a strong labor presence, HR reform erodes due process protections (Hays and Sowa 2006, 111). Moreover, in some states, excellent civil servants may be replaced by well-connected cronies (Condrey and Battaglio 2007). Public sector employees and citizens may come to view the way government is managed with distrust.

Although public HR managers face many challenges, there are also opportunities for practitioners to make a difference. *Reform* is not a bad word—change is a necessary and important part of improving government services. How we go about change is what matters.

Opportunities: The Future of PHRM

PHRM reforms are challenging for the public sector. However, they also present opportunities. Indeed, students and practitioners are operating in a dynamic time in the public sector. The many policy issues facing our nation—health care, the environment, transportation, the economy—have prompted novel solutions from noted scholars. This is true of PHRM as well. The reforms we have discussed throughout the text have ushered in an unprecedented era of PHRM research. The case studies and examples in each of the chapters highlight the many opportunities for improving PHRM. Below are a few of the more important opportunities for HR professionals.

Opportunity 1—Advances in information technology have ushered in a new era of managing human resources information. Computer networks and cloud-based software have given HR managers highly productive tools. HRIS allows HR staff to manage large amounts of employee information while making this information available to employees, management, and others. HRIS now provides an integrated platform for managing strategic planning, performance management, workforce planning, development, compensation and benefits, and risk management. With such information now readily available, the HR function can play a central role in strategic planning.

Managing vast amounts of employee information comes with a special responsibility to safeguard confidential data. Laws and regulations govern how sensitive information must be handled. Public HR managers and IT staff must be familiar with this body of law to protect employees' privacy and avoid legal liability.

Public HR managers seeking to drive performance in a dynamic environment must be able to analyze relevant data efficiently. HRIS gives managers the tools to meet this challenge, potentially contributing significantly and strategically to the future of the public service.

Opportunity 2—Strategic human resource management (SHRM) offers public managers an opportunity to invest in employees as part of the human capital initiative. SHRM views employees as organizational assets (GAO 2001). As such, training and development are crucial parts of any strategic plan to meet future workforce challenges.

It is true that public service reforms place HR systems under stress, making the implementation of SHRM challenging. For example, when taking on new responsibilities due to decentralization, agency-level HR professionals need extensive training. Moreover, differences across public agencies make system-wide SHRM efforts problematic, as when HR professionals must develop and administer performance-based pay according to a given standard despite agency differences (Hays and Sowa 2006; Kellough and Nigro 2002; Perry, Engbers, and Jun 2009). However, public managers invested in a strategic approach to HR practice will identify and analyze such differences in terms of the units' needs and potential for change, thus facilitating coordination of HR initiatives across work groups (Longo 2008, 7).

To coordinate SHRM efforts, HR professionals will need to align strategic plans to agency goals. For example, they must ensure the performance appraisal system accurately rewards high performance. Finally, taking a strategic approach to HRM means identifying appropriate metrics and devising ways to track them.

Opportunity 3—Improved HR instruction and curricula can prepare students for current and future trends in the field. Scholars and educators in the PHRM field are always reevaluating how best to prepare future professionals to meet organizations' human capital and management needs. Llorens and Battaglio (2010) suggested that recent reforms call for PHRM coursework to incorporate related content, such as how to design performance-based compensation systems that also acknowledge public service motivation. HR professionals also need to keep up with the evolving literature of the field.

Final Thoughts

The takeaway for public HR managers is that "one size does not fit all." When considering PHRM reforms, managers would be wise to begin with a trial effort—a "beta test," as it were—before pursuing system-wide efforts. Implementing a reform in a particular division or unit within an agency will allow its successes and shortcoming to be analyzed. The feedback derived from such a trial will allow HR managers to address problems before extending the initiative to other parts of the organization or other agencies. HR professionals must also communicate regularly with peers through professional associations as a way to discover best practices and learn from others' mistakes.

A lack of adequate funding will ultimately undermine the most well thought out PHRM reform. With regard to performance-based pay programs, for example, employees working under an insufficiently funded compensation plan will not expect their extra output to be appropriately awarded. However, public sector budgets are often constrained. Therefore, public HR managers will have to come to terms with the idea of doing more with less. Complicating the situation is the fact that HR managers in a decentralized environment will be required to handle numerous responsibilities efficiently. To meet this challenge, they will need an understanding of HRIS to use technology to do the work once performed by a larger number of staff. In a decentralized context, communication with counterparts in other government agencies will be important to avert equity concerns.

Public HR managers have a special responsibility to maintain a representative workforce, despite any countervailing influences arising from reform intiatives. This means investing in outreach efforts, especially to protected-class communities that have historically been discriminated against. For example, recruiting at historically black colleges or Hispanic chambers of commerce will help allay any concerns minorities might have about working in a reform environment. Moreover, HR managers should communicate clearly that diversity is a priority of their jurisdictions. Diversity plans are a notable tool for creating a workplace environment that values inclusion.

Finally, as students and instructors of PHRM, we have a duty to continuously improve our knowledge of research and practice. If we truly believe in bringing relevant research to bear on shaping practice for the better—and I do—then education is the lifeblood of improved management. The empirical research into the results of decentralization, performance-based pay, declassification, deregulation, and privatization suggests that organizations may encounter difficulties as they transition away from traditional HR practices (Risher 2005; Selden 2009). One way to avert such problems is to adopt new metrics for analyzing performance, especially in terms of how different work behaviors and job outcomes will be rewarded. SHRM encompasses a number of measures for organizing and assessing agency progress in a reform climate.

Recruiting and retaining a qualified public workforce may also prove difficult in an era of PHRM reform. The push toward deregulated and privatized systems may make this task particularly difficult. HR professionals should measure employee morale and turnover as reforms are implemented (Selden 2009). Recent scholarship (Battaglio 2010; Battaglio and Condrey 2009) suggests that EAW systems in particular may disrupt the employer/employee relationship, adversely affecting individual and organizational performance.

Public HR managers will also need to understand how to manage outsourced HR functions. They can find some practical instruction in published material, such as Chapter 10 in this book and general PHRM textbooks (Cohen & Eimicke 2008; Cooper 2003), as well as government reports. Given the many changes to PHRM over the last few decades, an excellent educational program as well as ongoing training and development will prove instrumental to contributing strongly to the 21st-century public service.

References

Battaglio, R. Paul, Jr. 2010. "Public Service Reform and Motivation: Evidence from an Employment At-Will Environment." *Review of Public Personnel Administration* 30:341–63.

Battaglio, R. Paul, Jr., and Stephen E. Condrey. 2006. "Civil Service Reform: Examining State and Local Government Cases." *Review of Public Personnel Administration* 26:118–38.

Battaglio, R. Paul, Jr., and Stephen E. Condrey. 2009. "Reforming Public Management: Analyzing the Impact of Public Service Reform on Organizational and Managerial Trust." *Journal of Public Administration Research & Theory* 19:689–707.

Battaglio, R. Paul, Jr., and Todd Jordan. 2012. "Public Human Resource Management Research Perspectives: Where Are We on Public Service Reform?" Unpublished manuscript, last modified October 8. Microsoft Word file.

Battaglio, R. Paul, Jr., and Christine Ledvinka. 2009. "Privatizing Human Resources in the Public Sector: Legal Challenges to Outsourcing the Human Resource Function." *Review of Public Personnel Administration* 29:293–307.

Bernhardt, Annette, and Laura Dresser. 2002. "Why Privatizing Government Services Would Hurt Women Workers." Washington, DC: Institute for Women's Policy Research. http://www.european-services-strategy.org.uk/outsourcing-ppp-library/equalities-and-social-justice-impacts/why-privatizing-government-services-would-hurt/women-impact-privatisation-us.pdf.

Bradbury, Mark D., R. Paul Battaglio Jr., and John L. Crum. 2010. "Continuity Amid Discontinuity? George W. Bush, Federal Employment Discrimination, and 'Big Government Conservatism.'" *Review of Public Personnel Administration* 30:445–66.

Brook, Douglas A., and Cynthia L. King. 2008. "Federal Personnel Management Reform: From Civil Service Reform Act to National Security Reforms." *Review of Public Personnel Administration* 28:205–21.

Coggburn, Jerrell D. 2001. "Is Deregulation the Answer for Public Personnel Management? Revisiting a Familiar Question: Introduction." *Review of Public Personnel Administration* 20:5–8.

Coggburn, Jerrell D. 2007. "Outsourcing Human Resources: The Case of Texas Health and Human Services Commission." *Review of Public Personnel Administration* 27: 315–35.

Coggburn, Jerrell D., R. Paul Battaglio Jr., James S. Bowman, Stephen E. Condrey, Doug Goodman, and Jonathan P. West. 2010. "State Government Human Resource Professionals' Commitment to Employment at Will." *American Review of Public Administration* 40:189–208.

Cohen, Steven, and William B. Eimicke. 2008. *The Responsible Contract Manager: Protecting the Public Interest in an Outsourced World.* Washington, DC: Georgetown University Press.

Condrey, Stephen E., and R. Paul Battaglio Jr. 2007. "A Return to Spoils? Revisiting Radical Civil Service Reform in the United States." *Public Administration Review* 67:425–36.

Cooper, Phillip J. 2003. *Governing by Contract: Challenges and Opportunities for Public Managers.* Washington, DC: CQ Press.

Daley, Dennis M., Michael L. Vasu, and Meredith Blackwell Weinstein. 2002. "Strategic Human Resource Management: Perceptions among North Carolina County Social Service Professionals." *Public Personnel Management* 31:359–75.

DiMaggio, Paul J., and Walter W. Powell. 1983. "The Iron Cage Revisited: Institutional Isomorphism and Collective Rationality in Organizational Fields." *American Sociological Review* 48:147–60.

Fernandez, Sergio, Hal G. Rainey, and Carol E. Lowman. 2006. "Privatization and Its Implications for Human Resources Management." In *Public Personnel Management: Current Concerns, Future Challenges,* 4th ed., edited by Norma M. Riccucci, 204–24. New York: Longman.

Grant, Adam M. 2008. "Employees Without a Cause: The Motivational Effects of Prosocial Impact in Public Service." *International Public Management Journal* 11:48–66.

Hays, Steven W., and Jessica E. Sowa. 2006. "A Broader Look at the 'Accountability' Movement: Some Grim Realities in State Civil Service Systems." *Review of Public Personnel Administration* 26:102–17.

Hou, Yilin, Patricia Ingraham, Stuart Bretschneider, and Sally Coleman Selden. 2000. "Decentralization of Human Resource Management: Driving Forces and Implications." *Review of Public Personnel Administration* 20:9–22.

Kellough, J. Edward, and Haoran Lu. 1993. "The Paradox of Merit Pay in the Public Sector: Persistence of a Problematic Procedure." *Review of Public Personnel Administration* 13:45–64.

Kellough, J. Edward, and Lloyd G. Nigro. 2002. "Pay for Performance in Georgia State Government: Employee Perspectives on GeorgiaGain After 5 Years." *Review of Public Personnel Administration* 22:146–66.

Kellough, J. Edward, and Lloyd G. Nigro. 2005. "Radical Civil Service Reform: Ideology, Politics, and Policy." In *Handbook of Human Resource Management in Government,* 2nd ed., edited by Stephen E. Condrey, 58–75. San Francisco, CA: Jossey-Bass.

Kellough, J. Edward, and Lloyd G. Nigro. 2006. "Dramatic Reform in the Public Service: At-Will Employment and the Creation of a New Public Workforce." *Journal of Public Administration Research and Theory* 16:447–66.

Kim, Jungjin. 2009. "Strategic Human Resource Practices: Introducing Alternatives for Organizational Performance Improvement in the Public Sector." *Public Administration Review* 70:38–49.

Leisink, Peter, and Bram Steijn. 2008. "Recruitment, Attraction, and Selection." In *Motivation in Public Management: The Call of Public Service,* edited by James L. Perry and Annie Hondeghem, 118–35. Oxford, UK: Oxford University Press.

Llorens, Jared J., and R. Paul Battaglio Jr. 2010. "Human Resources Management in a Changing World: Reassessing Public Human Resources Management Education." *Review of Public Personnel Administration* 30:112–32.

Longo, Francesco. 2008. "Managing Public Reforms Effectively: A Strategic Change Management Approach." In *Strategic Change Management in the Public Sector: An EFMD European Case Book,* edited by Francesco Longo and Daniela Cristofoli, 1–20. Hoboken, NJ: Wiley.

March, James G., and Johan P. Olsen. 1983. "Organizing Political Life: What Administrative Reorganization Tells Us about Government." *American Political Science Review* 77:281–96.

Maynard, Melissa. 2012. "States Push to Shake Up Personnel Practices." *Stateline: The Daily News of the Pew Charitable Trusts,* February 16. http://www.stateline.org/live/details/story?contentId=632584.

McCartin, Joseph A. 2011. "What's Really Going on in Wisconsin?" *The New Republic,* February 19. http://www.tnr.com/article/politics/83829/wisconsin-public-employees-walker-negotiate/.

Moe, Ronald C. 1987. "Exploring the Limits of Privatization." *Public Administration Review* 47:453–60.

Moe, Ronald C., and Robert S. Gilmour. 1995. "Rediscovering Principles of Public Administration: The Neglected Foundation of Public Law." *Public Administration Review* 55:135–46.

Mosher, Frederick C. 1982. *Democracy and the Public Service.* 2nd ed. Oxford, England: Oxford University Press.

Moynihan, Donald P. 2008. "The Normative Model in Decline? Public Service Motivation in the Age of Governance." In *Motivation in Public Management: The Call of Public Service,* edited by James L. Perry and Annie Hondeghem, 250–64. Oxford, England: Oxford University Press.

Moynihan, Donald P., and Noel Landuyt. 2008. "Explaining Turnover Intention in State Government: Explaining the Roles of Gender, Life Cycle, and Loyalty." *Review of Public Personnel Administration* 28:120–43.

Nigro, Lloyd G., and J. Edward Kellough. 2000. "Civil Service Reform in Georgia: Going to the Edge?" *Review of Public Personnel Administration* 20:41–54.

Perry, James L. 1988. "Making Policy by Trial and Error: Merit Pay in the Federal Service." *Policy Studies Journal* 17:389–405.

Perry, James L., Trent A. Engbers, and So Yun Jun. 2009. "Back to the Future? Performance-Related Pay, Empirical Research, and the Perils of Persistence." *Public Administration Review* 69:39–51.

Rainey, Hal G. 2009. *Understanding and Managing Organizations.* 4th ed. San Francisco, CA: Jossey-Bass.

Risher, Howard. 2005. "How Much Should Federal Employees Be Paid? The Problems with Using a Market Philosophy in a Broadband System." *Public Personnel Management* 34:121–40.

Schulz, Eric R., and Denise Marie Tanguay. 2006. "Merit Pay in a Public Higher Education Institution: Questions of Impact and Attitudes." *Public Personnel Management* 35:77–88.

Selden, Sally Coleman. 2009. *Human Capital: Tools and Strategies for the Public Sector.* Washington, DC: CQ Press.

Selden, Sally Coleman, Patricia W. Ingraham, and Willow Jacobson. 2001. "Human Resource Practices in State Government: Findings from a National Survey." *Public Administration Review* 61:598–607.

Selden, Sally Coleman, and Robert Wooters. 2011. "Structures in Public Human Resource Management: Shared Services in State Government." *Review of Public Personnel Administration* 31:349–68.

Shafritz, Jay M., David H. Rosenbloom, Norma A. Riccucci, Katherine C. Naff, and Al C. Hyde. 2001. *Personnel Management in Government: Politics and Process*, 5th ed. New York: Marcel Dekker.

Thompson, James R. 2001. "The Civil Service under Clinton: The Institutional Consequences of Disaggregation." *Review of Public Personnel Administration* 21:87–113.

US Government Accountability Office (GAO). 2001. "Human Capital: Meeting the Governmentwide High-Risk Challenge." GAO-01-357T. Washington, DC: Government Printing Office. http://www.gao.gov/assets/110/108710.pdf.

Whalen, Cortney, and Mary E. Guy. 2008. "Broadbanding Trends in the States." *Review of Public Personnel Administration* 28:349–66.

Wilson, George. 2006. "The Rise of At-Will Employment and Race Inequality in the Public Sector." *Review of Public Personnel Administration* 26:178–87.

Woodard, Colleen A. 2005. "Merit by Any Other Name: Reframing the Civil Service First Principle." *Public Administration Review* 65:109–16.

Note: In page references, b indicates boxes, f indicates figures, and t indicates tables.

Dr. R. Paul Battaglio, Jr. is an associate professor of public affairs at The University of Texas at Dallas. Dr. Battaglio's research interests include public human resource management, organization theory and behavior, public and nonprofit management, comparative public policy, and research methods. He teaches human resource courses in the master and Ph.D. programs of public affairs. Prior to working in academia, Dr. Battaglio was a policy analyst in the Louisiana Governor's Office for six years. As a policy analyst, he was responsible for state matters in energy, transportation, economic development, and higher education. His research on public human resource management is cited extensively in many of the top journals in the field, including, *Public Administration Review, Journal of Public Administration Research & Theory, American Review of Public Administration, Review of Public Personnel Administration,* and *Public Personnel Management.* He has consulted with local government and nonprofit officials in the areas of organizational change and development, ethics, project and contract management, and strategic human capital management. Dr. Battaglio is currently the editor-in-chief of the *Review of Public Personnel Administration,* the leading journal in public human resource management.

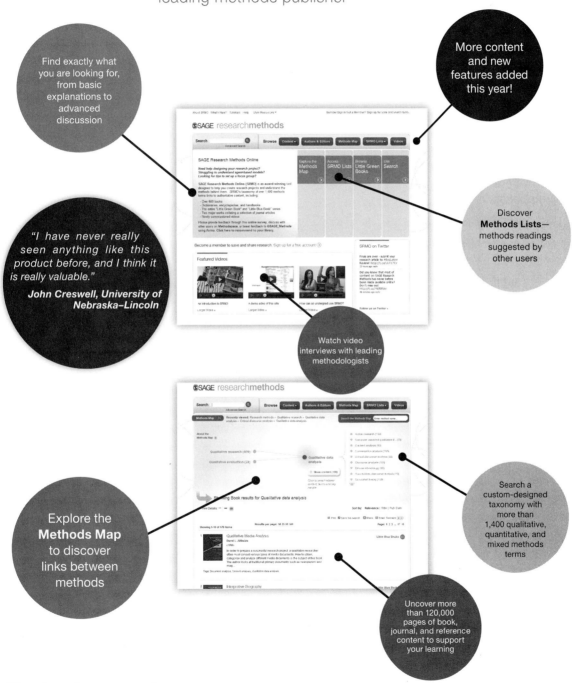

⑤SAGE research**methods**

The essential online tool for researchers from the world's leading methods publisher

Find exactly what you are looking for, from basic explanations to advanced discussion

More content and new features added this year!

"I have never really seen anything like this product before, and I think it is really valuable."

John Creswell, University of Nebraska–Lincoln

Discover **Methods Lists**— methods readings suggested by other users

Watch video interviews with leading methodologists

Explore the **Methods Map** to discover links between methods

Search a custom-designed taxonomy with more than 1,400 qualitative, quantitative, and mixed methods terms

Uncover more than 120,000 pages of book, journal, and reference content to support your learning

Find out more at
www.sageresearchmethods.com